CONSCIOUS ACTS OF CREATION:

THE EMERGENCE OF A NEW PHYSICS

BY

WILLIAM A. TILLER, PH.D., WALTER E. DIBBLE, JR., PH.D.

AND MICHAEL J. KOHANE, PH.D.

Publisher's Cataloging-in-Publication
(Provided by Quality Books, Inc.)

Tiller, William A.
  Conscious acts of creation : the emergence of a new physics / by William A. Tiller, Walter E. Dibble, Jr., and Michael J. Kohane. -- 1st ed.
    p. cm.
  Includes bibliographical references and index
  ISBN: 1-929331-05-3

  1. Physics--Philosophy. 2. Consciousness.
3. Parapsychology and science. I. Dibble, Walter E.
II. Kohane, Michael J. III. Title.

QC6.T55 2001   530'.01
                       QBI01-201024

LC – Library of Congress Catalogue Card Number:
2001-135246   8·1·08 CLC
                      530.01 TIL

SAN 299-4038

Printed in the United States of America

This book is dedicated

to our benefactor

Lynn ("*Buck*") Charlson

whose financial support nurtured

this work from the earliest days

of experimentation.

We are very grateful to him

for his faith in our dream!

CONTENTS

Preface xi

Foreword xiv

1. Introduction 1
    Specific Scientific Approaches to Consciousness 2
        Contributions From Medicine 2
        Contributions From Parapsychology 3
        Contributions From Consciousness Studies 3
        Contributions From Physics 8
        Considerations About "Space" 9
    What The Various Chapters Contribute 10
    For Whom Is This Book Written? 12
    The General Experimental Protocol 12
    Appendix 1.A: Some Device Essentials 17

2. Perspectives On A New Physics 21
        Some Limitations Of Present Quantum Mechanics 21
        De Broglie's Pilot Wave Concept 22
        A Biconformal Base-Space Approach 23
        A Higher Dimensional Framework 24
        Intention And Its Path Of Action 26
    Some Consequences Of High Deltron Activation 30
        Conditioning And Altered Gauge Symmetry 30
    Information Transfer Mechanisms 33
        Consciousness And Possible Vacuum Interactions 34
    Conditions For Repeatability 37
    Appendix 2.A: Pathways To Understanding Multidimensional Reality
    40
    Appendix 2.B: The Relativity Constraint On The De Broglie Concept
    46
    Appendix 2.C: Some Basic Concepts In Gauge Theory 48

3. Water And IIED-Generated pH Changes 54
    Some Anomalous Features Of Water 54

Molecular Nature 54
Volume/Entropy Bulk Water Anomalies 58
The Quantum Electrodynamic (QED) Perspective 61
Some Anomalous Features Of Electric/Magnetic Properties 62
    Weak AC Magnetic Field Effects 62
    Non-Inductive Coil-Induced Conductivity Changes 64
Simple, Long Time EM Frequency Storage In Water 65
Specific EM Molecular Information Transfer To Pure Water ... 67
Homeopathy As An Information-Specific Medical Therapeutic . 68
Significant Contributions from Colloid Surface Science Studies
.... 69
    Ice Crystal Patterns Materialize Specific Intentions In Water ... 70
Device-Mediated pH Changes In Water 70
    Early Days 70
    pH Measurement Procedures 71
    Evian Water 72
    Castle Rock Water Experiments 75
    ASTM Type 1, Purified Water Experiments 87
    Purified Water with $ZnCO_3$ Crystallites 88
Some Summary Findings 94
Appendix 3.A: The Chemical Evolution Of Evian Water In Our
Experiments 98
Appendix 3.B: Characteristics Of Type I Purified Water Used In Our
Experiments 99

4.   *In Vitro* **Enzyme And Coenzyme Activation By IIEDs**
.... **102**
Some General Background On Enzymes And Coenzymes 102
Experiments With Alkaline Phosphatase (ALP) 108
    Experiment I, The Influence Of IIEDs On ALP Activity 110
    Experiment II, ALP Activity As A Detector Of Subtle Energies
.... 113
        (a) Faraday Cage Layer Number Effect 114
        (b) Exposure Period And Faraday Cage (n=0,1) 115
        (c) Device Type, Position And Condition In The Faraday Cage
.... 116
        (d) Substituting ALP Vessels For Devices in (c) 118
        (e) ALP Detector Activity With Position For n=0 119
Experiments With Nicotinamide Adenine Dinucleotide (NAD) 119

     (i) [NAD] Change Over Time 120

     (ii) [ATP]/[ADP] Ratio In Fruit Fly Homogenates 122

    Some Summary Findings For The Enzyme/Coenzyme Experiments

    125

    Appendix 4.A: Our Use Of The Vitros DT System 127

    Appendix 4.B: Faraday Cage Construction And EM-Shielding 128

    Appendix 4.C: Box Plot Data For The Various Experiments 129

5. **An *In Vivo* Experiment With Fruit Flies 142**

    Introduction to *Drosophila Melanogaster* 142

    Bioenergetics 144

    Some Relevant Prior Baseline Studies With *Drosophila Melanogaster*

    147

    Experimental Procedures 148

       Biological Assay 148

       Energy Assay 148

       Fitness 150

       Energy Levels During Larval Development 152

    Experimental Results 153

    Appendix 5.A: Aspects Of Energy Metabolism 157

    Appendix 5.B: General Box Plot Representation Of The Data 159

       Intention-Augmented EMFs And The [ATP]/[ADP] Ratio 163

    Appendix 5.C: Numerical Data And Statistical Analysis 164

6. **Conditioning And Transformation Of The**
Experimental Space 169

    What Does Space Conditioning Mean? 169

    Some Experimental Indicators Of Space Conditioning 172

       DC Magnetic Field Polarity Effects 173

       Property Oscillations In The Water Vessel And The Air 174

       Air T-Oscillation Waveform Symmetry At Different Locations 180

       Wave Oscillation Trains 182

       Other Important Features Of These Oscillations 187

       Communication Between Distant Vessels Of Water 190

         First Transmission Experiment 192

         Second Transmission Experiment 192

         Third Transmission Experiment 193

    Some Specific Experiments With Conditioned Space 194

       Mechanical Fan Experiment 194

       Quiescent Air, Spatial Variation Of T-Oscillation Amplitude;

Case (a), With Faraday Cage 200
Case (b), After Removal Of The FC And Water Vessel, The
Phantom Effect 201
Air T-Oscillation Amplitude Perturbation Via A Natural Quartz
Crystal At Position Zero; 202
    Case (a), C-Axis Up 202
    Case (b), C-Axis Horizontal 203
The Use Of A Space-Conditioning IIED In A New Locale 206
Simultaneous Side-By-Side vs. Sequential Experiments In An
Initially Unconditioned Space 218
Oscillations In Random Number Generation And The
"Millennium" Effect 220
    The Millennium Effect 231
Experience With Conditioning Experiments At Two Remote Locations
.... 232
    Location 1 232
    Location 2 233
Some Summary Findings For The Locale Conditioning Experiments
.... 234
Appendix 6.A: Method Used for Random Number Generation Studies
.... 236

7. **Some Relevant, Quantitative Aspects Of 20th
Century Physics** **240**
The Reciprocal Lattice Concept 240
The Reciprocal Space Concept 243
The D-Space/R-Space Connection In Physical Reality 245
Experimentally Generated Fourier Transforms 250
Theoretically Generated Fourier Transforms 253
    1-D Objects 255
    2-D Objects 258
    3-D Objects 261
    4-D Objects 261
Experiment/Theory Comparison 261
    Limitations And Approximations 262
Information Transformation In The Brain 269
Thermodynamics And Kinetics 270
Chemical And Temperature Oscillations 275
    Natural Convection-Driven Oscillations 275

Chemical Reaction-Driven Oscillations 277
Coherence And Oscillating Electron Flows 286
Colloids, Clusters And Electromagnetic Fields 288
   External Field-Absence Case 290
   External Field-Presence Case 292
Appendix 7.A: Wave Diffraction And Interference Maxima From
Crystals 295
Appendix 7.B: Generalized Thermodynamics And Nature's Forces 302
Appendix 7.C: The Fourier Transform For N-Space And For
D-Space Shapes 304

8. Quantitative Theory For The New Paradigm 310

The New Framework's Foundation Stones 311
   The Key Elements From Tiller's Multidimensional Simulator
   Model 311
   Empowering The Pattern 314
   What Does An Experimental Observation Contain? 316
   What Does This Say About The Size Scale Factor In Quantum
   Mechanics? 319
   The Importance Of Increasing Deltron Coupling On the Gibb's
   Free Energy 319
   The R-Space/D-Space Connection Constraints 321
   Transforming δ-Functions Into Qualities 323
   R-Space Resonators 329
Electric/Magnetic Interactions In Different Symmetry States 331
   The Mirror Principle 331
   Electromagnetism (EM) And Magnetoelectrism (ME) 334
Some Applications Of The Theoretical Constructs 340
   Non-Local Forces 340
   Time-Dependent D-Space Oscillations 341
   Aspects Of Homeopathy 343
   A Possible D-Space Structural Mechanism For Homeopathic
   Action 348
      Nanobubbles In Water 350
      Artificial Enzymes 350
      Magnetic Cellular Automata 351
   IIEDs And SU(2)/U(1) Mixed Gauge Symmetry 352
   Long Distance Communication Between Vessels Of Water 355

Decay Of The Temperature Oscillation Amplitude With Distance
.... 356

Fine Structure Observed In Many Physical Processes 357

Biconformal Base Space As An Alternative Interpretation For
Quantum Mechanics 360

Some General "Wrapping Up" Comments 363

Appendix 8.A: Some R-Space Undulation Interval Recipes For Specific
D-Space δ-Function Loci 367

Appendix 8.B: Theoretically Matching Temporal D-Space
Oscillations 369

Appendix 8.C: Modulus Evaluation For Remedy Preparation In
Homeopathy 371

Appendix 8.D: Calculation of $\int_R \hat{k}_R dk_t$ for $10/\beta = 1\pm$ A Small

Constant 373

9. Some Implications For Religion, Philosophy, Psychology And Integrated Medicine 377

Religion 377

The Biobodysuit Metaphor 378

(a) The Vacuum 380

(b) Coherence 381

(c) Mindsets 381

(d) The Cause/Effect Process 381

Philosophy 383

Pathways To Scientific Understanding 384

Psychology 388

Integrated Medicine 391

10. Some Implications For Science And Technology 393

The General Experimental Facts 393

New Meaning For Humanity From These Facts 396

Implications For Some Fields Of Science 398

Physics 399

Biology 401

Electrical Engineering 402

Implications For Some Technologies 404
    Water Treatment For Health Care 405
    Enhancing Brain Coherence In Humans 405
    Chemical And Pharmaceutical Industries 406
    Semiconductor Fabrication Lab Facility 407
    Crystal Growth With An Ordered Internal Vacuum Phase 407
    Enhanced Computer Coherence 408
    Integrated Medicine Applications 408

PREFACE

This book marks a sharp dividing line between old ways of scientific thought and old experimental protocols, <u>wherein, human qualities of consciousness, intention, emotion, mind and spirit cannot significantly affect physical reality</u>, and a new paradigm wherein they can robustly do so!

For the past several centuries and up to the present day, the formal expressions for the various sub-fields of physics have contained no contributions arising from any human quality – as if the various human "broadcast-fields" in no meaningful way interacted with the substratum for nature's modes of expression. Because of this, the very large and growing body of experimental data confirming a contrary view has been conveniently ignored by most of today's establishment science. This book brings such robust experimental data to the table that only those of questionable integrity can continue such avoidance behavior. Further, and perhaps most important, this data shows that, in seemingly the same cognitive space, both basic chemical reactions and basic material properties can be strongly altered. Such remarkable changes appear to be related to transformations of the <u>vacuum substance</u> within each atom and molecule occupying that cognitive space. If so, it heralds an exciting era of new science, technology and human self-realization that awaits us "just around the corner" in our near future!

The first half of this book demonstrates, utilizing a unique experimental protocol on both inanimate and animate systems, that the human quality of <u>focused</u> <u>intention</u> can be made to act as a true thermodynamic potential and strongly influence experimental measurements for a variety of specific target experiments. In addition, continued use of this protocol in a given experimental locale leads to a unique conditioning of that space. This conditioning manifests itself in special ways, one of which is that the local physics Gauge symmetry is raised to a higher level than that of our normal cognitive space. It is this altered Gauge symmetry factor that is responsible for the altered material properties and processes in that space (which can be larger than 100 square feet of floor space, can be sustained for longer than a year or more and can be created in a variety of locales). And it clearly establishes a stable but modified reality.

Here, in addition to the experimental validation of this modified reality, we both conceptualize an expanded physics worldview for understanding this new experimental data vis à vis our normal cognitive reality and mathematically formalize a quantitative framework for testing this new worldview. The basic theory is not yet fully complete but enough of the foundation stones have been set in place for the reader to see that "a good beginning" has been made!

This book has been written for all people with a real interest in science and how science moves our world. In particular, that group of college graduates with a broad interest in self-development, metaphysical considerations and the spiritual path will rejoice in its content. All those involved in human health care, whether medical doctors, psychiatrists, psychologists, nurses or trained technicians, will come to appreciate how crucial are their attitudes of mind during performance of their daily ministrations. Finally, all those working in or studying the fields of physics, chemistry, biology and engineering who read this book will see a natural expansion of these fields from their present state to one with a much greater vista filled with great new adventures for questioning minds.

Chapter one provides an overall philosophical perspective with specific scientific approaches to the role of human consciousness in the experimental findings from a variety of fields. Since our view of the world we live in is strongly shaped by the way we think about "space", and since this book concentrates on a type of consciousness-field-conditioning of that "space", this topic is more than casually explored in our opening chapter. Chapter two is an attempt to forestall any "boggle" effect on the part of the reader as he/she tries to assimilate the experimental data of chapters three to six with that found in their conventional reality. Here, a fairly brief and qualitative theoretical perspective of a relevant theory is utilized to try and help the reader view the experimental data with a clear and open mind.

Chapter three introduces the reader to our unique experimental protocol wherein a specific intention is imprinted into a simple electrical device called an IIED (Intention Imprinted Electrical Device). And that device significantly influences a particular target experiment simply by putting the device close to the experimental apparatus and turning it on. The target experiment of this chapter is to either increase or decrease the pH of water by one full pH-unit with no chemical additions and with a measurement accuracy of ± 0.01 pH-unit. Chapter four extends this IIED-technique to the *in vitro* enhancement of specific enzymatic and co-enzyme activity with similar great success. Chapter five extends the technique into the living system realm by enhancing the [ATP]/[ADP] ratio in the cells of developing fruit fly larvae to make them more "fit" and thus shorten larval development times. Once again the experimental data reveals great success via use of this IIED technique.

Chapter six was a wonderful serendipitous surprise to us as it reveals important details of the slow "space conditioning" associated with continued use of our IIEDs. Here, many detailed experimental results are presented to show how this "space conditioning" manifests itself, to reveal important insights into some of the structural characteristics of what constitutes this type of space conditioning and both how long it takes to "condition" a new locale and how long this "conditioning" can endure after all IIEDs have been removed.

Chapter seven provides background conventional physics and chemistry of a quantitative nature that helps illuminate some aspects of the experimental data. Chapter eight provides a quantitative expansion of the conventional physics and chemistry model so that one can see how the qualitative perspective from Chapter two can be seriously put to work to both assess the new data and provide relevant explanation for a variety of "anomalous" experimental data (based on the prevailing paradigm) reported over the past century. Chapter nine looks at the implications of both this new experimental data and theoretical modeling to the fields of religion, philosophy, psychology and integrated medicine. The presence and "broadcast fields" of all the lifeforms connected to the experimental space significantly alter the framework for understanding these fields. Chapter ten looks at a variety of specific implications for the quantitative sciences and their output technologies. Our tentative conclusion to date is that this IIED-technology is capable of advancing every industry that humanity presently pursues as well as creating vast new technologies to serve a consciously evolving humanity.

Many readers find themselves unduly perturbed by the presence of any mathematical equations in material they are reading, feeling that it must be too technical for them and they should not pursue it further. For such readers of this book, they should just ignore the equations and focus on the text. Most of the mathematics has been relegated to appendices that can be completely ignored by those who do not wish to pursue the details. Chapters 7 and 8 are exceptions to this statement because, there, the mathematics is a key part of the text. However, to "downplay" their role, the equations have been largely grouped into tables so that they can be simply viewed visually without becoming entangled in the details. Many readers will simply wish to skip Chapters 7 and 8.

We owe a considerable debt to a number of individuals who helped make this a better book. To James Leckie and Ward Watt for providing lab space for WD and MK at Stanford. To Ed Schwarzkopf who created many of the original figures in this book and to Darlene Chiles, Nancy Nelson and others at Ditron, LLC and Durance Corporation who assisted us with this work. To Germaine Cornelissen for help with the box plots. To Greg Fandel for helpful suggestions and many other chores related to finalizing the book format. To my former student, Nicolas Cuendet who initially calculated and plotted Figures 7.6 to 7.13, plus appendix 7.C for a joint paper with me (unpublished). To James Dibble for help with creating the cover figure and other valuable assistance. To Wayne Jonas, Cyril Smith, Brian O'Leary, Stanislav O'Jack, Yasuhiko Kimura, Robert Jahn, Gordon Hansen, Bernard Williams, Ernest Pecci, Rustum Roy, John Young and Joie Jones for reviewing an earlier version of chapters 1-6 and providing useful comments for their rewrite. To George Sudarshan, Wayne Jonas and Rustum Roy for being willing to provide a critical reading of the entire book in its final draft form and for agreeing to each write a section of the "foreword" to this book. Finally, I thank my dear wife, Jean, for putting up with my preoccupied behavior during the past ~20 months spent in writing this manuscript.

William A. Tiller, April 30, 2001

FOREWORD

This foreword has been contributed by three very remarkable gentlemen, R.R., W.J. and G.S.

Rustum Roy (R.R.) is the Evan Pugh Professor Emeritus of Solid State at the Pennsylvania State University and Founding Director of its internationally renowned Materials Research Laboratory. He is a member of the U.S. Academy of Engineering, foreign member of the Royal Swedish and Japan's Academy of Engineering, the Russian Academy of Sciences and India's National Science Academy and has published over 900 papers and 5 books covering basic and applied science, science policy, science education, the science-religion interface and integrative medicine.

Wayne B. Jonas, M.D. (W.J.) is an Associate Professor, Departments of Family Medicine and Preventative Medicine/Biometrics at the Uniformed Services University of the Health Sciences (USUHS) in Bethesda, Maryland. He is the former Director of both the Office of Alternative Medicine at the National Institutes of Health and the Medical Research Fellowship at the Walter Reed Army Institute of Research. He has authored over 60 publications as well as the major textbook "Essentials of Complementary and Alternative Medicine" and is currently the founding Director of the Samueli Institute in Corona Del Mar, California.

E. C. George Sudarshan (<u>G.S.</u>) is the distinguished Professor of Physics and former Director of the Center for Particle Theory at the University of Texas, Austin. He has published numerous papers and 5 books and, among his many discoveries was the first theory of the weak nuclear force.

●   <u>R.R.</u>: This book by Tiller, Dibble and Kohane is at once a "magnum opus" and a "tour de force". The former appellation accurately describes what Bill Tiller and his co-authors have brought together in this volume, extensively packed with data, analysis and the beginning of a comprehensive theoretical framework. The latter appellation is justified because Tiller may indeed succeed, through this vehicle, in attracting the attention of the theoretical physics community to the necessity to open up their framework from their three dimensional U(1) Gauge physics to a wholly new multi-dimensional SU(2) Gauge physics (see pages 30-33 for the most accessible explanations).

As a materials scientist, deeply involved for 50 years in the study of the behavior and properties in matter subjected to extreme variations in the intensive thermodynamic variables, I have been studying the researchable data accrued for millennia by highly trained practitioners of traditional healing arts. This, "whole person healing" as I have termed it, has as it's key axiom the equation: $P=B+M+S$ (a person is "composed", literally as much as sulfuric acid is "composed" of hydrogen, sulfur and oxygen, of body (B) mind (M) and spirit (S)). This simple formulation immediately provides a framework to understand in a qualitative way, <u>all</u> the interactions ever proposed for any manifestation of, supposedly, extraordinary examples of healing. A healer (H) interacts with a patient (P) via many possible combinations in a 3x3 matrix each side with B, M, and S subdivisions.

Why I regard this book as being so important is that for the first time Tiller, Dibble and Kohane have put the argument in the language of physics. Also, more significantly, from my point of view, as a materials scientist they have provided what appear to be very solid and very extensive data on $S \rightarrow (M) \rightarrow B \rightarrow$ interactions.

Thus, data described in detail on Intention-Imprinted Electronic Device (IIED) effects on the pH of water are compelling to an experimentalist like myself. Because of the sign reversibility (pH up or down) and because of the myriad repetitions, it will take a very convoluted argument to explain the data from any U(1) Gauge stance. The chapter on water is worth the price of the entire book, and it's connection to a likely theoretical framework for explaining homeopathic effects may well become its best-known result.

The arrangement of the chapters and the sequencing of the arguments are not easy to follow for a novice. For the non-physicist I recommend starting with Chapter 10 and following with Chapters 3 and 6 before going into deeper waters. "The Whole Person Healing" community will be in deep debt to these authors for many years.

● W.J.: A distinguished psychology professor once told me that the biggest dilemma in human relationships is distinguishing between the "punk and the prophet". For the average person, they can appear remarkably the same. An identical dilemma faces science. Most scientific ideas never pan out. Of the hundreds of thousands of experiments conducted over the several centuries the vast majority have led nowhere. Knowing which will stand the test of time and usefulness seems to require divine discernment. While Director of the Office of Alternative Medicine at the NIH I saw many unconventional ideas. Every week a new cure for everything would be presented to the office. If even one in a thousand could do what it claimed, medicine would be revolutionized.

In this book, Professor Tiller makes a claim that would not only revolutionize medicine but our perception and approach to all reality. Professor Tiller has been exploring the subtle domains of energy, parapsychology and the implications of quantum physics for decades. These areas are among the most ancient and controversial in science. Unlike many who venture into these realms, Tiller has a distinguished career as a mainstream engineer at Stanford University and a solid grounding in physics. If there are prophets in our extraordinary times he is likely one of them. His claim is a bold one indeed: human consciousness contributes to the creation and direction of the universe.

That human consciousness can interact with unseen aspects of the universe in ways that influence matter and events is an assumption as old as humanity. Most religions and mystics assume that our prayers to the divine have an effect. Shamans and healers from all cultures enter meditative and trance states in order to influence illness, alter our thinking and redirect events. Over 80% of those in the hospital pray for help with their condition. But is there anything to these claims or are they simply more evidence of how easily we are deceived with wishful thinking?

Decades of rigorous experiments at Princeton University and elsewhere have demonstrated small effects from intention on random systems, and research sponsored by the Department of Defense has shown the ability of certain individuals to detect information through means outside the five accepted senses of the body. Proponents have pointed to the aggregate statistical significance of these findings that are well beyond chance. Skeptics, however, have pointed to the inconsistency of these effects from experiment to experiment and to the very small magnitude of such effects. If they exist what difference do they make? A good question indeed.

Professor Tiller says that he has discovered a way to make these effects more robust. By entering a deep meditative state and then sending or "imprinting" intentions onto electronic devices that are shielded from electromagnetic and human influences, these effects are maintained and even transferred to the space around them. Like the "sacred sites" of churches and special holy places, these "conditioned" spaces retain a certain quality about them that can be measured with simple pH or temperature meters. Intentions, previously so erratic and feeble, now become more consistent, more direct and more ordered.

Professor Tiller's model of how this works and the mathematical principles upon which it is based have yet to be proven. Yet, if his predictions are correct and if the procedures he describes can be used by the general population he will have made the discovery of the millennium and he will be a modern prophet indeed. Timely and careful exploration of these findings may reveal to us that divine discernment is closer than we have imagined.

G.S.: Physics is organized human experience that applies to all matter. It does it by controlled experiments and by interconnecting them by theories so that we can deduce the results from a small number of laws. As our experience expands, so does the field of physics. In Newton's time we had no scientific study of electricity, though lightning storms would have been seen. The sun shone, but the mechanism was beyond the domain of Newtonian physics although Newton had brought the motion of celestial bodies under physical laws.

The curious 'charging by friction' would have also been observed but it too was not subjected to scientific study; now we cannot imagine a world without electromagnetism as well as the mechanisms of the subatomic world.

There are some unusual effects of human intention on matter that many physicists do not study. The authors of this book have not only carried out careful experiments, but also provided us with a documentation of their various experiments. In this domain they are done with due care and have obtained reproducible results which are somewhat disconcerting to mainstream physics. The authors have taken special care to have extra controls so as to ensure the accuracy of the results. Since these results do not go well with conservative scientists, such scientists often deny the validity of these phenomena.

A large part of this book is devoted to a new theoretical framework going beyond the usual one. Physicists who are unfamiliar with the new language would wonder what "negative energy" means, and how to understand a formulation in which an x-space (coordinates) and a k-space (inverse distances) coexist. The new paradigm invites physical scientists to find a more acceptable theoretical framework, if they find the present framework inadequate or unacceptable for any reason.

In addition to the careful description of the experimental protocol and the impressive data gathered, this book has an introductory part that reviews 'classical' ('standard') physics and the possibility of a new physics that would include the "new" phenomena. Physics must deal with all physical manifestations.

Rustum Roy
Penn State University

Wayne B. Jonas
USUHS

E.C. George Sudarshan
University of Texas, Austin

CHAPTER 1

Introduction

The underlying message of this book is that, under at least some conditions, human intention acts like a typical potential capable of creating robust effects in what we call physical reality. This significantly broadens the purview of physics, challenges its present perspectives, mindsets and laws, and sets it on a new course toward understanding how physical matter and energy are connected to human consciousness. On the other hand, in today's world, the prevailing paradigm for science and technology is that focussed human intention cannot meaningfully interact with specific target experiments at an energy/information level. Even more strongly, its proponents would state that human intention cannot possibly be captured in a simple electronic device and <u>then</u> have that device meaningfully interact with a specific target experiment. These are both reasonable approximations to reality when the symmetry state of our local space exhibits U(1) Gauge symmetry†.

Abundant historical, technological as well as present day experience with expert systems, computer-aided design, reliable engineering, reliable machines, etc., all tend to buttress this prevailing scientific U(1) Gauge symmetry viewpoint. Over the past 4-5 centuries, this viewpoint has led humanity down a reductionist and materialistic path of development. On the other hand many have espoused a different evolutionary path for humanity. One can certainly conceive of a society whose consciousness is sufficiently developed that their focussed intentions could alter the Gauge symmetry state and thus strongly influence specific target experiments. In fact, there seems to exist fragmentary evidence to support such a contention, some of which will be highlighted in the next section. Of course, accepting such a perspective would require the development of a new scientific paradigm; such a perspective would awaken one to the fact that a significant transformation had occurred in the human species and that humans would further evolve down a very different path.

Over the past 3-4 years, the authors have conducted several very different target experiments using intention imprinted electrical devices

---

†The U(1) Gauge symmetry state means (1) Abelian algebra for all fields, x, y, etc., where xy-yx = 0, (2) substances are constructed from electric monopoles and <u>magnetic dipoles</u> and (3) Maxwellian electromagnetic field equations apply.

(IIEDs) and found <u>robust</u> interaction between these simple devices and the chosen target experiments. This is in <u>complete opposition</u> to the view of the prevailing U(1) Gauge symmetry paradigm or, at best, the materialistic/reductionist paradigm is a limiting case of the larger reality wherein intention/consciousness is a significant factor. This book is about telling the "story" of those experiments, how we can begin to understand them and what <u>profound</u> implications they hold for future science, technology, philosophy and religion. Whether or not these experimental results are indicative of some cosmological change, destined to move much of humanity towards an alternate path of evolution, it is too early to say. However, it seems abundantly clear that consciousness-directed intention is a powerful force that must be incorporated into any new scientific paradigm and that is the overview perspective of this book.

Specific Scientific Approaches to Consciousness

<u>Contributions from Medicine</u>: Through the years, mind-body medicine and remote healing have provided prime examples of human consciousness in action. Dossey's three eras of medicine model[1,2] begins with Era I -- medicine as allopathic medicine at the turn of the 20th century and Erlich's "magic bullets" (e.g., mercury for the treatment of syphilis). However, most diseases don't have magic bullets, they are mostly stress related, caused by being out of right relationship with ourselves, with others, with our environment and with a higher power. The statistics show that 90% of all illness does not require Era I-medicine. Era II-medicine is mind/body medicine with emotions being the interface between the mind and the body. The informational molecular links are the neuropeptides[3].

Era III-medicine is defined by <u>nonlocal</u> approaches to healing[1,4]. It views the mind as unbounded and unconfined to points in space and time so that this category of healing events may bridge persons who are widely separated from each other. This category of medicine goes beyond today's view of physics so that <u>mind</u>, not matter, is ultimately considered as being primary[1].

It appears to be the right temporal lobe of our brains that allow humans to interact with a seemingly timeless, spaceless, nonlocal reality. Studies of temporal lobe pathology, direct electrical stimulation, temporal lobe epileptics, near death experiences (NDEs), comparisons of ketamine and LSD experiences and the actions of associated neurotransmitters within the human brain all tend to implicate the mesial right temporal lobe, hippocampus and associated limbic lobe structures as biological substrates for (1) out-of-the-body experiences and (2) religious experiences[5-9].

Contributions From Parapsychology: Anyone who reads Dean Radin's book "The Conscious Universe"[10] from cover to cover and has intellectual integrity, can no longer doubt that there is incontrovertible evidence to support the existence of ESP capabilities in humans. He has done a masterful job in assembling, analyzing and criticizing a huge body of data that is presented in a clear and readable fashion. Such ESP-tools strongly reveal nonlocal accessing of information and nonlocal influencing of physical processes. Remote viewing, one of the best known capabilities via its modern-day originator, Ingo Swann, has been well documented in the laboratory and shown to be independent of both distance and time[11,12]. The similarities between mind-body healing, remote viewing and postulated interactions with a non-local universe[13] all point to a crucial need to expand our framework for doing physics.

Contributions From Consciousness Studies: Running through the work in this field is the assumption that we all share the same underlying consciousness and that there is no separation or boundary in space and time at a deep level. Grof[14] draws the important conclusion that his research and that of others is incompatible with materialistic monism or scientific materialism which claims that matter actually generates consciousness and that there is no creative intelligence at the heart of nature. He contends that there is abundant evidence to challenge this view and finds it remarkable how academic circles have managed to suppress or ignore this evidence. Probably Ravindra[15] has placed his finger on the reason why the orthodox professional establishment has avoided looking at the data that clearly shatters their most fundamental metaphysical assumptions. He quite properly points out that higher or more broadened consciousness cannot be understood in terms of, and by remaining at, a lower or more narrow consciousness. An analogy would come from our radio or television experience. One cannot know what is the content of another station or channel without tuning to it.

"True knowledge is obtained by participation and fusion of the knower with the object of study -- and the scientist is required to become higher in order to understand higher things. Such a science would demand and assist the preparation, integration and attunement of body, mind and heart of the scientists so that they would be able to participate in the vision revealed by higher consciousness. The important lesson here, from the perspective of any future science of consciousness, is the importance of knowledge by identity. We cannot remain separate and detached if we wish to understand. We need to

3

participate in and be one with what we wish to understand. But unwillingness or even a refusal of the need for radical transformation is ubiquitous. Unfortunately, even when the idea of transformation has an appeal, one generally wishes to be transformed without actually changing."

Serious research in this area requires the courage to cultivate and train one's mental and emotional states so that they are both disciplined and directed. This builds some type of reliable infrastructure into our systems, which allows us to "tune" to a broader spectrum of Nature's expression. In this regard, use of the adjectives narrower and broader is definitely preferable to lower and higher when referring to human consciousness. Further, the metaphysical assumption of most of today's scientists that <u>all</u> cause and effect follow certain immutable laws wherein consciousness plays no role seems to be just plain wrong!

For several decades, many researchers have investigated correlations between the mental intention of various subjects on other humans,[16] mice,[17] and electronic devices[12,18,19,25]. These include the statistical output of electronic random number generators[12,18] with an extension to consider the effects of mental intention on the level of background ionizing radiation from radioactive samples[19] with three main conclusions: (1) under proper conditions, mental intention seems to be able to influence naturally occurring levels of such radiation, (2) some aspects of the physiological state of the subject plus the local magnetic field appear to correlate with a successful result and (3) local environmental (baseline background radiation level) and geocosmic factors (sunspot number) also appear to influence success. Radin[19] proposed that matter-mind interaction (MMI) effects may be thought of as the creation of localized regions (immediate region of the target and for short times) wherein random noise character has been statistically organized to produce a space-time domain of partial order. From the theoretical structure to be discussed in Chapter 8, this might take the form of fluctuating patches of order in the generally disordered vacuum substratum of the target space-time region.

Using a poised gas-discharge device, one of us[25] showed that humans can robustly influence electron microavalanche formation and growth in the device, depending upon the focus of their mental intention, without needing to winnow the effect from a mass of statistics. It was found that, for fixed position of the subject relative to the device, only when the subject's intention was consciously drawn away from the device and directed elsewhere (e.g., focussing on a simple arithmetic problem), no influence on the discharge current was observed[25]. Fairly recently, a brief study was carried out on the ability of humans to alter the structure of either pure water or water plus DNA solutions so that its UV (ultraviolet) spectrum was altered[20]. In that study, there appeared to be two <u>necessary and sufficient</u> conditions required to produce the UV spectrum change: (1) the subject needed to be in an internal state that produces either of the two discerned <u>ordered</u> modes of heart function[30] (as determined by simultaneous electrocardiogram (EKG) analysis) and, (2) the subject needed to <u>intend</u> to influence the structure of water. For the case of the DNA solutions, the intention could be specified to either wind the DNA coils or unwind the DNA coils, and the corresponding UV spectral shift occurred -- provided the subject was in one of the ordered modes of heart function. Much additional research will be needed to both validate and clarify the details of this important study.

It is extremely interesting that the early animal studies by the Watkins'[17] showed that <u>places</u> could retain residual psychic intention (via their studies on reviving anesthetized mice more quickly). They found that, if you put another mouse down later in the <u>same place</u> where the first one had recovered, it revived more quickly (suggesting that the physical locale held some type of "charge"). One begins to wonder if this may be related to the profound observation that, during heart transplants, strong personality and habit characteristics of the donor are sometimes reported to be transferred to the recipient[21,22]. This data suggests that this pump, composed of human cells, has been powerfully altered by the intentions of the original user and that a residue of these "extra" characteristics are transferred with the "heart meat". One needs to ask if the space within the heart has been conditioned at subtle domain levels by the intentions of the user much as we find with the use of our Intention Imprinted Electrical Devices (see Chapter 6). If this general speculation is true, then one would expect some level of effect from other organ transplants and from blood transfusions.

As a side-comment to the above discussion, the inclusion of human consciousness as a factor in scientific research results has been explored recently by Sheldrake who pointed out how seldom this factor was considered to be an important one in physics, chemistry or much of biology[23]. The use of blind assessment was adopted in the mid-19th century by homeopathic physicians who recognized that our beliefs, desires and expectations can influence, often subconsciously, how we observe and interpret things. By the end of the 19th century, this blinded research approach was taken up by psychologists and by psychical researchers -- as a deterrent against the unconventional.

Table 1.1 *Numbers of papers reviewed and the number involving blind or double-blind methodologies in a range of scientific journals. Only papers reporting experimental results were included and all publications appeared from 1996 through 1998 unless otherwise noted.*

Journal	Volumes (and parts)	Number of papers	Blind methods
Physical Sciences			
Jour. of the Am. Chemical Society	118 (39-41)	86	0
Jour. of Applied Physics	80 (11)	76	0
Jour. of Phys.: Condensed Matter	8 (48-49)	75	0
Totals		237	0
Biological Sciences			
Biochemical Journal	318-319 (1-3;1)	191	0
Cell	87 (4-5)	29	0
Heredity	76 (1-5)	58	0
Jour. of Experimental Botany	46-47 (295-302)	132	0
Jour. of Molecular Biology	262 (2-5)	48	0
Jour. of Physiology	497-498 (1;1-2)	145	4
Nature	383-84 (6600-6610)	108	0
Proc. of the Nat. Acad. of Sciences	93 (22-23)	203	3
Totals		914	7 (0.8%)
Medical Sciences			
American Jour. of Medicine	103-104 (5-6; 1-3)	45	22
Annals of Internal Medicine	128 (2-7)	41	12
Brit. Jour. of Clinical Pharmacology	42 (3-5)	49	4
British Medical Journal	313 (7061-7068)	53	2
New England Jour. of Medicine	338 (9-16)	39	15
Totals		227	55 (24%)
Psychology and Animal Behavior			
Animal Behavior	52 (1-4)	72	2
British Journal of Psychology	87 (1-3)	21	0
J. of Experimental Psych.: General	125 (1-3)	23	2
Human Percept. and Performance	22 (5-6)	27	3
Totals		143	7 (4.9%)
Parapsychology			
J. Soc. of Psychical Res. (1993-96)	59-61 (830-845)	14	11
J. Parapsychology (1994-96)	58(3) – 60(2)	13	12
Totals		27	23 (85%)

In single-blind experiments, an investigator does not know which samples or treatments are which. In medicine and experimental psychology, where human subjects are involved, double-blind procedures are used to guard against the expectancy of both subjects and investigators. In a double-blind clinical trial, some patients are given tablets of a particular drug while others are given similar-looking placebo tablets that are pharmacologically inert. Neither researcher nor patients knows who gets which pill until the end of the study when the code is broken.

Sheldrake[23] utilized two surveys in an attempt to quantify the attention or inattention paid to possible experimenter effects in different fields of science. The most common view expressed by physical and biological scientists was that blind methodologies were unnecessary outside psychology and medicine, because "nature itself is blind". This "metaphysical" assumption about nature has led to gross neglect of the consciousness factor in both scientific journal publications (see Table 1.1) and in academic teaching establishments (see Table 1.2).

Table 1.2   Results of a survey of science departments carried out between Dec. 1996 and Feb. 1997 at the following British universities: Bristol, Cambridge, Edinburgh, Exeter, Imperial College (London), Manchester, Newcastle, Oxford, Reading, Sheffield, and University College (London). Members of the academic staff were interviewed by telephone and asked the following questions: (1) Do you ever use blind experimental methodologies in your department? (2) Are students taught about blind methodologies and experimenter effects in general?

Department	Number of departments surveyed	Blind methods used	Blind methods taught
Physical sciences			
Inorganic chemistry	7	0	0
Organic chemistry	7	0	0
Physics	9	1	1
Biological sciences			
Biochemistry	10	1	2
Molecular biology	6	1	0
Genetics	8	4	4
Physiology	8	6	6

A chronic problem for psychopharmacology is the "placebo" effect[24]. It has been shown on countless occasions that administering a simple sugar pill or injecting water can alleviate symptoms or even cure a disease, as long as the patients (and doctors) believe they could be getting a real drug. Enserink[24] points out that "when companies started testing drugs for obsessive-compulsive disorder back in the mid-1980's, the placebo response rate was almost zero. As time went on, this response rate began to creep upward, up to a point where one could reasonably conclude that some clinical trials failed because of high placebo response rates." A very recent meta-analysis of 19 antidepressent drug trials revealed that the "placebo effect" on average accounted for 75% of the effect of <u>real</u> drugs. Although many feel that this data represents a kind of soft underbelly that both academic and industry researchers are more comfortable leaving out of sight, others are fascinated by the power of the placebo effect viewing it not as a problem but as a source of insight into mental health. Going even further, what is it saying about the <u>actual</u> laws of nature, as distinct from our metaphysical assumptions about them, and <u>why</u> has the magnitude of the placebo effect increased so remarkably in the last 20 years?

<u>Contributions From Physics</u>: Only a few years ago, the idea of extra dimensions for explaining some phenomena inhabited a nebulous region somewhere between physics and science fiction. The background concerning the use of extra dimensions is described in an earlier book by one of us[25]. As researchers today explore extra dimensions, they are on the lookout for implications regarding unification of the four fundamental forces of today's physics and they have found this concept to be a useful tool (see Chapter 2).

Despite the hopes of many physicists to the contrary, it now appears more certain than ever that most of the universe is made from a kind of "unworldly" dark matter that can pass right through ordinary matter without leaving barely a trace[26]. Physicists are also coming to believe that empty space is pervaded by an equally mysterious "dark energy", a kind of antigravitational force (called quintessence) that is accelerating the universe's expansion. Some speculate on a type of matter called "mirror matter" (very different from anti-matter) that they think of as just regular matter that is trapped in another dimension. Although its light is also stuck inside what amounts to a parallel universe, its gravity comes shining through, bedeviling the astronomer's calculations [26]. This nether realm might also be the home of dark energy, the quintessence needed to give a boost to cosmic expansion, explaining why it is speeding up instead of slowing down. Interestingly enough, a type of "mirror" matter and its "space" for expression is just what we have found to be crucial for explaining a wide variety of psychoenergetic phenomena[25] as well as the experimental data presented in Chapters 3 to 6 of this book. The mechanism for explaining this is discussed in Chapters 2 and 8.

<u>Considerations About "Space"</u>: Our view of the world we live in is shaped by the way we think about space. In particular, the notion of space as a type of neutral container, a purely geometrical structure within which are located entirely separated objects, is the notion held by most present day philosophers of science[27]. In this construct, matter is the stuff that fills up space and gives curvature to the four-dimensional container, space-time, whose mathematical geometry and relativity characteristics have been described so well by Albert Einstein.

Paraphrasing Ansari,[28] a mathematician/physicist, space, any space, is defined as a medium for the manifestation of patterns or relationships. In simple cases, the elements are easily distinguishable pieces like the conceptual units of a paradigm or the parts of a conceptual model. A complex case requires a drastic rearrangement, or even the creation of newly distinguishable pieces. The analogy to a picture puzzle is useful here -- the pieces fit closely and their arrangement is constrained by their individual geometry. This analogy brings out rather graphically the process of science. Our picture of "reality" changes continuously as pieces are rearranged, replaced or added.

From a mathematics perspective, life provides us with convergent (ordinary) problems and divergent (non-ordinary) problems[28]. The daily preoccupation of all but a very small number of scientists is with ordinary problems via application of well-established theories. Divergent problems, on the other hand, are open-ended and have no unique solution or no solution at all within the confines of the conceptual framework. They require a new theory, usually in a larger conceptual framework, for their solution. That is the approach taken in Chapter 8 of this book.

In general, any theory may be said to contain two components, philosophical and technical. The philosophical component is concerned with meaning or effects in psychic space (why), while the technical component is concerned with manipulations or arrangements in physical/mathematical space (how)[28]. It is the technical component which provides the distinguishing characteristics of a scientific theory. In practice, the power to manipulate our environment depends on our ability to reliably produce desirable effects by suitably arranging environmental conditions. This means the ability to predict the subsequent course of events associated with a given initial set of events in the base space. Thus, a scientific theory is required to make predictions which can be tested.

Conceptual models provide an important link between the two components of science because the model acts as an open channel for the flow of meaning into the theory. The natural desire to attribute meaning to a model probably occurs as an expression of our being in the world. Thus, the geometry of causal relationships, as grasped by a comprehending mind, places the model as much in the world of meaning as in the world of technique[28].

In mathematics, space is abstractly defined as a collection of objects, which is fairly useless unless one says what the objects are and how they are interrelated; i.e., the objects and their relationships describe the space. A well-known example of a mathematical space is metric space in which the "distance" between two points, the elements of the space, is defined in a specific way as in the familiar case of Euclidian space. Over time, we have found that the application of this particular mathematical space to physical problems is extremely valuable, although why this should be so is not clear. In any event, mathematical analysis of physical problems can certainly be successfully carried out by treating space as a purely mathematical concept. Thus, space can be utilized as a philosophical device which merely allows us to put things together, to relate them to one another, and it is the nature of these relationships that prescribes the geometry of the particular space. This, of course, applies to what we call "physical space" which material objects must occupy and which exists between them[28]. This is such an ingrained notion in our minds that perhaps we should label it "vacuum space" as a base space through which physical particles may or may not transit.

In order to describe a physics that includes the forces of intention and consciousness on physical particles, it has been necessary to invent a specific higher dimensional space[25] which, since it is a work in progress, might be called a biconformal space as an approximation. It is a lower dimensional biconformal base space that includes the "mirror" [see Chapter 2] and this is the proper base space for what should be considered as physical reality. This includes both what we call physical particles plus the coarsest substructure of the vacuum. This will be qualitatively expressed in Chapter 2 and quantitatively applied in Chapter 8.

What the Various Chapters Contribute

The latter portion of this chapter lays out the common experimental protocol for Chapters 3 to 6. Chapter 2 provides a qualitative theoretical perspective of relevant theory needed for the reader to look at the experimental data with a clear and open mind without shutting down their sensory system because of the "boggle" effect. It has been our experience, when verbally describing our experimental results to many people, that a point is reached where the data so challenges their long-held mindset or belief system concerning how nature is supposed to behave that it all becomes mind-boggling for them and they lose the ability to continue assimilating the data. This is because it doesn't conform to their "world view" and they need to be able to either temporarily suspend this personal framework for data assimilation or accept (tentatively) a larger framework such as the one provided in Chapter 2.

Chapter 3 deals with our initial experiments on water and clearly shows that, merely by placing the activated IIED (intention imprinted electrical device) in the proximity of a vessel of water that is being monitored for pH level, the pH of the water can be moved upwards or downwards (depending on the specific intention imprinted into the device) by a large amount. Chapter 4 contains the data for the third target experiment rather than the chronologically next experiment that we conducted. It deals with our specific *in vitro* enzyme target experiments and, once again, we found that the specific activated IIED was able to significantly increase the thermodynamic activity of the enzyme in complete accord with the imprinted intention. We also found that this enzyme technique could be utilized as a meaningful detector of the subtle energies involved. Chapter 5 contains the data for the chronologically second target experiment that was an *in vivo* study with fruit flies. Here, the specific intention was to increase the [ATP]/[ADP] ratio in developing fruit fly larvae so as to make them more fit and thus reduce larval development time. Once again, great success was obtained using this particular IIED. Chapter 6 is a return to water experiments, but this time using the water as a probe to register the degree of "conditioning" taking place in the local space of the experiment. This data shows that the local symmetry, and thus the local physics, changes in very significant ways as a result of continued IIED use in that locale. This is thought to occur via changes in the degree of order present in the physical vacuum.

Chapter 7 provides background conventional physics of a quantitative nature that forms a part of the theoretical explanation for the experimental data of Chapters 3 to 6. Chapter 8 provides some of the quantitative new physics needed to largely explain this data. Chapter 9 looks at the implications of this experimental data plus the theoretical modeling to the fields of religion, philosophy, psychology and integrated medicine (complementary or alternative medicine) while Chapter 10 looks at a variety of specific implications for science and technology.

By the time Chapter 10 is reached, one can hopefully begin to see how a vast new technology could be unfolded for humanity by pursuing and applying all phases of the IIED concept. For example, we expect to be able to greatly increase the solubility of oxygen or nitrogen in purified water. The former can be utilized in some applications as a super-oxidant and in others as an energizing "boost" to healthy humans or medical patients at key times during the day. The latter might allow us to reduce or replace fertilizers in agricultural applications. One might also be able to tailor-make specific needed enzyme-like structures or key pharmaceutical-like structures in the purified water also of great therapeutic benefit to medical patients.

The whole concept of a "conditioned" space that might involve ordering and structural transformations in the "stuff" of the vacuum opens the door to direct influence of, and ultimately engineering advances of, every area of technology that humanity has created to date. In addition, it allows the possibility of engineering vast new technologies from those to be "spun" out from the ability to possibly create room temperature super-conducting materials to those involving machines that can pump energy from the vacuum and drive vehicles to the stars.

For Whom Is This Book Written?

This book is written for all professional people with an interest in science. In particular, one audience most immediately concerned with the material of this book is all those involved in human health care, whether medical doctors, psychiatrists, psychologists, nurses or trained technicians. The next most concerned audience is that group of college graduates with a broad interest in self-development, metaphysical considerations and the spiritual path. This book is also written for individuals working in or studying physics, chemistry, biology and engineering; however, today's prevailing mindset in these fields is such that only a few broad-gauge individuals would, at the moment, be interested in the opportunities presented by this book. This is because the present U(1) Gauge symmetry paradigm, which strongly dominates these latter fields, leaves all human qualities <u>outside</u> of the framework of physics. This book focuses on the emergence of a new physics where the human qualities of emotion, mind and intention are incorporated into the framework for meaningfully describing the various expressions of nature.

The General Experimental Protocol

The methods and procedures we followed for experiments described in this book were simple ones. For the most part our measurement apparatus could be set up on a standard laboratory benchtop using equipment readily available from well-known laboratory supply companies. In all our experiments the standard scientific method was employed. Even though our results (and some procedures) were far from conventional, to obtain them our intention was to use methods and procedures familiar to conventional science.

For each target experiment, we start with two identical physical devices (see Appendix 1.A). We isolate one from the other by storing it in an electrically-grounded Faraday cage and "charge" the other with the specific intention for the particular target experiment. The interior of a Faraday cage is just an electrically shielded volume wherein ambient electromagnetic field intensities have been substantially reduced. This charging process involved the services of four highly qualified meditators to imprint the device with the specific intention (there is probably nothing sacred about using four). The devices with the same imprint were then wrapped in aluminum (Al) foil and stored in their own electrically-grounded Faraday cage until the next step in the process. Next, when needed, the Al-foil wrapped devices were separately shipped on separate days, via Federal Express, to their laboratory destination about 2000 miles away. On arriving there, they were immediately placed in separate, electrically-grounded Faraday cages until their use in the actual target experiments conducted by others. The device was merely placed close to the particular target experiment and turned on for some time period.

Overview of the Experimental Results: For target experiment 1, changes of ~ 0.5 to 1.0 pH units increase or decrease, with a measurement accuracy of ± 0.01 pH units, was achieved (with an effect size of ~ 1000). For target experiment 2, reductions of $\sim 15\%$ in larval development time for the imprinted vs. the unimprinted device were obtained with strong statistical significance ($p < 0.001$ and an effect size of ~ 15). For target experiment 3, increases in thermodynamic activity for ALP of $\sim 10\%$ to 20% were achieved for the imprinted device vs. the unimprinted device and at a strong statistical significance level ($p < 0.001$ and an effect size of $\sim 10\text{-}20$). For target experiment 4, anomalously large oscillations in water of temperature, pH, electrical conductivity and DC magnetic field polarity effects heralded the onset of locale conditioning and the second phase of the new physics development was undeniably achieved.

Blinded vs. Unblinded Experiments: In the very beginning, while target experiments 1 and 2 were still being conducted at Stanford University, they were set up as a blinded experiment. The experimenters (Dibble and Kohane) did not know which devices were imprinted and which were unimprinted. Thus, our first successful results were obtained with this protocol. However, with the water pH-studies, the imprinted device revealed a very characteristic behavior difference with respect to the unimprinted device (see Figure 3.20) so a blinded experiment became untenable. For the biological experiments side-by-side simultaneous comparisons were made (see Figure 4.7) and we soon neglected to continue the blinded aspect of the protocol. Probably, for these studies it would have been better to stay with the blinded feature in the overall protocol. However, once the blinded feature was removed from the water studies and device reimprinting became a necessary part of the program, our uncertainties concerning the effectiveness of our device isolation technique caused us to choose the unblinded modality for the biological studies as well.

Inner Self-Management Practices of the Experimenters: Although this is not normally considered to be a protocol component for an experimental study, in future work of this type it should be. Dibble is a long-time Siddha Yoga practitioner with a regular regimen of physical exercise while Kohane restricts his activities to rigorous daily physical exercise. During the Stanford period of investigation, neither of them had any technician assistance. During the Minnesota phase of the experimentation, first a technician (competent, self-contained, only marginally interested in the scope of the work and with no inner self-management practice) was added to assist Kohane. About 6 months later, an assistant (a very capable, accomplished Siddha Yoga practitioner with a keen interest in the scope of the work) was added to the program to help Dibble. The reasons why this is considered to be a meaningful consideration in the protocol are addressed at the beginning of Chapter 6.

In closing this section and this chapter, it should perhaps also be stated that neither the Stanford environment, nor the dominating forces in the Minnesota facility (except in the very early days) provided much emotional or psychological support for these studies.

References

1. L. Dossey, <u>Meaning and Medicine: Lessons From a Doctor's Tales of Breakthrough and Healing</u> (Bantam Books, New York, NY, 1991).

2. J. Borysenko, "In Defense of a New Paradigm: The Science of Body, Mind and Spirit," Bridges, 9 (3), (1998) 4.

3. C. Pert, <u>Molecules of Emotion: Why You Feel The Way You Do</u> (Scribner, New York, NY, 1997).

4.   R. C. Bird, "Positive Therapeutic Effects of Intercessionary Prayer in a Coronary Care Unit Population," Southern Medical Journal, <u>81</u>:7 (1988) 826.

5.   M. L. Morse, "The Right Temporal Lobe and Associated Limbic Lobe Structures as the Biological Interface with an Interconnected Universe," Network, #68 (1998) 3.

6.   W. Penfield and T. Rasmussen, <u>The Cerebral Cortex of Man: A Clinical Study of Localization of Function</u> (MacMillan, New York, NY, 1950).

7.   W. Penfield, "The Role of the Temporal Cortex in Certain Psychical Phenomena," J. Ment. Sci., <u>101</u> (1955) 451.

8.   M. Persinger, <u>The Neuropsychological Basis of God Beliefs</u> (Praeger, New York, NY, 1987).

9.   M. L. Morse, D. Venecia and J. Milstein, "Near Death Experiences: A Neurophysiological Explanatory Model," J. Near Death Studies, <u>8</u> (1989) 45.

10.   D. I. Radin, <u>The Conscious Universe</u>, (Harper Edge, San Francisco, 1997).

11.   H. E. Puthoff and R. Targ, "A Perceptual Channel for Information Transfer Over Kilometer Distances: Historical Perspective and Recent Research," Proceedings of the IEEE, <u>64</u> (1976) 329.

12.   R. G. Jahn and B. J. Dunne, <u>Margins of Reality</u> (Harcourt Brace, New York, NY, 1987).

13.   R. Targ and J. Katra, <u>Miracles of Mind: Exploring Nonlocal Consciousness and Spiritual Healing</u> (New World Library, Novato, CA, 1998).

14.   S. Grof, <u>The Cosmic Game</u> (New Leaf, San Francisco, 1998).

15.   R. Ravindra, "Yoga and the Future Science of Consciousness: Some Notes," Network, #66 (1998) 8.

16. W. G. Braud and M. J. Schlitz, "Consciousness Interactions with Remote Biological Systems: Anomalous Intentionality Effects," Subtle Energies, 2 (1), (1991) 1.

17. G. K. Watkins and A. M. Watkins, "Possible PK Influence on the Resuscitation of Anesthetized Mice," J. Parapsychology, 35 (4), (1971) 257.

18. D. I. Radin and R. D. Nelson, "Evidence For Consciousness-Related Anomalies in Random Physical Systems," Foundations of Physics, 19 (1989) 1499.

19. D. I. Radin, "Beyond Belief: Exploring Interaction Among Body and Environment," Subtle Energies, 2 (1991); "Environmental Modulation and Statistical Equilibrium in Mind-Matter Interaction," Subtle Energies, 4 (1993) 1.

20. G. Rein and R. McCraty, "Structural Changes in Water and DNA Associated with New Physiologically Measurable States," J. Scientific Exploration, 8 (1994) 438.

21. P. Pearsall, The Heart's Code: Tapping the Wisdom and Power of Our Heart Energy (Broadway Books, New York, NY, 1998).

29. G. Schwartz and L. Russek, The Living Energy Universe: A Fundamental Discovery That Transforms Science and Medicine (Hampton Roads, Charlettesville, VA, 1999).

23. R. Sheldrake, "How Widely is Blind Assessment Used in Scientific Research?", Alternative Therapies, 5 (1999) 88.

24. M. Enserink, "Can the Placebo Be the Cure?", Science, 284 (1999) 238.

25. W. A. Tiller, Science and Human Transformation: Subtle Energies, Intentionality and Consciousness (Pavior Publishing, Walnut Creek, CA, 1997).

26. S. S. Holt and C. L. Bennett (eds) "Dark matter", Proceedings 336, American Institute of Physics, New York, 1995.

27. N. Huggett, Ed., <u>Space From Zeno to Einstein: Classical Readings With a Contemporary Commentary</u> (MIT Press, Boston, MA, 1999).

28. A. Ansari, "Higher Order Information and Energy Spaces -- A Conceptual Framework" (Unpublished Paper, 1998).

29. The "Ally," Clarus Products International, LLC, 1330 Lincoln Avenue Suite 210, San Rafael, California 94901.

30. C. W. Smith, "Is a Living System a Macroscopic Quantum System?", Frontier Perspectives, <u>7</u>,1 Fall/Winter (1998) 9.

31. W. A. Tiller, R. McCraty and M. Atkinson, "Cardiac Coherence: A New Noninvasive Measure of Autonomic Nervous System Order," Alternative Therapies, <u>2</u> (1996) 52.

Appendix 1.A: Some Device Essentials

<u>The Host Devices</u>: The physical size of the plastic case housing the electronics is $\sim$ 7 in. x 3 in. x 1 in. The electric circuits utilized are quite simple (see Figure 1A.1). They basically involve only an EEPROM (Electrically Erasable Programmable Read Only Memory) component (not conventionally connected into the circuit), an oscillator component (1-10 MHz range), no intentional antenna and either line voltage or battery power supply. We utilized both single oscillator devices (7.3 MHz) and three-oscillator devices (5.0, 8.0 and 9.3 MHz). The radiated electrical power for these devices was less than the order of $\sim$ 1 microwatt and they were generally placed at a distance of $\sim$ 3 in. - 6 in. from the target experiment. These devices were designed to be almost identical to a commercial device[29] that is readily available so that other investigators might more easily attempt to reproduce our experimental results.

<u>Device Isolation and Storage</u>: Early on in this experimental program, it was discovered that, even in the switched-off state, some form of information leakage was occurring between the imprinted device (IIED) and the unimprinted control device. This manifested as a temporally decreasing difference in the results found when these two types of devices were separately used in a particular target

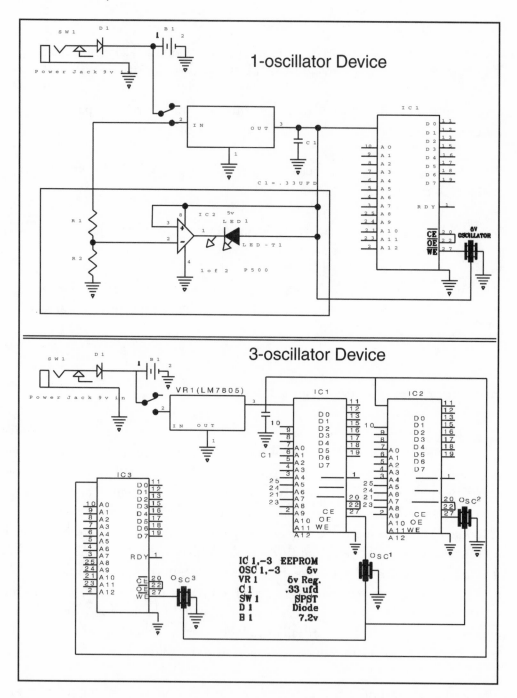

Figure 1A.1   Circuit diagrams for the electronic devices used as host devices for intention imprinting.

experiment so that, in essence, we lost our control after some relatively short period of time. The resolution of this difficulty, for the entire course of the present experiments, was to store each device with a unique category of imprint in its own electrically-grounded Faraday cage after first completely wrapping it in aluminum foil. Although not perfect, this procedure has allowed the intention charge to remain stored in the IIED for ~ 3-4 months and appears to have significantly diminished unwanted communication between the imprinted and unimprinted devices.

The Faraday cages were constructed from a fine mesh copper screen (0.16" grid) in a cylindrical geometry with diameters from 6 in. to 18 in. (mostly 12 in.) and with a close-fitting cylindrical cap that would close the top and slide down the side-wall about 6 in. Theoretically, such cages screen out the intensity of radio and higher electromagnetic (EM) frequencies by about a factor of 10. At the very high frequency end, EM-wavelengths smaller than the copper mesh size can readily pass into the interior of the cage and this is why we always wrap the devices in Al-foil (to stop such photons). At the very low frequency end (~ 60 Hz and below), the EM skin depth in copper is so large that our type of cages are only minimally effective for EM-shielding. We did not study the effectiveness of magnetic shielding, via the use of mu-metal containers, during this study but it is a procedure that should be seriously considered for future experiments. In related studies, Smith[30] has found that mu-metal shielding of the geomagnetic field erases both his specific electromagnetic frequency imprints in water as well as homeopathic potentials in water. In his studies, the imprinting threshold was found to be ~ 360 nT (nanotesla). As a final point on this topic, when one makes measurements using probes located <u>inside</u> the Faraday cage and recording instruments <u>outside</u> the Faraday cage, the overall EM-shielding effectiveness is reduced.

<u>**The Imprinting Process**</u>: The actual imprinting procedure for a particular target experiment was as follows: (a) place the single-oscillator or three-oscillator device, along with its current transformer (plugged in and turned on), on a table around which the imprinters sit, (b) four people (two men plus two women) who were all accomplished meditators (decades of regular practice), coherent, inner self-managed and readily capable of entering an ordered mode of heart function[25,31] plus sustaining it for an extended period of time, sat around the table ready to enter a deep meditative state, (c) a signal was then given to enter such an internal state, to mentally cleanse the environment and then create a sacred space for the intention (requiring about 10 to 15 minutes). Then, a signal was given by one of the four to put attention on the table-top objects to mentally erase any prior imprints from the device, (d) after 3 or 4 minutes, another signal was given by one of the four to begin focussing on the specific

prearranged intention statement (it was read aloud by one of the four) for about 15 minutes and then abruptly released, (e) next, a final signal was given to shift focus to a closing intention designed to seal the imprint into the device and minimize leakage of this essential energy/information from the device (requiring about 5 minutes) and (f) since this completed the process, the four people withdrew from the meditative state and returned to their normal state of consciousness. It should be obvious to the reader that a wide variety of options and variants exist with respect to the erasing, imprinting and sealing phases of the overall treatment process for these devices.

The specific intentions for the four target experiments are given below:

1. **Water Studies**: To activate the indwelling consciousness of the system so that the IIED decreases (or increases) the pH of the experimental water by one pH unit compared to the control; i.e., increase (or decrease) the H^+ content of this water by a factor of 10.

2. **In Vivo Fruit Fly Studies**: To synergistically influence (a) the availability of oxygen, protons and ADP (adenine diphosphate), (b) the activity of the available concentration of NAD (nicotinamide adenine dinucleotide) plus (c) the activity of the available enzymes, dehydrogenase and ATP-synthase, in the mitochondria so that the production of ATP (adenine triphosphate) in the fruit fly larvae is significantly increased (as much as possible without harming the life function of the larvae) and thus the larval development time significantly reduced relative to that with the control device.

3. **In Vitro Enzyme Studies**: To activate the indwelling consciousness of the device so as to increase by a significant factor (as much as possible), the thermodynamic activity coefficient of the specific liver enzyme, alkaline phosphatase (ALP). This activity coefficient increase is to occur relative to the same type of experiment conducted with an unimprinted device.

4. **Locale Conditioning Studies**: To activate the indwelling consciousness of the system so that this type of IIED becomes a powerful locale environment conditioning system. It is to activate such a high deltron content in the local environment that the strong coupling condition between D-space and R-space is quickly attained (see Chapter 2 for the meaning of these new words). Thus, any type of subsequent IIED or psychoenergetic experiment conducted in that conditioned locale is to be successful to a high degree.

CHAPTER 2

Perspectives on a New Physics

Most of us describe nearly all of our day-to-day experience of nature from the viewpoint of classical physics, the dominant physics paradigm of the 18th and 19th centuries. However, since the early part of the 20th century, quantum physics has become the dominant paradigm. Quantum mechanics (QM) and relativistic mechanics have, at a fundamental particle level, replaced Newtonian mechanics. Today, QM is the most exact and the most powerful theoretical procedure in the entire arsenal of physics. Thus, when we want to describe nature of any variety or expression, we would expect the most accurate description to arise from utilizing a QM viewpoint or an extension thereof.

Some Limitations of Present Quantum Mechanics

Although properly applied QM is very accurate, it has many limitations to its use, especially for macroscopic objects and macroscopic phenomena. Present day computer capacities limit the QM computations to only microscopic size objects containing a few atoms. This puts most phenomena of our day-to-day experience completely beyond the scope of today's QM computations. Perhaps even more limiting is the fact that QM, even for very small systems, doesn't provide much insight into, or intuition about, the fundamental interactions and processes taking place during an event being computationally treated. Thus, present-day QM behaves very much like a "black box" where one inputs the initial conditions, turns a mathematical crank on the black box and eventually receives a precise output from the box. To expand the usefulness of QM we need to invent some procedure for seeing something of the structures operating inside the black box! Before setting out to do this, let us first continue to list the shortcomings of QM. In Appendix 2.A we also provide general information concerning limitations of the normal path of progress for any science.

The black box aspect of QM seems to have come about because the originators constrained the formal representation of the theory to a single 4-dimensional space (3 distance plus 1 time), what we call physical space-time or our normal cognitive domain. Because of this restriction, a variety of conceptual dichotomies arose as residues of this approach. Three of these are

(1) the concept of wave/particle duality, (2) the concept of non-local forces and (3) the concept of broken symmetry between electric and magnetic monopoles. These have confounded our imagination for three-quarters of a century but perhaps they provide a clue for a place to start in order to modify present QM and actually look into its black box nature.

A second level of strange characteristics associated with QM related to (1) the Heisenberg uncertainty relationships that connected a particle's uncertainty of position, Δx, and its uncertainty of momentum, Δp, or the uncertainty in its energy, ΔE, with it's uncertainty of location in time, Δt, and (2) the dematerialization of the particle into the vacuum and its rematerialization again out of the vacuum at another position in space-time. These two characteristics may be intimately related; however, serious discussion of them is beyond the scope of this book. Here, we will only deal with a level of modeling that accounts for the three dichotomies mentioned in the previous paragraph.

De Broglie's Pilot Wave Concept

To achieve this worthy goal, we start with wave/particle duality and look at its origin. In the 1920s, de Broglie proposed the concept that every particle had a pilot wave envelope enclosing it and moving at the particle's velocity (see Figure 2.1).

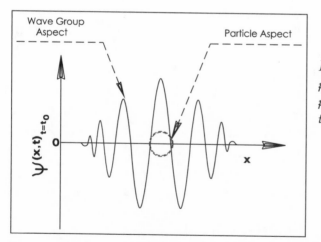

Figure 2.1   A group of pilot waves for a physical particle located somewhere in the group.

This concept required some new wave components to move into the envelope and some old wave components to move out as the envelope moved along. If we call the particle velocity, v_p, and the velocity of the individual wave components, V_w, then relativity theory requires that the following relationship hold (see Appendix 2.B)

$$V_p V_w = c^2 \qquad (2.1)$$

where c is the velocity of light. Since $V_p < c$ always, V_w must be $> c$ always and these waves were denoted "information" waves in order to not make trouble for relativity theory. Subsequent experiments showed that particles like neutrons, protons, electrons, helium atoms, etc., all exhibited wave-like behavior and de Broglie received a Nobel prize for his seminal work. Depending upon the design of a particular experiment, the results showed either particle-like or wave-like behavior so that this <u>simultaneous</u> particle/wave concept of de Broglie's was incorporated into QM as wave/particle <u>duality</u> and came to mean either/or rather than both for many physicists.

Here, in this book, we firmly return to the original concept of nature expressing itself <u>simultaneously</u> via its particle aspect <u>and</u> it's wave aspect and ask how we might formally express this without losing one aspect or the other. Long experience with the particle aspect has shown us that distance-time or (x,y,z,ict)-space, which we can call direct space or D-space, is a satisfactory coordinate system for describing the behavior of this aspect of substance. We have also used this coordinate system for describing wave motion, even though the waves of our cognitive experience are merely <u>modulations of particle fluxes</u> or <u>particle densities</u> in space-time. It is probably the misinterpreting of this class of particle modulation wave with the de Broglie pilot wave that caused QM's founding fathers to confine the theory to a purely (x,y,z,t)-formalism. The de Broglie pilot wave is thought to be a waveform of a much more continuum nature than particle modulation waves.

A Biconformal Base-space Approach

A more appropriate coordinate system for describing de Broglie-type waves is a reciprocal space or R-space system, $(x^{-1}, y^{-1}, z^{-1}, t^{-1})$. Each of these coordinates is a frequency; 1/distance equals number per unit distance or a spatial frequency and 1/time equals number per unit time or a temporal frequency. In solid state physics, wave behavior in R-space is described using a wave number, (k_x, k_y, k_z, k_t), descriptor (each $k_\alpha = 2\pi j/\alpha$ where $\alpha = $ x,y,z,ict and the quality indicator, j, may be different than i). Thus, although it is <u>not wrong</u> to describe both the particle aspect and the de Broglie wave aspect in terms of (x,y,z,ict)-space, as is done in QM, it entangles the two aspects in a very complex fashion and leads directly to the QM-black box nature. For this reason, a better approach would be to keep the particle aspect and the wave aspect separate, using the D-space coordinate system for the one and the R-space coordinate system for the other. Following this approach, any formal description of substance behavior would involve at least the eight coordinates (x, y, z, ict, k_x, k_y, k_z, k_t). However, since $V_p < C$ and $V_w > C$, the two aspects cannot directly interact with each other because of relativity theory; therefore it is necessary to invent the presence of an additional substance that is not constrained by relativity theory, because these two aspects clearly interact in the de Broglie particle/pilot wave picture. This will be more fully explained in Chapters 7 and 8.

The moieties of this coupling substance are thought to be from the domain of emotion and have been labeled deltrons, δ, by one of us[1]. This means that any formal description of substance behavior in nature, <u>without any human intervention</u>, involves at least 9 coordinates (x, y, z, ict; k_x, k_y, k_z, k_t; C_δ) where $C_{\delta o}$ is the cosmic background activated deltron concentration. When human intervention, via human consciousness in the form of the application of human intentionality acts on nature, one must add at least one more coordinate to any meaningful description of nature. Thus, formal description of nature, which includes human intention, involves at least ten coordinates (x, y, z, ict; k_x, k_y, k_z, k_t; $C_{\delta o}$; I*) where I* represents the intensity of human intention and it influences the magnitude of C_δ (Chapter 8 is devoted to showing how particles, expressing themselves in the dual 4-spaces, interact with each other).

A Higher Dimensional Framework

A diagrammatic representation of this functionality is given in Figure 2.2[1]. There, we see our cognitive domain that we call physical reality in the center and a dual or conjugate 4-space reality connected to it. In the esoteric literature, this has been labeled "etheric" reality. Here, we make the additional postulate that the moieties that write the waves in this etheric or (k_x, k_y, k_z, k_t)-space are the magnetic monopoles. Thus, the electric monopoles operate in direct-space while the magnetic monopoles operate in reciprocal space with a very special type of "mirror" relationship (not a reflection mirror) functioning between them[2] (see Chapters 7 and 8). Via this unique mirror, the magnetic monopoles of R-space generate magnetic dipole images in D-space while the electric monopoles of D-space generate electric dipole images in R-space. This

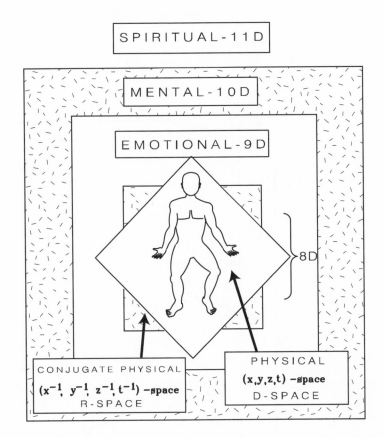

Figure 2.2   A visualization   of dual four-space frames imbedded in three higher dimensional frames.

leads to our normal Maxwell equations for electromagnetism functioning in D-space and another set of analogous equations for magnetoelectrism functioning in R-space[2,3]. This is illustrated in Table 2.1. We will see later in Chapter 8, where we deal with the <u>quantitative</u> physics perspective, that this procedure allows us to predict how the non-local forces vary from point-to-point in D-space (space-time) via natural events occurring in R-space. Thus, this general approach allows us to totally eliminate the three major dichotomies of QM listed earlier. We will also see later in Chapter 8 that a part of the R-space behavior is present in every physical measurement that anyone makes so that a new definition of what one takes to be a physical quality must eventually be made.

Returning to Figure 2.2, we find that the dual 4-spaces (D-space/R-space) are imbedded in the domain of emotion, the natural home for the deltrons, and this is called a 9-space domain (since it embeds the general 8-

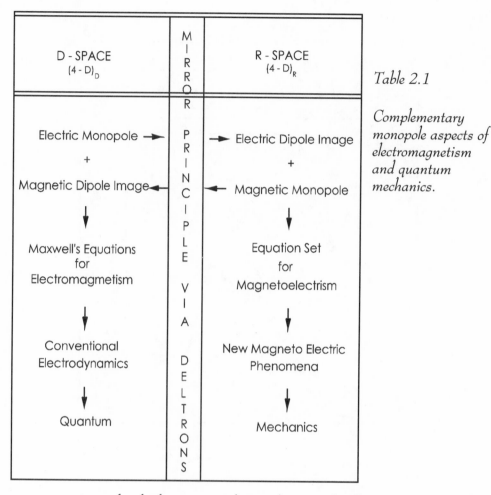

Table 2.1

Complementary monopole aspects of electromagnetism and quantum mechanics.

space containing the dual 4-spaces of D and R). It has been proposed earlier that this 9-space domain of emotion is itself imbedded in the domain of mind, a 10-dimensional construct. And all of this is proposed to be imbedded in the domain of spirit (a construct that is thought to be eleven dimensional and higher). The boundary between the 10-dimensional domain of mind and the 11-dimensional domain of spirit is thought to distinguish and separate the <u>relative</u> universe (10-dimensional and below) from the <u>absolute</u> universe (11-dimensional and above)[1-4].

Intention and Its Path of Action

To obtain some insight into how human intention can influence physical behavior and physical measurements, consider Figure 2.3. The following is the proposed mechanism[1]. A specific intention, projected from the level of spirit, imprints a detailed pattern on the domain of mind. This pattern is an information pattern that is a one-to-one representation of the original intention. Via the structural mechanism connecting the mind domain to R-space, this pattern imprints a second representation of the

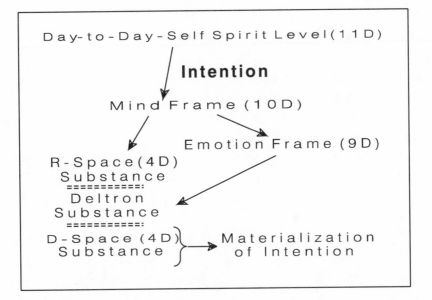

Figure 2.3   *Illustration of one possible process path whereby spirit produces action in the physical domain.*

information (of somewhat lower fidelity) onto the R-space domain[1]. In addition, an enhanced activation of deltrons from the emotion domain occurs, changing the activated deltron level from the cosmic background level, C_{δ_0} to a much higher level, C_δ (Chapter 8 shows how crucial this is to the mathematical development). This increased deltron activation strongly increases the coupling between the magnetic monopoles of R-space and the electric monopoles of D-space so that the R-space information pattern is transferred to D-space with still further reduction in fidelity (Chapter 7 shows how the geometry in one 4-space predicts the pattern geometry in the dual 4-space). These R-space/D-space information patterns engage the hard-wired mechanisms and processes of the physical body to materialize in physical reality the original intention. Let us now consider an interesting metaphor to illuminate the Figure 2.2 / Figure 2.3 construct.

At least one of us (WAT) has come to believe that we are all spirits having a physical experience as we "ride the river of life" together. Our spiritual parents dressed us in our biobodysuits and put us in this playpen that we call a universe in order to grow in coherence, in order to develop our gifts of intentionality and in order to become what we were originally intended to become – co-creators with our spiritual parents.

These biobodysuits come in a fairly wide variety of colors and in two basic morphological forms that we choose to call "genders". The biobodysuits are fabricated with four unique layers, (1) the outermost layer is fashioned from electric monopole substances (particulate substance), (2) the first inner layer is fashioned from magnetic monopole substances (de Broglie wave substance), (3) the second inner layer is fashioned from emotion domain substances and (4) the third inner layer is fashioned from mind domain substances. These three inner layers are all substructures of the physical vacuum! And inside this biobodysuit is a portion of our spirit self that drives the vehicle. Thus, this metaphorical device or biobodysuit resembles a "diving bell", with a human inside, that is utilized for deep-sea explorations. In our case, the biobodysuit is well designed for sensing and for expressing mobility in this strange earth environment.

Most of the general public hold the idea that the vacuum is not only the absence of physical matter but that it is also devoid of anything! However, this is not so. For QM and relativity theory to be internally self-consistent theories, the vacuum is <u>required</u> to contain an amazingly large inherent energy content. This vacuum energy density is calculated to be so large that the intrinsic energy contained within the volume of a <u>single</u> hydrogen atom is about one trillion times <u>larger</u> than that stored in <u>all</u> the physical mass of <u>all</u> the planets plus <u>all</u> the stars in the cosmos out to the present limits of detection, a radius of ~ 20 billion light-years (provided we neglect the gravitational constant factor which is unity for a "flat" space). This makes the energy stored in physical matter a mere whisper compared to that stored in the vacuum. Uncovering the secrets of the vacuum is obviously a very important part of humankind's future!

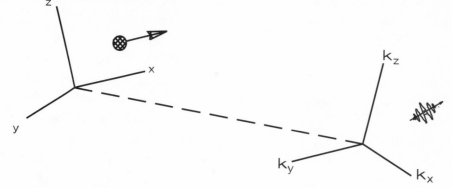

Figure 2.4   *D-space particle event (on left) connected to R-space pilot wave event (on right).*

Because of the conceptual separation of physical substance into D-space and R-space aspects with descriptors separated into (x,y,z,t)- vs (k_x, k_y, k_z, k_t)-behavior, the de Broglie particle/pilot wave concept of Figure 2.1 needs to be expanded to express a moving particle at the instantaneous location (x', y', z', t') in D-space and its connected pilot wave at the specific location (k'_x, k'_y, k'_z, k'_t) in R-space. This alteration will be developed more fully in Chapter 8. Here, we merely seed the new picture for the reader and utilize Figure 2.4 to concretize it somewhat. The implication is that the particle event in D-space is intimately and lawfully connected to the pilot wave event in R-space. From this, the reader can begin to qualitatively see how R-space wave events can influence remote D-space particle events (see Chapter 8).

It is useful to comment on the dimensionality of the spaces utilized in this description versus the minimum number of unique variables required for a meaningful description of nature. Our total dependence on a distance and time description of natural phenomena may be more related to the fact that these are major cognition parameters of brain functioning rather than something fundamental in nature. Nature may be expressing itself via a broad spectrum of parameters but we are only cognitively aware of a few of them because of brain development limitations at our present state of evolution. Thus, to try to circumvent this limitation, we propose a model that discriminates D-space from R-space plus from the 9-space of Emotion and the 10-space of Mind. Such a structural separation is not arbitrary, as will be more fully delineated in Chapters 7 and 8. These descriptors are largely a convenience to aid our progress towards expanded understanding and may ultimately be revealed not to be the most appropriate symmetry subsets of nature. However, for now, they correlate with our triune brain and have sufficient quantitative utility to allow us to reach that richer perspective.

The evolution of brain functioning may have produced limitations in addition to cognitive awareness of higher dimensions. One hypothesis is that the effect of our intention on physical reality is limited as a result of natural selection as well. The capacity to do real harm to each other could be significantly enhanced by human intentions manifesting robustly. This concept would tend to justify thinking that human intention can only produce small, barely perceptible effects on physical reality. Such a viewpoint needs to be replaced by one that is a bit more expansive; namely, that development of sufficient inner self-management allows one to circumvent these limitations[1] without serious side-effects.

Some Consequences of High Deltron Activation

A final but extremely important point to be made with respect to this basic perspective relates to the consequences to be anticipated if the degree of deltron activation can be increased by large values. This expectation is illustrated by Figure 2.5 for some generalized physical measurement, Q_M. As the reader will see from the following chapters, significant experimental data has been gathered to show that some type of conditioning process occurs in the local volume of physical space around an activated IIED (Intention Imprinted Electrical Device) as a function of processing time. It is useful, here, to think of this as the development of organization (order) in the vacuum within the interstices of all atoms and molecules inhabiting that local volume. One consequence of this is that a significantly stronger coupling appears between the physical domain and higher dimensional domains of nature. This manifests itself, after some initial incubation processing period, as altered physical behavior of water (and presumably also other materials) as measured in the processed locale and as contrasted with the same measurements being made in any of several locales located greater than 20 – 50 feet from the processed site. With sufficient locale processing, one attains the strong coupling condition associated with the upper plateau in Figure 2.5. Then, even with the IIED removed and stored in an electrically grounded Faraday cage, the same type of strong coupling behavior can be obtained in that locale for several months to a year or more.

As the reader will see in Chapter 6, when $Q_M = \Delta \, pH_S^N = pH$ (S-pole) – pH (N-pole) for a DC magnet placed under the vessel of water as in Figure 2.6 with either the north-pole pointing up or the south-pole pointing up, $\Delta \, pH_S^N = 0$ is observed to occur in a normal locale but $\Delta \, pH_S^N$ can be much greater than zero or much less than zero in a fully conditioned locale. pH is a measure of the hydrogen ion concentration in the water (see Chapter 3). This behavior seems to indicate some fundamental shift in the physics Gauge condition operating in the conditioned locale (see Appendix 2.C for a discussion of Gauge symmetry).

Conditioning and Altered Gauge Symmetry

The normal locale state is that described by the U(1) Gauge condition wherein observable nature expresses itself in terms of electric monopoles, magnetic dipoles and the standard Maxwell's equations for electrodynamics[5-6]. At this Gauge level, no DC magnetic field polarity effects are allowed because

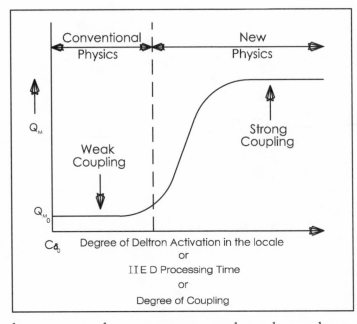

Figure 2.5

Q_M *(some generalized physical measurement) vs. Deltron activation (or time of operation of IIED).*

the magnetic force is proportional to the gradient of the square of the magnetic field strength ($-\nabla H^2$) and any possible polarity effect disappears when one changes H to H^2. We are all familiar with the fact that squaring a mathematically negative number produces a positive number (e.g. $(-2)^2 = 4 = (+2)^2$). For a strongly conditioned locale, the locale exhibits a characteristic that definitely belongs to the higher symmetry SU(2) Gauge condition. In the SU(2) Gauge condition, nature expresses itself in terms of both electric and magnetic monopoles with necessary modifications to Maxwell's equations. The reader is directed to Appendix 2.C for an expanded discussion of Gauge theory in physics.

In current physics, one of the key discussions that connects the Gauge condition to important concepts and hypotheses in physics is that revolving around the "big bang" concept. Here, one encounters a description of matter undergoing evolutionary changes of state, from states of higher fundamental symmetry to states of lower fundamental symmetry. At amazingly short times in this proposed process, Gauge transformations occur from very high symmetry states and progressively drop to the lower symmetry state of the SU(2) Gauge and then on down to the U(1) Gauge symmetry level.

Symmetry changes for matter still occur at the U(1) Gauge level but these all involve collective interactions described as changes of state of the plasma $\Rightarrow$ gas $\Rightarrow$ liquid $\Rightarrow$ solid kind. In the IIED locale conditioning experiments, we seem to be on a process path that involves a reversal of this

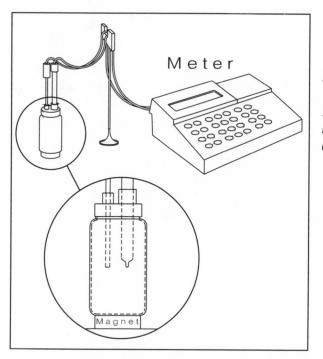

Figure 2.6

Experimental set-up for magnet-water experiments (see Chapter 6).

fundamental Gauge symmetry transition path occurring in the big bang picture!

At the U(1) Gauge symmetry level of our world, we have expert systems and intelligent machines plus hardware architecture with supportive written software that allows the machines to perform within precise, predictable limits. In relatively simple electronic systems, one has come to expect that the output performance of such systems can be completely and exactly characterized based upon the system design along with its specific material and electrical component parameters. In such cases, the output response/input signal ratio is independent of any other factors than these. Certainly, the great success of computer-aided design (CAD) for both electric circuit design and semiconductor processing procedures utilized for integrated circuit fabrication underscores the great utility of this paradigm in today's technology. In a world completely governed by this U(1) Gauge symmetry and thus the paradigm just enunciated, conventional science would state that humans could not meaningfully interact, at an energy/information level, with their experiments.

Based on this paradigm, conventional science would even more emphatically state that specific human intentions could not be embedded into a simple electronic device which is then used to meaningfully influence an experiment in complete accord with the specific intention. The experimental data of the following chapters show that, <u>under our conditions</u>, this conventional science paradigm or rather, this U(1) Gauge paradigm, does not hold or only partially holds depending upon where we are along the abscissa of Figure 2.5. Thus, in much of the work reported on in the following experimental chapters, the state of locale conditioning is not precisely known and it is slowly drifting upscale (Figure 2.5 abscissa) as the basic target experiment is repeated again and again. Only when the locale conditioning state reaches the upper plateau can one expect precise repeatability of the experimental results. It is important for the reader to realize these facts in order not to be confused by the confrontation between this data and the normal conventional experience in our day-to-day world.

Information Transfer Mechanisms

In conventional modes of information transfer between site A in D-space and site B, some distance removed in D-space, two main pathways are well known. One is based on the modulation of sound waves (as in speech, telephone, etc.) while the other is based on the modulation of electromagnetic (EM) waves (as in radio, fax, television, etc.). Perhaps not so well known is the fact that every material emits an EM spectrum of waves due to electrodynamic excitations at the atomic (UV and visible) and molecular (visible and IR) levels. These electrodynamic force-generated waves have an effective travel distance of $\sim 3 - 5$ wavelengths in D-space (~ 1 micron to 100 microns). Cooperative modes of vibrations for molecules in the material lead to longer wavelengths (IR to radio) and thus lower frequency emissions which could serve as carrier waves for the higher frequency modulations (such modulations may be amplitude, frequency, phase, or pulse). This leads to possible travel distances of $\sim$ centimeters but at weak signal strength. The piezoelectric nature of some materials, and particularly biological materials, leads to EM to sound transduction and even longer effective travel distances but probably at further reduced signal strength.

Discussion of unconventional modes of information transfer will be left to the concluding chapters; however, there are three areas of activity with enough experimental support to justify mentioning them here: (1) Remote Viewing, (2) Distant Healing and (3) Qi Gong. All three of these activities appear to be remarkably unimpeded by distance, and somewhat by time. In our modeling, all three of these activities, and many more, are thought to occur via the process paths of R-space (the coarsest level of the vacuum).

As will be seen in the subsequent chapters, the three target experiments conducted via IIED's with their meditation-imbedded intentions have been robustly successful in significantly modifying material properties. Of course, for a specific intention to be fulfilled in D-space, a certain set of D-space processes must be required to operate in a particular way. This, in turn, requires that a certain thermodynamic potential map be applied to D-space with the rate of fulfillment of the intention in D-space being determined by the D-space kinetics involved. We must eventually come to understand in detail exactly how this occurs. That is one of the goals of this work. If, for example, we take the pH-change in water as our target, then some of the D-space processes that might be involved would be: (1) the dissociation reaction of H_2O, (2) the solubility reactions of CO_2 and O_2 in water and (3) any acid or base dissociation reaction for dopant species in water. Intention-induced alterations at the physical vacuum level of reality probably change the equilibrium constants for these chemical reactions sufficiently to bring about the desired changes.

One of the relevant considerations here, from a thermodynamics perspective, comes from considering the Gibb's phase rule which tells us for equilibrium conditions the number of degrees of freedom, f, available to a chemical system of C components when there are p coexisting material phases present. For the U(1) Gauge reality and a pure material, nature generally has only the two thermodynamic extrinsic variables of temperature, T, and pressure, P, to deal with and this completely determines the equilibrium state. Let us assume, for the moment, that f, p and C are such that our system of purified water is in dynamic equilibrium at (T,P). From the experiments of the following chapters, they tell us that, at least under some conditions at a Gauge level between U(1) and SU(2), intentionality, I^*, and probably consciousness, C^*, are also true thermodynamic variables of D-space. Thus, in the Gibbs phase rule, our number of independent thermodynamic variables is now increased to four (T,P,C^*,I^*). For our water, which was at (P,T) equilibrium, we now have two more degrees of freedom available for chemical reactions and our water system is allowed to be temporarily out of (P,T) equilibrium with material phase transformations occurring at the D-space and R-space levels.

Consciousness and Possible Vacuum Interactions

Another relevant energetic consideration is how the basic energy levels of atoms and molecules can change by interaction with the vacuum. In the

1920's, Dirac utilized relativistic quantum mechanics to evaluate the interaction between a physical electron and the vacuum. His equations predicted not only positive energy states but also negative energy state solutions. From this, he postulated that the vacuum consisted of all these negative energy states that were all filled (occupied). Nevertheless, by stimulating this negative energy state distribution via an absorbed photon with sufficient energy, a particle (electron, say) may be promoted into one of the allowed positive energy states (see Figure 2.7) and become physically real (i.e., observable). The hole left behind in the negative energy spectrum is the antimatter particle (positron in this case). To date, antimatter particles have been found experimentally for all the particles known to today's physics.

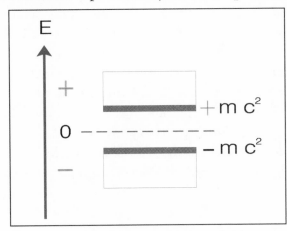

Figure 2.7   Schematic energy spectrum associated with the Dirac analysis[6]. A band gap of forbidden energies exists between $E = \pm mc^2$ for particle-antiparticle creation of mass 2m.

It is the QM interactions between the vacuum's virtual particle sea and the electron that constitutes the ground state energy, μ_0^e (e = electron) at (T,P). This same approach applies for all elementary particles which then may combine to form atoms and molecules. So the bottom line is that the standard state chemical potential, μ_0^j, for any physical species, j, involves the interaction of j with the non-physical <u>stuff</u> that constitutes the negative energy sea of the vacuum. In terms of our earlier discussion, this largely means the interaction between a D-space particle and its R-space counterpart, the coarsest substructure of the vacuum. A few years ago, one of us proposed that, if from a deep meditative state, focused human intention could shift the degree of coherence in the virtual particle sea of the vacuum by even a tiny amount, μ_0^j for the electron, other elementary particles, atoms and molecules, could be appreciably altered[7]. This, indeed, appears to be what we have done with the experiments to be described in Chapters 3-6. It is not magic, rather, it is just the physics of another Gauge reality than the U(1) Gauge!

The third relevant consideration is to see how IIED's, simply via an on/off switch, appear to be able to <u>broadcast</u> a "prime directive" to the different target experiments. The simplest postulate would seem to be that such effects are somehow related to the EM waves emitted by the oscillators in the devices. These EM waves are actually photons, albeit photons with very long wavelengths and quite low energy and, as such, each has a de Broglie pilot wave built from R-space components. Our postulate is that it is not the D-space interaction between the photons and the water, fruit fly larvae or enzyme that produces these unexpected results but, rather, it is the R-space components of the photons that are interacting with the R-space counterparts of the water, larvae or enzyme to drive these changes. From the aforedescribed theoretical model, the Maxwell equations in D-space couple to the analogous set of equations in R-space via deltron activation. The mathematically real part of this interaction, at very low deltron activation is what leads to electromagnetism. At significant deltron activation, new terms are thought to enter this non-linear coupling interaction, and it is these terms that lead to the present experimental results in D-space. The addition of the mathematically real part of these non-linear interactions to the conventional linear interactions we call "augmented-electromagnetism". We will hereafter use the rubric "Intention-Augmented" EMF's to indicate that some new type of association with EM-waves has occurred which allows a specific intention to interact with the target.

Early on in our experimental program it was discovered that, even in the electrically switched-off state, some degree of information leakage was occurring between the imprinted device and the unimprinted control device. This manifested as a temporally decreased difference in the results found when the two devices were separately used in a target experiment. The present solution to this difficulty was to store each device in its own electrically grounded Faraday cage after first completely wrapping it in aluminum foil. The theoretical rationale used here was that vacuum domain substances appear to interact with D-space substance via some process that manifests a magnetic vector potential contribution, $\Delta \overline{A}$, at the D-space/R-space interface. Since it is well known from standard electrodynamics that any $\Delta \overline{A}$ can produce an electric field effect, $\Delta \overline{E}$, and a magnetic field effect, $\Delta \overline{H}$, then augmented-EM radiation between the devices (even in the off-state due to fluctuating environmental EMF's) and the environment could allow both information transfer and energy dissipation (proportional to $(\Delta \overline{E})^2$ and $(\Delta \overline{H})^2$). Such energy dissipation would slowly reduce $\Delta \overline{A}$ which would, in turn, dissipate the intention "charge" in the subtle domain. In any event, although not perfect, this procedure has allowed the intention charge to be stored in the devices for ~ 3 – 4 months and significantly diminished the apparent communication between the imprinted and unimprinted devices.

Our normal physical experience is that, when we have a localized source of thermodynamic potential (heat, concentration, charge, etc.), its strength decays monotonically with time as the relevant moiety diffuses outwards from the source (a conservation requirement). However, in the experiments of the next four chapters, we must be prepared for the possibility that the source strength decays in time with an oscillatory component that depends upon the degree of coupling between D-space and R-space. We have come to this tentative conclusion because some of the data supports the postulate that the IIED "intention charge" source strength has not decayed to zero even after 6-8 months.

Conditions For Repeatability

It is well known that most individual humans have intentions that swing widely over time so that the time-averaged effect over weeks to months is usually of small magnitude. Individual humans having long practice with one of the available inner self-management techniques like Yoga, Qi Gong, Sufism, HeartMath, etc., do much better but there is still some time-averaging limitation involved. One may presume that most of these outwardly-directed fluctuations of intention from a large number of uncorrelated individuals tend to cancel each other out because their amplitudes lie in the linear regime. Inwardly-directed fluctuations of intention, being more local, influence their bodies at unconscious and autonomic nervous system levels. Specific experiments designed to reveal the effects of human intention, as recognized in Chapter 1, generally exhibit a larger signal amplitude with lower frequency oscillations in D-space so that physical measurements in the time-domain register <u>some</u> effect at satisfactory levels of statistical significance. However, very few of these results are truly robust without application of statistical methodology.

Precipitating a specific intention, held by a selected group of four meditators, into an electrical device during a 1-2 hour focused meditation session eliminates much of the swing or fluctuation nature of the outwardly-directed intention of an individual by themselves. After this focused session, the meditators need not give any thought to the outcome. Seemingly, all of the intention has been transferred to a surrogate, the IIED. However, one wonders why the experimental consequences have been so robust in our case.

Group intentional efforts, especially those focused on healing prayer, have been successful both locally and non-locally using our normal criteria for determining success. From studies in the area of individual healers, one generally finds that those who are most effective exhibit not only significant levels of inner self-management and physiological coherence of their bodies, but they acknowledge that it is "unseen" forces of the universe that do the healing work <u>through</u> them. They generally think of themselves as a participating conduit for the passage of this energy/information into and through R-space/D-space from higher dimensional levels. At our present level of human evolution, it is doubtful that we can <u>properly</u> articulate the true nature of this "unseen forces" factor. However, we can recognize that it is part of the higher dimensional infrastructure of the universe that may, <u>or may not</u>, cooperatively participate in our intention-stimulated events of physical reality.

Imbedding subtle energies into a device and then using that device in a particular experiment tends to partially "objectify" the subtle energy. If the subtle intention-charge can be retained in the device for many months, then this would allow many different laboratories to perform the same experiment with the same devices and with similarly processed devices imprinted by others. This would more fully objectify the subtle domain imprint influencing the course of D-space reality. However, before embarking on such an experimental path, it is absolutely necessary to understand the necessary and sufficient set of conditions needed for repeatability of our results in other locales.

From the authors' present perspective, the following is a list of discriminated factors influencing the subsequent chapters' experimental results: (1) The imprinter's training, degree of inner self-management, internal coherence, group cooperative coherence, heart focus and intentions, (2) the specific details of the imprinting protocol, (3) the unseen network of forces cooperating with the imprinters, (4) the D-space design, components and materials of the device, (5) the information isolation efficiency between the physically identical unimprinted and imprinted devices, including the shipping phase, (6) the particular D-space locale used for the experiments which affects the amount of conditioning needed to bring it to a specific level of coupling, (7) the degree of inner self-management and internal coherence of the actual experimenters, (8) the held attitudes of heart and mind of the experimenters during the course of the experiments and (9) the number of times the experiment is repeated in the particular locale.

For replication by others, to initially bypass items 1-4 of this list, it would be most efficient to utilize the same imprinters and devices as in the experiments reported on here. After some continued experience with this mode of operation, it would be useful to explore other possibilities. It is very easy to underestimate the importance of the individual items in this list. To illustrate, consider the following example. Let us suppose that some inventor has worked for years in his garage to construct and perfect a subtle energy conversion device of extremely high efficiency and eventually, to his satisfaction, he is successful in achieving his goal. He tries to sell his invention and prototype and, as part of the deal, the prototype is to be moved to a testing laboratory in another city for rigorous evaluation by others. The tests are carried out carefully in this new location and the high conversion efficiencies of the original tests are not substantiated. Only normal behavior is observed for the device. People conclude from this that the inventor was either not a careful experimenter, was imagining his results or was practicing fraud. However, in reality, he had probably conditioned both the original environment and the device with his sustained intention through the years of prototype development. He had created something approximating an $SU(2)$ Gauge condition in the original locale and it is not surprising that, when the device was moved to a $U(1)$ Gauge locale and a stranger did the testing, the original behavior was not repeated! This tends to imply that, at the $SU(2)$ Gauge symmetry level, the device and the locale are linked.

We can conclude this section with the statement that the properties of physical materials, both inanimate and animate, as determined by measurements registered in our normal cognitive domain, depend intimately on the physics Gauge conditions operating in the locale where the properties are measured. The experiments of the next four chapters show that, under some conditions, the consciousness of humans as represented by their focused intentions can alter the local Gauge condition and thus the properties of matter[1].

References

1.   W.A. Tiller, <u>Science and Human Transformation: Subtle Energies, Intentionality and Consciousness</u> (Pavior Publishing, Walnut Creek, CA, 1997).

2.   W.A. Tiller, "Energy Fields and the Human Body" in <u>Frontiers of Consciousness</u>, J. White editor (Julian Press, Inc. New York, 1974) p 229.

3.   W.A. Tiller, "The Positive and Negative Space/Time Frames as Conjugate Systems" in <u>Future Science</u>, J. White and S. Krippner editors (Anchor Books, Garden City, New York, 1977) p 257.

4.   W.A. Tiller, "A Lattice Model of Space", Phoenix, <u>2</u> (1978) 27.

5.   K. Moriyasu, <u>An Elementary Primer for Gauge Theory</u> (World Scientific Publishing Co. Pte. Ltd., Singapore, 1983).

6.   I.J.R. Aitchison and A.J.G. Hey, <u>Gauge Theories in Particle Physics</u> (Adam Hilger Ltd., Bristol, 1982).

7.   W.A. Tiller, "What are Subtle Energies?", J. Scientific Exploration, <u>7</u> (1993) 293.

8.   G. 't Hooft, "Gauge Theories of the Forces Between Elementary Particles", Scientific American, <u>242</u>, 6 (1980) 104.

9.   R.M. Eisberg, <u>Fundamentals of Modern Physics</u> (John Wiley & Sons, Inc., New York, 1961) pp 140-146.

Appendix 2.A: Pathways to Understanding Multidimensional Reality

There are two basic ways of approaching any technical phenomenon. The first is the time-honored method of inquiry that treats the phenomenon under study as a "black box" whose internal characteristics are unknown but are amenable to probing and analysis (only through the entry and exit ports). Such a situation always occurs in the early stages of development of a particular field of knowledge and is illustrated in Figure 2A.1(a). We apply some input stimulus (IS) to the box and determine some output response (OR). By correlating the OR with the IS, we deduce information about the most probable behavior of the box for this degree of stimulus. We then speculate on models that would reproduce such a spectrum of responses and design critical tests for discriminating between acceptable models.

Our first steps toward determining the behavior of the black box of Figure 2A.1(a) is to characterize it in the following form:

$$\frac{OR}{IS} = \widetilde{f}\,(\hat{\boldsymbol{\mathcal{E}}}_1, \hat{\boldsymbol{\mathcal{E}}}_2, \ldots, \hat{\boldsymbol{\mathcal{E}}}_n\,;\, x_1,\, x_2, \ldots, x_n) \tag{2A.1a}$$

$$\approx \widetilde{f}'\,(\hat{\boldsymbol{\mathcal{E}}}_1, \ldots, \hat{\boldsymbol{\mathcal{E}}}_j\,;\, x_1, \ldots x_k) \text{ with } \hat{\boldsymbol{\mathcal{E}}}_j^* < \hat{\boldsymbol{\mathcal{E}}}_j < \hat{\boldsymbol{\mathcal{E}}}_j^{**}$$

$$\text{and} \qquad x_k^* \bar{<}\ x_k \bar{<}\ x_k^{**} \tag{2A.1b}$$

for all indices j, k = 1, 2, ..., m. In Equation 2A.1a, $\widetilde{f}$ represents the true functional relationship between all the possible material parameters $\hat{\boldsymbol{\mathcal{E}}}_j$ and the experimental variables x_k of the system where unlimited range is allowed for these parameters and variables. In Equation 2A.1b, the observed functional relationship $\widetilde{f}'$ between a limited but seemingly sufficient number of the parameters and variables, for a given degree of reliability, is indicated for bounded ranges of the parameters and variables. Since the number of experiments, Q_1, needed to be performed to map OR/IS uniformly in this j + k space is

$$Q_1 = (d\,/\,\lambda)^{j+k}, \tag{2A.2}$$

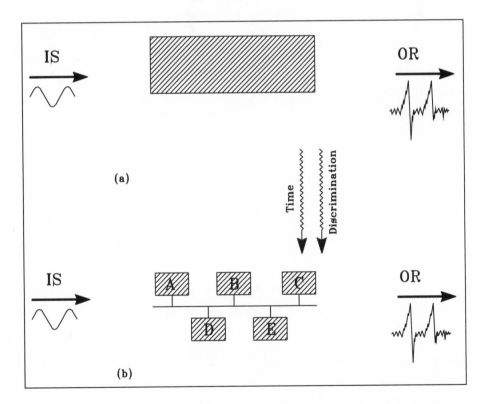

Figure 2A.1   *Schematic representation of (a) the "black box" approach and (b) the "system" approach for studying nature (IS = input stimulus; OR = output response).*

41

where λ is the average grid spacing for measurement along any coordinate axis and d is the total experimental range encompassed along that coordinate direction, we endeavor to reduce $j + k$ and d / λ as much as is practical since the time and cost involved in an experimental study are proportional to Q_1.

To obtain enough data along a given coordinate direction for the testing of a theory or for the fitting to a mathematical function, we take d / λ ~ 10. We thus find that a typical well-defined physics problem, for which $j + k \sim 3 - 4$, requires $\sim 10^3 - 10^4$ experiments. At $1 - 10$ data points collected per day, this is a typical thesis problem of ~ 3 man-years duration. For a typical engineering problem, $j + k$ increases to ~ 10 and, by using dimensionless groups, this may be reduced to 5-6 which requires the numbers of man-years of effort to increase for comparable reliability with the typical physics problem. For a typical physical/inanimate material problem, $j + k \sim 20$ so that d / λ must be reduced to $\sim 1 - 2$ for a comparable number of man-years investment. Because of this, one is confined to a "recipe" or "art" mode to obtain a successful result and the technology resulting from such efforts must be characterized as an "Art-Based Technology."

With the passage of time and experimentation we are usually led to the second way of approaching the particular technical area of study. We begin to discriminate the various unique phenomena and processes clustered together in the black box of Figure 2A.1(a) and choose to describe it as an interacting system as illustrated schematically in Figure 2A.1(b) and mathematically via the following equations:

$$\frac{OR}{IS} = \widetilde{g}\left[\widetilde{f}_1, ..., \widetilde{f}_k \right] \tag{2A.3a}$$

$$\approx \widetilde{g'}\left[\widetilde{f'}_1, ..., \widetilde{f'}_j \right] \tag{2A.3b}$$

where $\widetilde{f}_i$ and the $\widetilde{f}_i'$ are of the form represented by Equations 2A.1a and 2A.1b and where $\widetilde{g}$ and $\widetilde{g'}$ represent the exact and approximate functional relationships between the various $\widetilde{f}_i$ and $\widetilde{f}_i'$. For such clustered phenomena, in this representation the $\widetilde{f}_i'$ can be treated as elementary parts or subsets in the overall system or ensemble.

In order to develop a science of events that conforms to Equations 2A.3a and 2A.3b for a considerable range of variations of the $\hat{\varepsilon}_j$ and x_k, it is necessary to develop methods of systems analysis for analyzing the events (the phenomena). The steps to be taken appear to be: (i) identify the critical and individual phenomena included in the single black box that encompasses the clustered event, i.e., boxes A through E of Figure 2A.1(b); (ii) gain an understanding of the $\tilde{f}_i^{'}$ for each box in isolation so that a quantitative response spectrum can be determined for a quantitative input stimulus; (iii) gain an understanding of the $\tilde{f}_i^{'}$ as they interact with various other $\tilde{f}_i^{'}$ in pairs, triplets, etc. and (iv) partition the total potential for the clustered event into the partial potentials consumed by the various elemental $\tilde{f}_i^{'}$ as they interact with each other; and (v) given the total available input potential, assess the kinetics of change of the coupled system and the stability of the mode of change.

For a clustered event with n discriminated subsystems and $j + k$ total coordinate axes, the average number of required mapping experiments, Q_2, is given by

$$Q_2 = n\left(\frac{d}{\lambda}\right)^{\left(\frac{j+k}{n}\right)} + \frac{n}{2}(n-1)\left(\frac{d}{\lambda}\right)^{2\left(\frac{j+k}{n}\right)} + \ldots \qquad (2A.4)$$

where the second term arises from pair interactions. If one takes $j + k \sim 20$ and $n = 5$ with $d / \lambda \sim 10$, then $Q_1 \sim 10^{20}$ which is an impossibly large number while $Q_2 \sim 5 \times 10^4 + 10^9$ which is still large but appreciably smaller. If $j + k$ can be reduced to ~ 10 by forming dimensionless groups, then $Q_2 \sim 10^5$ which becomes a more manageable problem and we can expect reliable scientific studies to be forthcoming from this approach with a reasonable amount of effort. Such an approach leads to a "Science-Based Technology." In this approach, careful basic experiments on each of the subsystems in isolation can be performed so that the first term of Equation 2A.4 is readily known in any clustered event. This allows the *OR/IS* to be determined for the pair and higher order interactions.

As an illustrative example, suppose we want to predict the solid structure (grain size and shape, degree of macro- and micro-segregation, etc.) that arises from freezing a volume v of binary alloy liquid having a solute content, C_∞, initially superheated an amount $\hat{\Delta T}$ and then cooled at its outer surface at a given rate $\dot{T}$ per unit area of surface. Even to begin to make such a prediction, it is necessary to discriminate at least nine separate $\tilde{f}_i^{'}$ which are indicated in Figure 2A.2; moreover, at least twenty material parameters, at least seven interface variables which control the processes going on at the interface between the crystals and the liquid, and at least five major field equations must be considered. If one relied solely on the philosophy represented by Equations 2A.1a and 2A.1b, it would be relatively impossible to predict the behavior of one alloy system on the basis of the performance of another, since the variation of any one of the parameters or variables leads to large variability in the morphology of the growing crystals and thus in the

Figure 2A.2   Crystallization variables and parameters

	Boundary value problems	Material parameters	Interface variables	Macroscopic variables	Con-straints
Phase equilibria		ΔH, T_O, k_O, m_L		$TL\ (C_\infty)$	
Nucleation		N_h, ΔT_c		t	
Solute partitioning	Diffusion eq. (C)	D_{CS}, D_{CL}, k_i	C_I, $T_L(C_i)$ V, $\hat{s}$		
Fluid motion	Hydromdy-namic eq. (u)	v	δ_C	u_∞	C_∞
Excess solid free energy		γ, ΔS, E_j^f, n_j^f	T_E		$\dot{T}$
Interface attachment kinetics		β_1, β_2			
Heat transport	Heat eq. (T)	K_S, K_L	T_i	T_∞	
Interface morphology	Perturbation response and coupling eqs.	D_{TS}, D_{TL}			
Defect generation	Stress eq.				

resulting structure of the solid. This approach had been the dominant one in the casting industry until the 1950's.

When one uses the approach of Equations 2A.3a and 2A.3b, the problem begins to become manageable and one can partition the total excess free energy driving the total reaction at any time into a set of partial excess free energies consumed by the various elemental $\tilde{f}_i'$, in the system as a function of time. Following this approach, the basic multiparameter, multivariable metallurgical problem $(j + k \sim 20 - 40)$ has been reduced to the simultaneous solution of nine interrelated physics problems $(j + k \sim 3 - 4)$.

As one moves from areas of purely inanimate materials to animate materials, such as studied in biology or medicine, the number of relevant $j + k$ increases greatly, perhaps to ~ 100 if one seeks reliability of prediction on the order of today's typical engineering problem. As one moves towards considering the fields of psychology, psychiatry and onwards to sociology, the number of relevant $j + k$ increases still further. Thus, one can begin to understand why physics has been able to gain such a position of respect in the human community while many of the other technical activities have not. It is because the physics problems have been discriminated into subsystem problems of very few variables so that quite accurate analysis of these subsystems has been possible and thus high reliability achieved. For the other fields, the number of significant variables has been so huge that the Figure 2A.1(b) approach has not yet been possible for some of them, even after the investment of millions of man-years of effort by our world culture.

As humans expand their perspective, beyond the simple physical cognitive reality, to embrace the multidimensional reality that is the province of this book, the number of relevant variables in <u>any</u> technical area increases by a multiplier of perhaps 2 to 5. This is because the physics of the vacuum will be at least as rich and filled with complexity as the domain of inanimate physical matter. Since present-day QM, at the fundamental particle level, already is incorporating some vacuum behavior, about which it knows very little, into its prediction forecasting, the anticipated error bars can be large and thus the reliability of such predictions small. However, step by step, humanity moves forward, from the Figure 2A.1(a) procedures to the Figure 2A.1(b) procedures as nature gradually reveals her secrets.

Appendix 2.B: The Relativity Constraint on the de Broglie Concept [9]

Consider a beam of EM radiation containing quanta of total relativistic energy E. From Einstein, the frequency, ν, of this radiation is

$$\nu = E/h \qquad (2.B.1a)$$

where h is Planck's constant. From standard wave theory, the wavelength, λ, of this radiation in terms of the velocity of propagation of a wave, v', is just

$$\lambda = v'/\nu = h/p \qquad (2.B.1b)$$

since $v' = c$ for EM radiation and $E/c = p$, the momentum of the quantum. It was de Broglie who first postulated that <u>the wavelength, λ, and the frequency, ν, of the pilot wave associated with a particle of momentum, p, and total relativistic energy, E, are given by Equations 2.B1 and that the motion of the particle is governed by the wave propagation properties of the pilot waves</u>.

For a particle, as distinct from a photon, $v' \neq c$, so that

$$v' = \lambda\nu = E/p = [c^2p^2 + (m_0c^2)^2]^{1/2}/p \qquad (2.B.2a)$$
$$= c\,[1 + (m_0c/p)^2]^{1/2} \qquad (2.B.2b)$$

where the total relativistic energy for a particle of rest mass, m_0, has been utilized. From Equation 2.B.2b, one readily sees that $v' > c$. From Figure 2.1 of the main text, the amplitude of the pilot waves must be modulated in such a way that their value is non-zero only over a finite region of space in the vicinity of the particle. The pilot waves form a <u>group</u> of waves that must move along with the same velocity as the particle. Thus, one must distinguish between the group velocity, v_g, and the velocity, v', of the individual oscillations of the waves comprising the group ($v_g < v'$, generally).

For the Figure 2.1 configuration, a single wave of unit amplitude can be represented most simply by

$$\psi(x,t) = \sin[2\pi(k'x - \nu t)] \quad ; \quad k' = 1/\lambda. \qquad (2.B.3)$$

To form a minimal group, one need only consider two such waves so we use

$$\psi(x,t) = \psi_1(x,t) + \psi_2(x,t) \qquad (2.B.4a)$$

where

$$\psi_1(x,t) = \sin[2\pi(k'x-vt)] \qquad (2.B.4b)$$

$$\psi_2(x,t) = \sin[2\pi(k'+dk')x - (v+dv)t] \qquad (2.B.4c)$$

for $dv \ll v$ and $dk' \ll k'$, this yields

$$\psi(x,t) \approx 2\cos\left[2\pi\left(\frac{dk'}{2}x - \frac{dv}{2}t\right)\right]\sin[2\pi(k'x-vt)]. \qquad (2.B.4d)$$

This is our original wave of Equation 2.B.3 whose amplitude is modulated by the first term to form a series of beats. These two waves of slightly different frequency alternately interfere and reinforce each other so as to produce an infinite succession of groups. The velocity, v', of the individual waves can be evaluated by considering the second term on the RHS of Equation 2.B.4d while the velocity of the groups, v_g, can be evaluated from the first term. Thus, we find that

$$v' = v/\,k' \text{ and } v_g = \frac{dv/2}{dk'/2} = \frac{dv}{dk'} \qquad (2.B.5)$$

It can be shown that, for an infinitely large number of waves combining to form a single moving group, v' and v_g are identical to the results given by Equation 2.B.5.

From Equation 2.B.1a and our definition of k', we have

$$dv = dE/h \text{ and } dk' = dp/h \qquad (2.B.6a)$$

so that

$$v_g = dv/dk' = dE/dp \qquad (2.B.6b)$$

with E as

$$E^2 = c^2p^2 + (m_0c^2)^2 , \qquad (2.B.7a)$$

47

$$v_g = dE/dp = c^2(p/E). \qquad (2.B.7b)$$

With $E = mc^2$ and $p = mv_p$, we obtain

$$v_g = v_p. \qquad (2.B.8)$$

So the velocity of the group of pilot waves is just equal to the velocity of the particle, v_p. Combining Equations 2.B.1 and 2.B.7b, we also have

$$v' = c^2/v_g \qquad (2.B.9a)$$

which, in the nomenclature of Equation 2.1 of the main text, is

$$v_p v_w = c^2. \qquad (2.B.9b)$$

Since $v_w > v_p$, the individual waves are constantly moving through the group from the rear to the front[9].

Appendix 2.C: Some Basic Concepts in Gauge Theory

The concept of a "Gauge" was introduced in 1918 by Herman Weyl to mean a standard of length whereby the gravitational force could be formulated in terms of the curvature of space and the various geometries involved. In general, Gauge Theories were constructed to relate the properties of the four known fundamental forces of nature to the various symmetries of nature (see Figure 2C.1[8]). The most familiar symmetries are spatial or geometric in appearance, like the hexagonal symmetry of a snowflake. An invariance in the snowflake pattern occurs when it is rotated by 60 degrees. In general, the state of symmetry can be defined as an <u>invariance</u> in pattern that is observed when <u>some</u> transformation is applied to it (e.g., a 60° rotation for the snowflake or a 90° rotation for a square).

One example of a non-geometric symmetry is the charge symmetry of electromagnetism. For the case of a collection of electric dipoles, if the individual charges are suddenly reversed in sign, the energy of the ensemble is unchanged so the forces remain unchanged. The same behavior occurs for magnetic dipoles and electromagnetic fields in general (this is because the energy is proportional to E^2 and to H^2 so it does not change by a 180°

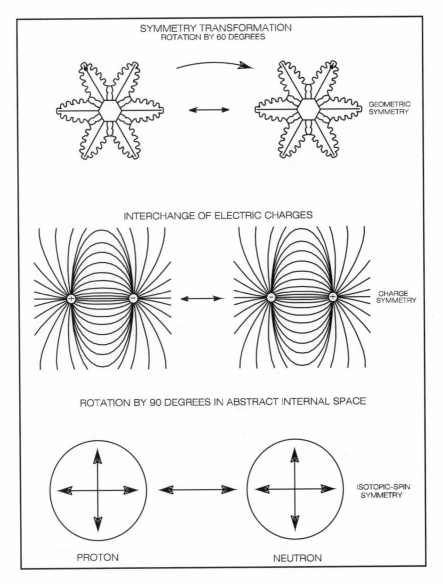

Figure 2C.1   Symmetries of nature determine the properties of forces in Gauge theories. The symmetry of a snowflake can be characterized by noting that the pattern is unchanged when it is rotated 60 degrees; the snowflake is said to be invariant with respect to such rotations. In physics, non-geometric symmetries are introduced. Charge symmetry, for example, is the invariance of the forces acting among a set of charged particles when the polarities of all the charges are reversed. Isotopic-spin symmetry is based on the observation that little would be changed in the strong interactions of matter if the identities of all protons and neutrons were interchanged. Hence proton and neutron become merely the alternative states of a single particle, the nucleon, and transitions between the states can be made (or imagined) by adjusting the orientation of an indicator in an internal space. It is symmetries of this kind, where the transformation is an internal rotation or a phase shift, which are referred to as Gauge symmetries.

49

rotation of the dipoles). Another symmetry of the non-geometric kind relates to <u>isotopic-spin</u> of particles, a property of neutrons, protons and hadrons (the only particles responsive to the strong nuclear force). The symmetry transformation associated with isotopic-spin rotates the <u>internal indicators</u> of all protons and neutrons everywhere in the universe by the same amount and at the same time. If the rotation is by exactly 90 degrees, every proton becomes a neutron and every neutron becomes a proton so that no effects of this transformation can be detected and this symmetry is invariant with respect to isotopic-spin transformation.

All of these described symmetries are <u>global symmetries</u> (happening everywhere at once). In addition to global symmetries, which are almost always present in a physical theory, it is possible to have a <u>local</u> symmetry[8]. For a local symmetry to be observed, some law of physics must retain its validity (remain invariant) even when a different transformation takes place at each separate point in space-time. Gauge Theories can be constructed with either a global symmetry or a local symmetry (or both). However, in order to make a theory invariant with respect to a local transformation something new must be added. This new something is a new force[8].

The first Gauge Theory with local symmetry was the theory of electric and magnetic fields, introduced in 1868 by James Clerk Maxwell. The character of the symmetry that makes Maxwell's theory a Gauge Theory is that the electric field is invariant with respect to the addition or subtraction of an arbitrary overall electric potential. However, this symmetry is a global one because the result of experiment remains constant only if the new potential is changed everywhere at once (there is no absolute potential and no zero reference point). A complete theory of electromagnetism requires that the global symmetry of the theory be converted into a local symmetry. Just as the electric field depends ultimately on the distribution of charges, but can conveniently be derived from an electrical potential, so the magnetic field generated by the motion of these charges can be conveniently described as resulting from a magnetic potential. It is in this system of potential fields that local transformations can be carried out leaving all the original electric and magnetic fields unaltered. This system of dual, interconnected fields has an exact local symmetry even though the electric field alone does not[8].

Maxwell's theory of electromagnetism is a classical one, but a related symmetry can be demonstrated in the quantum theory of EM interaction (called quantum field theory). In the quantum theory of electrons, a change in the electric potential entails a change in the <u>phase</u> of the electron wave and the phase measures the displacement of the wave from some arbitrary reference point (the difference is sufficient to yield an electron diffraction effect). Only differences in the phase of the electron field at two points or at two moments can be measured, but not the absolute phase. Thus, the phase of an electron wave is said to be inaccessible to measurement (requires a knowledge of both the real <u>and</u> the imaginary parts of the amplitude) so that the phase cannot have an influence on the outcome of any possible experiment. This means that the electron field exhibits a symmetry with respect to arbitrary changes of phase. Any phase angle can be added to or subtracted from the electron field and the results of all experiments will remain invariant. This is the essential ingredient found in the U(1) Gauge condition.

Although the absolute value of the phase is irrelevant to the outcome of experiment, in constructing a theory of electrons, it is still necessary to specify the phase. The choice of a particular value is called a Gauge convention. The symmetry of such an electron matter field is a global symmetry and the phase of the field must be shifted in the same way everywhere at once. It can be easily demonstrated that a theory of electron fields, along with no other forms of matter or radiation, is <u>not</u> invariant with respect to a corresponding local Gauge transformation. If one wanted to make the theory consistent with a local Gauge symmetry, one would need to add another field that would exactly compensate for the changes in electron phase. Mathematically, it turns out that the required field is one having infinite range corresponding to a field quantum with a spin of one unit. The need for infinite range implies that the field quantum be massless. These are just the properties of the EM field, whose quantum is the photon. When an electron absorbs or emits a photon, the phase of the electron field is shifted[8].

The freedom to move the origin of a coordinate system constitutes a symmetry of nature. Actually there are three related symmetries: All the laws of nature remain invariant when the coordinate system is transformed by translation, by rotation or by mirror reflection. However, these symmetries are only global ones and each symmetry transformation can be defined as a formula for finding the new coordinates of a point from the old coordinates. Those formulae must be applied simultaneously and in the same way to all the points. The general theory of relativity stems from the fundamental observation that the structure of space-time is not necessarily consistent with a coordinate system made up entirely of straight lines meeting at right angles. As in electrodynamics, for relativity theory, local symmetry can only be generated from the global symmetry condition by adding a new field to the theory. In general relativity, the field is that of gravitation[8].

The symmetry at issue for the SU(2) Gauge is the isotopic-spin symmetry with the rule that the strong interactions of matter remain invariant (or nearly so) when the identities of protons and neutrons are interchanged. In

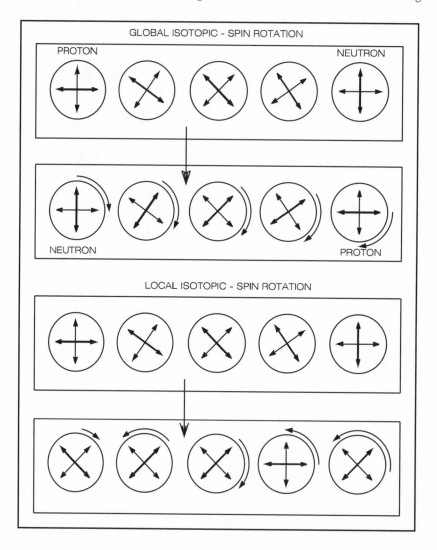

Figure 2C.2   Isotopic-spin symmetry serves as the basis of another gauge theory. If isotopic-spin symmetry is valid, the choices of which position of the internal arrow indicates a proton and which a neutron is entirely a matter of convention. Global symmetry (upper diagram) requires the same convention to be adopted everywhere, and any rotation of the arrow must be made in the same way at every point. In the Yang-Mills theory, isotopic spin is made a local symmetry (lower diagram), so that the orientation of the arrow is allowed to vary from place to place. In order to preserve the invariance of all observable quantities with respect to such local isotopic-spin transformations, it is necessary to introduce at least six fields, corresponding to three massless vector particles one of which can be identified as the photon.

the global symmetry, any rotation of the internal arrows that indicate the isotopic-spin state must be made simultaneously everywhere (see Figure 2C.2). A local symmetry allows the orientation of the arrows to vary independently from place to place and from moment to moment as an arbitrary function of position and time. As in other instances where a global symmetry is converted into a local one, the invariance can be maintained only if something else is added to the theory. Constructed on the model of electromagnetism, Yang and Mills found that, when isotopic-spin rotations are made arbitrary from place to place, the laws of physics remain invariant only if six new fields are introduced. They were all vector fields, they all had infinite range (and were therefore massless) and they were non-Abelian (the order of the rotations was important whereas for EM, and Abelian theory, the rotation order is not important). Although the Yang-Mills theory was of monumental importance, it needed considerable fine-tuning to describe the real world. One strategy adopted in an attempt to fix its defects was to artificially endow the charged field quanta with a mass greater than zero. Imposing a mass on the quanta of the charged fields confines them to a finite range and, if the mass is large enough, the range can be made as small as is wished. Ultimately, a way was found to endow some of the Yang-Mills fields with mass while retaining exact Gauge symmetry. This technique is now called the Higgs Mechanism[8].

The fundamental idea of the Higgs Mechanism was to include in the theory <u>an extra field,</u> one having the peculiar property that it does not vanish in vacuum. The Higgs field is unusual in that reducing it to zero costs energy. The energy of the field is smallest when the field has some uniform value <u>greater</u> than zero. The Higgs field is a scalar quantity, having only a magnitude (like temperature) and so the quantum of this field must have a spin of zero. The Higgs Mechanism is an example of a well-established process called spontaneous symmetry breaking. Over the last two decades, this approach has further evolved into quantum chromodynamics requiring an invariance with respect to local transformations of quark color leading to the quanta of the color being called gluons (because they glue the quarks together). As 't Hooft[8] states, many questions still remain unanswered "why do the quarks and the other elementary particles have the masses they do? What determines the mass of the Higgs particle? What determines the fundamental unit of electric charge or the strength of the color force?" The answers to these questions requires an even more comprehensive theory so one continues to search for other global symmetries and then explores the consequences of converting them to local symmetries.

CHAPTER 3

Water and IIED-generated pH Changes

The experimental platform of this chapter is a very simple one. It is merely the measurement of pH for a variety of waters – from commercial bottled water to laboratory purified water to purified water containing specific added particulates. Evian water was selected for the initial tests because of its published composition data and ready availability. Initial measurements on Evian water revealed large pH excursions as the water equilibrated with atmospheric CO_2 (it lost CO_2) followed by precipitation of Ca/Mg carbonate crystals. Subsequent experiments using pH-stable water allowed pH measurements to be made on a system not dynamically precipitating solids. The final segment of the experimental data deals with purified water containing a small-added mass of sparingly soluble $ZnCO_3$ crystallites.

From somewhat faltering beginnings when we first entered this new arena of activity and didn't know what to expect, our experiments eventually generated robust and reproducible changes of pH for the imprinted vs. the unimprinted devices. One caveat that the reader should keep in mind, when taking an overview of the entire data set of this chapter, is that the actual process of running the experiments time after time tended to condition the experimental locale so that the IIED results grew more robust as this unanticipated experimental variable continued to act. This "conditioning" process is the topic of chapter 6 so, for now, the reader need only realize that, although the physical environment was held constant throughout the experiments, an unseen and initially unappreciated factor was slowly changing over the ~30 months of these particular experiments. Before proceeding with a description of our IIED experiments, let us briefly review some relevant information concerning structural and property aspects of water.

Some Anomalous Features of Water

Molecular nature[1]: The H_2O molecule shape forms an isosceles triangle with the oxygen at the apex and the hydrogens at the base as illustrated in Figure 3.1. Because of electric charge transfer between the H and the O species, the molecule exhibits a strong electric dipole moment so that dipole-dipole interactions are expected to be important here and a fixed dipole alignment is to be expected at some temperature (this is what one finds for ice). However, such a fixed dipole alignment provides very little configurational entropy and an alternate possibility exists when the dipole alignment between

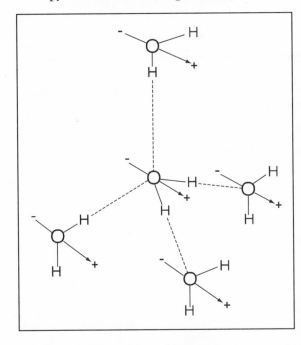

Figure 3.1   Here, an arbitrary central H_2O molecule in ice is shown with its four nearest neighbors. The electrostatic field, F, arising from the fixed neighbors induces an addition, aF, to the dipole moment of an isolated water molecule (a is the molecular polarizability). Each oxygen atom is surrounded tetrahedrally by four other oxygen atoms at a distance of 2.76 Å. The O-H distance, by comparison, is about 1 Å.

two H_2O molecules is in the head-to-tail configuration yielding an interaction energy close to the average thermal energy, kT (T is temperature and k is Boltzmann's constant). In such a case, the mutual orientation of any two dipoles may be destroyed by the thermal collisions occurring between molecules. At room temperature (T=25 °C), the energy, E, doesn't change much but now the system has abundant configurational entropy, S_c, due to the random orientation of the dipoles. Thus, the <u>free energy</u>, G, of the bulk H_2O

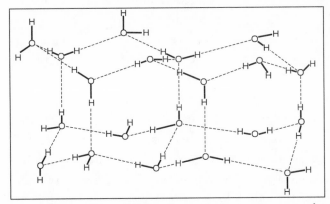

Figure 3.2   The structure of hexagonal ice, solid lines are covalent chemical bonds while dashed lines are hydrogen bonds.

(G = E + PV – TS, where P = pressure and V = volume) is lowered by changing from a fixed dipole alignment (ice) to a continuously varying dipole alignment (water).

Perhaps the major key to understanding liquid water and its various solutions lies in the concept of the "hydrogen bond". Hydrogen bonds are strongly directional but with a strength of only ~5 kilocalories per mole (~0.22 electron-volts). Because of this, the H_2O molecule can act as both an acceptor and a donor of hydrogen. This dual ability is most readily seen by considering the fragment of ice illustrated in Figure 3.2. There, one sees that each H_2O molecule in the ice has four nearest neighbors to which it is hydrogen bonded. It acts as a hydrogen (H) donor to two of the four and as an H-acceptor to the other two. These four H-bonds are spatially arranged with local tetrahedral symmetry (like silicon, Si, in a silicon crystal or like quartz, SiO_2, in one of its crystal forms) and these tetrahedra form a space-filling three dimensional network.

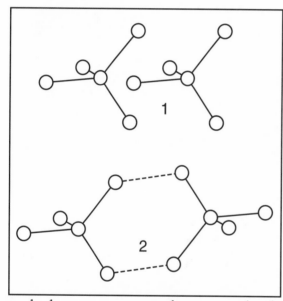

Figure 3.3 Two idealized water molecule interaction clusters.

The view of liquid water that emerges from this line of thinking is that of a random three-dimensional network of H-bonds. The network has a local preference for tetrahedral geometry with a mix of the two idealized clusters illustrated in Figure 3.3. However, this network contains a large portion of strained and broken bonds which play a strong role in the kinetic properties of water. Molecules can readily switch allegiances by trading a strained bond here for one there so that the network topology may be quickly altered.

The behavior of water towards nonpolar solutes (and nonpolar side-groups attached to biopolymers) or nanometer-size gas bubbles leads to what has been called a "hydrophobic" interaction. Because nonpolar solutes fill space, the random H-bond network must reorganize around them in such a way that not too much damage occurs to the already defective network[2]. Network rearrangement occurs towards a local clathrate-type cage that is far from perfect. The decrease in solution entropy associated with the presence of nonpolar molecules comes partially from the bond strengthening in the imperfect solvation cage and partially because the H_2O molecules in that cage layer around the solute have markedly reduced orientational options. Because of the energetic advantage associated with having H-bonds, each solvation sheath H_2O molecule prefers to "straddle" the nonpolar molecule (see Figure 3.4) with its OH covalent bonds so that they can bond to other solvation layer water molecules and not waste any H-bonds[2].

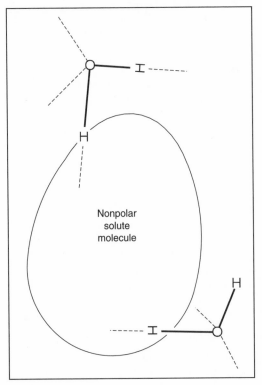

Figure 3.4   Orientational arrangement for water molecules surrounding a nonpolar solute. They tend to straddle the inert solute and create a cage with the maximum number of hydrogen bonds.

Pairs of nonpolar solutes in water experience an entropy-driven net attraction for one another via this so-called hydrophobic bond. This is thought to be an important factor for the native conformation of biopolymers containing both hydrophobic and hydrophilic side groups. Insertion of nonpolar solute molecules into water biases the configurational probabilities for water molecules in the immediate vicinity towards formation of a convex H-bond polyhedron of sufficient size to contain that solute. Very recent work using polarized infrared laser pulses of 200 femtosecond duration shows that the energy in an OH-bond definitely hops from one molecule to another at vibrational transfer rates more than twice current theoretical expectations[3]. It is thought that biological molecules in aqueous solution may exchange energy with each other via this previously unknown "fast track" through the solvent.

In closing this subtopic, we need to recognize and emphasize the different structural scales (polymer size) for H_2O in water. The first scale transition for H_2O seems to be from a single H_2O molecule to an $(H_2O)_5$

Figure 3.5 Physical arguments relating to the plausibility of the existence of the known liquid-gas critical point C *and the hypothesized* LDL-HDL *(high-density liquid/low-density liquid) critical point* C' *(see Figure 3.7).*

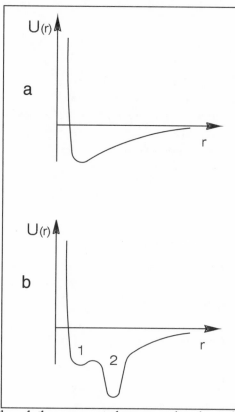

(a) *Idealized system characterized by a pair interaction potential with a single attractive well. At low enough* T *(*T<T$_c$*) and high enough* P *(*P>P$_c$*), the system condenses into the "liquid" well.*

(b) *Idealized system characterized by a pair interaction potential whose attractive well has two sub-wells, the outer of which is deeper and narrower. For low enough* T *(*T<T$_{c'}$*) and low enough* P *(*P>P$_{c'}$*), the one phase liquid can "condense" into the narrow, outer "low-density liquid" sub-well, thereby giving rise to a low-density liquid phase, and leaving behind the high-density liquid phase occupying predominantly the inner sub-well.*

molecule with four H_2O molecules located at the corners of a tetrahedron, that are hydrogen-bonded to a central H_2O molecule (called a pentamer). The corner molecules are separated from the central molecule by 2.8 angstroms, corresponding to the first peak in the oxygen-oxygen radial distribution function in water. Interaction of pentamers leads to the two well-defined pentamer cluster types of Figure 3.3[4] and one can readily imagine extensions to larger clusters of each type which would then correspond to local "high-density" and "low-density" structural heterogeneities in liquid water. Such a result is consistent with recent experimental data on the effect of high pressure on the $O=O$ radial distribution function and with detailed neutron structure data[5]. The idealized models of Figure 3.3 require an intermolecular potential for water of the core-softened type with a shallow, inner well of non-hydrogen-bonding nature plus a deeper, outer well of hydrogen-bonding nature (see Figure 3.5).

Volume/Entropy Bulk Water Anomalies[6]: If one considers the isothermal compressibility, K_T, which is related to the expectation value for fluctuations in average volume, $\bar{V}$, as the temperature is lowered for a normal liquid, one expects the fluctuations to decrease as indicated in Figure 3.6a. Water is anomalous in three respects: (1) It's normalized compressibility is rather larger than one would expect, (2) although at high T, K_T decreases as T decreases, below ~46 °C it starts to increase strongly with decreasing T and doubles in value by $T = -38$ °C and (3) $\log K_T$ vs. $\log |T\text{-}228|$ plots yield a region of straight-line behavior hinting at some sort of critical-point behavior for water.

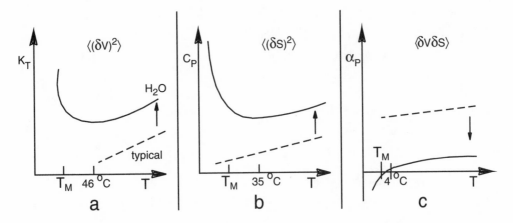

Figure 3.6   Schematic dependence on temperature of (a) the isothermal compressibility K_T, (b) the constant-pressure specific heat C_P, and (c) the thermal expansivity α_P. The behavior of a typical liquid is indicated by the dashed line, which is a rough extrapolation of the high-temperature behavior of liquid water. The anomalies exhibited by liquid water are apparent above the melting temperature, T_M, but become especially striking as one supercools below T_M.

When one considers the specific heat at constant pressure, C_P, which is related to the expectation value for entropy, S, fluctuations one again finds water to behave strangely. For a typical liquid, this quantity gently decreases as one lowers T (see dashed line in Figure 3.6b). Water is again anomalous in the same three respects: (1) C_P for water is very large, (2) below ~ 35°C, C_P actually starts to increase and (3) this increase in C_P can be approximated by a power law.

The third temperature response function to consider is the thermal expansion coefficient at constant pressure, α_P, (see Figure 3.6c). This coefficient is proportional to the cross-fluctuations of entropy and specific volume and which, for a typical liquid, is positive. $\langle \delta \bar{V} \delta \bar{S} \rangle$ is positive because, in local regions of the liquid in which the volume is larger than average ($\delta \bar{V}$ is positive), the local entropy is also larger (so $\delta\bar{s}$ is positive). Water is unusual in the same three aspects: (1) $\alpha_P \sim 3$ times smaller than that of a typical liquid (see dashed line in Figure 3.6c), (2) as one lowers T, the anomaly gets stronger and stronger and, at 4°C, α_P actually becomes negative and (3) once again, an imminent singularity appears to be close by.

The theoretical conclusion that Stanley[6] draws from the foregoing observations is that the basic structure of water is a hydrogen-bonded gel. However, because these hydrogen bonds have very, very short lifetimes (typically a picosecond), water doesn't behave at all like jelly. This is because hydrogen bonds are breaking and reforming much faster than transport process rates in the liquid. Further, the structure of water is influenced in high temperature regions by the critical point associated with the liquid/gas phase transition and at lower temperatures by another critical point associated with a high density liquid-low density liquid phase transition. This situation is schematically illustrated in Figure 3.7.

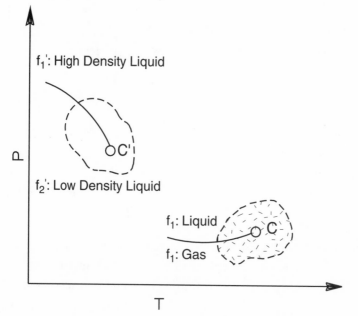

Figure 3.7   Schematic projection onto the P-T plane of the hypothesized equilibrium phase diagram for water. Shown is the well-known gas-liquid critical point C, which is the terminus of a line of first-order phase transitions separating two fluid phases: f_1 ("liquid") and f_2 ("gas"), which differ in $\bar{V}$, the first derivative of the Gibbs potential. The shaded area denotes the region of critical behavior. Also shown is the hypothesized HDL-LDL critical point C', which is the terminus of a line of first-order phase transition separating two new fluid phases: f_1' ("high-density liquid" or HDL) and f_2' ("low-density liquid" or LDL), which also differ in $\bar{V}$, the first derivative of the Gibbs potential.

The Quantum Electrodynamic (QED) Perspective: For the past 3-4 decades, computer simulations using effective molecular pair and many-body potentials have been utilized to meaningfully mimic the phenomenological H-bond array of water. All of these calculations have been performed under the assumption that the transverse EM field is in its ground state and that it only involves "zero point fluctuations". However, the very large experimentally measured dielectric relaxation times for many liquids[10] (three orders of magnitude larger than the single molecule rotation time) indicates that large groups of molecules are responding collectively to the externally applied EM field suggesting the existence of some type of coherence state in these liquids.

It is interesting to note that, as a result of statistical fluctuations in the position and motion of charges in any material body, spontaneous local electric and magnetic moments are generated which in turn create EM field emissions. These EM fields cover a wide range of frequencies, from ultraviolet to infrared, with the distribution being specific, like a finger print, for a given material. Thus, at any temperature, a fluid is internally driven by such a spectrum of EM fields.

An Italian group[7-9] considered the evolution of an assembly of initially independent molecules that, by QED instability of their electron ground states, are driven toward a coherent dynamical state where large intermolecular interactions emerge. This work exploits the coherent electrodynamic interaction of the water molecules with the transverse EM field.

Figure 3.8   Close-packed arrangement of low density regions of coherent water surrounded by peripheral, higher density regions of disordered water.

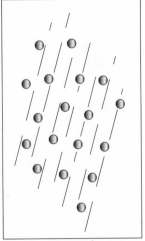

Specifically, QED requires the simultaneous solution of the Schroedinger equation coupled with the Maxwell equation (rather than the static Poisson equation as normally utilized). They find that, above a certain density threshold, the small quantum fluctuations of the wave field, between the ground state and a singled out excited state, will grow to a large value. This leads the quantum system, matter plus EM field, to a state where the matter is entrained to oscillate in-phase with the modes of the EM field that are in resonance with the matter transition over a long range.

Depending on the temperature, this leads to a two-fluid system, one ordered and the other gas-like. The minimum free energy for this combined two-phase system, coherent core phase (of low density) plus peripheral disordered phase (of higher density) in a close-packed arrangement such as illustrated in Figure 3.8, requires a specific volume fraction of each phase as a function of T (see Figure 3.9). As T is lowered, the size of the coherent domains increase (radius ~ 300 Å – 10,000 Å) until the transition occurs to a completely ordered phase of ice. As T is increased, the coherent domain size decreases while the peripheral disordered domain volume grows until the transition occurs to the completely disordered gas phase of water vapor. This theoretical model readily accounts for the anomalous behaviors of K_T, C_P and α_P discussed above as well as the water boiling temperature and the latent heat of vaporization.

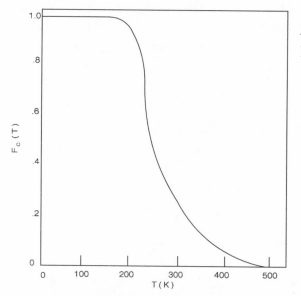

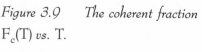

Figure 3.9   The coherent fraction $F_c(T)$ *vs. T.*

Some Anomalous Features of Electric/Magnetic Properties: Over the past two decades, a wide variety of experiments carried out around the world (particularly in Russia) have shown that the physico-chemical properties of water and ice can be appreciably altered by exposure to EMF's of a wide variety[11-20]. One rather remarkable result appearing from such studies is that the water solutions seem to retain a "memory" of these applied fields for hours to days. Only two examples will be mentioned to illustrate this point (Refs. 11 and 16).

Weak AC Magnetic Field Effects[11]: When the amplitude of an alternating magnetic field was only 12.3 A/m (the earth geomagnetic field intensity is 46 A/m = 0.58 gauss) it was found that the dielectric loss tangent, tan δ, which is a good measure of energy dissipation in water at the excitation frequency, showed a strong resonance at a frequency of 156 Hz for highly purified water and ice (see Figure 3.10) with the peaks being about 5 times higher in ice (T = -5 °C) than in water (T= 10 °C). In heavy ice, D_2O, the resonant frequency was 78 Hz, half that of water, while the peak height was about half of that for H_2O ice at the same low applied field strength and temperature. By varying the low field strength at fixed frequency, f, they found that the resonance peak always occurred when H_{App}/f = constant.

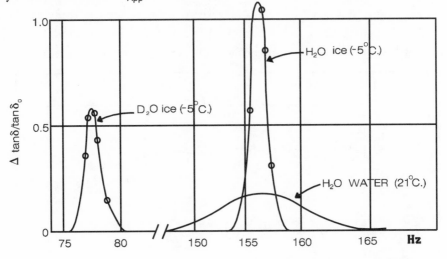

Figure 3.10   *Relative changes in tan δ for H_2O ice, D_2O ice at T = -5 °C, and liquid H_2O at T = 21 °C in an alternating field of 12.3 A/m amplitude as a function of field frequency.*

It is interesting to note that, from the theory of nuclear and spin resonance absorption in materials, the resonant frequency, f^*, is calculated to be directly proportional to H_{App}/m where m is the mass of the moiety (electron, proton, etc) that is exhibiting motion due to its magnetic moment in the material. This is consistent with the above experimental data and one may picture the magnetization vector of this mobile species as precessing around the static earth field vector axis at an angle that depends on the amplitude of H_{App}, the various damping factors, and the proximity to resonance. Although it appears that the proton is involved (D_2O vs. H_2O frequencies), the mass, m, for the mobile moiety needed to quantitatively match the data does not fit the unhindered proton mass (however, it does fit the nuclear mass as an interstitial species in the network). Finally, it should be noted that it requires several hours for this AC applied field effect to yield a maximum consequence on tan δ and that the effect persists for hours to days after H_{App} has been set to zero.

Non-Inductive Coil-Induced Conductivity Changes[16]: In this investigation, the authors studied the effects of a non-inductively wound solenoidal coil (NIC - a coil wound from a pair of intertwined wires connected so that current flows in opposite directions one to the other and the induced magnetic fields cancel) and a normal inductively wound solenoidal coil on the electrical conductivity of water placed within the coil for the same treatment times, t. The magnetic field strength for the NIC is expected to be zero because of the cancellation from the two reversely wound coils of this solenoid.

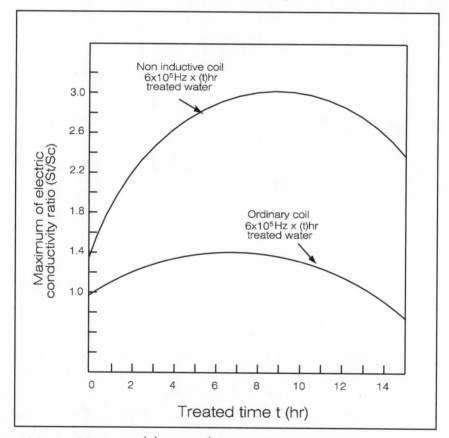

Figure 3.11   Maximum of electric conductivity ratio vs. treatment time

Distilled water was exposed to the field of the NIC (square wave, f = 0.6 MHz, voltage 4 volts and mean current 1 milliAmp) for t = 2 to 14 hr and its electrical conductivity (S_t) measured at T = 40 °C. The value for an untreated control water was also measured (S_c). The ratio, S_t/S_c, is shown plotted in

Figure 3.11 for both the NIC and the ordinary coil. One can see that S_t/S_c increased up to 25% after 8 hr of treatment for the ordinary coil. In contrast, the NIC-treated water increased its S_t/S_c ratio with time up to a maximum value of 3.0 after 8-11 hrs. When this NIC-treated water (10 hr treatment) was kept at room temperature for 7-8 days, the S_t/S_c ratio still showed a value of 3.0 but began decreasing for longer holding times. No ready explanation exists for such a result.

Simple Long Time EM Frequency Storage in Water: Smith[21] has demonstrated that electromagnetically sensitive individuals, known to respond to specific EM frequencies, respond similarly when the same frequencies are transferred to a sealed vial of water that has been exposed to the EM field from a solenoid coil for less than 1 minute. Later studies showed that it was the magnetic vector potential that caused the changes in the water. It was shown that a specific frequency could be imprinted (or potentized) into the water when an AC current of this frequency passed through the solenoid. The threshold strength for the AC magnetic field imprinting at an extremely low frequency (ELF) was found to be 7.6 μT (microteslas, 1 μT = 0.1 gauss) if the axis of the solenoid was aligned north-south and half this value if it was east-west. Succussing (banging) the vial of water against a wooden surface, near but external to the solenoid, imprints the water at a thousandth of this field strength.

Initially, a pendulum held over the water by Smith was used to indicate via a "dowsing" response when the water had been imprinted. More recently[22a], a known frequency of 1.0 KHz has been imprinted into the water and read out again a short time later (sometimes months later). After the readout, a slightly different frequency, 1.1 KHz was superimposed in the same water and then both frequencies were read out correctly. These chart recorder traces are given in Figure 3.12a. A block diagram of the apparatus used for making these traces is given in Figure 3.12b. In this case, the water was contained in a carefully cleaned, 75 ml beaker into which two gold wires were dipped and arranged parallel to the beaker axis with 5 mm spacing. They were directly connected to a low-noise preamplifier and then a high gain amplifier. Both systems were inside custom-built mu-metal or steel shielding boxes (see Figure 3.12b). The frequency imprint "resonances" were detected in the output of the amplifiers via use of an "active" multiplier circuit whose output frequency contains the sum and difference frequencies between the signal

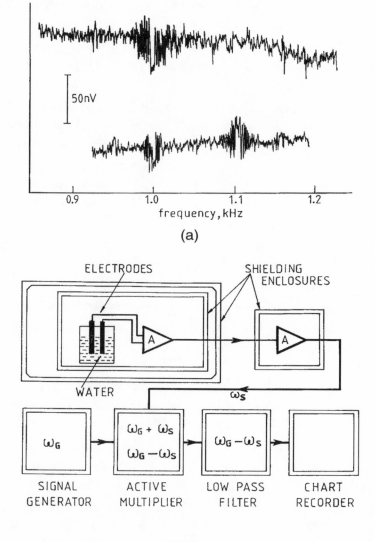

(a)

(b)

Figure 3.12   Resonances imprinted by an alternating magnetic field into a sample of bottled mineral water that originally exhibited only noise between 0.9 kHz and 1.1 kHz, (a) upper trace is the chart recorder output of a frequency scan after the water had been exposed to a 1.0 kHz magnetic signal. Subsequently, the same treated water was exposed to a 1.1 kHz magnetic signal and the lower trace shows the output of a later frequency scan revealing both imprints and (b) diagram of water measuring system showing electrodes, shielding and active filter placement.

generator output and the water imprint frequencies. The low-pass filter allows only the difference frequency component to pass through the chart recorder.

Smith found that some of the water was intrinsically more "noisy" than others for this type of experiment so they used a special mineral water (Volvic) for their tests. The appearance of the beat frequencies (a characteristic of the type of filters used) in Figure 3.12a, as the tuning oscillator approaches a resonance, is an indication that actively oscillating resonances are a permanent feature in the water.

Some may object to Smith's use of a "dowsing" technique to provide valid experimental data or to the Figure 3.12 data since it has not been published in a peer-reviewed journal. However, the former technique was successfully utilized by him in a double-blind medical study that was published[22b]. We hope we will not have to wait too long before others try to replicate this work.

Specific EM Molecular Information Transfer to Pure Water: In France, Benveniste[23] has been studying the effect of very dilute solutions on both in vitro cells and whole organs. In one typical experiment, he

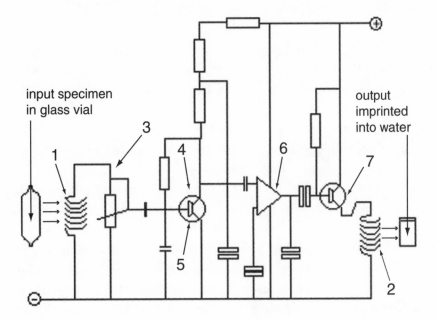

Figure 3.13   Amplifier circuit diagram (as used by Benveniste), (1) input EM coil, (2) output EM coil, (3) high frequency filter, (4) preamplifier, (5) transistor, (6) amplifier and (7) common transistor.

and his associates would innoculate guinea-pigs with new egg albumin to sensitize them before removing their hearts and suspending them in glass cylinders to keep them alive. He then dripped highly dilute solutions of egg albumin into the dismembered hearts. A typical immune reaction, wherein the coronary arteries dilated and the blood flowed faster, indicated that the disembodied heart had recognized the egg albumin. Even when a homeopathic dilution of egg albumin below the Avogadro limit ($1/(6 \times 10^{23})$ moles) was used, the blood vessels of the disembodied hearts responded by dilating a measurable amount (e.g., a fourfold increase in blood flow).

Benveniste and his colleagues then went on to build an electronic amplifier circuit (see Figure 3.13) fitted with one EM input coil and one EM output coil. In blind and open experiments, vials of ovalalbumin solution were placed in the input coil while purified water vials were placed in the output coil for 15 minutes. Water from the output coil vials was then tested via the perfused hearts and statistically significant coronary flow variations were observed in these hearts. It was as if this water contained egg albumin. From this, one can see that one physical carrier of this specific molecular signal can be an EM field somehow imprinted into the water in ways we do not yet fully understand. It is as if nature expresses itself simultaneously via a correlated information aspect and a molecular particulate aspect.

Homeopathy as an Information-Specific Medical Therapeutic[1]:

Hahneman was the first to come up with the idea that a substance which can produce a specific set of symptoms in a healthy person can cure a sick person manifesting the same set of symptoms. This has been called "the law of similars". Hahneman developed a systematic procedure for testing substances (called "proving") on healthy humans in order to elucidate the symptoms characterizing the actions of that particular substance.

During a proving, a substance is introduced into a healthy organism at a sufficiently high concentration to disturb the organism and mobilize its defense mechanisms. The body's defense mechanism then produces a spectrum of symptoms on the physical, emotional and mental levels of the organism. It is this spectrum of symptoms that characterizes the peculiar and unique nature of the substance. Fortunately for the therapeutic side of homeopathic practice, it is found that the symptom pictures of the remedies can be matched, often quite accurately, with the symptom pictures of most illnesses in existence, in all their variety.

Hahneman also discovered in the late 1700's that, when the remedy is diluted with water and, at the same time, succussed between dilutions, the effect of the diluted remedy is significantly increased. This dilution enhancement effect can continue well past the point when theoretically, no molecules of the original physical substance are still present in the solution (this happens for potencies above 12c), yet the solution is still observed to exert a significant action on a living organism.

Perhaps as important as the many studies of homeopathic remedies on humans are the few studies that have been made on other living organisms (particularly in veterinary medicine). Statistically significant effects have been found by using potentized (homeopathic) mercuric chloride in research on the activity of the enzyme diastase, an important component in the hydrolysis of starch. Likewise, homeopathic borax was found to give excellent protection to animals during an epidemic of hoof and mouth disease.

It has also been noted that a remedy loses potency when (a) it has been exposed to heat above 110 °F to 120 °F, (b) it has been exposed directly to the sun, (c) it has been exposed to a strong aromatic substance like camphor and (d) shielding the geomagnetic field with a steel box momentarily erases the potencies. This seems somewhat analogous to the destruction of specific chemical bonds in molecules via UV or γ-radiation but here much smaller photonic energies are involved. The therapeutic action of homeopathy appears to act at the information aspect rather than the particle aspect (water structure aspect) of nature. Hahnemann's potencies were clinically effective for as many as 15 years after preparation.

Significant Contributions from Colloid Surface Science Studies:

Very recent studies[24] using atomic force microscopy have shown that (1) DC magnetic field exposure reduces the electrical potential of a solid surface in contact with aqueous solutions, (2) this magnetic field also thickens the surface adsorbed layer, (3) these magnetic effects appear mostly in solutions of structure-disordering cations such as Cs^+, Rb^+ and K^+, (4) the magnetic memory effect in these solutions lasts long after the magnet exposure (at least a day), (5) this magnet effect decays with the increasing concentration of alcohol in solution as well as with increasing temperature (falls off to ~ 0 at T ~ 50 °C.) and (6) the magnet effects are easily disturbed by an external mechanical disturbance. It has also been shown[25] that the equilibrium pressure, P_0, of water vapor/solid systems changed upon applying relatively small magnetic fields (H < 10 kG) at 30 °C.

Most importantly, evidence has been found[26] that (1) the primary receptor for electromagnetic radiation effects is a gas/liquid interface and that a gas/liquid interface can require many hours to equilibrate (probably because it modifies the local hydrogen bonding network and ion hydration at the interfaces), (2) careful outgassing removes all EM field effects, including the magnetic memory effect, (3) the amplitude of the H-field influences many observed effects, (a) precipitation of $CaCO_3$, (b) zeta potential of suspended colloids, (c) rate of dissolution of colloidal silica, (d) attachment of colloidal silica to metal surfaces and (e) the solubility and diffusivity of gaseous species are also modified, (4) the addition of H_2O_2 or H_2 did not produce equivalent effects without additional gas/liquid interface perturbations via EMF's and (5) hydrophobic gases such as Ar or CO_2, which promote clathrate-like structuring of water, appear to be affected more significantly through the action of EMF's.

Ice Crystal Patterns Materialize Specific Intentions in Water: In his recent book[27], "The Message From Water", Masaru Emoto has shown that, under what appeared to be well controlled conditions, ice crystal formation in water appears to display relatively unique patterns dependent, not only on the chemical toxicity of various lakes, springs, glaciers and cities where the water is collected which is to be expected, but also upon (1) specific music played in a precise environment, (2) wrapping printed statements of appreciation, thanks, anger, hate, etc. on the jars of this water for a given time, (3) specific subtle energies (chi, hado) expressed in the water environment and (4) specific essence additions to water. In all of these examples, it is difficult to evaluate the proportion of the effect on ice crystal pattern formation that comes directly from the physical factors involved and the portion that comes indirectly from the held intentions of the humans involved in the process. It is our belief that a meaningful portion of these beautiful ice crystal patterns arise indirectly from the latter and this provides a perfect stage for us to now describe the details of our own experiments on IIED's with water.

Device-Mediated pH Changes in Water

Early Days: Our experiments began early in January, 1997, in the Materials Science Department at Stanford University. A cautious but tolerant association had been developed between a professor in civil engineering who had an on-going water research program and some extra laboratory space in the Terman Engineering building that he was willing to let WD temporarily occupy. Through him, we had access to a water purification system and a small amount of bench-top space that was located about 100 yards from the office in the Peterson laboratory where the measurements were conducted.

At first we did not want to mix exposure and measurement protocols. Thus, the Terman bench-top space was utilized for much of the preparation work and, in the earliest days, exposure of the water to the active devices. Then, the treated water samples would be walked to the Peterson office where, on the top of a desk, the pH measurements were carried out over subsequent days and weeks. Thus, in those early days, WD did a great deal of shuttling back and forth between the two work areas. We didn't know if this procedure was deleterious or not to the data gathering but we had to start somehow and this procedure was a viable beginning.

pH Measurement Procedures: The pH of an aqueous solution is a quantitative measure of the hydrogen ion concentration, C^{H+}, in the solution given by

$$pH = - \log_{10}(\gamma^{H+} C^{H+}) \tag{3.1}$$

A neutral solution has pH = 7, an acidic solution has pH < 7 while a basic solution has pH > 7 and a change of 1.0 pH units is equivalent to a change in C^{H+} by a factor of 10. In Equation 3.1, γ^{H+} is the activity coefficient for the hydrogen ion (~1 for dilute solutions).

In our studies, the solution pH-values were measured using Accumet 50 and 150 pH meters (Denver Instruments) and fast-response, high-performance, glass combination electrodes. This measurement equipment included automatic temperature measurement. Calibration involved using two buffer standards (pH 7 and either pH 10 or pH 4 depending on the pH range being tested) to determine both (1) the slope of the linear relationship between pH and meter electrical output and (2) the slope efficiency which involves a comparison with the ideal slope (100%). In these studies, the slope efficiencies ranged between 99.5% and 100.2%. The measurement resolution of these meters was 0.001 pH units with an accuracy of ±0.002 pH units. pH buffers have uncertainties of ±0.01 to ±0.02 pH units depending on manufacturer and pH. Measurement uncertainty for a properly calibrated electrode was ±0.02 pH units. Here, the reported pH-values were obtained after first placing the electrode in the solution and then tracking the registered pH reading over a period of time. Normally, the reading increases monotonically and approaches the reported value in 20-40 min. for unstirred solutions (see Figure 3.14). Temperature measurements with an accuracy of ±0.3 °C and resolution of 0.1 °C were made simultaneously with the pH measurements.

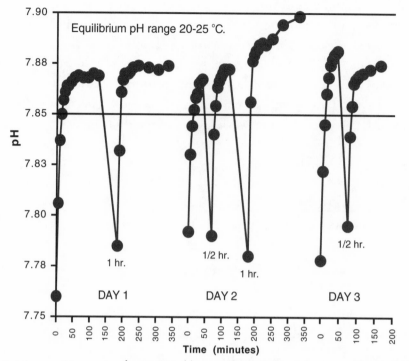

Figure 3.14   pH vs. time for 50/50 dilution of Castle Rock water with ASTM Type 1 (see Appendix 3.B) purified H_2O. The solution was in a closed bottle inside a Faraday Cage with a device (as in Figure 3.15 without meter). After exposure, the bottle was walked several hundred yards to a different laboratory where pH measurements were made. Exposures of varying duration to both types of <u>unimprinted</u> devices were performed. Downward spikes represent exposure intervals (duration marked). pH measurements were done on 3 consecutive days using solution prepared 2 months earlier in the same 125 ml PP bottle. Horizontal bars (at 7.85 and 7.9) mark the equilibrium pH range for temperatures between 20 and 25 °C. Note that the pH values enter the equilibrium range in just a few minutes after the electrode is placed in the unstirred solution.

Several types of water were utilized in this study. Two commercial bottled waters (Evian and Castle Rock), ASTM type 1 purified water and a 50/50 solution of the Castle Rock and ASTM type 1 purified water. The ASTM type 1 water that we used had a specific resistance (prior to exposure to air) of 18.2 to 18.3 megohms-cm. For a profile of ASTM type 1 purified water, see Appendix 3.B.

Evian Water: Evian water is a naturally occurring spring water with an initial pH of around 7.00. The first step in its preparation was to drive out excess CO_2 by stirring and this could increase the solution pH to over 8.0. It is initially a calcium/magnesium bicarbonate solution with total dissolved solids

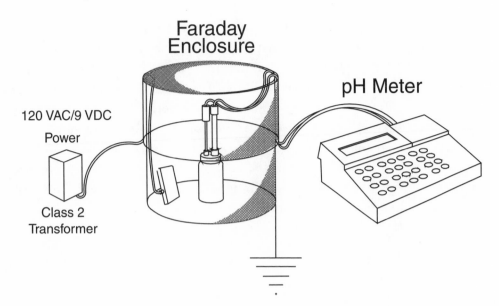

Figure 3.15   Schematic drawing of experimental set-up used in simultaneous exposure and pH measurement experiments (unshielded leads connected the water vessel to the pH-meter).

(TDS) of 300 mg/l and $[Ca^{++}]/[Mg^{++}] = 3.2$. The experimental conditions of temperature, pH and initial calcium concentration utilized here are very similar to those used in controlled calcite precipitation experiments[28]. Although our initial intention was not to grow $CaCO_3$ crystals, after discovering that stirring Evian water caused carbonate precipitation, studying the effect of IIED's on pH during crystal growth was considered worthwhile. The prepared solution was placed in plastic containers (125 ml clear polypropylene bottles) and, just before exposure to either an unimprinted or an imprinted device, had a pH in the range 8.35 to 8.55.

Device exposure was performed as soon after sample preparation as practical since nucleation of fine-grained carbonates can occur soon after stirring. Induction periods for nucleation are a strong function of the degree of supersaturation[28], which was relatively uncontrolled in these experiments. Nucleation and crystal growth are also affected by the sample container used and whether the container was or was not open to the atmosphere. The solid precipitate formed in these runs was expected to be a mix of stable and metastable carbonate phases.

After sample preparation, the solution was poured into two or more bottles with at least one of them being a "control" while the other was exposed to a device. For storage and waiting testing, each bottle was placed in its own electrically grounded Faraday cage (FC). To evaluate a device effect, a powered

IIED was placed in a FC with the bottle for periods of 30 minutes to several hours (same as in Figure 3.15 without meter). Soon after exposure to a device, the bottle was walked several hundred yards to the measurement site where repeated pH measurements were made over a period of about two weeks. In addition, some "seeded" experiments were performed in which stirred solution had been placed in previously used bottles containing a small residue of carbonate precipitate. These bottles had been rinsed and filled with deionized water to dissolve most of the fine-grained solid carbonate. No device exposure was involved in these precipitation "memory" experiments and freshly prepared solution placed in <u>new</u> containers served as the control.

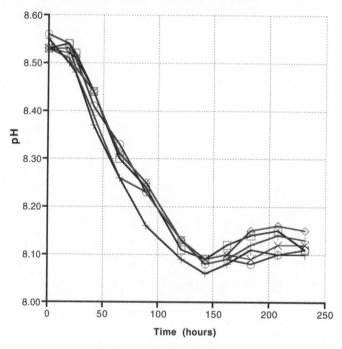

Figure 3.16   *pH vs. time for stirred undiluted Evian water in 6 control bottles. No device exposure was performed. Stirring removes excess CO_2 from this fluid and causes the pH to increase to a level where, after a short nucleation induction period, Ca/Mg carbonates crystallize. This crystallization causes the pH to drop to the levels shown. The magnitude of the drop in pH and amount of carbonate crystallization depends strongly on the initial pH among other factors.*

Figure 3.16 shows the pH vs. time data for the control samples. One notes that the long-time pH asymptote approaches 8.1 ±0.05 in six days. Other similarly prepared solutions were exposed to powered, imprinted, single-oscillator devices (IIEDs) soon after solution preparation with one bottle reserved as the control (see Figures 3.17). In all cases, the pH decreases in the device-exposed solutions exceed those in the control solutions, in accord with the imprinted intention (and EMF exposure (see Figure 3.14)). In some cases, pH changes of 0.25 pH units lower than the control solutions were measured. Qualitatively, the rates of pH decline (associated with particle growth rate) were also greater (Figure 3.17a) in the IIED-exposed solutions. The significant result of these initial experiments is that the more pronounced pH drops occurred in the solutions exposed to the IIEDs even though the best results were appreciably less than the prime directive intention of a 1.0 pH unit decrease.

The data of Figures 3.17 compared to Figure 3.16 suggests at least two things: (1) the imprinting effect somehow initiates the carbonate precipitation reaction at a smaller solution supersaturation than is found with the control solutions (the initial pH values are lower and the rate of pH change is higher in Figures. 3.17) and (2) some type of aging process may be occurring with respect to the family of heterogeneous nucleation catalysts present in the initial solution. This latter point is undoubtedly involved in the starting and ending pH differences between the various control solutions. The starting pH values will be strongly dependent on the degree of initial stirring that occurred before the pH measurements were initiated and, in turn, strongly influenced the final pH. This is probably associated with a particle agglomeration process which is well known to increase with stirring. This leads to the same total mass of solid having a smaller interfacial area (few particles of larger size) and therefore a smaller net mass accumulation rate.

In the seeded experiments, freshly prepared Evian solution was added to previously used bottles that contained carbonate precipitates in wall crevasses after imprinted device exposure. There was a small departure from the control pH (lower than control) only in bottles containing precipitate formed after exposure to IIEDs. When the same bottles were acid-soaked after initial use and the experiment repeated, no departure from the controls was noted. This confirms the "memory" of previous device exposure in the crystals.

The actual chemical evolution of the Evian solutions during these experiments may be important to understand before meaningful comparisons can be made between control experiments and experiments utilizing exposure to IIEDs. The reader interested in the details of this chemical evolution is referred to the discussion given in Appendix 3.A.

Castle Rock Water Experiments: To determine effects of IIED's on water not precipitating solids, we used a more dilute spring water than Evian, Castle

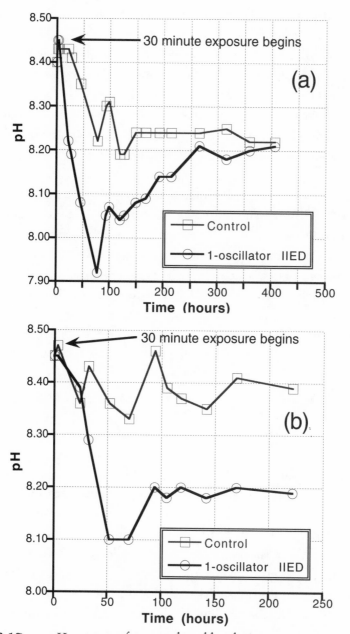

Figure 3.17   pH vs. time for stirred undiluted Evian water. (a) One bottle was a control and the other was exposed to the 1-oscillator IIED for 30 minutes. Note that the pH of the exposed solution dropped to a value lower than that of the control and the controls shown in Figure 3.16 even though the starting pH was lower. The initial rate of pH drop was also considerably greater than in the controls. (b) Another single-oscillator IIED exposure. Another freshly prepared solution was exposed for 30 minutes and compared with a control solution that was not exposed to devices. Again the pH of the exposed solution dropped to a value lower than that of the control but not lower than the control experiments depicted in Figure 3.16.

Rock, and diluted it further with purified water. Four sets of experiments using 50/50 dilutions of Castle Rock water with ASTM type 1 purified H_2O have been carried out, each with a different protocol. Figure 3.14 provides the pH-time plots for the control solution exposed to unimprinted devices. These measurements were carried out on three consecutive days using solution prepared nearly two months earlier. The dynamic pH values enter the equilibrium range in just a few minutes after the electrode is placed in the unstirred solution. The pH values remain in this range for months in the absence of exposure to imprinted devices or to solutions previously exposed to imprinted devices.

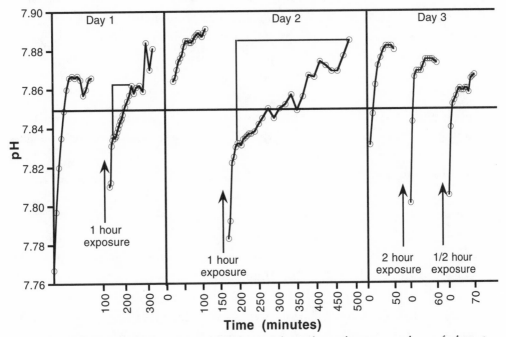

Figure 3.18   pH vs. time for 50/50 dilution of Castle Rock Water with purified H_2O. After exposure to a device, the bottles were taken to another laboratory where pH measurements were performed. Exposures of varying duration to an __imprinted__ 1-oscillator device were performed. Horizontal bars mark the equilibrium pH range for temperatures between 20 and 25 °C.

The Castle Rock water, obtained from retail outlets in plastic bottles, is a naturally occurring spring water with an initial pH of around 7.10, and total dissolved solids (TDS) of about 95 mg/l and $[Ca^{++}]/[Mg^{++}] = 2.0$. Prior to bottling, it is ozonated and filtered through 0.2 μm pharmaceutical grade filters. The 50/50 dilution with ASTM type 1 purified water lowered the total $Ca^{++} + Mg^{++}$ concentration to ensure that no precipitation reactions could occur. Stirring was then used to increase the pH by driving out the excess CO_2. This prepared solution was placed in 125 ml clear polypropylene (PP) bottles and it had a stable pH of 7.875 ± 0.025 in equilibrium with atmospheric CO_2 between 20°C and 25°C.

Experiment (i):   In the first set of experiments using imprinted devices, the sample bottles were exposed in the Terman Site and then walked the several hundred yards to the Peterson Site for measurement. The results, depicted in Figure 3.18, show that a small but measurable effect of the imprinted devices was observed. Compared with the control measurements of Figure 3.14, we observed a much delayed approach of the pH to a stable value in the equilibrium range on days 1 and 2. The areas delimited by the triangle-forming lines in Figure 3.18 represent the total effect of the device exposure on the pH measurement. The magnitude of the effect increased from day 1 to day 2 but almost disappeared on day 3.

Experiment (ii):   We changed the experimental protocol significantly by deciding, in the second set of experiments, to expose the solution to devices simultaneously with pH measurement at the Peterson site (no jostling convection induced by walking several hundred yards, see Figure 3.15 for experimental set-up). Because the pH electrode had now been exposed to an active device, it was kept for use with that device only. Thus, many pH electrodes were eventually used, each for a specific measurement situation. In the first experiment of this set, we used the same solution as in Figure 3.14 (which was two months old by this time). The results shown in Figure 3.19a indicate very little change in pH as a result of imprinted device exposure. Because of the age of this solution, we reasoned that this might be having an effect on the results and so we prepared some fresh solution and repeated the experiment about 10 days later. The result shown in Figure 3.19b demonstrates a meaningful effect of device exposure. For the first time, some "curious" structure appeared in the pH - time behavior - with shoulders plus maxima and minima reminiscent of more conventional "spectra". In the two days following the last data point (420 min.), the pH asymptotically approached a value of 7.70.

This same experiment was repeated three weeks later on the same prepared solution and yielded the result in Figure 3.19c. Once again a curious structure is seen but muted somewhat in magnitude. Comparing Figures 3.19b and 3.19c, in the first 200 min. there is an initial pH drop followed by two "shoulders", the second being somewhat subdued compared to

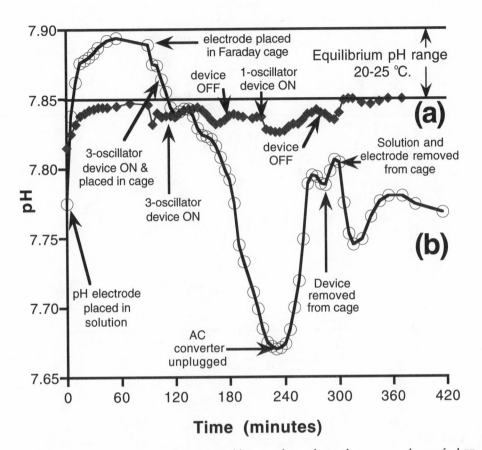

Figure 3.19 (a) pH vs. time for 50/50 dilution of Castle Rock Water with purified H₂O.
Measurement of pH was done simultaneously with 1-hour sequential exposure to both
single-oscillator and three-oscillator imprinted devices. The solution used was identical to
that used in the experiments depicted in Figure 3.14 (prepared on 4/11/97); these
measurements were made on 6/12/97. (b) Measurement of pH was done simultaneously
with 2-hour exposure to an imprinted 3-oscillator device. Solution was prepared 3 days
before measurement and exposure which began on 6/23/97.

the first. The pH-decline then goes through a maximum rate, followed by
another shoulder and another decline into a minimum.

A week after the measurements depicted in Figure 3.19c, they were
repeated again using the same solution and device. The result shown in Figure
3.19d indicates that the device effect is waning (or the water is significantly
aging) but some small suggestion of structure is still present. An additional
week later, this experiment was repeated (Figure 3.19e) and the imprinting
effect seemed to have disappeared. At the time, we interpreted this final result
to mean that the "imprint-charge" had been dissipated from the device so we
sent it back for re-imprinting.

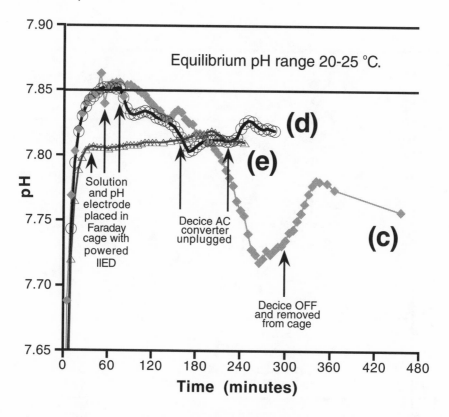

Figure 3.19 (c)pH vs. time for 50/50 dilution of Castle Rock Water with purified H₂O. Measurement of pH was done simultaneously with exposure to the imprinted three-oscillator device. 4-hour exposure on 7/13/97; (d) 2.5 hour exposure on 7/20/97; (e) 1.5 hour exposure on 7/27/97.

Experiment (iii): Following experiment (ii), an exposure of the previously unexposed "control" solution to the <u>unimprinted</u> three-oscillator device was performed simultaneously with pH measurement. An initial pH decrease below the equilibrium range was noted followed by an irregular pH increase on succeeding days. Figure 3.20 (top) shows the results of these measurements on the days following exposure. Not only does the pH vary with time on the scale of days, but a significant variation is observed on the scale of hours as well.

One can contrast this result with exposure of the same initial solution to an <u>imprinted</u> three-oscillator device about one month later (see figure 3.20, bottom). Measurements were made the same way as before. Note the monotonically increasing pH behavior and steady increase of pH in the days following exposure. This contrast in pH behavior with time between the unimprinted vs. imprinted devices was consistently observed for these two

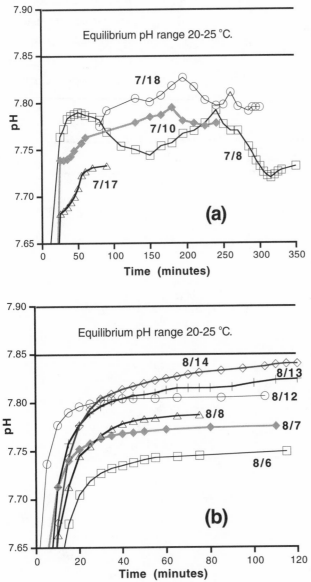

Figure 3.20   pH vs. time for 50/50 dilution of Castle Rock Water with purified H_2O.

(a) Measurements were made on a solution that had been exposed to an unimprinted three-oscillator device on 7/7/97. Note irregular pH behavior and oscillation of pH in the days following exposure (solution prepared on 6/28/97).

(b) Measurements were made on a solution that had been exposed to the imprinted three-oscillator device on 8/5/97. Note monotonically increasing pH behavior and steady increase in pH in the days following exposure (solution prepared on 6/28/97).

device variants. For solutions exposed to imprinted devices, this coherent-like behavior was a consistent marker.

<u>Experiment (iv):</u>   Experiments measuring the pH of water with IIED exposure can be carried out in at least two different ways: (1) the pH can be measured simultaneously with IIED exposure or (2) the pH can be measured <u>after</u> the water has first been exposed to the IIED. An example of simultaneous exposure and measurement of a freshly prepared solution is given in Figure 3.21a. Note that, here, the IIED was turned on early in the

81

measurement process when the pH of the solution was still in its equilibrium range. The pH then declined in accordance with the pH-decreasing intention, even after the device's battery had been electrically discharged. Recharging the device's battery and continuing the solution exposure resulted in a further marginal drop. A total decrease of about 0.5 ± 0.05 pH units occurred during

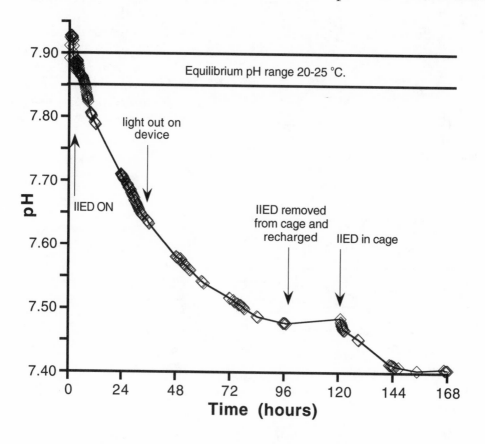

Figure 3.21 (a) pH vs. time for 50/50 dilution of Castle Rock Water with purified H_2O. Measurement of pH was done simultaneously with exposure to an imprinted 1-oscillator device starting 8/18/97. Only the internal battery (which loses charge in ~30 hours) powered the device. The device's battery was recharged and the device was placed back in the cage (solution prepared on 8/16/97).

its simultaneous exposure/measurement experiment with a single oscillator IIED. The relatively large uncertainty is due to the long measurement period without pH calibration. The pH of this particular bottle of solution, measured after its exposure and moved to a different location 5 miles away, using completely unexposed equipment, ranged between 7.50 on the next day and 7.60 one month later even though the local ambient equilibrium pH-range was

~7.85 to 7.90. This substantiated the long-term stability of this profound pH change.

In another experiment, a bottle from the same batch of new solution was exposed to the pH-lowering IIED (without pH measurement) in a Faraday cage for 5 days. The container holding the solution was tightly capped during most of that exposure time and, after this 5 day interval, the IIED was removed to storage and pH measurements commenced. It is perhaps reasonable for one to expect (based on Figure 3.21a) that the pH would have already dropped significantly in 5 days, in accordance with the specific intention of the IIED. However, this was not the case! Figure 3.21b shows the result for this sequential exposure/measurement experiment. Once again,

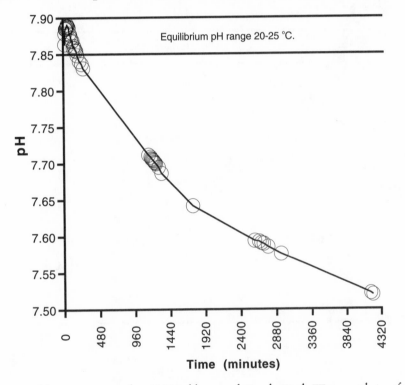

Figure 3.21 (b) pH vs. time for 50/50 dilution of Castle Rock Water with purified H_2O. pH measurements made on solution previously exposed to pH-lowering device for 5 days. Measurements on 9/22/97 through 9/25/97 involved no device exposure.

the pH-values first measured are in the equilibrium range and then decline steadily reaching a level at 4320 min very similar to that noted in Figure 3.21a for the simultaneous exposure/measurement protocols. This comparison of the two protocol results is shown in Figure 3.21c for the first 3-day period. During the measurement period of the sequential protocol, no device exposure occurred so it seems as if the "potential" for pH change was generated and passively stored at some level of the solution and was only actualized in space-time after the triggering event associated with the physical act of pH measurement.

The results in Figure 3.21 are somewhat analogous to the results described in a later section involving purified water and $ZnCO_3$ particles (see Figure 3.22). There, the pH of this solution was approaching its equilibrium range above pH=8 with no observable effect of the pH-lowering device exposure until a triggering event occurred associated with shaking the container to re-suspend the $ZnCO_3$ particles. After the shaking event, the pH

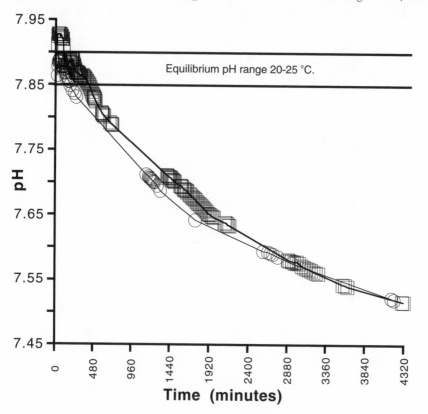

Figure 3.21 (c) pH vs. time for 50/50 dilution of Castle Rock Water with purified H₂O. Measurement of pH was done simultaneously with exposure to the imprinted one-oscillator device for the data points depicted by squares but only after exposure for the data points depicted by circles. These curves represent the same data depicted in Figures 3.21a and 3.21b above for the initial 72 hour (4320 minute period).

briefly spiked upward into the equilibrium range and then declined in accordance with the pH-lowering intention imprinted into the IIED. In experiments with control solutions (and no IIED involvement), no such long-term pH lowering ever occurred after shaking events.

To summarize the results for the Castle Rock water solution presented in this section, we observed significant pH-lowering with solutions exposed to IIEDs when the measurement and exposure occurred simultaneously. Some

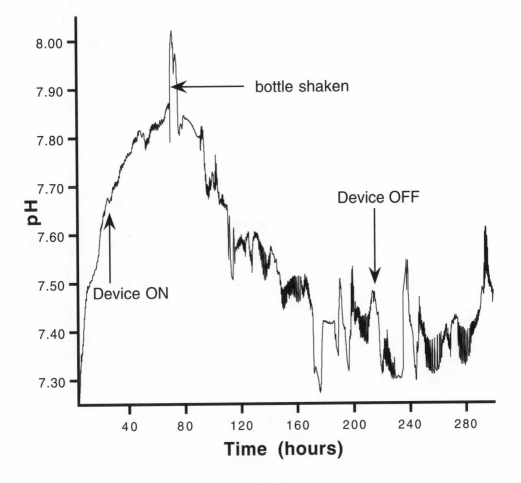

Figure 3.22   pH vs. time plot for ZnCO₃ particles in pure water. pH-lowering device was operated and deactivated, as indicated, in a location in a different building (156 feet away) from where the measurements shown were performed. The bottle containing ZnCO₃ particles and water was shaken to suspend the particles as shown.

pH-lowering also occurred in solutions where the measurement was performed in one location after prior exposure to IIEDs in another. There were also indications of some pH-lowering as a result of (1) exposure to solutions that had previously experienced prior device exposure and (2) unintentional exposure to devices operating at a remote location. In all cases, the pH drop was observed to be the greatest for solutions exposed to nearby powered imprinted devices.

The consistent result of these experiments is that a pH lowering was produced by the IIED's, although this did not always occur in the manner expected, perhaps for reasons related to the history and aging of the solutions. Also, the details of the observed pH-lowering changed during the course of the experiments making it difficult to ascribe completely reproducible characteristics to the pH-time behavior. The fading of the pH-lowering effect illustrated in Figures 3.19b to 3.19d may relate to the leakage rate from the device or to the fact that an aged, previously exposed solution becomes more refractory with time with respect to registering and recording effects of imprinted devices.

Some of these results may relate to the slow conditioning of the experimental system to the effects of imprinted IIEDs. As such, this conditioning may be ongoing but variable in ways we do not yet understand, so that somewhat different results manifest with the passage of time. This topic is so important and so profound that chapter 6 is entirely devoted to it. It may also be possible that the devices somehow "drive" the output of the pH-electrode and meter to produce a pH-lowering that is simply an artifact. This particular possibility seems to be ruled out by the results shown in Figures 3.21a and 3.21b where the sequential exposure and measurement protocol was utilized and yielded an almost identical result to that found using the simultaneous protocol (Figure 3.21c). Of course, some "cross-talk" between measurement system and devices cannot be completely ruled out.

Finally, there is also the possibility that, in long simultaneous exposure/measurement experiments, the slow flow of KCl solution from the electrode filling solution may cause a decrease in pH. However, measuring the pH of this filling solution and calculating the expected pH change in the bottle of water due to the small observed drop in the level of electrode filling solution indicates that only a slight pH-lowering can be expected from this source. Such a result is confirmed by our electrode recalibration tests which reveal only a very small drift from start to completion of a long experiment. Such an electrode drift effect was observed to be a factor of 20-50 smaller than the maximum pH-lowering of 0.5 ± 0.05 observed in these Castle Rock Water experiments.

At this point in time, about 10 months had passed and we decided to move our experimental studies to a laboratory in Minnesota (near Minneapolis) for the remaining 26 months of the contract period). We also decided to work with pH-raising IIEDs as well as with our pH-lowering IIEDs.

Our first few months in the Minnesota lab were spent replicating and confirming the earlier Stanford experiments.

ASTM Type 1, Purified Water Experiments: By early in 1998, we had our new lab and a good water purification system set up in Minnesota and began some new experiments with 100% ASTM Type 1 purified water (see Appendix 3.B) in equilibrium with laboratory air using the same protocols as earlier but now with IIEDs imprinted with the intention that they <u>raise</u> the pH of water by 1 pH unit. The devices were imprinted in California on April

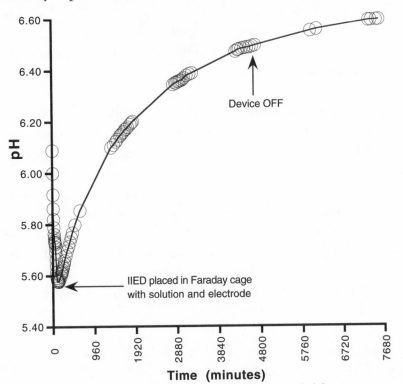

Figure 3.23   pH vs. time of pure water in equilibrium with laboratory air and in the presence of an IIED imprinted to raise the pH by one pH unit.

4, 1998 (it was subjectively felt to be a very "powerful" imprinting session), shipped to Minnesota a few days later and the experiments began on April 14, 1998. Figure 3.23 shows the first five days of data collection with a single-oscillator device. The initial relatively rapid drop in pH is associated with the electrode equilibration with the very dilute unbuffered water. The initial pH of this water was 5.6, consistent with pure water in equilibrium with the CO_2 in laboratory air. This initial pH drop into the equilibrium range was followed by a pH rise that asymptotically approached a pH of 6.6 five days later. This showed <u>conclusively</u> that the pH changes induced by imprinted device exposure are not an artifact of the measurement system. Here, we see the pH increasing by almost exactly one pH unit in complete accord with the prime directive for that IIED. A factor of 10 decrease in H^+ content via an IIED is a robust signature indeed!

A second experiment with this purified water was an investigation of the distance-effect for IIED interaction with the vessel of water as a function of separation between the two. What we found was that the effect of the IIED on the pH of pure water was less at a separation distance of 6 in. than at 1 to 2 feet where the effect was the greatest. At greater separation distances than 2 feet, the IIED effect decreased rapidly (see Figure 6.21). This result is consistent with previous work with IIED's on cell multiplication rates where similar IIED effects as a function of position were reported[1, p 273].

<u>Purified Water with ZnCO₃ Crystallites</u>: To test an idea suggested from the Evian water studies, that the imprinted water (after treatment by an activated IIED) might transfer an imprint effect to crystals grown from that water which, in-turn, might transfer the imprint-effect to unexposed water, we utilized some of the Ca/Mg carbonate crystals obtained from earlier studies. These crystals were carefully washed and then added to a vessel of new, untreated purified water. The crystals dissolved partially in this water and indeed transferred the imprint-effect to this new water. However, even though a transfer effect had been observed, it was difficult to determine if it was due to partitioning of the original imprint to these crystals as they grew from the imprinted solution or to the entrainment of some of the original water at defect surfaces formed as a consequence of their uncontrolled mode of growth. Further, because of unanticipated metastable phase formation from uncontrolled solution supersaturation and precipitation, even if real imprint partitioning had occurred, we didn't know which crystalline phase was the culprit.

To correct this deficiency, we set about to carefully grow specific crystals under well-defined conditions to test this imprint partitioning hypothesis. The sparingly soluble material, $ZnCO_3$, was chosen as the first test material and, during the course of that investigation, phenomena arose which sent the experimentation down a completely different path than anticipated. Serendipitously, it was observed that quite long-range (~ 150 feet) communication occurred between vessels of water when the water contained a suspension of small $ZnCO_3$ crystallites. In addition, pH and temperature oscillations of a particular periodic and repetitive nature began to be observed (to be discussed at length in chapter 6). Thus, the crystal-partitioning study was left unfinished while we explored these new research directions.

We will end this chapter by discussing some of the data on apparent communication between two vessels, containing purified water plus fine-grained $ZnCO_3$ particles, at a separation distance of 156 ft. By this time, we were simultaneously measuring both temperature and pH. Data was collected using the output from a pH-meter linked, via RS-232 cable, to a desktop computer and the sample interval ranged from 1 to 3 minutes. The IIED was placed near one vessel (designated the transmitter) while the other vessel has no nearby IIED (designated the receiver). In chapter 6, we will return to this topic and consider a four-vessel experiment with one transmitter and three receivers at remote locations from each other and from the transmitter (separation distances from 150 feet to 900 feet). There, we will also show (1) the strong observed correlation between pH-oscillations and temperature oscillations in the vessel, (2) successful communication to the receiver vessels even when the transmitter vessel is <u>inside</u> a faraday cage and (3) most importantly, a conditioning effect with time that occurs with continued exposure of the experimental locale to the augmented-EM waves associated with an activated IIED.

<u>$ZnCO_3$ Experiment I</u>: This experiment was carried out at two locations. At the location designated as the receiving station (called station B), one gram of a fine-grained, commercial $ZnCO_3$ powder[33] with a surface area of 21.4 m^2/gm was added to 250 ml ASTM-type 1 purified water in a polypropylene bottle. A pH electrode and temperature probe were both placed in the open bottle and pH and temperature were continuously monitored for periods of up to two weeks. Initially, the particles were completely suspended by shaking and, with the passage of time, settling occurred to produce a layer of $ZnCO_3$ sediment at the bottom of the vessel with clear water above.

At the sending station (location A), 156 feet away from B, a solution of Na_2CO_3 was added dropwise via a slow flow pump to an aqueous solution of $Zn(NO_3)_2$ at 90°C (see Figure 3.24). The IIED, imprinted to lower the pH, was placed 1 foot from this Erlenmeyer flask and turned on at about the same time the pump was activated to deliver the Na_2CO_3 solution. Nucleation of $ZnCO_3$ crystals began within hours and growth of the small crystallites was completed in 7 days. Approximately 1 gram of total solids was collected from the flask at the end of this growth cycle and the IIED was turned off.

At location B, the pH measurements began two days after powering the IIED at location A. pH measurements continued at location B for some time after the IIED had been turned off at location A and stored in its own Faraday cage (FC). After 13 days, the pH electrode was removed from the vessel and placed in buffer solution which revealed that the instrumental drift over this 13 day period was less than 0.02 pH units.

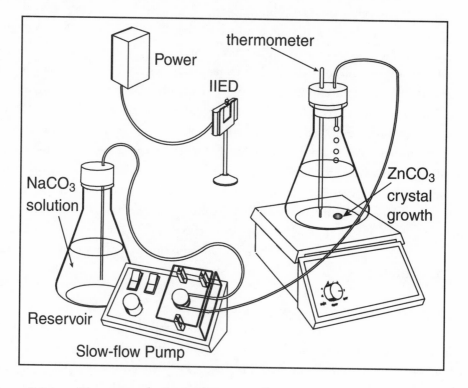

Figure 3.24   Experimental set-up at location A for ZnCO$_3$ Experiment I. The powered IIED is shown 1 foot from the heated flask where ZnCO$_3$ crystallites were growing. The set-up for ZnCO$_3$ Experiment II included only the powered IIED.

From Figure 3.25 one sees that, except for an initial exponential rise during the first 4-5 hours, the pH trend at location B was a general decrease over time but modulated by both highly periodic short-period ($\leq$ 2 hours) and long period ($\geq$ 20 hours) oscillations. During the first 120 hours of this experiment, ZnCO$_3$ crystallites were growing in the vessel at location A. It was noted that the short period oscillations at location B ceased $\sim$ 12 hours after the IIED was turned off at location A (they returned a few days later). However, the well-defined longer period pH-oscillations ($\sim$ diurnal) continued and, near the end of this experiment, the pH increased rapidly (see Figure 3.25).

ZnCO₃ Experiment II: About 30 hours after the pH-monitoring equipment at location B described above was re-calibrated, a repeat experiment was initiated. However, this time there was no vessel at location A containing

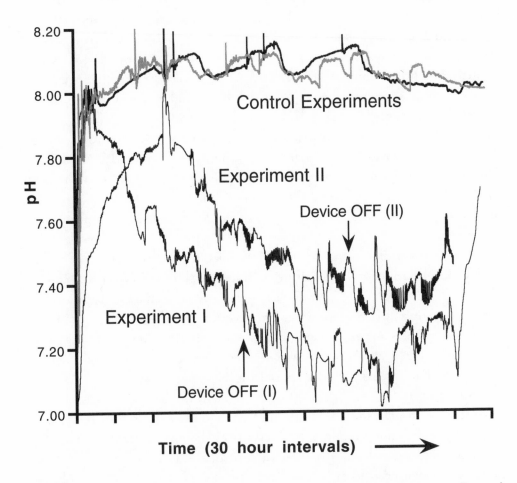

Figure 3.25   pH versus time plot summaries for ZnCO₃ experiments. All vessels contained 250 ml pure water and 1 g ZnCO₃ crystallites from a commercial source. Time scales differ between control experiments and Experiments I and II. Two intervals of 14 days of the latter are shown while two intervals of 5 days of the former are depicted. Experiment II was performed after Experiment I. The control experiments were performed at remote locations 1 to 2 months following Experiment II. A powered pH-lowering IIED was operating at a location A and was turned off as indicated. No IIED's were operated during the control experiments. Sharp upward pH spikes identify shaking events during these latter experiments. Experiment II data is the same as that depicted in Figure 3.22.

water plus ZnCO₃ crystallites – only the activated, unshielded, pH-lowering IIED.

At the end of $ZnCO_3$ Experiment I, the solution pH at location B had been drifting upwards towards its initial value. Here, in Experiment II, the pH of this suspension increased exponentially and approached pH $\sim$ 7.9 asymptotically over a period of 3 days even though the unshielded IIED at location A was turned on just after the end of day 1. Therefore, the pH increase at the end of experiment I was no fluke and, even with a powered IIED 156 feet away, the pH of the solution continued upwards towards the normal equilibrium range (possibly suggesting a very long coherence length between water samples). No downward pH trend was initially observed; however, some small amplitude but well-defined pH oscillations became apparent. After 3 days of measurement, the bottle was shaken to re-suspend the fine-grained $ZnCO_3$ powder in the solution (see Figures 3.22 and 3.25). This initiated a sharp increase in pH to just above pH = 8 (near the previous equilibrium value), followed by a sharp drop, a leveling out at a slightly lower pH level and finally a slow decline with well-developed large amplitude, pH oscillations.

The effect of shaking on *control solutions* of 1 gram $ZnCO_3$ crystallites in 250 ml of purified water (with no activated IIED) is shown in the top part of Figure 3.25. One set of measurements was performed at location C (a nearby site in a different building from A or B) while the other set was performed by the same experimenter at a remote location about 9 miles distant (gray overlay). In all, over two weeks of continuous measurements with 20 separate shaking events were carried out on these control solutions. As can be observed from Figure 3.25, the effect of shaking, in all cases, was to cause an upward spike in pH, a leveling out and then a gradual decline to the previous or slightly lower value. No long term effects of shaking, such as prolonged pH declines, were ever observed for these control solutions where no activated IIED was involved. No highly-periodic pH oscillations were ever observed either.

Discussion of Experiments I and II: The pH of pure water in equilibrium with atmospheric CO_2 plus coarse-grained, well-crystallized $ZnCO_3$ is calculated to be below pH = 7. At a pH of 8, the equilibrium concentration of Zn^{++} in such solutions should be very low, less than the concentrations of all other ions including H^+ ($C^{H+} < 10^{-8}$ molar). The rise in pH to about pH = 8.1 ± 0.2 that we have seen in numerous dissolution experiments performed using both commercially-obtained and in-house synthesized $ZnCO_3$ is almost certainly a result of dissolution of very fine-grained $ZnCO_3$ with its capillary-enhanced solubility. Also, the presence of metastable, hydroxyl-bearing, solid phases of significantly higher solubility cannot be ruled out.

The pH-time behavior of the control experiments shown in Figure 3.25 is entirely consistent with kinetically-enhanced dissolution of higher solubility material followed by subsequent slow growth of $ZnCO_3$ onto a somewhat less soluble $ZnCO_3$ substrate via the well-known process called "Ostwald ripening". Thus, the equilibrium pH for dissolution of very fine-grained $ZnCO_3$ from the sources described has been established as pH = 8.1 ± 0.2 and, when the pH deviates significantly from this range, <u>some external mechanism driving such a change must be invoked</u>. For $ZnCO_3$ Experiment I, Figure 3.25 shows a total pH decline of one full pH unit, consistent with the intention for the particular IIED used in the experiment at a remote location 156 feet away.

It appears that the unique phenomena described here are associated with the broadcast of a specific human intention manifesting itself in a solution at some distance from the transmitter site. Since earlier experiments revealed that, for unshielded vessels of <u>pure water</u> located at various distances from an activated IIED, negligible pH change occurred for vessels more than 3-4 feet from the device, the small $ZnCO_3$ crystallites must be critically involved in this overall communication process.

One interpretation of the "shaking-effect" shown in Figure 3.22 is that the water was kinetically "stuck" for some reason and could not keep up with the thermodynamic driving force for pH-change generated by the specific intention broadcast from the activated IIED. An analogy would be the common observation of the substantial supersaturation sometimes needed for crystal growth in a solution before a phase change can be nucleated in that solution. In our case, it is probably some basic property of water (see the early pages of this chapter) that allows and causes it to "stick" at some metastable pH level. Perhaps this represents a phase transition to a more stable phase of water, one that is more stable in the presence of our <u>augmented</u>-EM field. In such a case, the convection generated by shaking may allow heterogeneous nucleation of small domains of this new phase at key sites on the original binary water phases and, it is this new water phase that allows the pH to decrease so greatly.

Finally, the locale conditioning effect and the pH plus temperature-oscillation effects have been noted here but detailed consideration is projected to Chapter 6.

Some Summary Findings

- The IIEDs are able to cause a pH increase or decrease in various waters in accord with the imbedded intention and up to the maximum level projected in some cases.

- The physically identical unimprinted devices do not produce a significant pH change in these waters.

- These activated IIEDs appear to generate an enhanced degree of coherence in the water pH measurements while powering a physically identical unimprinted device appears to generate (or maintain) a degree of incoherence in the water pH measurements.

- With a pH-decreasing IIED both (a) simultaneous 5-day exposure/pH measurement and (b) sequential 5-day exposure/pH measurement produced almost identical pH vs. time curves.

- The addition of fine-grained $ZnCO_3$ particulates to purified water appears to enhance communication of intention and pH-time correlations between distant vessels of such solutions. Shaking the vessels appears to enhance the solution's approach to the intention-projected pH.

References

1.   W. A Tiller, <u>Science and Human Transformation: Subtle Energies, Intentionality and Consciousness</u> (Pavior Publishing, Walnut Creek, CA, 1997), pp. 243-246.

2.   F.S. Stillinger, "Water Revisited", Science, <u>209</u> (1980) 451.

3.   S. Woutersen and H.J. Bakker, Nature, <u>402</u> (1999) 507.

4.   G.E. Walrafen, J. Chem. Phys. <u>40</u> (1964) 3249; ibid <u>47</u> (1967) 114.

5.   W.B. Monosmith and G.E. Walrafen, J. Chem. Phys., <u>81</u> (1984) 669; M.C. Bellissent-Funel, Europhys. Lett., <u>42</u> (1998) 161.

6.   H.E.Stanley, "Unsolved Mysteries of Water in its Liquid and Glass States", MRS Bulletin, May 1999, 22.

7.   G. Preparata, <u>QED Coherence in Matter</u>, (World Scientific, Singapore, 1995).

8.   E. Del Giudice and G. Preparata, "Coherent Dynamics in Water", J. Biol. Physics, <u>202</u> (1994) 105.

9.   R. Arani, I. Bono, E. Del Giudice and G. Preparata, "QED Coherence and the Thermodynamic Properties of Water", Int. J. Mod. Phys. B, <u>9</u> (1995) 1813.

10.   G. Salvetti, "Dielectric Measurements of Water", in <u>Alcohols and Their Mixtures, in Hydrogen-Bonded Liquids</u>, Eds. J.C. Dore and J. Teixeira (Kluwer Academic Publishers, Dondrecht, 1991), p. 369.

11.   L.P. Semikhina and V.P. Kiselev, "Effect of Weak Magnetic Fields on the Properties of Water and Ice", Zavedenii, Fizika, <u>5</u>, May 1988, pp. 13-17.

12.   L.P. Semikhana and Yu, A. Lyubinov, "Effects of Weak Fmagnetic Fields on Dielectric Loss in Ordinary Water and Heavy Water", Moscow University Physics Bulletin, <u>43</u> (1998) 60-64.

13.   V.P. Kiselev, A.M. Saletskii and L.P. Semikhina, "Structural Changes in Water Exposed to Weak variable Magnetic Fields", Moscow University Physics Bulletin, <u>45</u> (1990) 53-58.

14.   K.M. Joshi and P.V. Kamat, <u>Effect of Magnetic Field on the Physical Properties of Water</u>, J. Indian Chem Soc., <u>43</u> (1966) 620-622.

15.   S. Rai, N.N. Singh and R.N. Mishra, "Magnetic Restructuring of Water", Med. Biol. Eng. & Comp., <u>33</u> (1995) 613-617.

16.   S. Sasaki, T. Kobayashi and M. Ohashi, "Changes of Water Conductivity Induced by Non-Inductive Coil", Soc. For Mind-Body Science, <u>1</u> (1992) 23.

17.   I.J. Lin and J. Yotvat, "Exposure of Irrigation and Drinking Water to a Magnetic Field with Controlled Power and Direction", J. Magnetism and Magnetic Materials, 83 (1990) 525-526.

18.   N.N. Krasikov, V.K. Koyekin and I.V. Slyusar, "Biological Activation of Water by a Non-Contacting Electric Field", Biophysics, 39 (1994) 965-969.

19.   L.D. Gapochka, M.G. Gapochka, A.F. Korolev and A.I. Kostienko, "The Effect of Microwave Radiation on Liquid Water", Moscow University Physics Bulletin, 49 (1994) 67-71.

20.   E.E. Fesenko and A. Ya Glustein, "Changes in the State of Water Induced by Radiofrequency EM Fields", FEBS Letters, 367 (1995) 53-55.

21.   C.W. Smith, "Electromagnetic Bioinformation and Water" in Ultra High Dilutions – Physiology and Physics, Eds. Endler and Schulte (Kluwer Acad. Pub., New York, 1992).

22.a   P. Tsouris and C.W. Smith, "The Detection of LF Resonances in Water", Private Communication from Smith, 1992.

22.b   W. J. Rea, Y. Fan, E. J. Fenyves, I. Sujisawa, H. Suyama, N. Samadi and G. H. Ross, " Electromagnetic Field Sensitivity", J. Bioelectricity, 10 (1991) 241.

23.   J. Benveniste, B. Armoux and L. Hadji, "Highly Dilute Antigen Increases Coronary Flow of Isolated Heart from Immunized Guinea-Pigs", Fased J., G. (1992) A, 1610.

24.   I. K. Higashitani and J. Oshitani, "Measurement of Magnetic Effects on Electrolyte Solutions by Atomic Force Microscope", Trans. I Chem. E., 75 B (1997) 115; "Magnetic Effects on Thickness of Adsorbed Layer in Aqueous Solutions Evaluated Directly by Atomic Force Microscope", J. Colloid and Interface Science, 204 (1998) 363.

25.   S. Ozeki, J. Miyamoto, S. Ono, C. Wakai and T. Watanabe, "Water-Solid Interactions under Steady Magnetic Fields: Magnetic Field-induced Adsorption and Desorption of Water", J. Phys. Chem., 100 (1996) 4205.

26.   M. Colic and D. Morse, "Effects of Amplitude of RF EM Radiation on Aqueous Suspensions and Solutions", J. Colloid and Interface Science, 200 (1998) 265; "Mechanism of the Long-term Effects of EM Radiation on Solutions and Suspended Colloids", Langmuire, 14 (1998) 783; "Influence of Resonant RF Radiation on Gas:Liquid Interface: Can It Be Quantum Vacuum Radiation?", Phys. Rev. Lett., 80 (1998) 2465.

27.   M. Emoto, "The Message From Water", (HADO Kyokusha, Tokyo, 1999).

28.   P.G. Koutsoukos and C.G. Kontoyannis, Precipitation of Calcium Carbonate in Aqueous Solutions, J. Chem. Soc., Faraday Transactions I, 80 (1984) 1181.

29.   W. Stumm and J. Morgan, Aquatic Chemistry: Chemical Equilibria and Rates in Natural Waters, (John Wiley & sons, New York, 1996).

30.   W. Dreybrodt, J. Lauckner, L. Zaihua, U. Svensson and D. Buhmann, "The Kinetics of the Reaction as One of the Rate Limiting Steps for the Dissolution of Calcite in the Syustem H_2O-CO_2-$CaCO_3$", Geochimica et Cosmochimica ACTA, 60 (1996) 3375.

31.   W.E. Dibble Jr., and W.A. Tiller, "Electronic Device-Mediated pH Changes in Water", J. Sci. Exploration, 13 (1999) 155.

32.   A. Katz, "The Interaction of Magnesium with Calcite During Crystal Growth at 25-90°C and One Atmosphere", Geochimica et Cosmochimica ACTA, 37 (1973) 1563.

33.   Baker Analyzed® reagent grade Zinc Carbonate.

34.   M. Brush, "Water, Water, Everywhere: A Profile of Water Purification Systems", The Scientist, 12 [12] (June 8, 1998) 18.

Appendix 3.A: The Chemical Evolution of Evian Water in Our Experiments

The Evian solution used here is a Ca/Mg bicarbonate solution that is oversaturated with CO_2 compared with the same water in equilibrium with the atmosphere. The amount of CO_2 in solution, above that in equilibrium with atmospheric CO_2, is termed "excess" CO_2. It should also be noted that the dissolved CO_2 is actually in the form of carbonic acid[29]. In the observed pH range, stirring removes the excess CO_2 via the following reaction [30]

$$HCO_3^- + H^+ \rightarrow H_2O + CO_2 \uparrow \quad . \qquad (3A.1)$$

Thus, as excess CO_2 is removed, the pH increases (H^+ decreases via Equation 3A.1) and the solution eventually supersaturates with respect to the formation of crystalline Ca/Mg carbonates. In fact, if the pH approaches or exceeds about 8.6, a carbonate precipitate forms while stirring, an observation consistent with the precipitation threshold established by others[28]. Such precipitation was avoided by not exceeding that pH while the solution was being stirred. The control solutions approached this pH closely (see Figure 3.16) and showed a greater pH lowering than other control experiments consistent with a greater degree of supersaturation with respect to the carbonate phases. If the Evian solution is not stirred enough to raise the pH to a value where carbonates crystallize spontaneously, then the solution remains oversaturated to varying degrees with CO_2 and, for a time, does not precipitate carbonates even if the solution is supersaturated with respect to them. If the supersaturation is below a certain threshold, nucleation induction periods can be very long[28].

The dissolved CO_2 excess itself can contribute to supersaturation with respect to Ca/Mg carbonates. Reactions that produce both stable (calcite) and metastable (hydromagnesite) phases can be readily formulated[31]. Once excess CO_2 is removed from the solution either by stirring or by precipitation of solids or both, the change in solution pH is consistent with a reaction such as

$$Ca^{++} + HCO_3^- \rightarrow CaCO_3 + H^+ \qquad (3A.2)$$

The rate of pH decrease, $d[H^+]/dt$, is approximately equal to $d[Ca^{++}]/dt$ which, in turn, is directly related to the total mass rate of calcium carbonate formation. The carbonate crystallization rate is relatively uncontrolled in our experiments because of (1) the variable heterogeneous nucleation on the walls of the container, (2) the variable degree of supersaturation (which is a function of both pH and dissolved CO_2), and (3) the effects of Mg^{++} plus other ions on the kinetics of the process.

The drop in pH from 8.55 to 8.05 shown in Figure 3.16 parallels the drop measured by others[28] in solutions with similar starting compositions (pH and total $Ca^{++} + Mg^{++}$). However, their reaction was complete in hours as opposed to several days in our experiments. The presence of Mg^{++} in large amounts for our experiments probably accounts for the decrease in rates, since Mg^{++} is known to inhibit the crystallization of $CaCO_3$[32]. In any case, the retardation in deposition rates compared with strictly controlled "pristine" $CaCO_3$ growth experiments[28] allowed us to very easily observe the effect of exposure to IIEDs on growth rates. If the rate of pH drop had been as rapid as in more conventional $CaCO_3$ growth rate experiments, there would have been no opportunity to observe the long-term effect of IIED exposure on these rates. Thus, simply stirring Evian water was a remarkably good experimental vehicle for our initial IIED work.

Appendix 3.B: Characteristics of Type I Purified Water Used in Our Experiments

Purified, reagent grade water is broken down into four types: Type I, Type II, Type III, or Type IV. Type I, or ultrapure water, is the most pure. Five major standards organizations, CAP (College of American Pathologists), NCCLS (National Committee for Clinical Laboratory Standards), ASTM (American Society of Testing and Materials), USP (United States Pharmocopeia), and ISO (International Organization for Standardization) define the characteristics of these water types. Type I water has varying qualities depending on which guidelines are used[34].

The various water types are defined in terms of specific resistance (megohm-cm), specific conductance (microhms per centimeter), total silica, total organic carbon (TOC), and bacterial count, among other attributes. ASTM Type I water has a specific resistance of at least 18 megohms-cm, a maximum TOC of 100 ppb (parts-per-billion), a maximum dissolved silica content of 3 ppb and a maximum bacterial colony count of 10/liter. Purified water produced by the water polishing apparatus we used typically exceeded the ASTM standards for Type I water. The manufacturer claims the unit we purchased produced water with a TOC of less than 5 ppb with a maximum specific resistance of 18.3 megohm-cm. This apparatus included ultraviolet irradiation, a TOC flush and advanced filtration options (see discussion below).

The production of Type I water using water purification systems involves the successful removal of a variety of impurities and contaminants[34]. These are generally lumped into the following groups.

- Particulate matter: This includes suspended particles, such as silt, sand, and clay particles, ranging between 1 micron and 20 microns in size, and colloidal particles, which fall between 0.01 micron and 1.0 micron in size. Altogether, these particles cause water to appear unclear or cloudy.

- Microorganisms: Bacteria, protozoa, viruses, and algae are among the organisms that contaminate water. Microorganisms give rise to pyrogens, which are thermostable, lipopolysaccharide fragments of cell walls. Pyrogens cause immune responses such as fevers when injected into mammals, and hinder cell and tissue cultures. DNA, DNase, RNase, and the normal biological materials and waste products produced by living and dying organisms are also impurities that must be dealt with.

- Dissolved nonionized solids and gases: This group includes man-made organic chemicals and the natural organic remains from decaying plants and animals. Together, these may include proteins, tannins and chloramines, in addition to pesticide, herbicide and detergent residues. Oxygen and nitrogen also fall within this group.

- Dissolved ionized solids and gases: These come from the exposure of water to rocks and minerals, and include sodium chloride, calcium carbonate, silicates, nitrates, sulfates, phosphates, and other compounds. Carbon dioxide is the main ionized gas.

Five major technologies exist to remove these impurities from water:

- Distillation: Distillation is the oldest and most widespread technology for the production of reagent grade water. This technology heats water to boiling, and then condenses the vapor back to liquid. The phase change from liquid to vapor separates water from its impurities. Distillation removes the widest range of impurities from water. We always used distilled water as the <u>starting</u> feed in the water polishing apparatus that produced purified water for our experiments.

- Adsorption by activated carbon: Chlorine and organic compounds are removed from water by adsorption to high surface area activated carbon filters. Adsorption is generally employed as a first or second step in water purification systems.

- Ultraviolet irradiation: The irradiation of water by UV light at 254 nanometers and 185 nanometers kills microorganisms and reduces trace organics by photochemical oxidation, respectively. UV irradiation plays an important role in maintaining the sterility of purified water once the biocides, such as chlorine, have been removed by other purification methods.

- Deionization: Also known as ion exchange or demineralization, deionization uses both cationic and anionic exchange resins to remove ionized salts from water. The resins may be used separately or combined into mixed-bed systems. The mixture of the two resins promotes efficient removal of inorganic ions.

- Filtration: Filtration can be broken down into subcategories based on the pore size of the filter devices. Particle filtration employs filters with pore sizes at least 1 micron in diameter. Microfiltration uses filter devices with pore sizes between 1 and 0.5 microns. These filters remove bacteria and submicron particles from water and are often used as a final step in water purification systems to ensure the removal of microorganisms from the final purified water.

CHAPTER 4

In Vitro Enzyme and Coenzyme Activation by IIEDs

All the significant properties of a system via which we define <u>life</u>, such as motility, growth, responsiveness, reproduction, etc., require energy. Thus, life requires a constant flow of energy, channeled by various organisms, to do the work of living. Each viable biological system requires many specialized subsystems interconnected in such a way as to optimize the overall functioning of the organism. These important subsystems are, in turn, comprised of cells which have their own internal subsystems which allow them to work efficiently and thus cooperatively serve the functioning of the total system.

The key ingredient of cells that are of particular interest to us in this chapter are enzymes and coenzymes. Of special interest are (1) the liver enzyme, alkaline phosphatase (ALP) and (2) the coenzyme, nicotinamide adenine dinucleotide (NAD) with which we have performed some *in vitro* experiments utilizing specifically imprinted IIEDs. This work is a natural extension of the water studies discussed in the previous chapter and a useful preparation for the *in vivo* studies with flies of the next chapter. Thus, let us lay out a bit of general background understanding on the indispensable importance of enzymes and coenzymes in cells before proceeding to discuss our specific experiments.

Some General Background on Enzymes and Coenzymes

All of the activities of a cell at the physical level are driven by energy, supplied either internally or externally by fluxes of photons or gained from the annihilation of specific local chemical bonds. However, before such a bond-breaking event can occur, a local energy fluctuation larger than some minimum value, called the "activation barrier" for the specific reaction, must be supplied. This is illustrated in Figures 4.1.

Enzymes significantly lower the magnitude of the critical size energy fluctuation needed for specific chemical bond breaking and thus are said to catalyze certain chemical reactions in the cell (see Figure 4.1c)[1]. A particular enzyme catalyzes only one or a few particular chemical reactions.

102

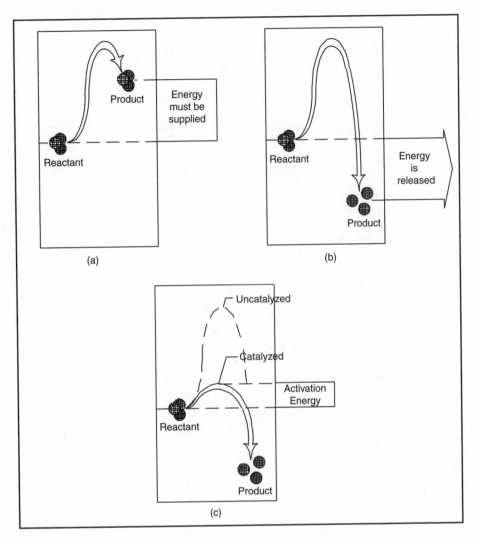

Figure 4.1   Energy, chemical reactions and catalysis: Extra energy must be supplied for endergonic reactions to occur. Excess energy is released in exergonic reactions. The amount of energy needed to begin a reaction can be lowered by catalysts.

The numerical rate of a specific reaction depends on the activation energy necessary for the process (this is the difference between the actual barrier height and the reactant level in Figure 4.1). Catalysts reduce the height of the activation barrier and so greatly increase the numerical rates of reaction without themselves being consumed in the process. This means that only a small amount of the catalyst is needed and it can be used over and over again.

One of the most rapidly acting enzymes in the human body is <u>carbonic anhydrase</u>, which plays a key role in blood by converting dissolved CO_2 into bicarbonate ion via the following reaction:

$$H_2O + CO_2 \Leftrightarrow H_2CO_3 \Leftrightarrow HCO_3^- + H^+. \quad (4.1)$$

Fully 70% of the CO_2 transported by blood is transported as bicarbonate ion. Although as indicated, this reaction may proceed in either direction. Because it has an appreciable activation barrier the reaction is very slow in the absence of

Figure 4.2   *The role of an enzyme as a template for catalysis.*

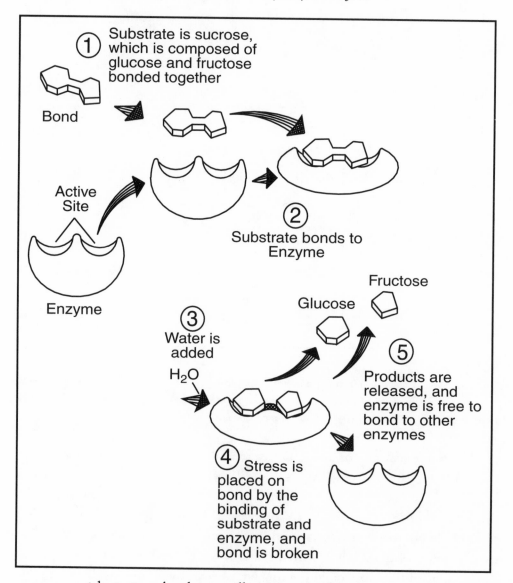

an enzyme (about 1 molecule per cell in 20 seconds). Reactions that proceed this slowly are of little use to a cell. However, cells can overcome this problem by employing an enzyme within their cytoplasm (carbonic anhydrase) which increases the rate of the above reaction by more than 10 million times (to an estimated 600,000 molecules of carbonic acid per second).

Shown in step 1 of Figure 4.2 is the example of the enzyme sucrase splitting the sugar substrate, sucrose, into simpler sugars, glucose and fructose. In step 2, the enzyme binds the substrate to its active site. In step 3, this binding causes the sucrase molecule to alter its shape. In step 4, the bond between the components, glucose and fructose is broken by amino acid residues present in the enzyme's active site. In step 5, the products of the reaction are released and the enzyme, which is unchanged by the process, is available to catalyze another reaction.

Most enzymes are globular proteins with one or more pockets or clefts on their surface called <u>active sites</u> where specific foreign molecules (substrates) can readily bind to the enzyme. For catalysis to occur, this substrate must fit very closely into an active site and, when that happens, amino acid side groups of the enzyme are configured in close proximity to key bonds in the substrate. These side-groups chemically interact with the substrate, significantly stressing these key bonds so that a much smaller activation energy than normal is needed for their breakage (see Figure 4.2)[1].

The numerical magnitude of the catalytic activity for a particular enzyme is influenced by temperature, pH and the presence of inhibitors or activators in the solution. Most human enzymes have their optimum temperature and pH for catalysis between 35 °C and 40 °C plus pH=6 to pH=8. Below this temperature, the H-bonds and hydrophobic interactions that determine the enzyme's shape are not flexible enough to allow the proper "fit" to substrates and, above this temperature range, they are too weak to maintain the required shape. In addition, the ionic interactions that hold the enzyme together (glutamic acid (-) and lysine (+)) are very sensitive to the H^+ concentration and thus to pH. Finally, the enzyme activity is sensitive to the presence of specific substances (inhibitors/activators) that bind to the enzyme and cause important changes to its shape. By means of such substances, a cell is able to regulate which enzymes are active and which are inactive at a particular time. This allows the cell to increase its efficiency and to control changes in its characteristics during development.

The function of enzymes is often assisted by certain chemical components known as cofactors (e.g. zinc, manganese, molybdenum, etc.). When the cofactor is a nonprotein organic molecule, it is called a coenzyme (many vitamins are parts of coenzymes). In many oxidation-reduction reactions (electron donating – electron accepting reactions) catalyzed by enzymes, the electrons are passed in pairs from the active site of an enzyme to a <u>coenzyme</u> that serves as an electron acceptor. The coenzyme then transfers these electrons to a different enzyme which releases both them and the energy they carry to the substrates in a subsequent reaction. These electrons are often paired with protons as hydrogen atoms and, in this way, coenzymes shuttle energy in the form of hydrogen atoms from one enzyme to another in a cell. This is called the electron transport chain.

Organisms contain thousands of different kinds of enzymes that catalyze a bewildering variety of reactions, many of which occur in sequences called <u>biochemical pathways</u>. Here, the product of one reaction with one type of enzyme becomes the substrate for another reaction with a second type of enzyme, etc.

One of the most important coenzymes is the hydrogen acceptor, nicotinamide adenine dinucleotide (NAD$^+$) indicated in Figure 4.3. When

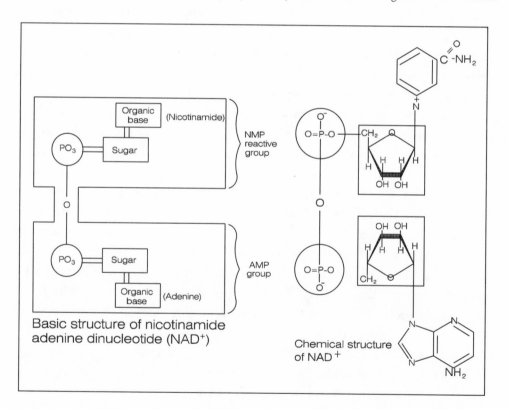

Figure 4.3   The structure of NAD$^+$. NAD$^+$ is composed of two nucleotides, nicotinamide monophosphate (NMP) and adenine monophosphate (AMP). AMP functions as a molecular core. NMP functions as the active portion since it contains a site that is easily reduced.

NAD$^+$ acquires two electrons and a proton from an active site of an enzyme, it is reduced to NADH. The two electrons and the proton are now carried by the NADH molecule to be later transferred to another molecule in the transport chain.

In closing this section, it is important to briefly mention the universal energy donor of all cells, adenosine triphosphate (ATP). ATP is able to power almost all of a cell's energy-requiring activities. However, the same factor that makes it an effective energy donor, the instability of its phosphate bonds, precludes it from being a good long-term energy storage molecule. In a cell, the function of long-term energy storage is better served by fats and carbohydrates.

From Figure 4.4[1], one sees that each ATP molecule is composed of three subunits, (1) a five-carbon sugar, called ribose, serves as the backbone to which the other two are attached, (2) adenine is composed of two carbon-nitrogen rings where each nitrogen in the ring weakly attracts hydrogen ions and (3) a triphosphate group where, due to electrostatic repulsion between the charged phosphate molecules, the covalent bonds joining the phosphates are unstable. These covalent bonds have a low activation barrier for breaking into

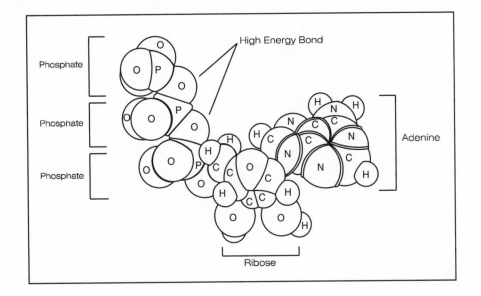

Figure 4.4   The structure of ATP. ATP has a molecular core of AMP. The reactive group is a chain of two phosphate groups which incorporate high-energy bonds. 7.3 kcal/mole of energy is released when adenine diphosphate (ADP) and phosphate (P) are produced by the cleaving of the outer bond of ATP. An additional 7.3 kcal/mole of energy is released when the second bond is cleaved, producing AMP and P or PP (inorganic phosphate ion).

P + ADP (adenosine diphosphate) with a concommittent energy release of 7.3 kilocalories per mole (~0.3 eV) under standard conditions.

Experiments with Alkaline Phosphatase (ALP)

ALP is present in nearly all tissues of the body, especially at or in the cell membranes and at particularly high levels in intestinal epithelium, kidney tubules, bone, liver and placenta[2]. Although its precise metabolic function is not yet understood, this enzyme is closely associated with the calcification process in bone. The two or three variants of ALP present in the sera of normal adults originate in the liver or the biliary tract while up to half of the total activity comes from the skeleton. Serum ALP measurements are of particular interest in the investigation of hepatobiliary disease and bone disease associated with increased osteoblastic activity.

The response of the liver to <u>any</u> form of biliary obstruction is to synthesize more ALP (increase its thermodynamic activity). These increases in ALP activity can be greater than three-fold in the case of an obstructing stone or cancer. However, liver diseases such as infectious hepatitis show only normal levels or moderate elevations. Among the bone diseases, the highest

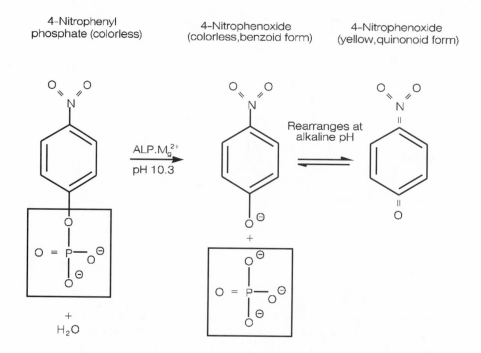

Figure 4.5   Colorimetric method for the determination of alkaline phosphatase (ALP) activity.

levels of serum ALP are found as a result of the action of osteoblastic cells as they try to rebuild bone that is being reabsorbed by uncontrolled activity of osteoclasts (values of 10-25 times normal are not unusual). Physiological bone growth elevates ALP in serum to about 1.2 to 2.5 times normal adult values and transient elevations are often found during the healing of bone fractures. Thus, overall, the human body has a variety of natural pathways for increasing the thermodynamic activity of ALP.

The most widely used substrate for assaying the thermodynamic activity of ALP is 4-nitrophenyl phosphate (4-NPP). This ester is colorless, but 4-nitrophenol (4-NP), the product of enzyme action (see Figure 4.5), is yellow at the pH of the reaction. Thus, the enzyme reactivity can be followed continuously by observing the rate of increase of yellow color spectrophotometrically.

In our studies, we measured enzymatic activity with a commercial system, the Vitros DT 60 chemistry system plus the DT 6011 analyzer and the DTSC 11 module[3]. This is a system that is widely used in physician's offices, clinics, hospitals and reference labs. This system provides results in 2-5 minutes. It provides an extensive test menu, including basic chemistries, electrolytes, enzymes, full lipid profile and derived tests. In addition, it is a dry-slide operation, which minimizes the effects of common interference to

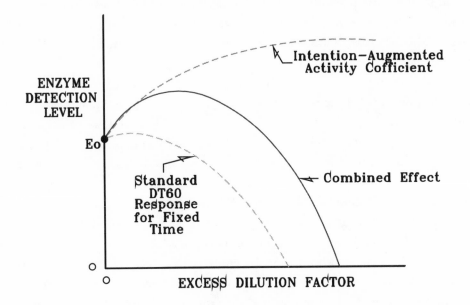

Figure 4.6   Experiments with ALP. Vitros DT60 system: The anticipated consequences of diluting the target enzyme.

provide accurate results with small sample volumes. A detailed description of this system is given in Appendix 4.A.

Our ALP was derived from porcine kidney and the experiments were performed at 4 °C in an incubator. All the Faraday cages plus the control were situated adjacent to each other in this incubator. Enzymatic activity determinations via the Vitros DT 60 system naturally involves concentrated solutions of the enzyme so that definitive and accurate results can be obtained in a short time. In such a case, one might presume that the chemical activity of the target enzyme approaches unity. On the other hand, one wishes here to demonstrate the effect of intention-augmented EM fields from the IIED used in the experiment which needs as much "thermodynamic room" as possible to allow the intention-induced thermodynamic pathways to significantly increase the chemical activity coefficient of the target enzyme. We proceeded to do this by diluting the ALP in purified water. This approach has a down-side which is an impairment of the Vitros DT 60 detection mechanism, the anticipated consequence of which is illustrated in Figure 4.6.

Experiment I, **The Influence of IIEDs on ALP Activity:**   In   this first experiment, we generally assess whether electromagnetic fields (EMF's) modify *in vitro* enzyme (ALP) activity by ~25% via several unique comparisons. Comparisons are made between the control ALP solution (C), placed in the normal incubator environment and (1) ALP solution placed in a small and otherwise empty Faraday cage (F) located adjacent to (C) on the shelf of the incubator (constructional details and EMF shielding efficiency of Faraday cages are given in Appendix 4.B) and (2) the same as (1) but with an activated, <u>imprinted</u> device (d,j) present and (3) the same as (1) but with an active, <u>unimprinted</u> device (d,o) present. All four experimental states (C, F, d,j and d,o) were located adjacent (with ~6" gaps between walls of adjacent Faraday cages) to each other in the incubator environment at 4 °C (see Figure 4.7). The first comparison, (C) with (F), allows one to assess the effect of the broad band, ambient EMF's on ALP activity. The second comparison, (F) with (d,o), allows one to assess the effect of low power (less than 1 micro-watt), specific frequency (one or three frequencies in the 1 to 10 megahertz range) EMF's on ALP activity. The third comparison, (d,j), augmented EMFs, with (d,o), normal EMFs, allows one to assess the effect of imprinted human intention on ALP activity. Finally, since all comparisons are being carried out simultaneously in the same external environment, correlations between any and all of the four experimental states are available.

110

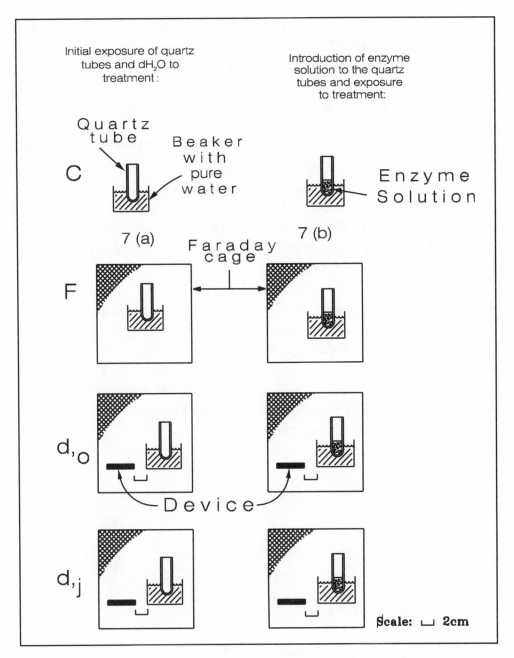

Figure 4.7   Experiments with ALP. Experiment configuration of the core system (C = control, F = Faraday cage, (d,o) = F + unimprinted device and (d,j) = F + imprinted device).

Our core experimental system, comprising 100 ml quartz tubes containing 100 ml of purified water, is illustrated in Figure 4.7 (a). The individual steps in the experimental protocol were as follows: (1) place the devices, (d,j) and (d,o), in their respective Faraday cages (electrically grounded) and leave them in the "on" position for 120 days (may not need to be nearly this long) prior to the experiment, (2) then expose the core experimental system for 2 days prior to adding new ALP solution to the quartz tubes, (3) then, with the new ALP solution added to the quartz tubes, expose this total system for 30 minutes (see Figure 4.7b) and (4) immediately, or as soon as possible, assay the ALP activity using the Vitros DT 60 system. A re-imprinted IIED was utilized for steps (2) and (3).

The beakers, empty tubes and tubes containing ALP solution were placed 2 cm from the devices and the treatments were assayed in the order (d,o), (d,j), (F) and (C) at the same time during any one day. We did not detect any meaningful temperature variation between treatments and the ALP dilutions were as follows: 100 µl stock ALP solution plus either 150 µl, 200 µl or 250 µl purified water. There were 7 replicate assays per treatment for each dilution with the data being collected over two consecutive days.

The experimental results have been presented here in Figure 4.8 in the form of means with their standard deviations for only two dilutions. A more detailed representation of the results has been presented in the form of a notched box plot[4] in Appendix 4.C and log-transformed data assessment via the ANOVA statistical procedure[4] with pair-wise Tukey post hoc test comparisons[4] being given in Appendix 4.D.

Figure 4.8

Untransformed means for two dilutions.

[dilution 1 – 100 µl ALP solution plus 150 µl purified water, dilution 2 – 100 µl ALP solution plus 200 µl purified water]

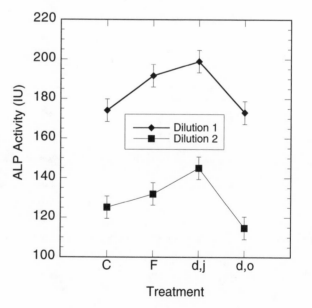

Visual inspection of the means plots (see Figure 4.8) and the ANOVA (see Table 4.1 in Appendix 4.D) indicated that both the treatment and the dilution significantly modified ALP activity. Higher ALP values were observed for the lower dilution of 100 μl ALP to 150 μl water. The treatment rankings for both dilutions were (d,j) > (F) > (C) > (d,o) and, Tukey post hoc comparisons between treatments indicated (1) that (d,j) was significantly greater than both (d,o) ($p < 0.000$) and (C) ($p < 0.005$) (2) that (F) was significantly greater than (C) ($p < 0.011$). For the various comparisons, Figure 4.8 shows the effect sizes to be ~10-15.

From these results, we see that the changes fall well within the normal range of human variations so that standard cellular processes are probably being utilized to produce such changes even though these are all *in vitro* experiments. However, although the changes observed are smaller than in living humans, these results are all statistically significant and it was a definite surprise to us to find that shielding the ALP solution from the ambient EMF's via a Faraday cage made a significant difference relative to the unshielded control. In the same vein, it was also a surprise to learn that the very low power, 1-10 MHz device made a significant lowering effect on ALP activity in the shielded environment – (d,o) vs. (F). Finally, we were pleased (indicating our bias) to see that the result with the highest statistical significance occurred for the comparison of the IIED (d,j) with the unimprinted device (d,o) in the otherwise shielded environment. Thus, the initial goal of this chapter has been established – our device imprinting technique works with a diluted *in vitro* enzyme! Now, we can go forward and try to learn something about the process whereby such effects occur by using the ALP solution as an experimental probe or detector of such anomalous events[5].

Experiment II, ALP Activity as a Detector of Subtle Energies: The basic experimental layout is illustrated by Figure 4.9. With this new equipment set-up, the ALP activity was measured in an ALP "detector", designated C at position ⓪ fixed in the incubator. The Faraday cage was located 13.5 cm away on the incubator shelf. The variety of experiments we subsequently carried out in this environment are listed below (note that for Experiment (d), the distances between the vessels at positions 1, 2, and 3 were all 20 cm).

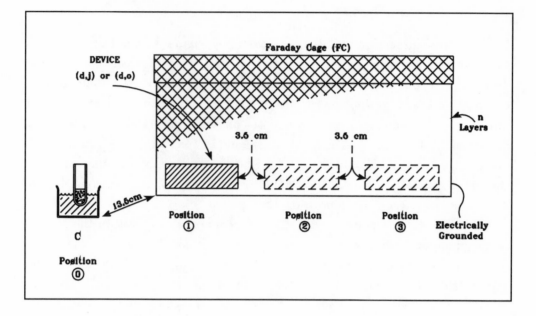

Figure 4.9   Experiment II configuration. When devices are replaced by enzyme vessels, the distances between the vessels at positions 1, 2 and 3 was 20 cm.

(a) Faraday Cage Layer Number Effect: The ALP activity in the detector (C) was measured for different number of layers, n, of copper mesh for the walls of the Faraday cage (F) where n = 0 refers to no Faraday cage. Values of n = 0, 1, 2, 3, 4, 5 and 6 were studied. We found that the presence of (F, n = 1) significantly modified the ALP activity of the detector (C). These results

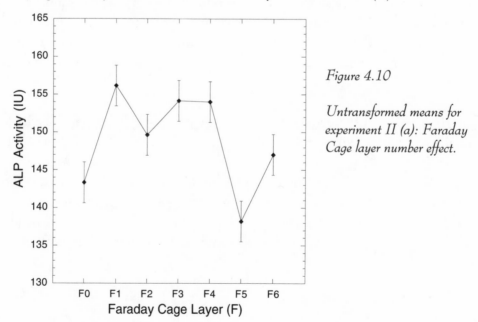

Figure 4.10

Untransformed means for experiment II (a): Faraday Cage layer number effect.

114

are shown in Figure 4.10 plus Appendix 4.C and Table 4.2 in Appendix 4.D.

The largest number of significant pairwise comparisons were observed for the 5-layer cage (see Table 4.2 in Appendix 4.D). Although, based on our physical understanding of reality, one would not expect that (F) should influence (C) when it is spatially so far removed (unless it somehow changes the local electrostatic potential). However, from Figure 10, one sees that a single layer cage significantly increases the activity of the ALP detector (p < 0.000 and an effect size of about 8) while a 5-layer cage reduces it somewhat. From Table 4.2 in Appendix 4.D, when comparing the 5-layer cage with cages of different n, the most significant comparison is between n = 1 and n = 5 at p < 0.000 and an effect size of about 12.

(b) **Exposure Period and Faraday Cage (n = 0 and n = 1):** In this experiment, we investigated variations in the ALP detector (C) activity associated with exposure periods of 15, 30 and 45 minutes and n = 0 or n = 1. The results are shown in Figure 4.11 plus Appendix 4.C and Table 4.3 in

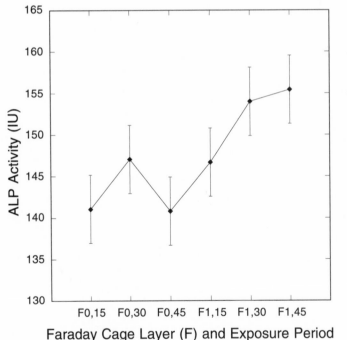

Figure 4.11

Untransformed means for Experiment II(b): Exposure Period and Faraday Cage (n=0 and n=1) effects.

Appendix 4.D. Certainly, exposure period did not significantly alter the ALP activity for n = 0; however, there was an indication that it did somewhat for n = 1, although the p value was not greatly significant. We again confirm the results of experiment (a) and note that treatment (the presence of the Faraday cage) significantly increases the ALP activity of (C). The mean values were 142.98 IU for n = 0 and 152.71 IU for n = 1.

We conclude from this that a 30-minute exposure period for all subsequent experiments was a reasonable choice even though a longer exposure period would probably have yielded somewhat larger differences.

(c) Device Type, Position and Condition in the Faraday Cage:

In this experiment, the ALP detector activity in (C) was assessed for devices (d,j) or (d,o) at positions 1, 2 and 3 in Figure 4.9 in both the "off" and "on" states and for the cage conditions n = 0 and n = 1. The data was collected for each position and treatment on two consecutive days and it can be analyzed from four unique perspectives: the data were organized by pooling for (1) both day and position, (2) position only, (3) day only and (4) the data is displayed for each day and position combination. This approach has led to voluminous numbers of plots and statistics which are all extremely interesting but more appropriate for a scientific paper than a book. Thus, here, we will just present the results for perspective (1) and describe some of the more significant changes that arise from pursuing the other three perspectives.

Perspective (1) gives an overall view of this experiment and Figure 4.12 provides the means for the data. The box plot presentation of the data is given in Appendix 4.C. The ANOVA and TUKEY post hoc tests are given in Table 4.4 of Appendix 4.D. We note from Figure 4.12 that, for n = 0, (d,j) and (d,o) produced similar effects when in the off condition. However, when the devices were turned on, the ALP detector at (C) showed an increase for (d,j) but a decrease for (d,o). For n = 1 and the devices in the off condition, the ALP activity at (C) was greater for (d,o) in comparison to (d,j). However, this was reversed for the on condition. Overall, this is a remarkable result with great statistical significance ($p < 0.001$ mostly with effect sizes of $\sim$ 8-10) and we are still scratching our heads as to what it is trying to tell us.

When we consider perspective (2), where the data is pooled for position only, and examine the influence of the first and second days of experimentation, the n = 0, device "on" condition shows the largest change compared to Figure 4.12. If we just look at the difference in detector activity, Δ ALP (on, o), it is ~17 IU in Figure 4.12 but it is reduced to $\sim$ 8 IU for day 1 and increased to $\sim$ 27 IU for day 2 with perspective (2). When we consider perspective (3), where the data is pooled for day only, and examine the influence of positions 1, 2 and 3 on the data, position 1 gives similar results to Figure 4.12 but with Δ ALP activity between the two devices being appreciably larger (almost a factor of two) at treatments on, o; off, 1 and on, 1. At the other two positions, some of the Δ ALP increased and some decreased.

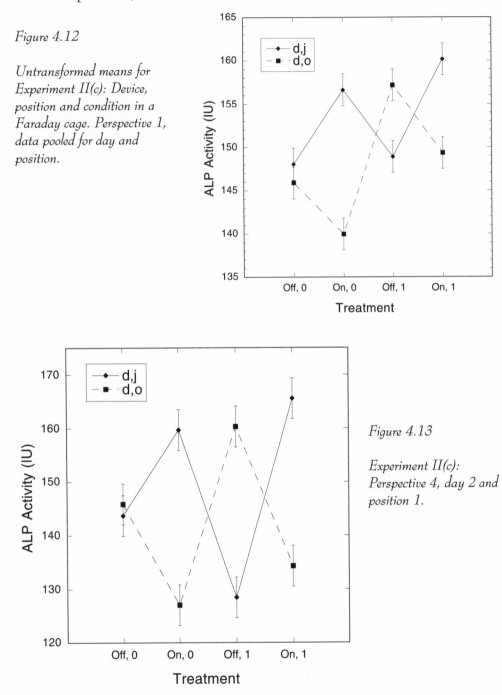

Figure 4.12

Untransformed means for Experiment II(c): Device, position and condition in a Faraday cage. Perspective 1, data pooled for day and position.

Figure 4.13

Experiment II(c): Perspective 4, day 2 and position 1.

Finally, when we consider perspective (4) and the unpooled data, a huge data set is obtained with many detailed features to be sifted through. However, in comparison with Figure 4.12, Figure 4.13 plots the ALP activity for day 2 with the devices at position 1 and we note that all three of the Δ ALP activity values have more than doubled the values found in Figure 4.12. Thus, the effect size is now increased to ~20.

(d) <u>Substituting ALP Vessels for Devices in (c)</u>: In this experiment, the devices were removed and replaced at the positions 1, 2 or 3 by either a single ALP vessel identical to that present at (C), two such vessels or three such vessels that we identify as v1, v2 and v3, respectively. This treatment involved both n = 0 and n = 1 Faraday cages with the untransformed means for the data being given in Figure 4.14 The data is presented as box plots in Figure 4.C.6 of Appendix 4.C. The ANOVA and Tukey post hoc comparisons for

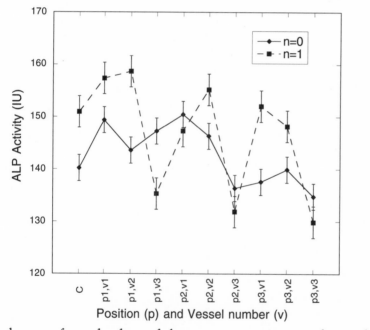

Figure 4.14

Experiment II (d)
n=0, n=1.

the transformed values of these means are presented in Table 4.5 of Appendix 4.D.

These results indicated that the number of ALP vessels and the position of those vessels modified the ALP activity in the detector (C), with the higher ALP activity occurring for n = 1 compared to n = 0. The Tukey post hoc test indicated that the ALP detector (C) activity was highest for the ALP vessels located at position 1 and this result was significantly greater than when the vessels were located at positions 2 and 3. Comparisons between the

ALP vessels located at positions 2 and 3 were <u>not</u> significant. For the n = 1 case, v3 was significantly lower than v1 or v2 at all three positions. The only treatment interaction effect that was observed was between the Faraday cage and the ALP vessels.

(e) ALP Detector Activity for Positioning at Locations 0, 1, 2, 3 in Figure 4.9 (n = 0): This final experiment with no Faraday cage, no devices and no additional ALP vessels was to test the effect of moving the ALP detector to various locations in the incubator. Our result, given in Figures 4.15, 4.C.7 of Appendix 4.C and Table 4.6 in Appendix 4.D, indicated that the ALP detector activity did not vary with respect to position. The mean values for these four positions were (0) 144.13, (1) 145.69, (2) 137.94 and (3) 144.69.

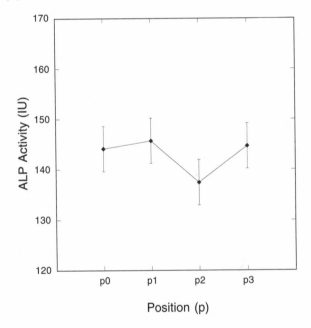

Figure 4.15

Experiment II(e): ALP activity in the detector (C) at positions 0, 1, 2 and 3 (untransformed means).

As a summary comment on this entire section, we have noted some remarkable and statistically significant effects that appear to have no ready explanation based upon the accepted, present day, scientific paradigm.

Experiments with Nicotinamide Adenine Dinucleotide (NAD)

As described in an earlier section of this chapter, NAD is a key molecule in intermediary metabolism and for the flow of energy in biological systems. It has been shown that a significant association exists between fruit fly larval development time, NAD and [ATP]/[ADP] ratio[6]. Furthermore, very recently, variation in NAD concentration has been associated with both Aids and Alzheimer's disease in humans [7, 8]. This recent study[7] has favorably implicated the coenzyme, NAD, as a medication for patients suffering from dementia of the Alzheimer type. For all patients evaluated in that study, an improvement in their cognitive function was observed. In the other study[8], it was shown that HIV-1 infection of human cells *in vitro* leads to significant decreases in the intracellular concentration of NAD. This decrease has been shown to vary with viral load and HIV strain. These authors conclude from their study that HIV induces a state of intracellular pellagra which is reversed by the administration of nicotinamide. This, in turn, maintains increased intracellular NAD concentration in HIV – infected cells with subsequent metabolic and energy changes for the patient.

In this final section of the chapter, we examine the possibility that both EMFs and intention – augmented EMFs significantly alter the condition of the water used for preparing NAD solutions to be subsequently utilized for *in vitro* fruit fly studies. Here, we show that NAD activity and the [ATP]/[ADP] ratio significantly depend on the four treatments given to the water.

(i) [NAD] Change Over Time: We initially exposed purified water for 2 weeks to the four separate treatments discussed earlier, (C), (F), (d,j) and (d,o) and designated the waters W,C; W,F; W,j and W,o. We then dissolved sufficient NAD (Sigma brand) in 5 ml of the respective waters to produce a 0.01M concentration and named these solutions NAD,C; NAD,F; NAD,j and NAD,o. We then placed these NAD solutions in the four treatments and measured the evolving NAD concentrations over time. Finally, on days 78 and 105, respectively, we also prepared four replicate NAD solutions but with untreated purified water and named these C-F and C-C (for controls inside a Faraday cage or with no cage and both with no devices) and stored them in the incubator.

The change in [NAD] activity over a period of 200 days is given in Figure 4.16. If we consider just the first 100 days it is clear that the [NAD] activity changes with time in somewhat of an oscillatory fashion and much more so than the two controls. Overall, the general trend was a decrease in [NAD] activity with significant treatment rankings of (F) > (d,j) > (d,o) > (C). All treatments were assayed in random order in a 36 hour period and the "day of assay" in Figure 4.16 refers to the time of the first assay in the sequence. We assessed treatment effects for each day of assay using ANOVAS and Tukey post hoc tests (not given but available on request).

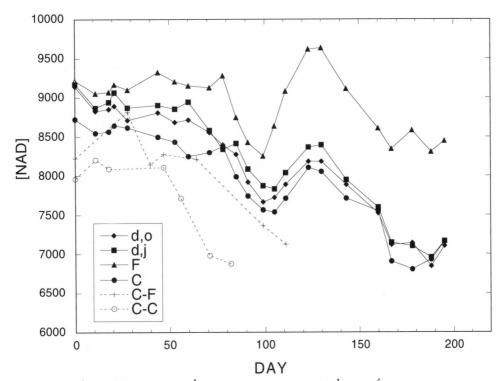

Figure 4.16 [NAD] means change in concentration with time for various treatments. ([NAD] is given as the area under the NAD peaks detected).

Considering day zero, significantly (p < 0.000) higher values were observed for (F), (d,j) and (d,o) in comparison to (C) whereas the first three did not significantly differ. ANOVAs were significant (p < 0.000) for all subsequent days of the assay. The highest and lowest [NAD] activity were uniformly observed for (F) and (C), respectively, at p < 0.000. Values for (d,j) were significantly (p < 0.000) greater than for (d,o) for assay days 21, 28, 53, 60, 85, 91 and 99 but not for days 11, 18, 44, 71 and 78.

During days 100-150, (F) and (C) continued to exhibit the highest and lowest NAD activity values, respectively. All ANOVAs were significant with a single maximum value around day 130. Around day 160, the NAD values for (d,j), (d,o) and (C) converged and did not differ significantly thereafter. (F) remained significantly higher than the other treatments during this final period with some suggestion of oscillatory behavior still being present. In all probability, the imprint "charge" in (d,j) had totally leaked away by day 130 (unless an oscillatory component of sufficient magnitude was present). Finally, considering (C-F) and (C-C), the former maintained its higher NAD activity level for an appreciably longer period than the latter.

(ii) [ATP]/[ADP] Ratio in Homogenates of the Fruit Fly, *Drosophila melanogaster*:

In this experiment with our *in vitro* fruit fly model system, both [NAD] activity and [ATP]/[ADP] ratio are measured in third instar larval homogenates which are supplemented with NAD. The experimental procedure for preparing these homogenates is fully described in the next chapter (see page 152).

At convenient times during experiment (i) above, we assessed the influence of (a) both these source waters plus NAD solutions upon the [ATP]/[ADP] ratio in the larval homogenates and (b) just the source waters alone upon the [ATP]/[ADP] ratio. The source waters, W,o; W,j; W,F and W,C, described above were used to prepare the larval homogenates at 2-4 °C. For (a) only, aliquots from these homogenates were than added to equal volumes of the respective NAD solutions, NAD,o; NAD,j; NAD,F and NAD,C at 2-4 °C. For example, homogenates were prepared using 250 µl of ice-cold W,o. 50 µl of this homogenate was then immediately added to

Figure 4.17

Untransformed means for [ATP]/[ADP] ratio in the in vitro fruit fly homogenates for (a) source-water plus NAD and (b) source-water only treatments.

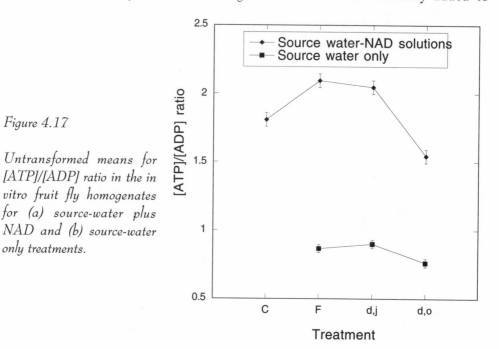

centrifuge tubes containing 50 μl of ice-cold NAD,o. After a 7 minute reaction period, during which the added NAD drives the electron transport chain *in vitro* and thus increases the [ATP]/[ADP] ratio, metabolic activity was stopped by freezing the centrifuge tubes in liquid nitrogen. ATP, ADP and NAD were then extracted and quantified using standard procedures and the HPLC[6] (see Chapter 5).

All experimental steps were carried out on ice at 2-4 °C. and on a laboratory bench in a room immediately adjacent to the incubator room. We assayed all possible combinations by randomly performing the above procedure in a time period from day 30—38 of experiment (i) above. We adjusted larval mass in each homogenate to be approximately 20 mg and there were no significant differences (p > 0.100) between homogenates. There were 8 replicate assays for each source water-NAD solution combination. The same set of procedures was followed for (b) but, now, only the waters W,o, W,j and WF, were used to prepare the homogenates and the NAD solutions were not supplemented.

All of our data are shown as box plots in Figure 4.C.8 of Appendix 4.C with the untransformed means derived from these data being given in Figure 4.17. The ANOVA and TUKEY post hoc comparisons are given in Table 4.7 in Appendix 4.D for the variation of [ATP]/[ADP] ratios with the data being transformed (square root) prior to analysis.

From this, one can see that both (a) the source water-NAD solution combination and (b) the source water alone, significantly (p < 0.000) influenced the [ATP]/[ADP] ratio in the larval homogenates. Treatment rankings for (a) were (F) ≥ (d,j) > (C) > (d,o) whereas, for (b), they were (d,j) > (F) > (d,o). From this, we may deduce that treated source water itself carried the enhancement factor which was amplified by the additional NAD. Finally, as a closing note to this section, Figures 4.18 (a) and (b), provide us with a time evolution picture of the "breakdown products" in the NAD. Once again, one can readily discern the strong EMF-shielding factor associated with the use of Faraday cages in this work.

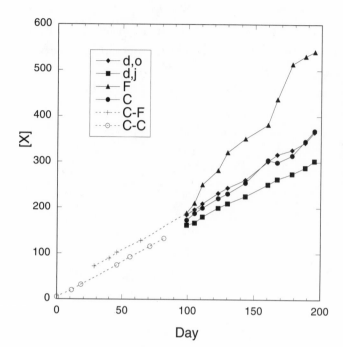

Figure 4.18 (a)

[NAD] change with time for an as yet unidentified breakdown product, X. Means are given for levels (area) of this breakdown product in the 0.01M solutions of NAD of Figure 4.16.

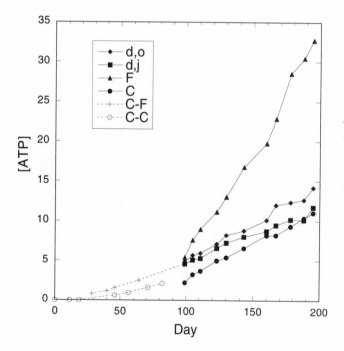

Figure 4.18 (b)

[NAD] change with time fot the breakdown product ATP. Means are given for the levels of ATP in the 0.01M solutions of NAD of Figure 4.16.

Some Summary Findings for the Enzyme/Coenzyme Experiments

- Figures 4.8 show that, not only does Faraday cage (FC) shielding from ambient environmental EMF's significantly increase ALP activity while the low power/specific frequency EMF's from an unimprinted device significantly reduces ALP activity. However, the specific intention imprint of the IIED more than compensates for these normal EMF effects and increases the ALP activity most of all. Thus, it has been clearly shown that the IIED effects on water described in Chapter 3 can be extended to an *in vitro* biological material, the liver enzyme alkaline phosphatase.

- The ALP can serve as a significant detector of novel energies, thought to be R-space vacuum energy effects in the detector's local environment. It clearly detects the presence of a FC in the incubator at an appreciable distance from itself (relative to normal atomic force field distances), presumably because the EM nature of the copper in the FC constructively/destructively interferes with that of the incubator itself at the R-space level (see Chapter 7, Figure 7). Changing the number of layers of copper mesh in the FC significantly alters the ALP detector activity, presumably also by local interference interactions between the copper layers at the R-space level. An exposure period effect is also indicated with ALP activity increasing with exposure period.

- When one of our electrical devices was placed in the FC, a series of very significant differences were noted by the ALP detector activity as a result of the following comparisons: (1) fixed device (j or o), (2) fixed device position (1, 2, or 3) relative to the ALP detector, (3) fixed ALP assay period (day 1 or day 2), (4) fixed device condition (off or on) and (5) fixed number of copper layers in the FC (1 or 0). The largest differential effects occurred when the device was in position 1 and the ALP detector assaying occurred on day 2 of the exposure to the particular treatment. Overall, this is thus at least a 5-variable phenomenon and, since the new physics involved is largely R-space physics, we are probably dealing here with multiple interference effects in that domain with the major portion of the collective R-space modulus contribution coming from the low frequency (low wave number, k_t) region of R-space (see chapter 8 for the connection between R-space patterns in particular wave number regions and their D-space consequence unfoldment in the time domain).

- Substituting one to several ALP-vessels for the electrical devices provides statistically significant additional substantiation for the $n = 0/n = 1$ layer FC comparison effect with significant R-space interference effects coming from grouping 3 ALP vessels at the various positions.

- The *in vitro* effect on the fruit fly larval homogenates by the four water treatments, with or without the supplemental NAD, have been shown to generate a very significant influence on the [ATP]/[ADP] ratios for the homogenates. Clearly, the various water treatments by themselves produce a statistically significant effect while the coenzyme, NAD, appears to largely act as an amplifier for the water treatment effect.

- Finally, the very robust ALP detector results shown here only scratch the surface of all the relevant factors involved in the R-space/D-space interactive physics. Much more work needs to be done in this area before serious conclusions can be drawn but this appears to be a useful beginning.

References

1.   P.H. Raven, and G. B. Johnson, <u>Biology</u>. (Wm. C. Brown Publishers, Boston,1996).

2.   C.A. Burtis and E.R. Ashwood, (eds), Tietz: <u>Fundamentals of Clinical Chemisitry</u>, 4th Edition, (WB Saunders, Philadelphia, 1996).

3.   Vitros Chemistry Products. Ortho-Clinical Diagnostics. Johnson and Johnson. 100 Indigo Creek Drive Rochester, NY, 14626, USA.

4.   R.R. Sokal, and F.J. Rohlf, <u>Biometry</u>, (WH Freeman and Company, San Francisco, 1995); L. Wilkinson, <u>Systat: Statistics Version 5.2 Edition</u>, (SYSTAT Inc.,Evanston, Il., 1992); R.A.J. Matthews, "Significance levels for the assessment of anomalous phenomena," J. Sci. Expl., <u>13</u> (1999) 1.

5.   W. A Tiller, <u>Science and Human Transformation: Subtle Energies, Intentionality and Consciousness</u> (Pavior Publishing, Walnut Creek, CA, 1997).

6.   M.J. Kohane, "Stress, altered energy availability and larval fitness in *Drosophila melanogaster*", Heredity, <u>60</u> (1988) 273-281; M.J. Kohane, "Energy, development and fitness in *Drosophila melanogaster*". Proc. Roy. Soc. (B), <u>257</u> (1994) 185-191.

7.   J.G.D. Birkmayer, "Coenzyme Nicotinamide adenine dinucleotide. New Therapeutic approach for improving dementia of the Alzheimer type", Annals of Clinical and Laboratory Science, <u>26</u> (1996) 1-9.

8.   M.F. Murray, M. Nohiem and A. Sprinivasan, "HIV infection decreases intracellular nicotinamide adenine dinucleotide (NAD)", Biochemical and Biophysical Research Communications, <u>212</u> (1995) 126.

Appendix 4.A: Our Use of the Vitros DT System

Vitros DT Controls, designed for use in monitoring the precision and accuracy of the Vitros DT Chemistry System, were used as the experimental material. The Vitros DT Controls are available[3] as vials of frozen lyophilate and serum. Enzymes are present in the lyophilate and ALP was derived from porcine kidney. The lyophilate and serum vials were stored at 2-8 °C for no longer than 6 months. Reconstitution was achieved as follows: the lyophilate and dilute vials were thawed at room temperature for about 1 hour. A specific volume of diluent (see below) was then added to a lyophilate vial. This vial was then inverted and gently mixed for 30 minutes at room temperature. Expected values were then determined and verified prior to use of the solution in the experiments (see main text). A fresh solution was prepared and used for each experiment. However, if necessary, reconstituted Vitros DT Control solutions can be used for up to 7 days if stored at 2-8 °C. Reporting units were U/L (where U is the international unit or quantity of enzyme that will catalyze the reaction of one μmole of substrate per minute and L is litre).

The Vitros ALP DT system is based on a slide which is a dry, multilayered film in a plastic support. It contains all the reagents necessary to determine activity in 10 μl serum or plasma. The reaction is based on alkaline phosphatase catalyzing the hydrolysis of p-nitrophenyl phosphate to p-nitrophenol. A 10 μl drop of solution is deposited on the slide and evenly distributed by the spreading layer, which contains the p-nitrophenyl phosphate substrate and other components required for the reaction. The ALP in the solution catalyzes the hydrolysis of p-nitrophenyl phosphate to p-nitrophenol at alkaline pH as follows:

$$\text{p-nitrophenol phosphate} \xrightarrow[\text{Mg}^{2+}]{\text{ALP}} \text{p-nitrophenol} + \text{H}_3\text{PO}_4.$$

The p-nitrophenol is then diffused into the underlying layer where it is monitored by reflectance spectrophotometry. The change in the reflection density is monitored at 37 °C and the rate of change is used to calculate enzyme activity. Slide reagents were as follows: p-nitrophenyl phosphate, 2-amino-2-methyl-1-propanol and magnesium sulphate, polymer beads, binders, buffer, surfactants, polymer across-linking agent and preservative. The wavelength used was 400 nanometers and the assay time and temperature were a maximum of 5 minutes at 37 °C. Standard curves are available from Johnson and Johnson.

Appendix 4.B: Faraday Cage Construction and EM-Shielding

The Faraday cages were constructed from a fine mesh copper screen (a 0.16" grid size) in a cylindrical geometry with diameters from 6 in. to 18 in. but mostly 12 in. diameter cages were used. The bottom of the cage had a radially extending lip to which a grounding lead could be easily attached. A close-fitting cylindrical cap was made to close the top of the cage and slide down the side-wall about 6 in.

In qualitative terms, such cages are thought to screen the intensity of radio, microwave and GHz EM-frequencies by about a factor of 10. At the very high frequency end, EM wavelengths smaller than the mesh size can readily pass into the cage and this is why we always wrap the devices in aluminum foil (to stop such photons). At the very low frequency end ($\sim$60 Hz and below), the EM-skin depth in copper is so large that our type of cages are only minimally effective for EM-shielding.

In quantitative terms, for the high frequency region, it is important to take into account both conduction current density effects (depends on electrical conductivity, σ) and displacement current density effects (depends on the product $\omega\varepsilon$, where ε is the electrical permittivity and $\omega = 2\pi f$ (f=frequency)). For different materials, the relevant parameter of choice is $\sigma/\omega\varepsilon$ and we arbitrarily place materials in the following three categories

$$\text{Conductors: } \sigma/\omega\varepsilon > 10^2 \qquad\qquad (4.\text{B}.1\text{a})$$

Quasi-conductors: $10^{-2} < \sigma/\omega\varepsilon < 10^2$ (4.B.1b)

Dielectrics: $\sigma/\omega\varepsilon < 10^2$.   (4.B.1c)

We thus see that frequency is important in determining whether a particular material acts like a conductor or a dielectric. For example, sea water is a conductor at frequencies less than $\sim 10^7$ Hz (radio range) but is a dielectric above $\sim 10^{11}$ Hz (infrared range). For a conducting medium (e.g. copper) with an EM-wave impinging on it from the air, the wave penetrates into the conductor a distance called the skin depth, δ_s, where the amplitude has decayed a factor of ~ 2.3 (intensity decays ~ 5.3) while both its wavelength, λ_c, and propagation velocity, v_c, in the conductor have changed in the following way

$$\delta_s = (2/\omega\mu\sigma)^{1/2} = (2\sigma/\omega\varepsilon)^{1/2}(\varepsilon/\sigma c) \qquad (4.B.2a)$$

$$\lambda_c = 2\pi\delta_s \qquad (4.B.2b)$$

$$v_c = \omega\delta_s. \qquad (4B.2c)$$

For copper, at 60 Hz, 1 MHz and 30 GHz, respectively, $\delta_s = 8.5 \times 10^{-3}$ m, 6.6×10^{-5} m and 3.8×10^{-7} m. Thus, since our single layer Faraday cages have a copper thickness of $\sim 1/32$ in. $\sim 10^{-3}$ m, the EM-wave amplitude reductions are $\sim 10\%$, x10 and x10^3, respectively so the EM-intensity reductions are $\sim 1\%$, x100 and x10^6, respectively, for 60 Hz, 1 MHz and 30 GHz. This means that at 6000 Hz and above, our cages reduce the penetrating EM-intensity by factors of 10 or more.

Appendix 4.C: Box Plot Data for the Various Experiments

For the various experiments of this chapter, all of the data are shown as notched box plots. The box plot is a visual display method for representing a batch of data while perceptually implementing confidence limits (CL) on the shown median values (see Figure 4.C.1). Each specific aspect of the data distribution that is encoded, medians, upper and lower quartiles, 95% CL's, etc., can be quite readily decoded visually. For example, it is quite easy to see the medians (a measure of the center of the distribution) as a whole and visually assess their relative values. The upper and lower ends of the box are the upper and lower quartiles. The interquartile range (IQR) is the distance

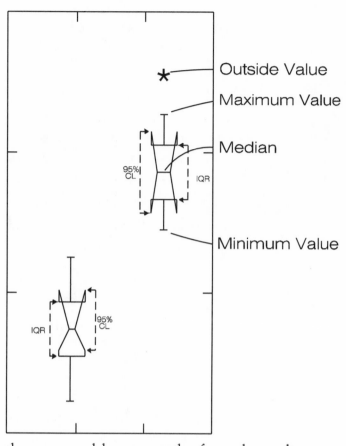

Figure 4.C.1 Defining diagram for the box plot method of data representation.

between these two values and is a measure of the spread of the distribution. The middle 50% of the data lie between the upper and lower quartiles. If the interquartile range is small, the middle data are tightly packed around the median. If the interquartile range is large, the middle data spread far out from the median. The relative distances of the upper and lower quartiles from the median give information about the shape of the data distribution; if one distance is much larger than the other then the distribution is skewed. The 95% confidence level (CL) for the median means that, if two 95% CL's do not overlap, one can be 95% confident that the two medians differ from each other. Outside values are reported via an asterisk and far outside values via an open circle.

Experiment I, Influence of IIEDs on ALP Activity: Figure 4.C.2 shows the experimental results whereby visual inspection indicates that both the treatment and the dilution significantly modified ALP activity. Higher ALP values were observed for the lower dilution of 100 μl ALP to 150 μl water. The treatment rankings for both dilutions were (d,j)> (F) > (C) > (d,o) and Tukey post hoc comparisons between treatments (see Appendix 4.D) indicated (1) that (d,j) was significantly greater than both (d,o) ($p < 0.000$) and (C) ($p < 0.005$) and (2) that (F) was significantly greater than (C) ($p < 0.011$).

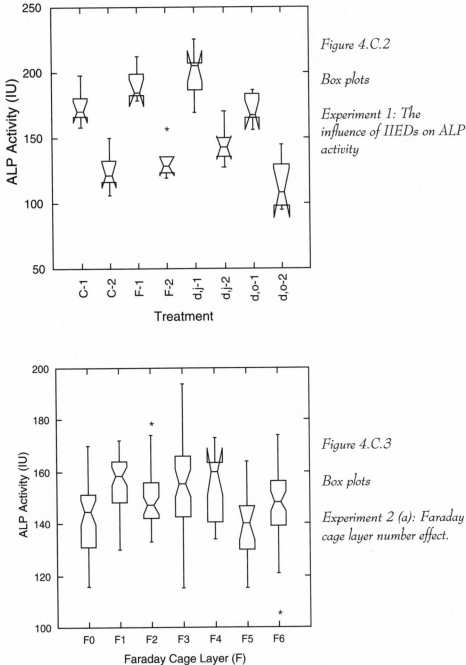

Figure 4.C.2

Box plots

Experiment 1: The influence of IIEDs on ALP activity

Figure 4.C.3

Box plots

Experiment 2 (a): Faraday cage layer number effect.

Experiment II, ALP Activity as a Detector of Subtle Energies:

(a) Faraday Cage Layer Number Effect: The experimental results are shown in Figure 4.C.3. From Table 4.2 in Appendix 4D, one sees that (1) a single layer cage (F1) significantly ($p < 0.000$) increases the activity of the detector relative to the control (F0) and (2) the most significant ($p < 0.000$) comparison is between $n = 1$ and $n = 5$.

(b) Exposure Period and Faraday Cage ($n = 0$ and $n = 1$): The experimental results are shown in Figure 4.C.4 and, from Table 4.3 in Appendix 4.D one sees that, although F1 > F0 is quite significant ($p < 0.000$) at both the 30 minute and 45 minute exposure, comparing both FC layer number (0,1) <u>and</u> exposure period was only marginally significant.

Figure 4.C.4

Experiment II(b): Exposure period and Faraday cage (n=0 and n=1) effects.

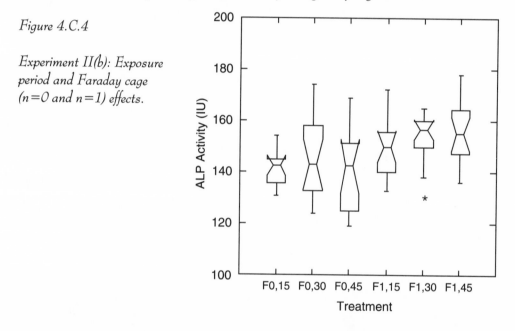

(c) Device Type, Position and Power Condition in the Faraday Cage: The device types were (d,o) and (d,j), located in positions 1, 2 or 3 in Figure 4.9, in either the "on" or "off" state with $n = 0$ or 1 for the FC and with the data being collected on two consecutive days. The box plot presentation of the data, pooled for <u>both</u> day and position only, is provided in Figure 4.C.5. The ANOVA and Tukey post hoc tests are given in Table 4.4 of Appendix 4.D.

(d) Substituting ALP Vessels for Devices in (c): Here, the devices were removed and replaced at positions 1, 2 or 3 in Figure 4.9 by either a single

ALP vessel identical to that present at (C), two such vessels or three such vessels that we identify as v1, v2 and v3, respectively. The box plot data for n=0 and n=1 is presented in Figures 4.C.6. The ANOVA and Tukey post

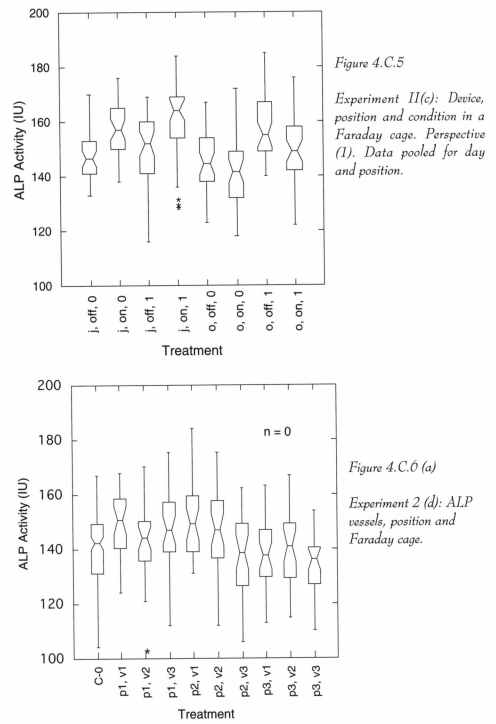

Figure 4.C.5

Experiment II(c): Device, position and condition in a Faraday cage. Perspective (1). Data pooled for day and position.

Figure 4.C.6 (a)

Experiment 2 (d): ALP vessels, position and Faraday cage.

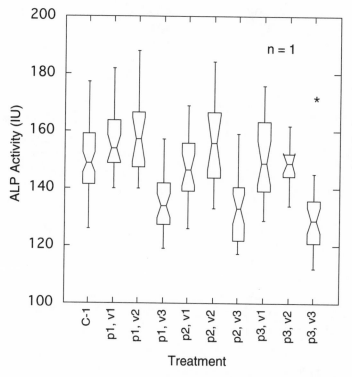

Figure 4.C.6 (b)

Experiment 2 (d): ALP vessels, position and Faraday cage.

hoc comparisons for the transformed means are presented in Table 4.5 of Appendix 4.D

(e) ALP Detector Activity for Positioning at Locations 0, 1, 2, 3 in Figure 4.9 with n=0:

The box plot data for this experiment is given in Figure 4.C.7 augmented by the data of Table 4.6 of Appendix 4.D. It clearly shows that the ALP detector activity does not vary significantly with position on the shelf.

Experiments with NAD: Figure 4.C.8 provides box plots for the [ATP]/[ADP] ratio in *in vitro* fruit fly homogenates for the two cases: (1) source-water plus NAD solutions and (2) source water only. The various treatments, o-1, j-1, F-1 and C-1 are described in the main text. The ANOVA and Tukey post hoc comparisons are given in Table 4.7 of Appendix 4.D.

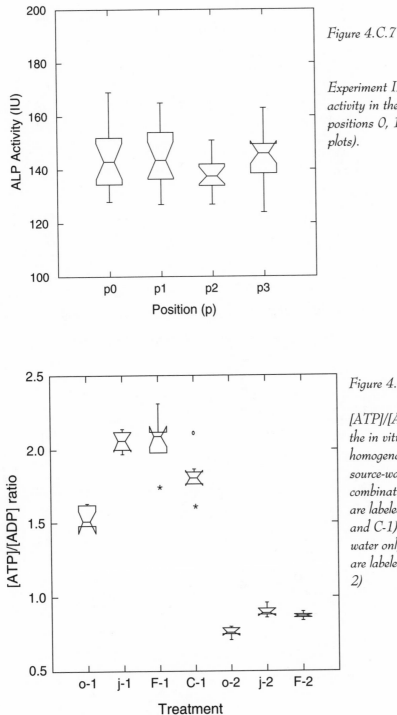

Figure 4.C.7

Experiment II(e): ALP activity in the detector (C) at positions 0, 1, 2 and 3 (box plots).

Figure 4.C.8 Box plots

[ATP]/[ADP] ratio in the in vitro fruit fly homogenates for (1) source-water-NAD combinations (treatments are labeled o-1, j-1, F-1 and C-1) and (2) source-water only (treatments are labeled o-2, j-2 and F-2)

Appendix 4.D: Specific Data

Table 4.1   *ANOVA for the influence of IIEDs on ALP activity.*

source	df	mean square	F
device/ treatment	3	0.097	9.217**
dilution	1	1.840	173.985**
device/ treatment × dilution	3	0.007	0.700
error	48	0.011	

** indicates p< 0.001

Tukey post hoc tests significant at p<0.05

Comparison	p-value
d,j > d,o > C	0.000 0.005
F > C	0.011

Table 4.2   *ANOVA for the (F) layer number effect.*

source	df	mean square	F
F	6	0.059	6.626**
error	265	0.009	

** indicates p<0.001.

Tukey post hoc tests significant at p<0.05

Comparison	p-value
0	
< 1	0.000
< 3	0.005
5	
< 1	0.000
< 3	0.002
< 4	0.018
< 2	0.047
6	
< 1	0.000

Table 4.3   ANOVA for exposure period and FC (n=0, 1).

source	df	mean square	F
F	1	0.111	15.537**
exposure	2	0.011	1.486
F×exposure	2	0.007	1.005
error	90	0.007	

** indicates $p < 0.001$.

Tukey post hoc tests significant at $p < 0.05$

(i)   (F) layer for 30 and 45 min. exposure

Comparison	p-value
F1	
> F0	0.000

(ii)   (F) layer and specific exposure periods

Comparison	p-value
F1, 45	
> F0, 45	0.011
> F0, 15	0.024
F1, 30	
> F0, 45	0.025
> F0, 15	0.050

Table 4.4   ANOVA for device, condition and (F) with n=0 or 1 (pooled for day and position).

source	df	mean square	F
device (d)	1	0.107	16.492**
treatment	3	0.048	7.483**
treatment×(d)	3	0.111	17.216**
error	327	0.006	

** indicates p<0.001.

Tukey post hoc comparisons significant at p<0.05:

Comparison and p-value	Comparison and p-value
d,j, on, n=1: > d,j, off, n=0 - p=0.000 > d,j, off, n=1 – p=0.001 > d,o, off, n=0 - p=0.000 > d,o, on, n=0 – p=0.000 > d,o, on, n=1 – p=0.002	d,j, on, n=0: > d,j, off, n=0 – p=0.034 > d,j, off, n=1 – p=0.059
d,j, on, n=0: > d,o, off, n=0 – p=0.001 > d,o, on, n=0 – p=0.000	d,o off, n=1: > d,j, off, n=0 – p=0.018 > d,j, off, n=1 – p=0.032 > d,o, on, n=1 - p= 0.058
d,o, off n=1: > d,o, off, n=0 – p=0.001 > d,o, on, n=0 – p=0.000	d,o, on, n=0: < d,j, off, n=0 – p=0.022 < d,j off, n=1 – p=0.012 < d,o, on, n=1 – p=0.006

Table 4.5   *ANOVA for ALP vessels, position and (F) for n=0 or 1.*

source	df	mean square	F
position (p)	2	0.121	13.964**
FC	1	0.059	6.856
vessel (v)	2	0.471	54.364**
p×FC	2	0.013	1.531
p×v	4	0.008	0.878
FC×v	2	0.163	18.843**
p×FC×v	4	0.025	2.914
error	470	0.009	** indicates $p < 0.001$

Tukey post hoc tests significant at $p < 0.05$:

Position only

Comparison	p-value
1	
> 3	0.000
> 2	0.022
2	
> 3	0.022

Position and vessel number, n=0

Comparison	p-value
p2, v1	
> p3, v3	0.000
> p2, v3	0.002
> C-O	0.008
> p3, v1	0.011
p1, v1	
> p3, v3	0.001
> p2, v3	0.004
> C-O	0.025
> p3, v1	0.027
p1, v3	
> p3, v3	0.020
p2, v2	
> p3, v3	0.039

n=1

Comparison	p-value
C-1	
> p1, v3	0.000
> p2, v3	0.000
> p3, v3	0.000
p1, v1	
> p1, v3	0.000
> p2, v3	0.000
> p3, v3	0.000
p1,v2	
> p1, v3	0.000
> p2, v3	0.000
> p3, v3	0.000
p1,v3	
< p2, v2	0.000
< p3, v1	0.000
< p2, v1	0.008
< p3, v2	0.017
p2, v1	
> p2, v3	0.000
> p3, v3	0.000
p2, v2	
> p2, v3	0.000
> p3, v3	0.000
p2, v3	
< p3, v1	0.000
< p3, v2	0.000
p3, v3	
< p3,v1	0.000
< p3,v2	0.000

Table 4.6   ANOVA for Experiment 2(e).

source	df	mean square	F
position	3	0.009	1.954**
error	60	0.005	

** indicates $p<0.001$.

Table 4.7   [ATP]/[ADP] ratio in the in vitro fruit fly homogenates: (a) source-water-NAD combinations and (b) source-water only.

(a)   ANOVA

source	df	Mean square	F
Source water-NAD solution	3	0.072	49.761**
error	28	0.001	

** indicates $p < 0.001$

Tukey post hoc tests significant at $p<0.05$.

Comparison	p-value
d,o < d,j < F < C	0.000 0.000 0.000
d,j > C	0.000
F > C	0.000

(b)   ANOVA

source	df	mean square	F
Source water-NAD solution	2	0.142	38.641**
error	21	0.004	

** indicates $p < 0.001$

Tukey post hoc tests significant at $p<0.05$.

Comparison	p-value
d,o < d,j < F	0.000 0.000
d,j > F	0.05

CHAPTER 5

An *In Vivo* Experiment with Fruit Flies

Introduction to *Drosophila melanogaster*

A natural extension of the experiments discussed in chapters 3 and 4 is to look at IIED effects on a fairly simple and well studied living system. We chose a common species of fruit fly, *Drosophila melanogaster*, for this purpose. This fruit fly, which we all recognize as being prevalent around ripening and fermenting fruit or decaying vegetation, has been studied in detail by scientists for almost a century. During that period, most of the fruit fly's genes have been identified while details of its physiology and biochemistry have been well characterized. Furthermore, the fruit fly has been extensively utilized in studies of both fitness plus evolutionary and developmental genetics. Thus, this seemed to be an ideal candidate with which to test the postulate that human intention, via IIED-influenced experiments, is also effective for living systems.

There are four distinct stages in the life cycle of the fruit fly: egg, larva, pupa and adult as illustrated in Figure 5.1. At 21 °C, a fresh culture of *D. melanogaster* will produce new adults in about two weeks; eight days in the egg and larval stages plus six days in the pupal stage. The adult flies may live for several weeks.

The day after the egg is laid, the larva hatches and it then molts twice (sheds the cuticle, mouth hooks and spiracles). During the periods of growth before and after molting, the larva is called an instar so, from Figure 5.1, the fruit fly has three instars. The cuticle of the third instar hardens and darkens to become the puparium. Metamorphosis occurs within the puparium with the pupa beginning to darken just prior to the emergence of an adult fly. About one day before emergence, the folded wings appear as two dark elliptical shapes and the pigment in the eyes becomes visible through the puparium. When metamorphosis is complete, the adult emerges. At first the fly is light in color, the wings are contracted and the abdomen is long. In a few hours the wings expand, the abdomen becomes more rotund and the color gradually darkens. Two days after emerging, a female can start laying eggs and, after maturity, are fertile as long as they live.

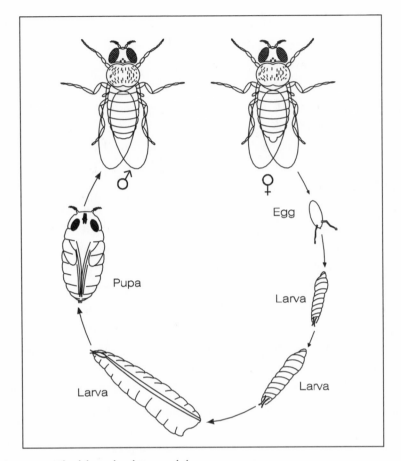

Figure 5.1   The life cycle of Drosophila.

In our study of *D. melanogaster*, we adopt an evolutionary genetics perspective. That is, we commence at the whole organism or phenotypic level and study fitness in the fruit fly. In general, total Darwinian fitness is divided into several components of fitness and, for the fruit fly, each component of the life cycle in Figure 5.1 can be considered as a fitness component.

In this chapter, we focus on the particular fitness component, <u>larval to adult fly development time</u>, which is an important developmental phenotype (genetic expression). We utilize isofemale strains (strains from a single female captured in the field) which are maintained in sequential discrete generations in the laboratory. These isofemale strains were chosen on the basis of differences in larval to adult development time.[1] Such strains are assessed in different environments in an attempt to identify change in fitness and developmental phenotype that may be caused by novel interactions between genes and the environment. It is thought that these changes may be the consequence of novel relationships between energy availability and gene expression which may be subsequently assessed at genetic and molecular levels.

143

Larval development time is given as $\tau_{1/2}$, the time taken for half of the surviving adults to emerge, thus, larval development rate in *D. melanogaster* is readily assayed and varies with respect to both genetic and environmental variation. For strains differing in their $\tau_{1/2}$ values, environmentally determined changes, $\Delta\tau_{1/2}$, are likely to be caused by modifications in gene expression, expressed in the context of the basic genetic differences existing between the strains.[2] Therefore, $\Delta\tau_{1/2}$ is assumed to be a useful initial indicator of differential gene expression during larval development, the molecular basis of which can be subsequently determined.[2, 3]

It is thought that analyses of strains which express modified developmental phenotypes in response to energy availability may elucidate the causal genetic and energetic events involved. Additionally, the response of strains to <u>treatments which modify energy availability</u> may indicate the treatments' dependence on genetic variation, metabolic and physiological effects. Fly development is complex and the effects of a modified energy source upon single loci or microscopic development process path is difficult to define (see the next section). However, by commencing at the level of development rate, relationships between single locus expression and energy availability may be resolvable. Finally, since earlier sexual maturation has been shown to lead to higher fitness [4-6], larval development rate is an important fitness component.

Bioenergetics

The work of the great German scientist, Otto Warburg, leads one to the idea that a functional continuum operates between energy availability and gene expression. This leads to integrated biological organization, precise development and high fitness. Warburg [7] emphasized the importance of (i) the relationship between respiration and structure, (ii) the nature of the energy derived from respiration for the maintenance of organic integrity and (iii) the important role of the molecule, nicotinamide adenine dinucleotide (NAD), in the above. In fact, energy metabolism has been considered to serve as both a regulatory process and a thermodynamic driving process in the biological system.[8]

NAD participates in the electron transport chain, in oxidative phosphorylation and in the production of the key biological energy molecule, ATP. As may be deduced from Figure 5.2, NAD collects electrons from various metabolic reactions (see Appendix 5.A for a brief technical review of

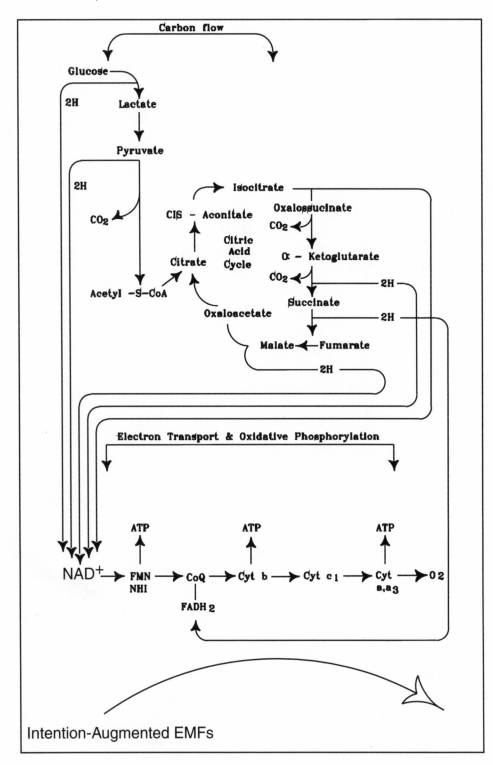

Figure 5.2   Diagram of Intermediary Metabolism, illustrating the pivotal role of NAD.

energy metabolism) and cycles them through the final energy producing pathway. A wide variety of studies indicate the presence of specific and limited variation in cellular NAD levels, suggesting that changes in these NAD levels may have profound consequences for the organism. In this context, modified cellular energy availability, and specifically a change in electron transport chain activity mediated by NAD, may modify gene expression. This has novel consequences for biological organization.

In Figure 5.2, FMN represents flaven mononucleotide, NHI-nonheme ion prosthetic group, $FADH_2$-flaven adenine dinucleotide reduced form, CoQ-coenzyme Q or ubiquinone, Cyt b, c_1, a ,a_3 the cytochrome system, EMF, the electromagnetic field and ATP, the probable points at which energy is conserved by coupling electron transport to the phosphorylation of ADP:

$$ADP^{-3} + P^{-2} + H^+ \rightarrow ATP^{-4}.$$

If it is possible to generate novel modifications in cellular energy availability, then novel alterations in gene expression and organism development should follow. The consequences of novel gene expression are many with some of the important ones being the following: (i) alteration of the basic rates of gene expression, (ii) the expression of hitherto inactive genes yielding new sensitivities to certain carcinogenic processes, to alteration medical therapies or to unusual physico-biological phenomena, (iii) the dissociation of gene/environment interactions such that gene expression becomes refractory to, and independent of, contemporary environments in contrast to historical or future environments and (iv) general and very subtle modification of metabolic pathways which, on the basis of metabolic network theory, may lead to new biological equilibria, modified homeostasis, disease resistance, etc.

An important aspect of the foregoing is the likelihood that novel modifications of biological energy availability may uniquely alter biological organization. We suggest that just such a situation may arise from the new physics involved in application of specific IIED's to biological systems. Our central hypothesis is that intention-augmented EMF's, with their associated magnetic vector potential nature, may interact with NAD, the electron transport chain and ATP production. This, in turn, should modulate gene expression, organism development and organism fitness.

Some Relevant Prior Baseline Studies with *D. melanogaster*

About a decade ago, Kohane[9] investigated NAD supplementation and larval development in field-derived larvae of *D. melanogaster*. Evidence was found for a novel phenotypic effect from supplemental NAD during larval development in terms of a significantly decreased $\tau_{1/2}$ value in the temperature range 18 °C to 29 °C. This result was discussed in the context of NAD functioning as (i) an additional energy source similar to glucose, (ii) a substrate for dehydrogenases and (iii) a direct electron flow enhancement into the electron transport chain and hence an enhanced energy availability, possibly circumventing intermediary metabolism. Enhanced energy availability at the cellular level was regarded as being equivalent to enhanced gene expression such that developmental processes were accelerated.

More recently, Kohane[10] extended the earlier work to isofemale strains of *D. melanogaster* - chosen on the basis of development rate differences. In this study, the following were assessed: (i) modifying the NAD-pool, moving the NAD concentration, and hence the redox state, beyond the boundary levels established during normal fly development, (ii) the effects of this altered state upon both the adenylate pool and the [ATP]/[ADP] ratio, (iii) correlation of these changes with changes in T, (iv) the developmental and fitness effects associated with low levels of supplemental NAD, (v) comparison of the effects of supplemental NAD glucose on $\tau_{1/2}$ and (vi) the effect of supplemental NAD upon $\tau_{1/2}$ in relation to genetic and phenotypic variation in a study of the extreme strains and their hybrids.

The results of these studies indicated that, under nutritional stress, perturbation of the energy metabolism via NAD supplementation modified the larval development time, a genetically-based trait relevant to fly development and fly fitness. Energetic studies, both *in vitro* and *in vivo*, indicated that supplemental NAD increased the proportion of ATP and the [ATP]/[ADP] ratio present during larval development. The decrease in $\tau_{1/2}$ mediated by NAD was attributed to the supplemental NAD modifying the NAD pool beyond the levels present during normal development.

Bioelectromagnetic studies have advanced considerably in the past decade and clearly indicate that electromagnetic fields (EMF's) influence cellular energy metabolism.[10] For example, magnetic field influences have been reported on the *in vitro* redox activity of cytochrome oxidase.[11] Additionally, weak EMF's stimulate ATP synthesis and alter Na, K-ATPase activity.[12-14] Interestingly, Menendez [15] has suggested that an EMF coupling process may explain the proton translocation mechanism in cellular energy transfer. Thus, a good foundation exists for our basic hypothesis that EMF's and intention-augumented EMF's may influence biological processes via interaction with the electron transport chain (see Figure 5.2).

Experimental Procedures

Biological Assay: This assay utilizes the response of developing larvae to specific treatments and couples these effects to the energy assay to be described next. Thus, the assay couples the metabolic basis of the treatments' effects on larval development *in vivo* to NAD's metabolic effects on *in vitro* larval homogenates (see below), and assays the effects in terms of changes in [ATP]/[ADP] ratio. In general, newly hatched larvae are cultured in food of controlled nutrition content in the presence of the various treatments. Larval density and non-stressful food composition may be varied with the typical composition being: 36 grams agar, 108 g sugar, 72 g dry yeast, 10 ml propionic acid and 24 ml nipagen in 200 ml water. Larvae obtained from two isofemale strains, strains 1 and 2 from ref. 10 were utilized. Larvae for energy analysis were collected at the appropriate age and assessed while, for development rate and other fitness tests, the larvae are allowed to complete their development and the survivors are collected. Separate constant temperature rooms (18 °C, 55% relative humidity) were utilized for (i) device storage, (ii) strain culture and unexposed adult culture storage and (iii) all experiments.

Energy assay: The energy assay is based upon (i) Warburg's manometric procedures for measurement of the overall metabolic processes for respiration and glycolysis and (ii) the fact that the endogenous metabolism of various homogenates (ground-up organisms) is modified in terms of changes in respiration following the addition of NAD.[16] Hence, the addition of NAD to larval homogenates, maintaining an endogenous metabolism in the presence of oxygen, may still modify the respiration of that homogenate state and cause changes to occur in the levels of ATP, ADP and AMP present (and thus in the [ATP]/[ADP] ratio). The homogenate formation process that we utilized did not appear to seriously damage the ATP or ADP molecules.

Our energy assay uses high performance liquid chromatography (HPLC) to measure changes in the levels of ATP, ADP and AMP present in the sample. From this, the [ATP]/[ADP] ratio is readily determined. HPLC is a technology that enables simultaneous separation, detection and concentration determination of the various biological molecules present in an originally heterogeneous solution. The separation principle involves charge and molecular mass differences so that different biological molecules (having different charges and molecular weights) are caused to accumulate at unique locations on a linear strip of medium (small beads) according to their relative charge and molecular weights (see Figure 5.3). The total concentration for particular species present is given by the area under the curve (relative to a baseline reading) around a unique mass location. Thus, from Figure 5.3 type data, one can readily determine the [ATP]/[ADP] ratio.

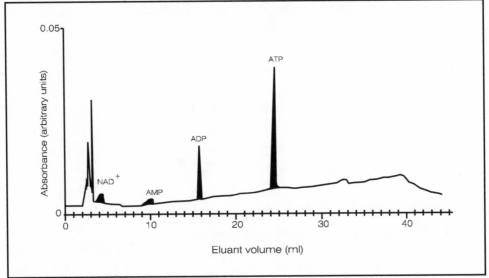

Figure 5.3   High-performance liquid chromatography separation of adenylates from D. melanogaster. Adenylates were detected at 260 nanometers; methods are described in the text. Shaded peaks and positions in the separation are, left to right: NAD at 4.0 ml, AMP at 9.8 ml, ADP at 16.0 ml and ATP at 24.2 ml.

For our assay, we use homogenates prepared from the larvae. The concentration levels of the specific molecules of interest in these homogenates are determined in the presence of either a specific added amount of NAD or pure water for a set time period, τ. Differences and ratio changes between the NAD-added homogenates and the water-added homogenates are particularly important to us. The value observed for the pure water case reflects the activity of the larval homogenate <u>prior</u> to the homogenization step while the value observed for the NAD-added case reflect the electron transport chain capability and degree of activity <u>during the time interval, τ</u>, since the added NAD activates the electron transport chain in the homogenate.

Considering *D. melanogaster*, the effect of supplemental NAD upon ATP, ADP and AMP-levels in larval homogenates is defined by the larval genetic structure or genotype, the experimental environment and fly phenotype. Further, this effect depends upon (i) the initial ATP, ADP and AMP levels at the time of homogenization and (ii) the metabolic capacity of the endogenous metabolism of the larval homogenate to react with NAD thereby changing the levels of ATP, ADP and AMP. Thus, this procedure provides a dynamic assay (but not a continuous assay) of energy metabolism in larval homogenates, in contrast to the conventional static procedures.[17] It should also be noted that (i) ATP production in larval homogenates should not be coupled to ATP demand by metabolic and physiological processes as it is for the *in vivo* case and (ii) the procedure is an assay at an overall metabolic level.

Fitness: Here is where we test our hypothesis that EMF's and intention-augmented EMF's may influence biological processes via interaction with the electron transport chain (see Figure 5.2). We investigated this idea with four individual experiments (the data is tabulated in Table 5.1 of Appendix 5.B).

We studied $\tau_{1/2}$ and [ATP]/[ADP] ratio under non-stressful nutrient conditions in both the presence and absence of electronic devices. These devices produced low power EMF's of frequencies appreciably higher than those utilized in previous biological studies and they certainly have an effect. We assessed these frequency effects using exposure periods of four hours to one life-cycle in order to detect EMF effects possibly hidden in the previous studies. The total study involved approximately 10,000 larvae and 7,000 adults assessed over an 8 month period.

While our main focus was development rate, we also measured adult survival, surviving adult weight and larval weight – other components of fitness. We incorporated Faraday cages and IIEDs into the basic design. The four treatments investigated in these experiments were as follows: (i) (C)-culture in the random EMF environment of the laboratory, (ii) (F)-culture inside the relatively muted EMF environment of a Faraday cage with no device present, (iii) (d,o)-culture inside a Faraday cage but in the presence of a control device, not treated by human intention, in the "on" state and (iv) (d,j)-culture inside a Faraday cage but in the presence of an IIED in the "on" state. These four treatments were conducted simultaneously in a side-by-side condition at 18 °C on a laboratory bench as illustrated in Figure 5.4. Since $\tau_{1/2}$ differences have, in the past, been detected at this temperature for the strains studied here[10], our present protocol bypassed such potential artifacts in the gathered data.

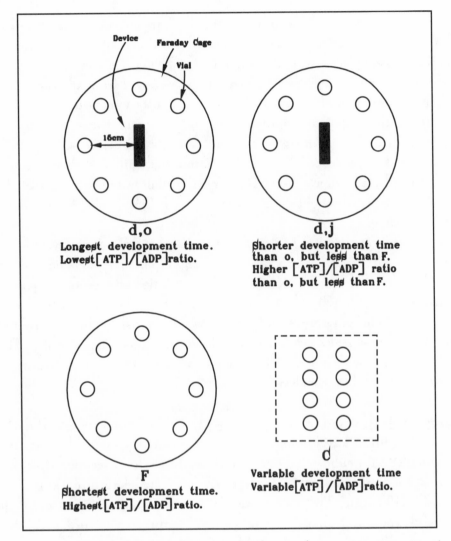

Figure 5.4   Experimental configuration for the simultaneous 4-treatment situation adjacent to each other on a table top.

A single replicate involved 30 larvae (0-4 hours old and counted by hand) transferred to a single silica vial containing non-stressful food. For each experiment, all vials were established within a three-hour period. The vials were transferred to Faraday cages and these were placed in the arrangement of Figure 5.4 with wall to wall separation of 6" between faraday cages. Treatment (C) involved vials transferred to a tray which was placed on the top of the treatment (F) Faraday cage. In a separate experiment, we used vial cultures as surrogate thermocouples and could statistically detect no temperature variation between the four treatments of this experiment.

Exposure of the vials to devices in the Faraday cages was achieved as follows: The respective device was placed in the center of a cage and vials/bottles were placed around its perimeter. The device was then turned on for a specific time period, then turned off and removed from the cage. Then the larval development proceeded until the adults enclosed. The device position in the cage was approximately 15 cm from the vials/bottles on average. The total electromagnetic output power of the device was expected to be less than 1 microwatt. The vials were monitored daily and surviving adults were both collected and weighed. The surviving adult weight was calculated for each vial as the total weight of the surviving adult flies divided by the number of flies surviving.

In experiments 1-3 (Table 5.1 in Appendix 5.B), larvae were derived from unexposed adults. In experiment 4 (Table 5.1), larvae were derived from exposed adults of strain 1 as follows: replicate bottle cultures were exposed to the treatments (C), (F), (d,j), (d,o) for one life cycle (one bottle for one treatment). The emerging adults were synchronously collected from the respective cultures and used to generate larvae for experimental vials. These new larvae were then exposed to the same treatment as their parents using a 4 day exposure period for the devices.

Energy levels during larval development: We measured the [ATP]/[ADP] ratio in third instar larval homogenates.[10] We stored the larval homogenates, supplemented with either NAD or pure H_2O, on ice for a reaction time of 40 minutes to facilitate metabolic activity prior to determination of the [ATP]/[ADP] ratio. This is a more conservative approach than the earlier successful work of Kohane[10] who used 7 minutes. In order to assess treatment, fitness and [ATP]/[ADP] ratio in the same experiment, experimental vials were established for energy assays concurrently with experiment 4 of Table 5.1. We avoided age-dependent effects on energy metabolism by preparing larval homogenates on the same day as follows: 15 third instar larvae were collected, transferred to micro-centrifuge tubes, weighed and homogenized in 250 µl ice-cold pure water to which 250 µl of ice-cold 0.01 molar NAD or pure water were immediately added.

The solutions were mixed and transferred to each treatment for a reaction time of 40 minutes to facilitate metabolic activity. The micro-centrifuge tubes were then freeze-clamped in liquid nitrogen. ATP, ADP and AMP were extracted using 4.2 M formic acid and 4.2 M ammonium hydroxide.[10] They were then quantified using an automated Isco HPLC apparatus, a Vydac Column (3021C4.6) and a pre-programmed gradient from

0.025 M sodium phosphate monobasic, pH 2.8 to 0.5 M sodium phosphate monobasic, pH 2.8 [18]. There were 8 replicates per treatment for both supplemental NAD and pure H_2O. All extractions were completed within a 4 hour period. The replicates were stored at 2-4 °C and assayed in random order over a 3 day period.

Experimental Results

The raw data, aggregated at the batch level, is presented in Appendix 5.B as "notched" box plots and in Appendix 5.C as tabulations based on the ANOVA statistical view. Figure 5.5 presents the means from this analysis for

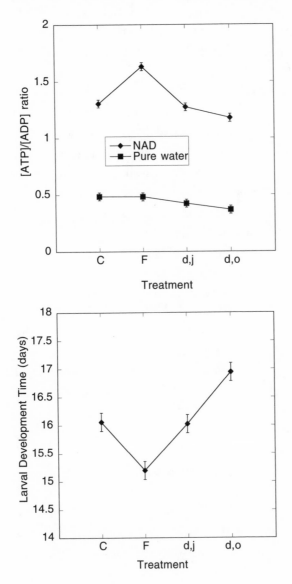

Figure 5.5 (a)

[ATP]/[ADP] ratio vs. treatment (means).

Figure 5.5 (b)

Means for larval development time vs. treatment.

[ATP]/[ADP] ratio (see Figure 5.5a) and for larval development time, $\tau_{1/2}$, (see Figure 5.5b). In assessing the degree of correlation between [ATP]/[ADP] ratio and $\tau_{1/2}$, we obtained a Pearson correlation coefficient of –0.856 (highly correlated). This provides additional evidence for a strong relationship between energetics and fitness since higher [ATP]/[ADP] ratios produced smaller $\tau_{1/2}$ values.

For both variables, the ANOVA gives $p<0.001$ overall with an effect size of ~5-12. In terms of our basic hypothesis for both variables, the ANOVA gives $p<0.001$ overall. In terms of our basic hypothesis concerning the influence of intention-augmented EMF's on larval fitness, this data provides robust support ($\tau_{1/2}$) with (d,j) < (d,o) at the $p<0.001$ level of statistical significance. The unexpected finding that (F) < (C) at $p<0.001$ and that (F) << (d,o) at $p<0.0001$ illustrates that both random ambient EMF's and specific high frequency EMF's (even at quite low power levels) are significant stressors for *D. melanogaster*.[10] The finding that the [ATP]/[ADP] ratio practically mirrors the $\tau_{1/2}$ data for the added-NAD case at a high Pearson correlation value strongly supports the connection between energy availability to the cells and organism fitness[10] as well as the profound importance of NAD to overall metabolic activity.

In terms of NAD effects on metabolic activity, both ambient levels of EMF's and our low power device levels of EMF's appear to significantly reduce the thermodynamic activity of the NAD in the organism. The intention-effect appears to increase the thermodynamic activity of the available NAD in the systems, so it is a fitness booster for the organism. Thus, in general, we must consider the sum of the stressor contributions and the booster contributions on the overall fitness of the organism and there is no *a priori* reason why the booster contribution need be smaller than the stressor contribution to the fitness of an organism. A goal of future research on *in vivo* systems should obviously be to understand how to achieve a booster/stressor ratio of >>1 and <<1 for a variety of life forms.

An additional comment that should be made about Figure. 5.5 is that, even for the added-pure water case, the different treatments gave an overall statistically significant effect ($p<0.001$ albeit at small effect size). Even comparing the (d,j) treatment to the (d,o) treatment, one finds marginal significance ($p<0.05$). Thus, ambient EMF's, the specific 1-10 MHz EMF's and the intention-augmented EMF's are either modifying the ambient NAD in the cells of the organism or they are impacting some other factor in the electron transport chain of Figure 5.2.

We did not observe a significant Faraday cage effect for adult survival or larval weight (see Appendix 5.B). However, considering surviving adult weight, a significantly higher weight ($p < 0.001$) was observed in experiments 3 and 4 for (F) in comparison to (C).

In closing this chapter, we point out that in Chapter 7, the EMF intensity is shown to be a thermodynamic contribution to the generalized potential for any molecular species while, in Chapter 8 it is shown that intention-induced coherence in the vacuum changes the ground state generalized potential for such molecular species. Thus, some fundamental science support exists for the experimental findings of this chapter.

References

1.   P.A. Parsons, "Isofemale Strains and Evolutionary Strategies in Natural Populations", Evol. Biol., 13 (1980) 175-217.

2.   L.I. Korochkin, Gene Interactions in Development, (Springer-Verlag, Berlin, 1981).

3.   W.J. Gehring, "Homeotic Genes, the Homeobox and the Spatial Organization of the Embryo", Harvey Lectures, 81 (1987) 153-172.

4.   L.C. Cole, "The Population Consequences of Life-history Phenomena", Q. Rev. Biol., 29 (1954) 103-107.

5.   R. C. Lewontin, "Selection for Colonizing Ability", in The Genetics of Colonizing Species , H. G. Bauer and G. L. Stebbins editors, (Academic Press,1965).

6.   P.A. Parsons, The Evolutionary Biology of Colonizing Species, (Cambridge University Press, New York, 1983).

7.   0. Warburg, New Methods of Cell Physiology Applied to Cancer and Mechanism of X-ray Action, (John Wiley and Sons, New York, 1962).

8.   F. Lipmann, "Metabolic Generation and Utilization of Phosphate Bond Energy", Advances in Enzymology, 1 (1941) 99-162.

9.   M.J. Kohane, "Stress, Altered Energy Availability and Larval Fitness in *Drosophila melanogaster*", Heredity, <u>60</u> (1988) 273-281.

10.   M.J. Kohane, "Energy, Development and Fitness in *Drosophila melanogaster*", Proc. Roy. Soc. (B), <u>257</u> (1994) 185-191.

11.   E.M. Goodman, B. Greenbaum, and M.T. Marron, "Effects of Electromagnetic Fields on Molecules and Cells", International Review of Cytology, <u>158</u> (1995) 279-338.

12.   B. Nossol, G. Buse and J. Silny, "Influence of Weak Static and 50 Hz Magnetic Fields on the Redox Activity of Cytochrome-C Oxidase", Bioelectromagnetics, <u>14</u> (1993) 361-372.

13.   C. Lei and H. Berg, "Electromagnetic Window Effects on Proliferation Rate of *Corynebacterium glutamicum*", Bioelectrochemistry and Bioenergetics, <u>45</u> 1998) 261-265.

14.   M. Blank, L. Soo and V. Papstein, "Effects of Low Frequency Magnetic Fields on Na,K-ATPase Activity", Bioelectrochemistry and Bioenergetics, <u>38</u> (1995) 267-273.

15.   R.G. Menendez, "An Electromagnetic Coupling Hypothesis to Explain the Proton Translocation Mechanism in Mitochondria, Bacteria and Chloroplasts", Medical Hypotheses, <u>47</u> (1996) 179-182.

16.   A. Harden, <u>Alcoholic Fermentation</u>, (Longmans, Green and Co., London, 1923).

17.   B. Sacktor, and E.C. Hurlbut, "Regulation of Metabolism in Working Muscle *in vivo*. II. Concentrations of Adenine Nucleotides, Arginine Phosphate and Inorganic Phosphate in Flight Muscle During Flight", J. Biol. Chem., <u>241</u> (1966) 632-634.

18.   M. J. Kohane and W. B. Watt, "Flight Muscle Adenylate Pool Responses to Flight Demands and Thermal Constraints in Individual *Colias Eurytheme* (Lepidoptea, Pieridae)", J. of Experimental Zoology, <u>302</u> (1999) 3145.

19.   L. Wilkinson, <u>Systat: Statistics Version 5.2 Edition</u>, (SYSTAT Inc., Evanston, Il., 1992).

20.   M.D. Brand and M.P. Murphy, "Control of Electron Flux through the Respiratory Chain in Mitochondria and Cells", Biol. Rev., <u>62</u> (1987) 141-193.

21.   P. Mitchell, "Coupling of Phosphorylation to Electron and Hydrogen Transfer by a Chemi-osmotic Type of Mechanism", Nature, <u>191</u> (1961) 144-148.

22.   B. Chance, "Enzymes in Action in Living Cells: The Steady State of Reduced Pyridine Nucleotides", Harvey Lecture, <u>49</u> (1953,1954) 145-175.

23.   O. Warburg, "Oxygen, the Creator of Differentiation", in <u>Current Aspects of Biochemical Energetics</u>, N.O. Kaplan and E.P. Kennedy editors, pages 103-109, (Academic Press, New York, 1966).

24.   M.J. Kohane, "Stress, Altered Energy Availability and Larval Fitness in *Drosophila melanogaster*", Heredity, <u>60</u> (1988) 273-281.

Appendix 5.A: Aspects of Energy Metabolism

The control of electron flux through the respiratory chain in the mitochondria of cells, and hence the rate of ATP synthesis in cells can be considered in terms of the following system: the electron transport chain, the H^+-ATPase, the adenine nucleotide carrier, the intra-mitochondrial adenine nucleotide and phosphate pools plus the proton motive force and the proton leak across the mitochondrial membrane.[20] This system interacts with the environment via the redox states of the NAD, ubiquinone (Q) and oxygen (O) plus the phosphorylation states of the extra mitochondrial adenine nucleotides. External effectors which cross the system boundary are few and include acyl-CoA. These inhibit the nucleotide carrier and fatty acids which activate an uncoupling protein found only in brown adipose tissue. At this level, the respiration rate is a consequence of the interactive internal properties of this system.

The respiration rate within cells is largely controlled by the rates of the reactions which feed electrons to the electron transport chain so as to consume or provide ATP. The former function through their effects upon the NADH/NAD and QH_2/Q ratios while the latter, via the cytosolic phosphorylation potential, adjust the [ATP]/[ADP] ratio. Reducible equivalent supply is controlled by the availability of oxidizable substrates which, in turn, depends upon diet and hormonal status. This control arises through regulation of pathways such as gleolysis and fatty acid catabolism plus Ca^{2+} activation of intramitochondrial dehydrogenases. Finally, hormonal control of respiration can occur at all of the above levels.

The chemiosmotic model of Mitchell[20,21] states that, at the level of the transport chain, the respiration rate is a function of the overall thermodynamic driving force acting on the electron transport chain. This is defined in terms of (i) the difference in redox potential between two carriers of reducing equivalents and (ii) the proton motive force across the mitochondrial inner membrane. The latter is defined in terms of the pH gradient and the electrical potential across the inner mitochondrial membrane. The redox potential is controlled by the electron supply and consumption rates while the proton motive force is controlled by the cytosolic phosphorylation state via the activity of the adenine nucleotide carrier and the H^+- ATPase.

An increase in the respiration rate in response to extra-mitochondrial phosphorylation status is considered to be due to an increase in redox state and a decrease in the proton motive force. The redox potential change is considered to be due to the effect of adenine nucleotides upon enzymes functioning beyond the electron transport chain. A decrease in proton motive force may be due to increased electron transfer from the H^+-ATPase during ATP synthesis.

Considering energy availability, it has been noted[20] that significant constraints are placed upon the control of respiration in cells and organs. There is the requirement that the cytoplasmic and mitochondrial [ATP]/[ADP] ratios do not significantly vary. In this way, the available free energy generated from the hydrolysis of ATP remains constant. Also, it is important that the metabolic changes required to modify ATP production do not significantly disturb those metabolic processes which respond directly to the [ATP]/[ADP] ratio. For example, AMP formed by adenylate kinase affects ATP demand in glycolysis and in oxidative phosphorylation while Ca^{2+} activation of dehydrogenases may signal ATP demand without changes in cytoplasmic phosphorylation status. Similar arguments may be made for the homeostasis of the intra-mitochondrial [ATP]/[ADP] ratio.

Studies indicate specific and limited variations in redox states for various experimental systems.[22] This observation of approximate redox state "locking" suggests that this is possibly established by specific boundary concentrations of NAD (but that may be transcended). Therefore, a focus has been given to the modification of energy availability via NAD, both *in vivo* and *in vitro* [23,24] on the basis of (i) boundary concentrations of NAD (ii) the controlling effect of NAD upon respiration, the electron transport chain, oxidative phosphorylation plus ATP, ADP and AMP levels.

Appendix 5.B: General Box Plot Representation of the Data

In this Appendix, the raw data, aggregated at the batch level, is presented as "notched" Box Plots (see Figures 5B.1 and 5B.2) which provide

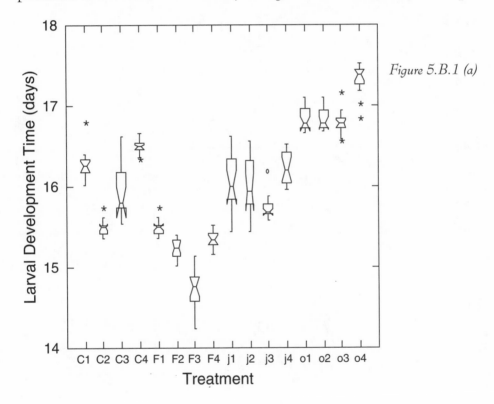

Figure 5.B.1 (a)

a simple graphical presentation of a batch of data. This type of plot implements confidence intervals on the shown median values. The boxes are notched at the median and return to full width at the lower and upper confidence interval values. If the intervals around two medians do not overlap, then one can be confident at about the 95% level that the two population medians are different. Outside values are presented by an asterisk, and far-outside values by an open circle. Thus, this visual approach is considered to be very useful for judging differences between treatments [19] (see Appendix 4.B).

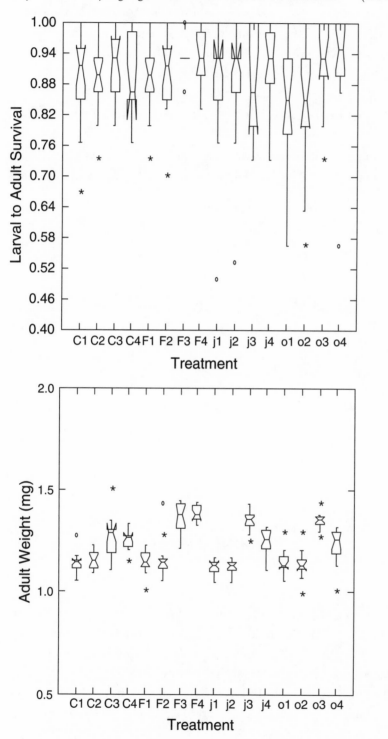

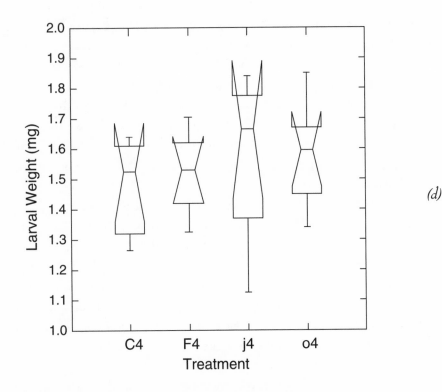

(d)

Figure 5.B.1 Box plot presentations of the collected data.

We have used visual inspection of Figures 5.B.1 and 5.B.2 to assess homogeneity with respect to the experiments as well as contrasts between the different treatments (o), (j), (F) and (C). We also present means and medians in Table 5.C.2 in Appendix 5.C. These data were transformed as follows: (i) larval development time - normal (the means are given), (ii) proportion survival – both the data and the log transformed data are not normal (the medians are given), (iii) surviving adult weight and larval weight – both essentially normal and improved after log transformation (the means are given) and (iv) [ATP]/[ADP] ratio – essentially normal and improved after arcsine – square root transformation (the means are given). The values given in Table 5.C.2 (Appendix 5.C) for each experiment and treatment are the untransformed values.

Intention – augmented EMF's and fitness: From Figure 5.B.1, one of the most striking comparisons is between (F) and (C), the Faraday cage effect, indicating that a strong effect ($p < 0.001$) exists when exposure to ambient random EMFs is appreciably reduced in intensity. We found that the presence of the Faraday cage significantly decreased $\tau_{1/2}$, in comparison to the control, in all experiments (Figure 5.B.1a). We did not observe a significant Faraday cage effect for adult survival (Figure 5.B.1b) or larval weight (Figure 5.B.1d). However, considering surviving adult weight, a significantly higher weight ($p < 0.001$) was observed in experiments 3 and 4 for (F) in comparison to (C).

From Figure 5.B.1 (a), a striking comparison occurs between (d,o) and (d,j) indicating the importance of the intention effect (at fixed specific EMF intensity level) on larval development. The presence of (d,j) significantly ($p < 0.001$) decreased $\tau_{1/2}$ in comparison to (d,o) in all four experiments. No significant device effect of either type was observed for adult survival, surviving adult weight or larval weight.

From Figure 5.B.1 (a), the most striking comparison is between (F) and (d,o), the oscillator effect. In all experiments, the presence of the Faraday cage without a device (F) significantly ($p < 0.001$) decreased $\tau_{1/2}$ in comparison to (d,o) with its three specific oscillators in the 1-10 MHz range and total output power of less than one microwatt. We did not detect any significant comparisons for both adult survival and larval weight. However, considering surviving adult weight, although no treatment effects were observed for experiments 1, 2 and 3, in experiment four the treatment ranking was (F) > (d,o) at $p < 0.001$.

Now we turn to the consideration of homogeneity of the data in our treatments across the four experiments. Considering $\tau_{1/2}$, neither (C) nor (F) were homogeneous with the rankings being (i) (C2) < (C3) ≤ (C1) < (C4) and (ii) (F3) < (F2) ≤ (F4) ≤ (F1). Considering (d,o), the rankings were (01) = (02) = (03) < (04); while (d,j) was essentially homogeneous. All treatments appeared to be homogeneous across the four experiments for adult survival while larval weight was only assessed in experiment 4 (see Table 5.C.2 in Appendix 5.C) but, considering surviving adult weight, the treatments were not homogeneous across all experiments. Surviving adult weight exhibited the following rankings: (i) (C1) ≤ (C2) ≤ (C4) ≤ (C3), (ii) (F1) = (F2) < (F3) = (F4), (iii) (j1) = (j2) < (j4) < (j3) and (iv) (01) = (02) < (04) < (03).

The relative homogeneity of the (d,j) effect on $\tau_{1/2}$ suggests that the intention somehow reduces fluctuations in the various metabolic processes so as to give an "ordering" constraint to the larval development time. Further, the smaller $\tau_{1/2}$ observed for all treatments in experiment 3, in comparison with experiment 4, suggests that exposure period to (d,j) may influence this fitness component. Considering surviving adult weight, significant differences were only observed in experiments 3 and 4, where the Faraday cage effect produced the highest weights. The results from experiment 4 suggest that cross-generational exposure to EMF's may affect fitness in ways that differ from single generation exposure. However, in general there did not appear to be any specific pattern to the heterogeneity.

Intention-augmented EMF's and the [ATP]/[ADP] ratio: From Figure 5.B.2, we see that the [ATP]/[ADP] ratio versus treatment for the added-NAD case almost mirrors the $\tau_{1/2}$ data of Figure. 5.B.1, whereas the added-pure water case reveals an almost uniform baseline. Comparisons between (F) and (C) reveal a significant ($p<0.001$) difference for the added-NAD case where   (F1) > (C) but not for the added- pure water case where (F1) $\cong$ (C). Comparisons between (d,j) and (d,o) showed significant differences for both assays, ($p<0.001$) for added-NAD and ($p<0.05$) for added- pure water with (d,j) > (d,o) in both cases. The greatest difference was again found to be between (F) and (d,o) with $p<0.001$ for the added-NAD case and $p<0.001$ For the added- pure water case.

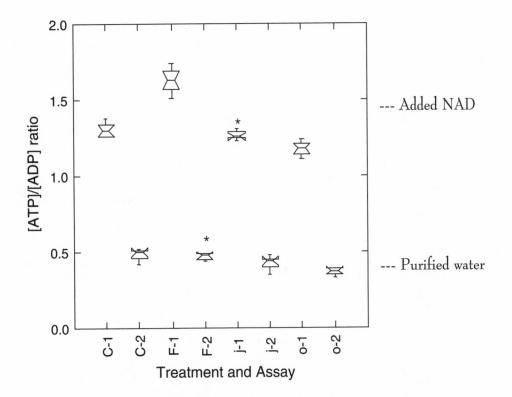

Figure 5.B.2   Box plot of [ATP]/[ADP] ratio versus treatment and assay for the two cases of (a) added-NAD and (b) purified water.

Appendix 5.C: Numerical Data and Statistical Analysis

Table 5.C.1   Summary of fitness experiments. Fitness components assessed were larval development time, adult survival and surviving adult weight.

Experiment Date	Strain	Device	Treatment and replicate number				Exposure period
			C	F	d,j	d,o	
1 2/97	2	d1	16	15	15	16	4 hours
2 2/97	1	d2	16	15	15	16	4 hours
3 7/97	1	d1	15	14	15	15	4 days
4* days	1 7/97	d1	15	15	16	16	Life-cycle plus 4

* the [ATP]/[ADP] ratio and third instar larval weight were assessed in experiment 4 (see text).

(1) Strain 1 and strain 2 refer to two isofemale strains.

(2) Experiments were conducted at 18 °C. Experimental vial cultures involved 30 larvae (0-4 hours old) transferred to a single vial containing non-stressful food.

(3) For Experiments 1-3, larvae were derived from unexposed adults; and for Experiment 4, larvae were derived from exposed adults.

Table 5.C.2 (a)Larval development time ($\tau_{1/2}$ in days). Means and standard deviations (in brackets) are given.

Experiment	C	F	j	o
			Treatment	
1	16.276 (0.170)	15.503 (0.097)	16.080 (0.351)	16.838 (0.145)
2	15.504 (0.097)	15.238 (0.111)	16.047 (0.336)	16.837 (0.141)
3	15.964 (0.315)	14.703 (0.248)	15.739 (0.151)	16.778 (0.152)
4	16.507 (0.087)	15.348 (0.106)	16.228 (0.197)	17.323 (0.186)

Table 5.C.2 (b)Larval to adult Survival (given as proportions for an input of 30 larvae). Medians and 25 and 75 percentiles (in brackets) are shown for adult survival since the data distribution curves for each batch were not normal. The 25 percentiles are given above the 75 percentiles.

Experiment	C	F	j	o
			Treatment	
1	0.917 (0.833) (0.933)	0.900 (0.842) (0.915)	0.933 (0.800) (0.933)	0.850 (0.767) (0.900)
2	0.900 (0.842) (0.915)	0.917 (0.833) (0.933)	0.933 (0.833) (0.933)	0.850 (0.779) (0.900)
3	0.933 (0.830) (0.938)	0.933 (0.871) (0.941)	0.867 (0.778) (0.917)	0.933 (0.867) (0.958)
4	0.867 (0.833) (0.967)	0.933 (0.879) (0.969)	0.933 (0.867) (0.967)	0.950 (0.890) (0.975)

Table 5.C.2 (c) Adult Weight (mg). Means and standard deviations (in brackets) are given.

Experiment	Treatment			
	C	F	j	o
1	1.140 (0.049)	1.148 (0.057)	1.124 (0.036)	1.147 (0.056)
2	1.155 (0.045)	1.158 (0.089)	1.125 (0.036)	1.136 (0.063)
3	1.267 (0.099)	1.360 (0.083)	1.349 (0.056)	1.352 (0.039)
4	1.254 (0.047)	1.388 (0.037)	1.249 (0.066)	1.238 (0.085)

Table 5.C.2 (d) Larval Weight (mg). Means and standard deviations (in brackets) are given.

Experiment	Treatment			
	C	F	j	o
4	1.478 (0.157)	1.524 (0.138)	1.575 (0.277)	1.579 (0.163)

Table 5.C.2 (e) [ATP]/[ADP] ratio. Means and standard deviations, in brackets, are given.

Assay	Treatment			
	C	F	j	o
NAD	1.305 (0.046)	1.630 (0.077)	1.273 (0.039)	1.177 (0.043)
pure water	0.486 (0.035)	0.482 (0.046)	0.424 (0.042)	0.368 (0.024)

Table 5.C.3   ANOVA for larval development time.

source	df	mean square	F
device/ treatment	3	0.008	19.175**
error	12	0.001	

** indicates $p < 0.001$.

Tukey post hoc tests significant at p < 0.05

Comparison	p-value
F	
< d,o	0.000
< C	0.010
< d,j	0.014
d,j	
< d,o	0.010
C	
< d,o	0.013

Table 5.C.4   ANOVA for [ATP]/[ADP] ratio.
(a) NAD assay - assay 1 of Figure 5.B.2.

source	df	Mean square	F
device/ treatment	3	0.055	108.477**
error	28	0.001	

** indicates p<0.001

Tukey post hoc tests significant at p < 0.05

Comparison	p-value
F-1	
> C-1	0.000
> j-1	0.000
> o-1	0.000
C-1	
> o-1	0.000
j-1	
> o-1	0.003

(b) pure water assay – assay 2 of Figure 5.B.2.

source	df	Mean square	F
device/ treatment	3	0.015	18.297**
error	28	0.001	

Tukey post hoc tests significant at p < 0.05.

Comparison	p-value
F-2	
> o-2	0.000
> j-2	0.023
C-2	
> o-2	0.000
> j-2	0.015
j-2	0.020
> o-2	

CHAPTER 6

Conditioning and Transformation of the Experimental Space

What Does Space Conditioning Mean?

This chapter is directed to the recording of an important milestone in our ongoing research concerning IIED's. In particular, significant experimental data has been gathered to show that some type of "conditioning" process occurs in a local volume of D-space (see Chapter 2) around an activated IIED as a function of processing time. One consequence of this is that a significantly stronger coupling appears to occur between the physical domain and higher dimensional domains of nature (particularly R-space, see Chapter 2). This conditioning effect manifests itself, after some initial incubation-processing period, as significantly altered D-space behavior as measured over time in the processed locale. This is contrasted with the same measurements being made in any of several locales more than 20-50 feet removed from the processed site. Figure 6.1 illustrates a version of this

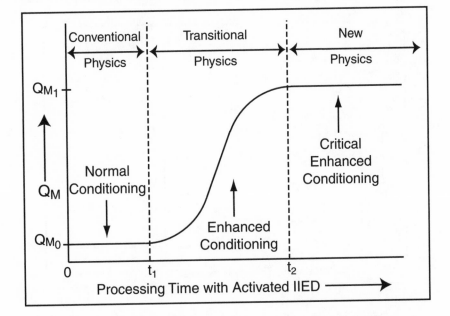

Figure 6.1   *For any typical physical measurement, **Q**, the qualitative magnitude change, **Q$_M$**, is plotted versus the degree of locale conditioning produced by continued IIED use.*

behavior for some generalized physical measurement of magnitude Q_M. Here, for processing times less than t_1, no change is detectable by our instruments and $Q_M = Q_{M_0}$. However, for processing times between t_1 and t_2, a variety of transitional behaviors (many of an oscillatory nature) are observed for Q_M. Finally, for processing times longer than t_2, the space conditioning seems to have reached a plateau wherein, even with the IIED removed and stored in an electrically grounded Faraday cage, the conditioning seems to remain fairly constant for very long periods of time in that locale (for over a year in one of our conditioned spaces). It is certainly possible that a series of successively higher plateaus may exist at even longer processing times.

Because of the time-varying conditioning associated with the consciousness imbedded in the IIED's, a dynamical change in properties of the medium is occurring during the course of our measurements. On the one hand, this is difficult to deal with since one likes to achieve easy reproducibility of measured data. On the other hand, it is exciting because it implies that the locale level of "effective" consciousness provides a moving baseline upon which physical measurements rest. This is, perhaps, what one should expect if this effective consciousness is able to change the level of order inherent in the R-space band of the vacuum. Such changes in the coherence level of the vacuum automatically change the ground state values of fundamental particles, atoms

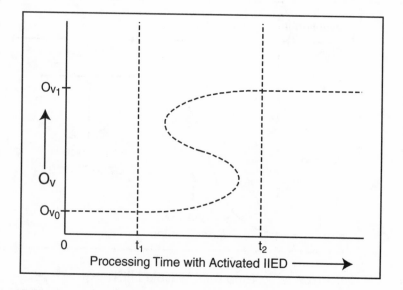

Figure 6.2 Qualitative illustration of how the degree of ordering in the vacuum, O_{v}, changes with conditioning time by an activated IIED.

and molecules of D-space matter. In fact, here, we may be seeing a kind of ordering transition or structural phase change occurring at the coarsest level of the vacuum (R-space) with increasing IIED processing of the locale. If we define the degree of vacuum order as O_V, then Figure 6.2 might illustrate how O_V changes from O_{V_0} to O_{V_1} via a classical, non-linear, cooperative phenomenon. This phase transition to a two-phase vacuum domain, with changing volume fraction of the more ordered phase, would indeed lead to transitional property measurements with our physical instruments.

As we presently see it, the total coupling effect, Q_C, between D-space materials and the vacuum appears to involve three main contributions that are loosely connected in the following approximate relationship:

$$Q_C \approx Q_D + Q_{LS} + Q_E \approx \tag{6.1a}$$

$$(Q_D' - \int_{t_1}^{t_2} q_D dt) + (Q_{LS}' - \int_{t_1}^{t_2} q_{LS} dt) + (\int_{t_1}^{t_3} Q_E' dt - \int_{t_1}^{t_2} q_E dt) \tag{6.1b}$$

where the subscripts D, LS and E stand for device, local space and experimenter, respectively. If Q_E is positive (inner self-managed and optimistic experimenters as distinct from negative experimenters) and Q_D is positive (still retains some of its imprint charge), then Q_{LS} grows with time and appears to behave as a consciousness storage system. Thus, Q_C grows with time because the locale is being "pumped" by both the IIED and the experimenter (just as optical pumping can produce excited states in a collection of atoms which, under the proper conditions, can emit bursts or continuous streams of coherent light). In the experimental data to follow, all three of the terms on the RHS of Equation 6.1a are important and $Q_C(t)$ is an increasing, and seemingly nonlinearly-increasing, function of time.

Equation 6.1b has been written to express two important facts, (1) each of the terms in Equation 6.1a contains an intrinsic leakage rate factor with the particular q_j being that rate over the time interval t_1 to t_2 with the Q_j' being the Q_j-value at the time t_1 and (2) the Q_E term involves not just the experimenter, who may be present in the locale only for the time increment (t_3-t_1), much smaller than the experiment interval (t_2-t_1), but the other humans who enter/leave/reside in that space. Thus, although Q_E may be strongly positive, for a small ratio $(t_3-t_1)/t_2-t_1)$ and a significant negative value for q_E, what we have called the Q_E-factor may turn out to be appreciably negative. By the end of this chapter we will see that all the equipment must enter Equations 6.1 as a fourth contributing factor.

Some Experimental Indicators of Space Conditioning

In this section, three branches of experimental measurements of Q_M in the transitional region of Figure 6.1 are reported on: (1) the pH of water is found to be significantly different in the presence of a DC north-pole vs. a south-pole magnet facing the water. Such a DC magnet polarity behavior is absolutely denied by the existing U(1) gauge theory of magnetism where the magnetic force is proportional to the divergence of the <u>square</u> of the magnetic field strength (so the sign of the field disappears), (2) Temperature (T)-oscillations, pH-oscillations and electrical conductivity (σ)-oscillations of significant magnitude and meaningful shape are observed in this conditioned locale and (3) strongly correlated oscillation behavior appears to be readily transferable from one conditioned locale to another conditioned locale ~ 25 to 125 feet apart even when both vessels of water were located inside their own electrically grounded Faraday cages.

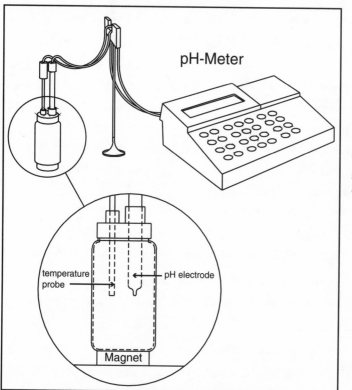

Figure 6.3

Experimental set-up for testing changes due to a DC magnet placed under the water vessel with either the N-pole or the S-pole axially and vertically aligned.

<u>DC Magnetic Field Polarity Effects</u>:   Although this was not the chronologically first evidence for conditioning to be discovered, à la Figure 6.1, it is the most revealing because it flies so strongly in the face of conventional physics. Using the experimental apparatus illustrated in Figure 6.3, one can easily change the DC magnetic field polarity without altering the basic cylindrical symmetry of this field.

     When one conducts this pH experiment in a typical laboratory environment where normal coupling holds, one observes two things, (a) there is no measurable difference between the north-pole "up" case versus the south-pole "up" case and (b) there is no measurable pH change in the water for either

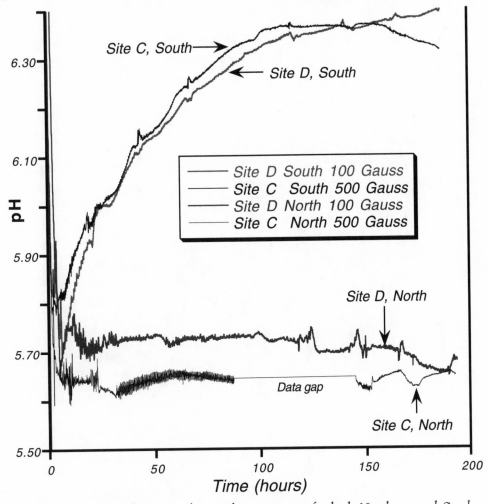

Figure 6.4   pH changes with time for pure water for both N-pole up and S-pole up axially aligned DC magnetic fields at 100 and 500 gauss. See Figure 6.10 for relative locations of sites C and D.

field polarity for field strengths less than 500 Gauss ($\delta pH = \pm\, 0.02$ pH unit is the measurement accuracy, the resolution being 0.001 pH unit). On the other hand, when one makes such measurements in a conditioned locale, the results can be remarkably different. There, one may find a marked difference for $\Delta pH_S^N = pH(S) - pH(N)$. Figure 6.4 shows an example wherein ΔpH_S^N grows in magnitude with the passage of time attaining a maximum value of $\sim$ 0.6 pH units after about 6 days. In other partially conditioned locales, ΔpH_S^N ~ 1.0 pH units and ~ -0.15 pH units have been observed. Later, in another section, we return to conditioning effects on ΔpH_S^N and DC magnetic field polarity effects on conditioning.

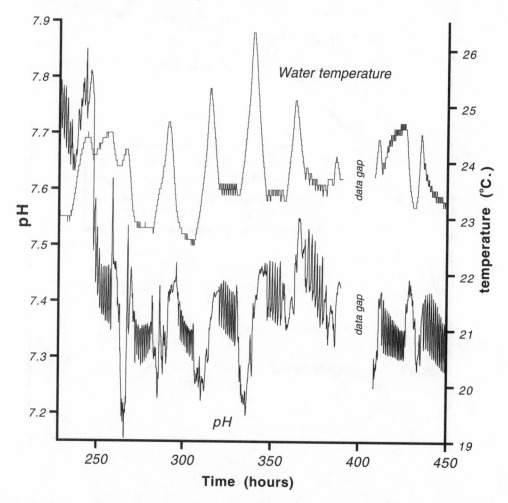

Figure 6.5   *pH and temperature changes with time for pure water containing fine-grained $ZnCO_3$ particulates in a partially conditioned space. The plots reveal both long, τ_L, and short, τ_S, periods of undulation.*

<u>Property Oscillations in the Water Vessel and in the Air:</u>   Picking up on the story where Chapter 3 left off, the second branch of experimental data confirming the existence of locale conditioning is that associated with time-varying oscillations in pH, temperature (T) and electrical conductivity (σ) of the water with both short term periods, τ_S, in the 20-100 minute range (1 cycle/hour = 0.28 millihertz) and long term periods, τ_L, on the time scale of ~1 day. Figure 6.5 provides us with a long time record of T- and pH-oscillations with some obvious correlation between them. The presence of the small $ZnCO_3$ particulates in the water appears to enhance the oscillation amplitude.   These τ_S oscillations exhibit amplitudes ~ 25 times the measurement accuracy of the monitoring system with a chemical energy fluctuation magnitude sometimes as large as ~ 0.6 kT for pH oscillations alone. For water temperature oscillations, thermal energy fluctuation magnitudes up to 2.5 kT have been recorded, a truly robust figure.

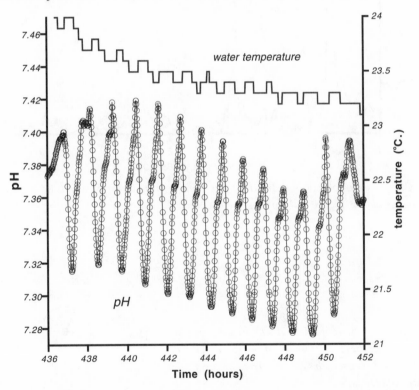

Figure 6.6   *An expanded short interval from Figure 6.5 to illustrate the regularity of the τ_S-oscillations. Note the inverse correlation between pH-oscillations and temperature fluctuations.*

Figure 6.6 shows an expanded waveset of pH-oscillations from the pH time plot depicted in Figure 6.5 (near the end) and one can note the well-

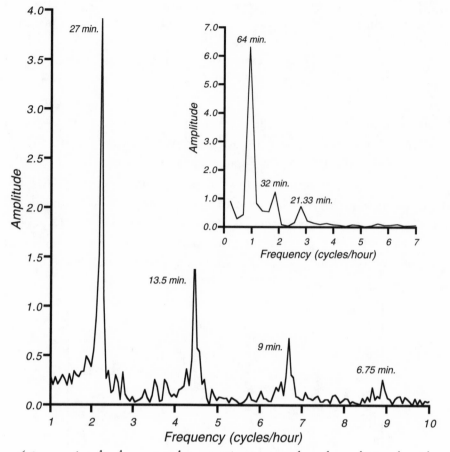

Figure 6.7   Amplitude spectra data via Fourier transform for real-time data depicted in the lowest plot in Figure 6.4 and Figure 6.6 (inset).

Figure 6.8   Schematic illustration of air temperature probe locations relative to a centrally located water vessel in an electrically grounded Faraday cage.

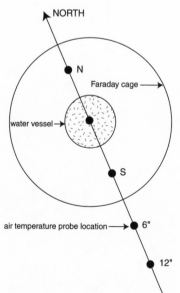

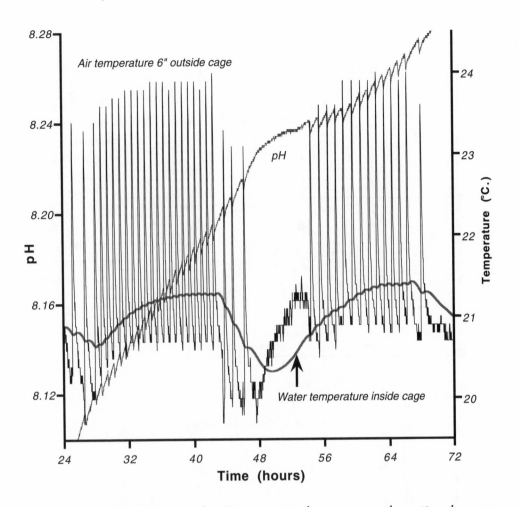

Figure 6.9a   Pure water with ZnCO₃ particulates in vessel in Faraday cage. Simultaneous measurement of air and water temperature plus pH in the Figure 6.8 configuration at the Barn location (location A in Figure 6.10) on 5/12/99 to 5/13/99. Note the precise frequency correlation for the three variables.

defined and characteristic wave shape. A frequency spectrum for the wave components making up this wave shape can be obtained by determining the amplitude spectrum for the data shown in Figure 6.6. This result is shown in Figure 6.7 (inset) where the fundamental and the first few harmonics are seen (64 minute fundamental period). Another example of such an amplitude spectrum is shown in the main part of Figure 6.7 that is calculated for the pH oscillations shown in the lowest plot of Figure 6.4. Typically, the short period waveforms involve ~ 1-6 major harmonics. <u>In a locale with normal conditioning, no such oscillations have ever been observed.</u> For completeness, see Figure 6.14 for an example of σ-oscillations (the upper plot).

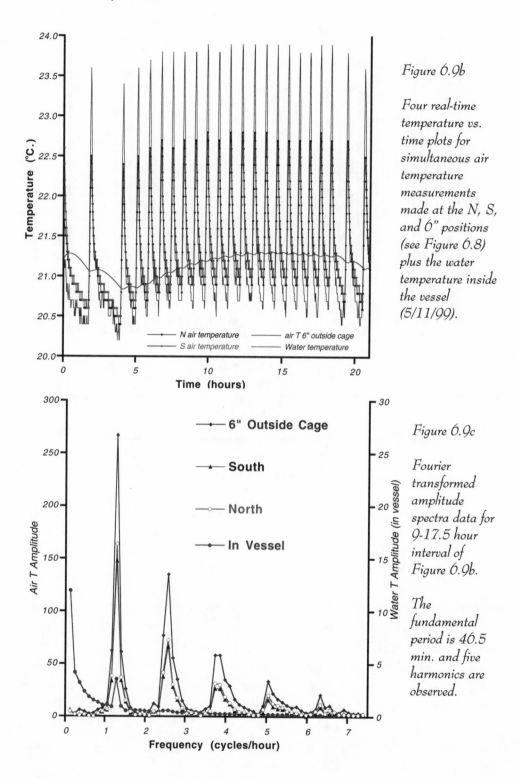

Figure 6.9b

Four real-time temperature vs. time plots for simultaneous air temperature measurements made at the N, S, and 6" positions (see Figure 6.8) plus the water temperature inside the vessel (5/11/99).

Figure 6.9c

Fourier transformed amplitude spectra data for 9-17.5 hour interval of Figure 6.9b.

The fundamental period is 46.5 min. and five harmonics are observed.

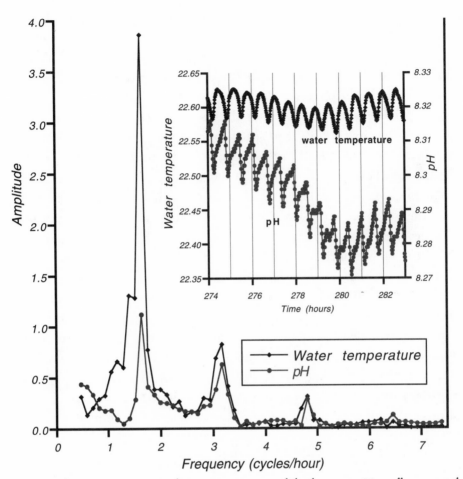

Figure 6.9d   Fourier transform comparison of both water T-oscillation and pH-oscillation data in the water vessel of Figure 6.8 on 5/10/99. Real-time oscillation data shown in inset. The fundamental period is 36.6 min. and three harmonics can be easily discerned.

To demonstrate both simultaneous water and air T- oscillations and the correlation between them, a Faraday cage with a central water vessel (containing $ZnCO_3$ particulates) was set up in the conditioned space. High-resolution digital thermometers were located with the local geometry shown in Figure 6.8. Figure 6.9a shows the air T-oscillations at the 6 inch location outside the cage plus the water temperature and pH in the vessel inside the cage. Figure 6.9b is an expanded view of data collected just before that shown in Figure 6.9a. Figure 6.9c shows the amplitude spectrum for part of this data (from hour 9 to hour 17.5) plus that for the simultaneous water data. These air T-oscillations are huge ($\sim$ 230 times our best measurement accuracy and $\sim$ 3500 times the resolution) and all have the same well-defined waveform. Figure 6.9d illustrates comparative amplitude spectra data for simultaneous T- and pH-oscillations taken in this vessel of water two days earlier (oscillation data shown in inset). Again, the same wave shape is exhibited for these two material properties. This is <u>not</u> the expected behavior for a purely D-space phenomenon.

One of the major discoveries of this work was the onset of air T-oscillations as the first indicator of space conditioning. These oscillations (as well as pH- and σ-oscillations) often continue long after the IIED causing the conditioning has been removed and the oscillations often continue to grow in amplitude somewhat thereafter (but it is also common experience that they decay in amplitude in some locations). Every different experimental space seems to develop somewhat unique behavior relative to the type, magnitude and duration of oscillations resulting from IIED-use experiments. The temperatures were measured using three different kinds of probes, (1) least often, we employed manual measurements based on the thermal expansion of mercury (a mercury thermometer), (2) often, computer-monitored measurements using high-resolution thermister-based, digital thermometers were used and (3) low-resolution thermisters were often used as well. <u>These different methods, depending on relative accuracy and resolution, produced basically the same results</u>. This important fact strongly suggests that the oscillations observed are not an artifact of the measuring equipment.

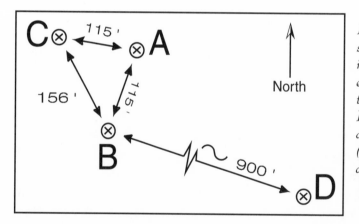

Figure 6.10 Geometrical site map (D-space) for intention-transmission experiments. Site A is the transmitting site with IIED while sites B, C, and D are receiving sites (no IIED), all located in different buildings.

<u>Air T-Oscillation Waveform Symmetry At Different Locations</u>: At the Minnesota facility, our experiments were conducted at four well-separated sites which we will designate as A, B, C and D (A=barn ~ 115 feet from B=Ditron office which is ~ 156 feet from C=lab and ~ 900 feet from D=Life Science office) located geometrically as shown in Figure 6.10. At each site, water pH-IIED's had been operated and, after site conditioning occurred and oscillations appeared, it became clear that each site was unique regarding the <u>shape</u> of oscillation waveform that developed and persisted there.

Three basic waveforms, related to the various kinds of T-oscillation triggering and annihilation mechanisms operating at sites A and B, have been observed. These are depicted in Figure 6.11a and are typical of air T-oscillations with periods of 45 minutes or greater. One often observes changes from type ii to it's mirror image, type i, as the oscillation frequency declines. The relationship between type i and type iii is more complicated. Which oscillation waveform type develops appears to depend upon its periodicity and, to complicate matters, on what objects are brought into the space (see Figure 6.25). Further, the type i oscillation waveform is triggered by temperature increases from some minimum value and annihilated by a sudden decrease in temperature while type iii oscillations are triggered by falling temperatures and annihilated by a sudden temperature increase. The A-

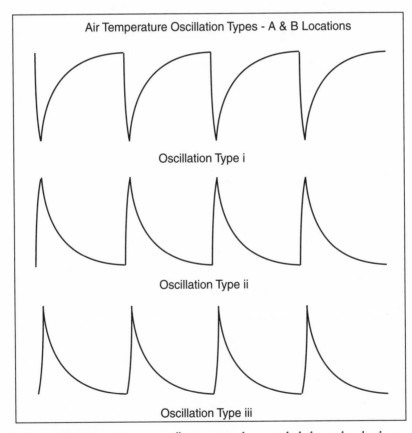

Figure 6.11a   Air temperature oscillation waveforms (slightly stylized) that superpose the diurnal variation. Recordings from the A & B locations.

location is a converted barn and large amplitude air, T-oscillations developed there after IIED use. However, after discontinuing use of IIED's in that space, after 3 months, the air, T-oscillation amplitude decreased and faded out to zero by the end of 6 months. Such behavior is in marked contrast to that at site B where large amplitude oscillations continued for well over a year after discontinuing IIED use at this location. At the moment, we attribute this difference to the Q_E-term in Equation 6.1; however, site B predominantly exhibits the type i, air, T-oscillation type while site A exhibits the type ii, air, T-oscillation type.

Two different rooms at site D were utilized for the water-IIED research and each eventually manifested high-amplitude air, T-oscillations. Room (a) at site D is the location of the space conditioning experiment shown in Figure 6.27a while Room (b) at site D corresponds to the location for the pH-lowering IIED experiment, 25 feet away. The types of air, T-oscillation waveforms manifesting in these two rooms at site D are substantially different from <u>any</u> oscillation observed at site B (see Figure 6.11b). The D-site came into use much later than site B and did not have as much history concerning IIED use. The frequency-modulated wave trains (discussed below) seen at site B were only very rarely observed at site D. At site D, mainly air, T-oscillation triggering via temperature increases was seen while oscillation-annihilation via temperature declines was the norm.

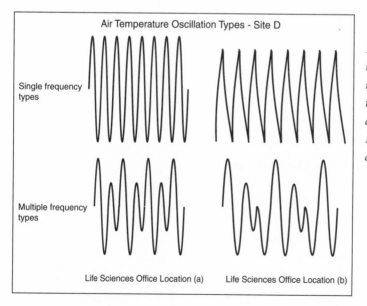

Figure 6.11b   Air temperature oscillation waveforms (stylized) that superpose the diurnal variation. Recordings from 2 sites at the D location.

<u>**Wave Oscillation Trains**</u>: A question that might be asked when the oscillations described in this work are closely examined is "Do these oscillations

look similar to anything anyone else has observed?" The answer is both yes and no. These oscillations are, on the surface, remarkably similar to oscillations discovered by chemical engineers and chemists working with relatively complex chemical reactions that begin at a thermodynamic state far from equilibrium. However, in our case we are working with the very simple systems of purified water and standard air at what is supposed to be at least very close to thermodynamic equilibrium (provided one neglects the "intention" statement). We will discuss the industrial chemical oscillation phenomenon as a part of Chapter 7 while, here, our remarks will be limited to the type of wave envelope modulation and overall envelope shape that are observed in our oscillation wave trains that often appear to occur as bursts.

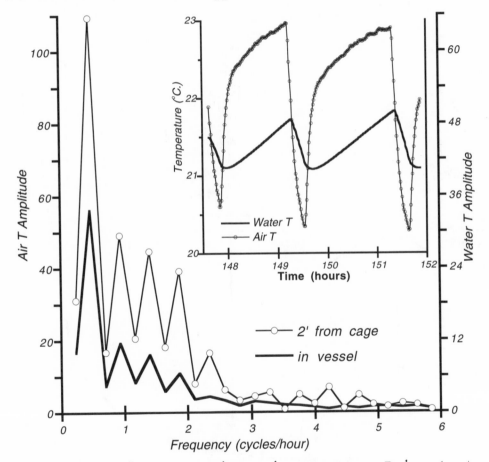

Figure 6.12a   Oscillation sequences for air and water temperature. Real-time (inset) and amplitude spectra data for site B with 0.01 M MgSO₄ solution inside a Faraday cage (Aug. 21-22, 1999). The air temperature probe is 2 feet outside the cage.

Figure 6.12a is an expanded view of two waves in a wave train of oscillations, for both the water temperature in a vessel centered in a Faraday cage and for the air temperature two feet outside the cage. Note the air temperature oscillation waveform is Type i from Figure 6.11a. In Figure 6.12b, from measurements made two days later, the right hand insert shows a complete wave train where the oscillation period increases almost exponentially with oscillation cycle in the wave train. The change of oscillation period with oscillation cycle in the wave train is given in the main portion of Figure 6.12b while mathematical analysis (left inset) of the oscillation frequency vs. oscillation cycle in the wave train shows that a parabolic relationship holds between these two characteristics with a very high level of accuracy. Further, from this left inset, extrapolating to a 10th oscillation in this wave train would require a <u>negative</u> oscillation frequency. This is probably why the wave train terminates after the 9th oscillation.

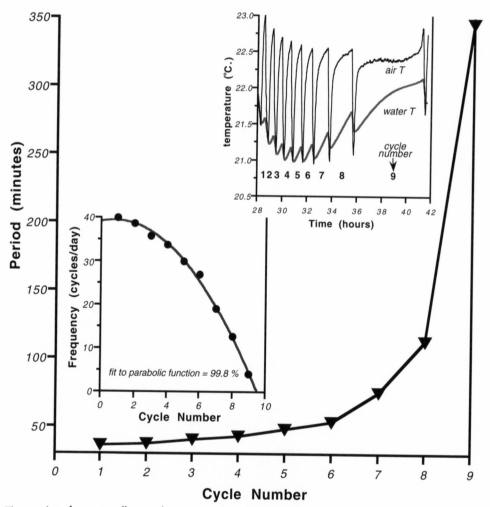

Figure 6.12b   Oscillation form, period and parabolic fit for frequency as a function of oscillation cycle in the wave (Aug. 24-25, 1999).

Figure 6.12c, from measurements made a few days later, shows another highly accurate parabolic fit between oscillation frequency and cycle number in the wave train. This time, however, we find both an ascending and a descending branch in this parabolic relationship. The important point to be drawn from the data shown in Figs. 6.12b and 6.12c is that something very lawful is causing these wave trains to exhibit the cycle characteristics that they

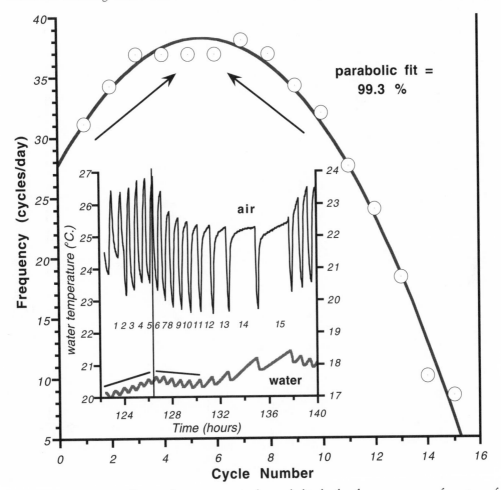

Figure 6.12c   Oscillation form (inset) and parabolic fit for frequency as a function of oscillation cycle in the wave (Aug. 28-29, 1999). An analogue in chemical oscillations would have the reaction affinity increasing and decreasing. The increasing limb of the parabola (increasing reaction affinity in the chemical oscillation case) meets the decreasing limb (decreasing reaction affinity) near cycle number 6. From the inset it can be observed that the change in the slope of temperature change (dT/dt) also occurs near cycle number 6. If this were an oscillating chemical system, therefore, the sign of the reaction affinity would depend on the sign of dT/dt. Also, once again, the frequency goes negative after cycle number 15.

do. Some, yet to be discovered, process in nature is causing this behavior. As a preview of the chemical oscillation segment given in Chapter 7, Figure 6.13 reveals a startling comparison between our data and a particular chemical oscillation model. However, a direct correspondence between the oscillations we observe and standard chemical oscillations is unlikely considering the characteristics of the data presented in Figure 6.12c.

As a space evolves from normal conditioning to enhanced conditioning to critically enhanced conditioning (Figure 6.1) we expect to see oscillation characteristics also evolve with time in some way. As coupling between D-space and R-space increases into the transitional region illustrated in Figure 6.2, considerable complexity is expected to manifest in the measurement of physical

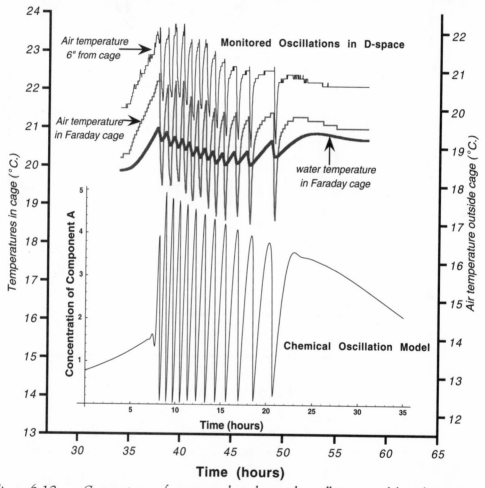

Figure 6.13   Comparison of a particular chemical oscillation model with air T-oscillations inside and outside a Faraday cage that contains a vessel of aqueous solution. Water T-oscillations inside cage also shown.

properties which is perhaps reflected in the richness and complexity of the oscillations we have observed.

Table 6.1   Oscillation Characteristics in Strongly-coupled Spaces

1.   A variety of simultaneous, correlated oscillations in material properties occur only in strongly coupled conditioned spaces.

2.   Oscillations have very well-defined and easily characterized frequency, amplitude and waveform behavior.

3.   Oscillations exhibit a well-defined triggering signature usually related to the sign of dT/dt.

4.   Frequency modulation is commonly observed and, if present, well-defined.

5.   Oscillations are affected by:
     a.   Water composition (both ionic and solid particulate components).
     b.   Experimental-setup and position and composition of parts of the experimental apparatus in the near-field (strong-coupling) region.
     c.   Temperature of immediate environment (near field) and sometimes direction of temperature change (sign of dT/dt).

6.   Oscillations are unaffected by:
     a.   Presence of objects and people just outside strong-coupling region (far field).
     b.   Motion of objects or people just outside strong-coupling region (far field).
     c.   Opening/closing of doors and windows outside strongly coupled region (far field) except as it affects 5c.
     d.   Running of heaters, air conditioners or fans except as they affect 5c.
     e.   Experiments operating in far field.
     f.   Downloading data from experimental apparatus and other periodic monitoring procedures.

Other Important Features of These Oscillations: Table 6.1 provides a list of the oscillation characteristics for conditioned locales. The first four items have already been addressed, so let us now briefly consider item 5 in Table 6.1. For purely ionic solutions at 0.01 M concentration, $MgSO_4$ additions increase the oscillation amplitude over that found for purified water, KCl additions do not change the oscillation amplitude much and $KClO_4$ additions decrease the oscillation amplitude. This is exactly the ordering of the structure temperature, t_{str}, at 20°C found for aqueous solutions of electrolytes (at 1 mole/liter); i.e., $t_{str}(KClO_4) > t_{str}(KCl) > t_{str}(MgSO_4)$.

Most of the earlier experiments were conducted with a small addition of $ZnCO_3$ particles added to the purified water (see also Chapter 3) and this type of solution was found to exhibit both expanding and contracting oscillation trains with a pH-decreasing IIED. On the other hand, solutions with colloid/sediment size particles of SiO_2 were found to exhibit primarily expanding (undamped) oscillation trains with use of a pH-increasing IIED. To further test the idea that the presence of particulates of high specific surface area (small particle size) might somehow influence the action of an IIED on the pH of the solution, one gram of high purity (Merck grade 7754) silica powder (surface area 550 m^2/gm) was added to 250 ml of purified water. Measurements were initiated immediately after the particles had settled and a pH-increasing IIED turned on in an already partially conditioned locale. As a

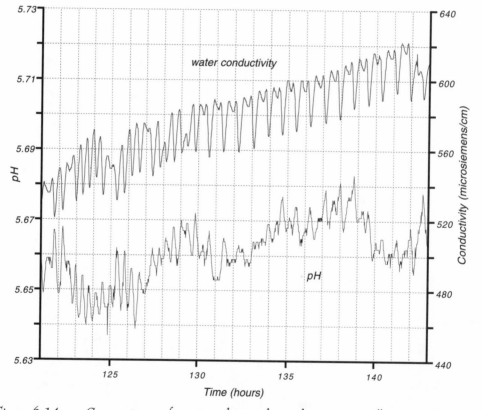

Figure 6.14   Comparison of water electrical conductivity oscillations with pH oscillations in a control solution (no IIED exposure) consisting of silica particles in purified water (ASTM Type 1). Note oscillations are π out-of-phase between pH and σ.

result, pH oscillations were observed immediately and eventually developed some of the largest amplitudes seen to date.

Three control experiments were conducted without the IIED and no pH changes markedly different from the equilibrium pH were noted in this partially conditioned locale. In two of the controls, both pH-oscillations and σ-oscillations (π out-of-phase) were observed (see Figure 6.14). Both of these are consistent with an oscillating dissociation constant so that, as the pH decreases, the ion concentration increases and the electrical conductivity also increases. In the third control, at a remote location, no oscillations were ever observed. In that experiment, the container was shaken a few times to re-suspend the particles. This led to downward pH spikes that shortly returned to the value present before shaking.

In the SiO_2-particle experiment performed with the pH-increasing IIED, a robust effect quickly occurred in accord with the imprinted intention with a maximum pH increase of 0.6 pH units and pH-oscillations of 0.125 pH units. In a later experiment using the pH-increasing IIED, the pH-oscillation amplitude increased to 0.25 pH units as the pH rose in accord with the imprinted intention. The addition of particulates to water may make the solution a more sensitive indicator of space conditioning via pH measurements. A common observation during experiments monitoring the water pH was the consistent and repeated decrease in pH-oscillation amplitudes with time particularly for <u>pure water</u>. For pure water with added particulates, the decrease in oscillation amplitudes with time was less evident (see Figure 6.5).

As indicated in Table 6.1, these oscillations appear to be unaffected by the presence of motion of objects or people located just outside the conditioned locale (the far-field region). Likewise, the running of heaters, air conditioners, fans or experiments in this far-field seems to produce no appreciable change in the oscillations within the conditioned locale so long as they do not measurably alter the ambient rate of temperature change within the conditioned locale.

For a critically conditioned locale ($t > t_2$ in Figure 6.2), the IIED can be removed from the locale, wrapped in aluminum foil and stored in a grounded Faraday cage and, still, the locale will continue to exhibit oscillations. This is a defining signature for a critically conditioned locale. A closing but important observation to this section is that a conditioned locale seems to be behaving very much like a finely tuned system which depends on both the positional configuration as well as the chemical and structural composition of the various parts for the whole experimental set-up. For example, if the conditioned computer is removed and replaced with a new one, the oscillations generally disappear for ~ 10 hours before returning. Likewise, the introduction of certain specific materials, even of very small volume, into a conditioned locale can cause the oscillations to disappear for weeks.

Communication Between Distant Vessels of Water: Figure 6.10 indicates the geometrical and spatial arrangement of the four experimental sites involved in this particular study. Temperature and pH were recorded at each site using purified water with added $ZnCO_3$ particulates as the intention transmitting and receiving medium. Placing a pH-monitored vessel

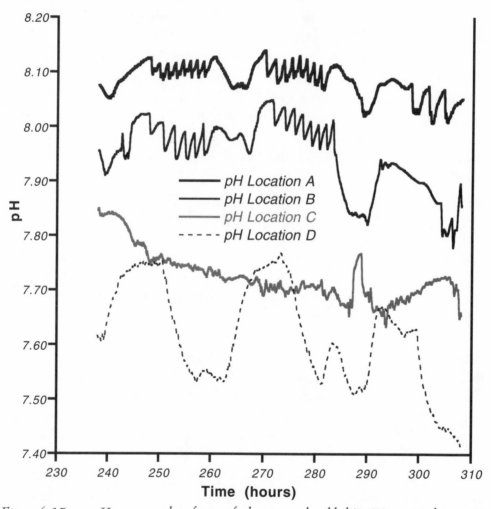

Figure 6.15a   pH vs. time plots for purified water with added $ZnCO_3$ particulates. pH oscillation correlation between the various sites of Figure 6.10. The IIED was located only at site A with site B being strongly conditioned while sites C and D were only marginally conditioned.

at position A and another pH-monitored vessel at position B, we found that for the two sites being conditioned locales and no IIEDs being used, when oscillations appear in the water vessel at site A, synchronized oscillations appear in the vessel of water at site B. When locale B is conditioned but locale D is not, then synchronized oscillations still appear at site B highly correlated with those at A but unsynchronized activity appears in the vessel of water at D (see Figure 6.15a and a smaller segment in Fig 6.15b).

A very significant add-on to these observations regarding spatially distant but correlated oscillation behavior is that the correlations still occur when the water vessels at sites A, B, C and D are inside individual, electrically-grounded Faraday cages. However, the actual pH-meter is outside the cage in each case. In all, 12 intention-transmission measurements were performed (three experiments at four sites) with their important results being summarized

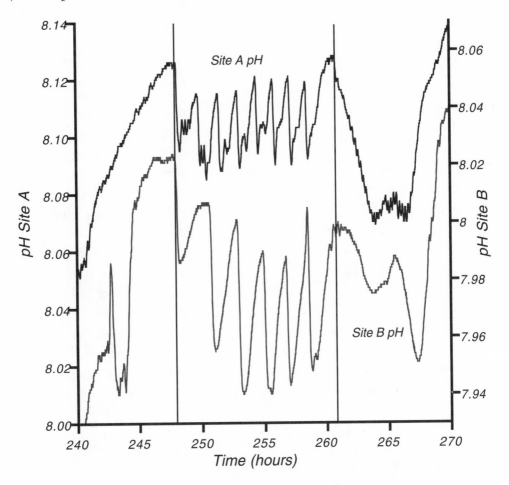

Figure 6.15b   More detailed view of a segment of Figure 6.15a.

in Table 6.2. These results are affected to a large extent by the previous history of each site relative to local IIED use. At the beginning, sites A and C were completely new experimental locations and, early on, showed no evidence of site conditioning. Site D had a very small amount of prior use while site B had, by far, the longest IIED use history.

Table 6.2   Results for the three intention-transmission experiments.

Location	First Transmission		Second Transmission		Third Transmission	
	% drop	Amplitude	% drop	Amplitude	% drop	Amplitude
A	60	0	90	0.1	>100	0.11
B	60	0.05	100	0.1	90	0.085
C	50	0	65	0.005	60	0.015
D	30	0.015	70	0	80	0

In Table 6.2, the % drop represents the maximum measured decrease in pH as a percentage of the imprinted intention. The amplitude represents the maximum amplitude (in pH units) observed (peak to trough) of higher frequency (period < 1 hour) pH oscillations.

First Transmission Experiment: This first series of experiments utilized an unshielded IIED placed next to a water bottle containing $ZnCO_3$ particles at site A as transmitter with similar bottles at the other three sites as receivers. At site A, although appreciable pH lowering occurred, no short-period pH-oscillations developed in 18 days of monitoring and 9 days of IIED operation (consistent with zero initial conditioning). During this same time frame, site C exhibited no short-period pH-oscillations consistent with it being an unconditioned site; however, it did exhibit significant pH lowering. This implies either that pH lowering doesn't require any locale conditioning provided an activated IIED is ~ 115 feet away or that pH lowering and pH-oscillations are involved with distinctly different types of locale conditioning.

An interesting observation regarding the oscillations was that, for pH drops less than 80% of the imprinted intention, the oscillation amplitudes are trivially small. However, for pH drops more than 80% of the intention target, the oscillation amplitude and continuity increased dramatically.

Second Transmission Experiment: Using   freshly   prepared, unshielded samples of purified water plus $ZnCO_3$ particles at all sites, Table 6.2 shows us that significant pH-oscillations began appearing at sites A, B and C but disappeared at site D. At site A, where oscillations had never appeared before, pH-oscillations with well-developed waveforms suddenly appeared and

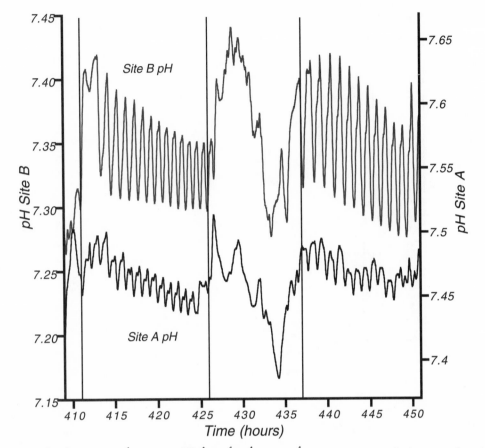

Figure 6.16a   Simultaneous pH data for the second intention-transmission experiment. Real-time data for sites A and B.

eventually developed amplitudes of 0.1 pH units. The most significant difference between this experiment and its predecessor was the much larger pH drops relative to the imprinted intention observed in this series.

<u>**Third Transmission Experiment**</u>:   Here, the freshly prepared bottle of purified water plus $ZnCO_3$ particles at site A was placed in a Faraday cage while those at sites B, C and D were unshielded. Oscillations in both pH and T appeared immediately in the water of sites A and B and eventually at site C but not at site D. Figures 6.16a and 6.16b reveal pH-oscillation correlations between sites A and B. One notes the larger amplitude oscillations at site B (a well-conditioned site) compared to site A (a partially-conditioned site) with the

IIED located nearby. This suggests that conditioning generates some type of amplification process for the basic oscillations.

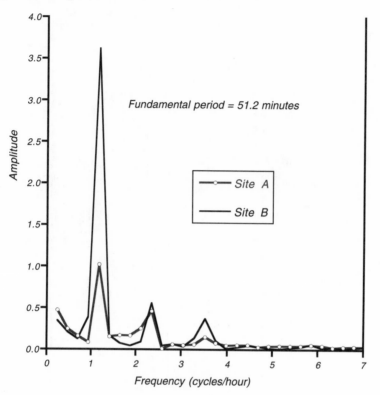

Figure 6.16b   Amplitude spectra via Fourier transform of a 4.25 hour segment of data shown in Figure 6.16a starting at hour 420.

Some Specific Experiments with Conditioned Spaces

<u>Mechanical Fan Experiment</u>:   This experiment was conducted in an already conditioned space (site B of Figure 6.10) which had been manifesting significant, high-amplitude oscillations in T and pH for over a year (because many IIED-water experiments had been previously conducted in that room for ~ 1 1/2 years). The focus of this experiment was to see if the air T-oscillations would be strongly influenced by forced air convection from a mechanical fan. If it were a typical D-space, air density phenomenon, one would expect the oscillations to disappear. If they did not disappear, then we should learn something about the domain wherein these oscillations were being generated.

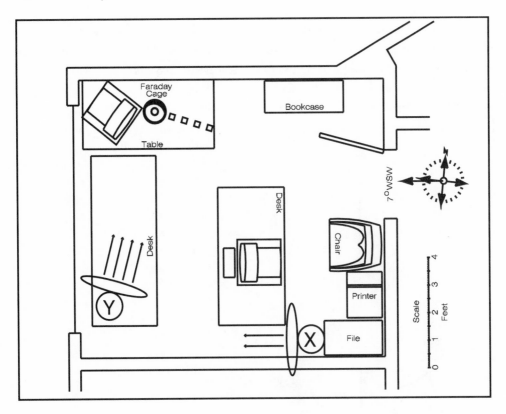

Figure 6.17a   Forced convection experiment at site B. A mechanical fan was positioned to perturb the air around a series of aligned temperature measurement probes. Fan location positions (X is on the floor, Y is on a desk) relative to the water vessel in a Faraday cage on upper left table top and a line of temperature probes (small boxes) 6 inches apart.

The furniture arrangement in the experiment room, including both the location of the water vessel inside its Faraday cage (FC) adjacent to its computer and the two fan locations, X (on the floor) and Y (on a desktop) is shown in Figure 6.17a. Figure 6.17b is an expanded view of the FC with its water vessel plus a few locations along a radial line at which temperature probes were placed for T-oscillation measurement. Initial measurements outside the FC occurred at 6-inch intervals out to 2 feet (about 8 in. above the tabletop). Later, measurements were extended out to 11 feet. High resolution, digital-thermometers (resolution = 0.001°C) were used in the water and at 1 foot outside the cage. Lower resolution, digital-thermometers (resolution = 0.1°C) were used in the air inside the cage and at 1.5 and 2.0 feet outside the cage. All measurements were computer monitored. Earlier measurements showed that the major floor-ceiling air temperature gradients occurred between the floor and ~ 3-4 feet above the floor so we started with the fan at position X (on the floor) and operated it for 55 hours. Later, the fan was moved to position Y and operated for 42 hours. For most of the data to be shown in subsequent figures, the peak to trough ΔT for the T-oscillations was averaged over 6-12 cycles and recorded.

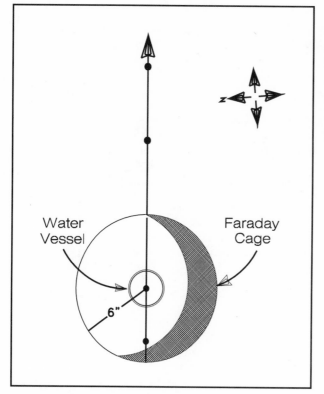

Figure 6.17b   Detailed schematic drawing of temperature probes relative to Faraday cage and water vessel and their relationship to true North. Position of temperature probes shown as black circles.

For comparison purposes, a 24-hour period, real-time record of the T-oscillations for the three cases of (1) no fan, (2) fan at X and (3) fan at Y are given in Figure 6.18. Thus, it seems clear that these oscillations neither cease nor change in a significant way due to the operation of the fan. It is also clear that the oscillation ΔT-excursion is a large percentage (sometimes 100%) of the total diurnal temperature variation in this room.

In contrast to the relatively unchanging waveform behavior, the relative amplitude (peak-to-trough) distribution with distance from the edge of the FC was modified in an interesting and significant manner. Such averages were determined for a position 2 in. inside the cage and at several positions outside the cage (see Figure 6.19a for the pre-fan case and Figure 6.19b for the post-fan case). The same basic pattern is observed for both cases. Here, the highest amplitudes are always observed in the air inside the cage with the minimum amplitude at one foot outside the cage. The amplitude then increases at greater distances from the cage. Interestingly, the only effect of the fan was to

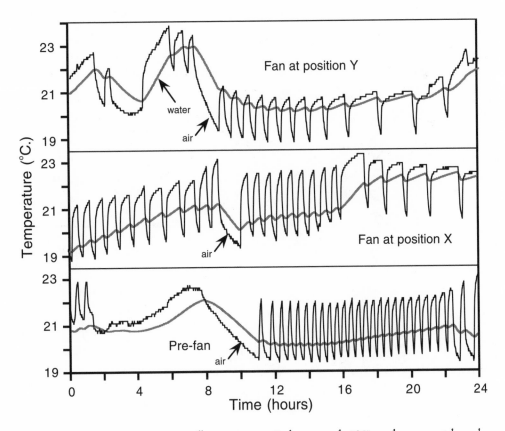

Figure 6.18   Temperature oscillations in air (1 foot outside FC) and water, with and without the fan operating.

produce an increased day-to-day variance in the amplitude distribution.

Using a shorter time scale for initial observations, an oscillation amplitude perturbation with distance was observed (see Figures 6.20a & 6.20b). From Figure 6.20a, with the fan at position X, the first oscillation observations after the fan started operating (1st sequence, Δt ~ 5-10 hrs.) gave the lowest amplitude inside the cage and this increased to a maximum at one foot outside the cage. However, with continued use of the fan at X for a number of days (sequences 2 to 4), the results of Figs. 6.19 were gradually reestablished. Moving the fan to Y, about 7 feet from the temperature probes and with the air flowing directly towards the T-probes, the velocity of airflow was sufficient to displace letter-sized pieces of paper lying next to the T-probes. Again a temperature amplitude vs. distance inversion occurred just as in Figure 6.20a, but much more subdued. Immediately after the fan was deactivated, the former amplitude/distance relationship was reestablished (see Figure 6.20b).

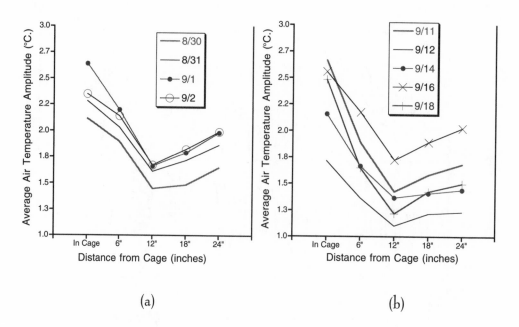

Figure 6.19   Average air, T-oscillation amplitude vs. position relative to the FC in Figure 6.17, (a) pre-fan condition and (b) post-fan condition.

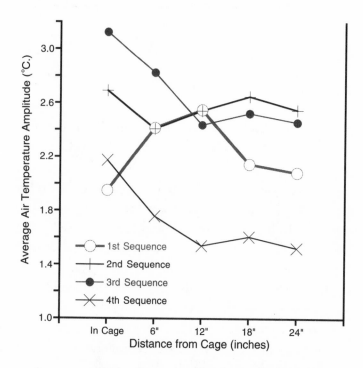

Figure 20a   Average air, T-oscillation amplitude vs. position relative to the FC in Figure 6.17 <u>during</u> the period of fan operation with the oscillation sequences (Δt ~ 5-10 hours) measured from the start of fan operation for fan at position X.

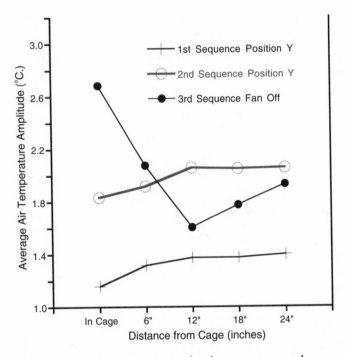

Figure 20b   Average air, T-oscillation amplitude vs. position relative to the FC. Fan at position Y (last sequence with fan off).

To summarize the main results of these forced convection experiments, we find that:

(1)   The "normal" air temperature oscillation amplitude was always highest inside the cage and fell to a minimum one foot from the cage before rising again,

(2)   This normal amplitude-distance relationship becomes initially inverted as a result of fan operation before returning to the pre-fan condition and

(3)   There is no serious alteration to the oscillation waveform as a result of fan operation.

These results suggest a non D-space origin for these temperature oscillations and are somewhat reminiscent of the von Reichenback observations[1] that magnetic "flames" emanating from the poles of DC magnets, observed by sensitive humans, could be diverted by blowing on them.

Quiescent Air, Spatial Variation of T-Oscillation Amplitude; Case (a), With Faraday Cage:

The experimental set-up was as in Figure 6.17 with six computer-monitored digital thermometers, one in the water, one 2 in. from the inner cage wall, one at 6 in. outside the cage, one at 2 feet (high resolution) outside the cage and the two others further out. We performed 6-12 cycle amplitude averaging as before. The other two thermometers (low resolution) were placed one foot apart at various distances from the cage ranging from 3-4 feet to 10-11 feet. Although it was not possible to obtain simultaneous T-oscillation data at all positions at once (that would require 14 thermometers), it was possible to piece together data from different sequences on different days at different distances to locate relative maxima and minima in the amplitude-distance relationship.

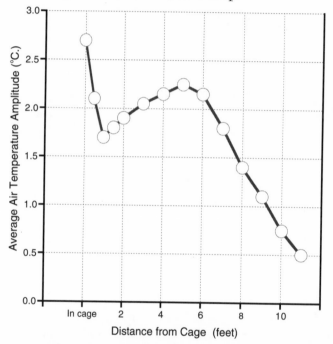

Figure 6.21 Composite amplitude vs. distance plot for air, T-oscillations in the Figure 6.17 geometry (between August and September 1999).

The combined results, given in Figure 6.21, show a decline from a maximum in the cage to a minimum, 12 in. outside the cage, and a gradual rise again to another but lower maximum at about 5 feet before declining to a small value at 11 feet (our furthest measurement point). In contrast to the minimum amplitude at 12 in. from the cage, which never varied from one oscillation sequence to another, the secondary maximum at about 5 feet varied in position from ~ 4 feet to ~ 6 feet from day to day. No additional extrema (minima or maxima) were ever observed in this far-field region using the low-resolution thermometers. With the Figure 6.21 data, it should be realized

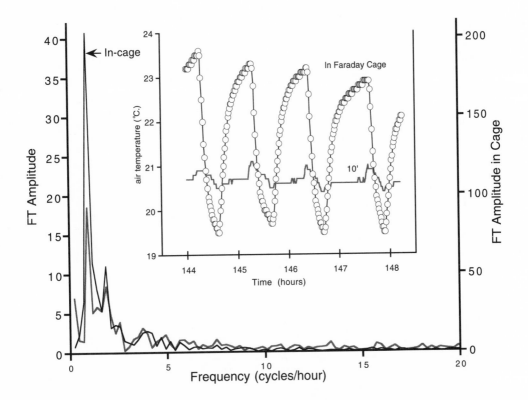

Figure 6.22   Amplitude spectra from Fourier analysis of air, T-oscillation real-time data (see inset) both in the FC and 10 feet away <u>outside</u> the closed door of Figure 6.17a. Note the high correlation between the oscillations measured at locations separated by ten feet, a closed door and a FC.

that, on any given day, the average amplitudes could be somewhat higher or lower than those shown in this typical composite.

Since the 10-foot measuring point in Figure 6.21 was in the hallway outside the office (see Figure 6.17a), it was possible to close the office door and compare the oscillations inside the Faraday cage with those outside in the hallway at this location. The inset in Fig 6.22 shows the simultaneous real-time data at these two positions while Fourier analysis of these two oscillation data sets reveals that they have the same frequency and basic waveform despite the fact that they are separated by a 10 foot distance, a closed door and a Faraday cage!

<u>**Case (b), After Removal of the FC and Water Vessel -- The Phantom Effect**</u>: Case (a) firmly established a type of conditioning center in the space of Figure 6.17 and IIED experiments had been performed with this cage over a span of 18 months prior to the forced convection experiment. Our next goal

was to see how this T-oscillation distribution might change after removal of the Faraday cage and its water vessel.

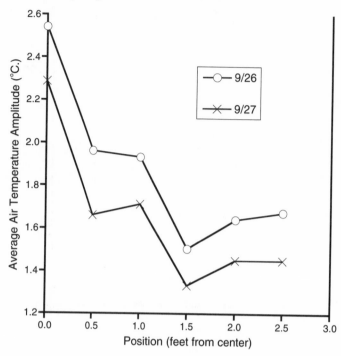

Figure 6.23   Average air, T-oscillation amplitude vs. distance plot for Figure 6.17 geometry one and two days after removal of the FC and water vessel (the former FC edge was located at 0.5 feet).

After removing this D-space "conditioning center", the temperature probe which had been at 2" from the interior wall of the FC was moved to the former cage-edge position. Now, the six temperature probes were all placed 6 in. apart along the line shown in Figure 6.17. The first important result was then immediately noticed -- the air T-oscillation profile remained despite the removal of the FC and water vessel. For this "phantom" profile shown in Figure 6.23, the minimum at 1 foot outside the cage of Figure 6.21 is still there at 1.5 feet from the central thermometer with the surrounding profile being very similar to that of Figure 6.21 (except for the cage interior, of course). With the passage of time, this phantom profile slowly decayed while developing an additional minimum at the former cage-edge position. This result is very reminiscent of the DNA phantom effect reported by Gariaev, et. al.[2]

Air T-Oscillation Amplitude Perturbation via a Natural Quartz Crystal at Position Zero; Case (a), C-Axis Up: Following the previous experiment that was ended on 9/27/99, we wanted to see how the results of Figure 6.23 might be altered by perturbing the conditioned space differently. From previous experience, we had learned that oscillations could be erased for weeks by introducing specific man-made materials into the conditioned space so, to be prudent, we decided to stick with a natural material as the perturbing element. We selected a natural quartz crystal for the purpose (6 in. long in the c-axis direction and 3" in diameter).

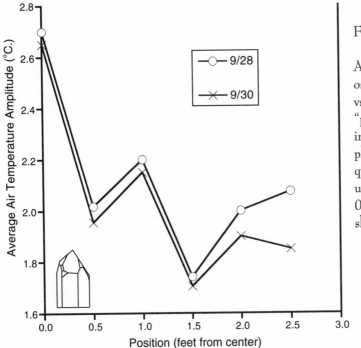

Figure 6.24

Average air, T-oscillation amplitude vs. distance plot on the "phantom" profile immediately after placing a natural quartz crystal (c-axis up) between position 0.0 and 0.5 feet as shown.

The crystal was initially placed near the former cage-center with it's c-axis perpendicular to the table top, and a prism plane parallel to the line of thermometers, it's apex pointing upwards. Figure 6.24 shows the results of the T-oscillation amplitudes on the subsequent two days. One can note the sharpened definition of amplitude structure for the maxima and minima plus a general upward shift to larger magnitudes than present in Figure 6.23. It should be noted here that there was no change in basic waveform and frequency range for the air temperature oscillations from the pre-quartz case to the case where the quartz crystal was placed c-axis up (see Figure 6.25, top).

Case (b), C-Axis Horizontal: Next, while keeping the crystal near the center position, it was rotated to lay with a prism face flat on the table, its c-axis aligned with the row of thermometers and its apex pointing away from the center position. Immediately, the oscillation waveform changed dramatically (see Figure 6.25) and the oscillation amplitude was significantly diminished

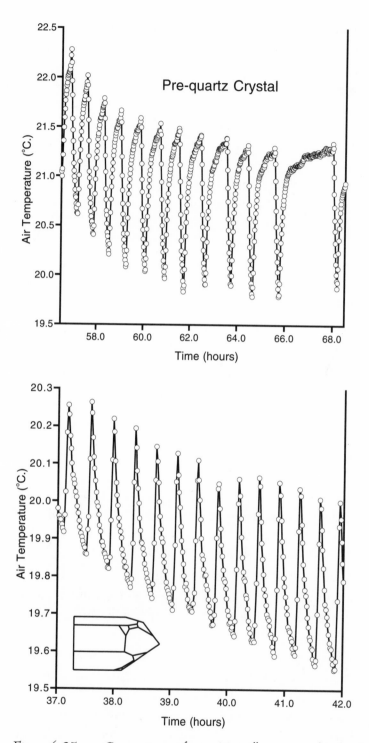

Figure 6.25   Comparison of air, T-oscillation amplitude, frequency and waveform between the pre-quartz crystal condition and the condition immediately after changing the orientation of the quartz crystal to the c-axis horizontal position.

(see Figs. 6.25, 6.26) while the frequency more than doubled. In addition, although room temperature increases had previously triggered oscillations, now temperature increases tended to annihilate them. Interestingly, Figure 6.25 (bottom) shows an inversion of the waveform shape seen in Figs. 6.18, 6.22 and 6.25 (top) while Figure 6.26 shows a spatial profile inversion compared to those of Figs. 6.19, 6.23 and 6.24. On the first full day with the crystal in this new orientation (10/2), the amplitude-distance relationship out to 2.5 feet was essentially flat. On succeeding days with the crystal in this orientation, the inverted amplitude-distance relation slowly developed with the former minimum at 1.5 feet becoming a maximum at 1.0 feet.

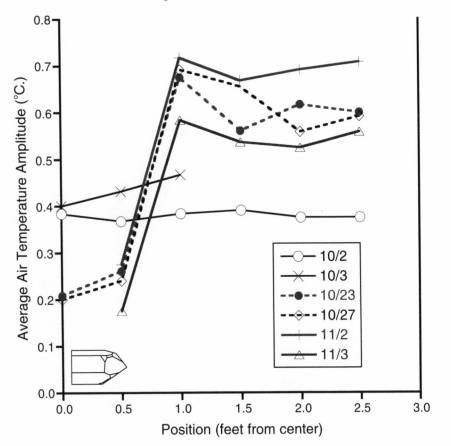

Figure 6.26   Average air, T-oscillation amplitude vs. distance plot over the month immediately following the change in the quartz crystal c-axis alignment on 10/2/99. The crystal was placed between position 0.0 and 0.5 feet as shown.

A curiously mixed oscillation mode was observed in the days following the onset of this completely new oscillation behavior. The new low-amplitude, high-frequency, oscillation behavior alternated for a time with the previous high-amplitude, low-frequency behavior and the amplitude-distance relationships also alternated between those of Figs. 6.19 and 6.20. Eventually the new oscillations and their amplitude profile became permanently established.

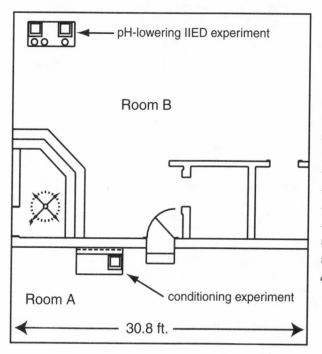

Figure 6.27a

Plan view, spatial geometry used in the space-conditioning IIED-DC magnetic field polarity experiment (Room A). Space conditioning device location separated by wall and 25 feet from a pH-lowering IIED experiment location in Room B (the latter overlapped in time by two months the 9.5 month space conditioning experiment).

The Use of a Space-Conditioning IIED in a New Locale: Figure 6.27a shows the site used for testing the new space-conditioning IIED relative to a formerly lightly used pH-lowering IIED experimental site. The space-conditioning IIED was imprinted specifically to increase the D-space/R-space coupling so as to move the locale in the direction of increased vacuum ordering as illustrated in Figure 6.2. A distance of 25 feet, a wall and a closed door separated these two sites. The experimental set-up for the site conditioning is shown in Figure 6.27b. Although we had already found air temperature-oscillation amplitude to be the most responsive correlate with site conditioning and water pH-oscillations to be the next, we wanted to also investigate the possible effect of DC magnetic field polarity on the site conditioning process. Thus, we utilized the experimental configuration of Figure 6.3 with a 480 Gauss magnet placed at the center, left or right position of Figure 6.27b to test both position (C, L, R) effects and DC magnet (S-pole up, N-pole up and no magnet designated (S, N, 0)) effects. The testing was carried out after

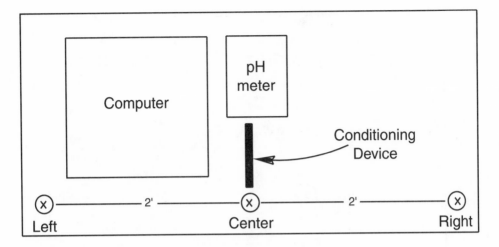

Figure 6.27b Space-conditioning IIED-DC magnetic field polarity experiment. Magnet and water vessel locations, X, relative to the position of the conditioning IIED.

periodic one-week exposures of the site to the conditioning IIED. Thus, there were 9 measurements performed per series (0,C; N,C; S,C; 0,L; N,L; S,L; 0,R; N,R; S,R) with a week-long exposure to the IIED between each series of measurements (see Figure 6.30-top). Series 1 provided the baseline conditioning <u>before</u> using this specific IIED. Series 6 (neglecting S,R and N,R) occurred after 5 weeks of site conditioning with this IIED at the central location and, after Series 4, a pH-lowering experiment was initiated at the other experimental site in Figure 6.27a (Room B) to determine how it might interfere with events occurring at the conditioning site.

To monitor the effects of the IIED and magnets on the conditioning of the space, real-time measurements of temperature and pH for a vessel of purified water (ASTM Type 1, no particulates) took place over a period of 3-7 days during each series. The computer monitoring was done using a sampling interval of one minute. Two pH-parameters were drawn from these measurements as correlation vehicles to tell us something about the site conditioning: (1) the pH-oscillation data of ~68 hours duration was Fourier analyzed and converted to an amplitude spectrum for which the maximum amplitude in six ranges of oscillation periods was determined and tabulated (8-15 min., 15-30 min., 30-60 min., 1-3 hr., 3-7 hr. and 7-12 hr.) and (2) the maximum pH deviation over this ~ 68 hours from its calculated equilibrium value (pure water in contact with air), ΔpH, was determined and tabulated.

Series 1 measurements showed us that some small amount of

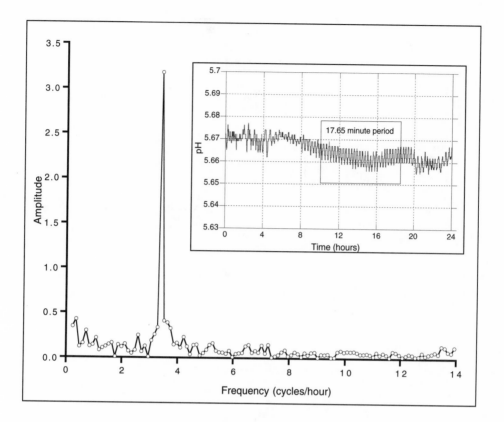

Figure 6.28   Baseline pH real-time data (inset) and amplitude spectrum at the central position of Figure 6.27b immediately prior to the site conditioning IIED exposure experiment.

conditioning had already occurred at this site. As can be seen from the inset in Figure 6.28, these pH oscillations were highly periodic but of very low amplitude. An 8.5-hour segment of the data (shown in box of inset) was used for the Fourier analysis to yield this amplitude spectrum. [It should be noted here that the oscillation data selected in Figure 6.28 (inset) for Fourier analysis was from a particularly periodic time segment. The average FT amplitude over a time segment as long as 68 hours would be considerably lower than the maximum amplitude depicted in Figure 6.28 (for example see Figure 6.30).] Figure 6.29, from Series 5 shows how the ΔpH parameter was obtained for a typical measurement.

From the set of 52 measurements, for the more periodic oscillation sequences, the maximum amplitude for each of the six ranges mentioned above normally occurred near the center of a cluster of higher amplitude frequency peaks. The fundamental frequency (highest amplitude) tended to occur mostly in the 15-30 min. period range (see Figure 6.28). If the harmonic content of

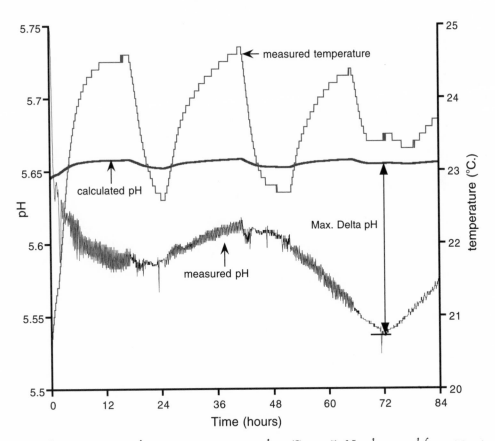

Figure 6.29   pH and temperature vs. time plots (Series 5, N-pole up at left position in Figure 6.27b) for defining the maximum ΔpH. The nearly flat pH curve represents the calculated pH for the measured temperature (curve above it).

a particular harmonic sequence was high, the maximum amplitude in the 8-15 min. period range tended to be high as well. At the lower frequency ranges, any amplitude peaks were sporadic. In all cases analyzed, a maximum amplitude could be determined consistently only for the four highest frequency ranges (shortest periods).

In Figure 6.29, the pH-oscillation and triggering characteristics can be observed. Note that the pH-oscillations are triggered and tend to grow when the temperature rises. These highly periodic oscillations end when the temperature falls. We have noticed that these triggering and annihilation mechanisms reverse themselves roughly as a result of changes in the forced heating/cooling cycle changes with the seasons. In fall/winter/spring periods, furnace heating controls these characteristics while, in summer, air-conditioned cooling reverses the triggering mechanism. In the summer, for

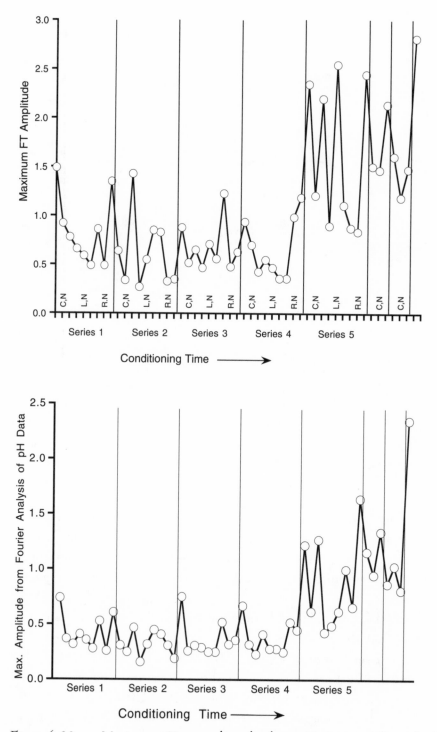

Figure 6.30   Maximum pH spectral amplitudes via Fourier transform of real-time data for all measurement series (each vertical line indicates a one week IIED conditioning period), (top) for the period range 15-30 min. and (bottom) for the period range of 8-15 min.

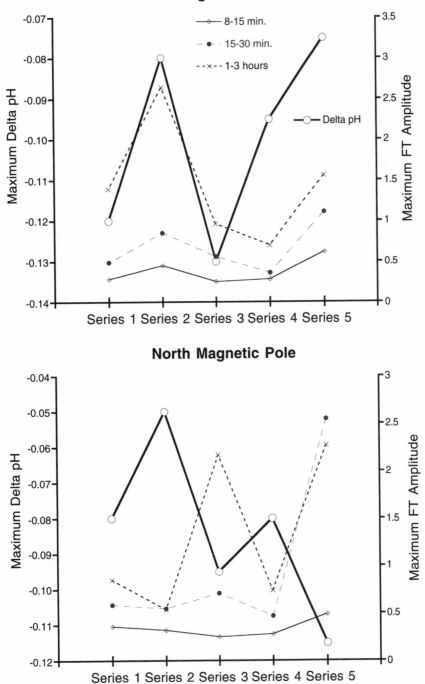

Figure 6.31   Maximum Δ pH and maximum spectral amplitudes for three spectral period ranges plotted for the first five series of measurements, (top) S-pole up at the left position and (bottom) N-pole up at the left position.

example, the highly periodic oscillations end when the temperature increases and are triggered to begin when the temperature falls.

From Figure 6.30, it can be seen how the maximum pH-oscillation amplitudes, periodicity and harmonic content change with conditioning time. For the first 4 series, little growth occurred in the maximum amplitude with the conditioning IIED. The data perhaps suggests that magnets may actually hinder the development of pH-oscillations. Of the total of 52 experiments, 34 used magnets of which 10 were performed in the "left" position and these gave much more significant statistical results than did those from the other two positions. Figure 6.30 shows an abrupt increase in maximum amplitude for the conditioning cycle at the end of Series 4. This could either be due to a strongly non-linear conditioning effect associated with this IIED or it could be due to the start-up of the pH-lowering IIED experiment at the 25 foot distant location indicated in Figure 6.27a. At this point in time, we cannot decide which is the proper explanation. For the magnet effects, it probably doesn't matter what is the source of the conditioning. In any event, for the south and north magnetic pole pointing upwards, Figure 6.31 presents the data for maximum ΔpH and Fourier transform (FT) amplitudes versus conditioning time through series 5.

Table 6.3   *Average ΔpH values for the 2 magnet polarities at all positions.*

Magnet and Position	Mean Δ pH
South Pole Left	-0.10
North Pole Left	-0.084
No Magnet Left	-0.043
South Pole Right	-0.074
North Pole Right	-0.070
No Magnet Right	-0.052
South Pole Center	-0.038
North Pole Center	-0.036
No Magnet Center	-0.036

At the left position, Figure 6.31 shows us that (1) for the south pole upwards, ΔpH becomes less negative with increased conditioning time while (2) for the north pole upwards, ΔpH becomes more negative with conditioning time. Using ΔpH-averages over the first 5 series for both magnet and no magnet exposure cases, Table 6.3 shows that magnets in the "left" position had the largest effect on the ΔpH of purified water. Likewise, compared to the no

Table 6.4   Statistical comparison between average Δ pH values for the no magnet exposure case compared with exposure to magnets at the 3 positions.

Magnet Exposure vs. No Exposure Comparisons	
Position	*one-tail p-value*
Left	0.00119197
Right	0.02237855
Center	0.46900659

magnet case, the "left" position always produced the greatest <u>difference</u> in ΔpH values and yielded a lower p-value (p = 0.0012) than at the other sites (see Table 6.4). Another indication that the trends that are revealed in Figure 6.31 for the "left" position are not "flukes" comes from the correlation coefficient data shown in Table 6.5. This data shows that very strong correlations exist between ΔpH and pH-oscillation amplitudes. The maximum amplitudes for the 4 frequency ranges shown were taken from the amplitude spectra (determined via Fourier analysis of pH oscillation data over a 68 hour time interval). The time of minimum indicates the number of hours that elapsed before the pH-minimum occurred in a particular measurement time sequence (see Figure 6.29). This minimum was used since almost all pH deviations from the equilibrium value were negative (lower). Note the high positive correlations between ΔpH, pH-oscillation amplitude and time of minimum for south-pole exposure (S-pole drives the pH upward) plus the high negative correlations for north-pole exposure (N-pole drives the pH downward).

Table 6.5   Correlation coefficient data showing correlation between Δ pH and variable X (at the left position) for two magnetic polarity exposures.

X	S Pole exposure	N Pole exposure
time of minimum	0.70953751	-0.8139105
Maximum FT Amplitude 8-15 min.	0.83783343	-0.5048537
Maximum FT Amplitude15-30 min.	0.67976708	-0.7577474
Maximum FT Amplitude 30-60 min.	0.38909361	-0.3602026
Maximum FT Amplitude1-3 hours	0.53406802	-0.8734826
averages:	0.63005993	-0.6620394

An important consideration for this book is that both IIEDs as well as magnets appear to influence space conditioning and these two effects may not always act cooperatively to enhance D-space/R-space coupling. In some instances, it appears as if the DC magnet effects on the space partially erase the IIED conditioning effect. For future work, a better experimental design might be to significantly separate the no magnet from the magnet locations and to further separate the S-pole location from the N-pole location.

Two quantitative measures of the magnitude of site conditioning using air, T-oscillations were found to be meaningful. The first, as might be expected, was the maximum amplitude of the oscillations (measured peak to trough). The second was the total number of hours in a 24-hour period that air T-oscillations occurred and we call this oscillation continuity. For a site, the oscillation continuity can vary from zero hours/day, when no oscillations at all occurred, to 24 hours/day when the oscillations were continuous. This is somewhat analogous to the coherence length of an optical laser.

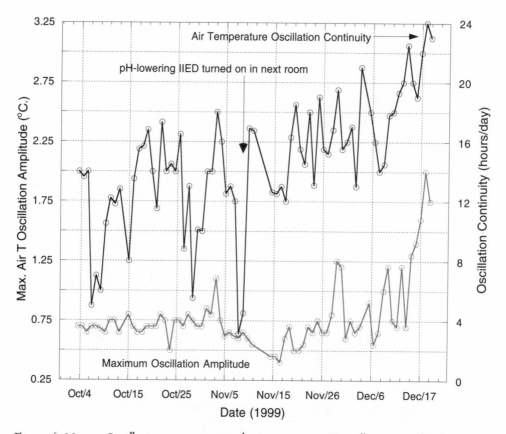

Figure 6.32   Oscillation continuity and maximum air T-oscillation amplitude vs. time over the last 11 weeks of the site conditioning experiment.

The air temperature data for this particular conditioning experiment was obtained by determining both the maximum air T-oscillation amplitude for each 24 hour period and the oscillation continuity for the same time interval. This data is provided in Figure 6.32 for the last 11 weeks of the conditioning experiment. One notes that both measures of site conditioning had increased significantly by the end of the experiment. The air T-oscillations had become nearly continuous and had attained a maximum amplitude of 2 °C by the last day of measurement (at some sites, the maximum amplitude has attained 4 °C). From Figure 6.32, the average oscillation continuity value was about 12.5 hours per day for the first 35 days and about

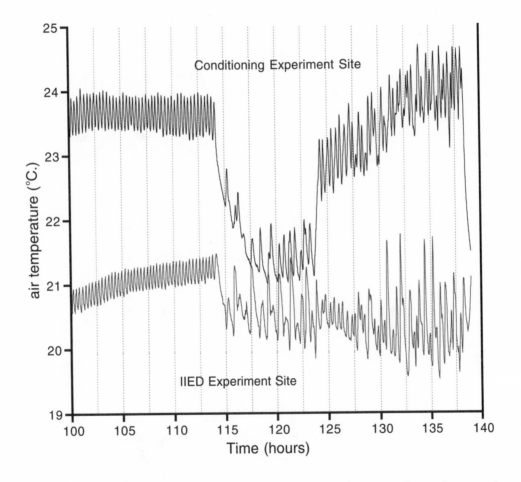

Figure 6.33   *Air T-oscillation data comparison as a function of time between the conditioning experiment site and the IIED experiment site of Figure 6.27a.*

18.3 hours per day for the remainder of the experiment. This represents, on average, over 1206 hours of air T-oscillations at this locale with an amplitude maximum above 0.4 °C.

A possible effect of the nearby pH-lowering IIED experiment (25 feet away) on the conditioning results is evidenced by the appreciable increase in the magnitude of the conditioning indicators after the pH-lowering IIED was turned on in the next room (see Figure 6.30 after Series 5). However, from Figure 6.30, each vertical line indicates a 7-day conditioning interval so the application frequency of the conditioning IIED was also greater during this time interval. Further, as indicated in Figures 6.1 and 6.2, the conditioning process is thought to be a very non-linear one.

Simultaneous air T-oscillation monitoring at both the new conditioning site <u>and</u> the pH-lowering IIED experiment site of Figure 6.27a allows us to discriminate, somewhat, the contribution of the pH-lowering IIED to the site conditioning data of Figure 6.30 after the Series 4 measurements had been completed. Figure 6.33 provides a segment of this data which obviously relate very strongly to one another and, since the air T-oscillation amplitude was larger for the conditioning site than for the pH-lowering site, one may conclude that much of the rise in amplitude seen in Figure 6.30 is due to the non-linearity of the conditioning process itself rather than due to the distant pH-lowering IIED.

Table 6.6   Summary Findings for the site-conditioning experiment

1. Oscillations in air temperature develop that are always larger than pH oscillations.
2. pH oscillations tend to fade out during a measurement sequence whereas this never occurs with air temperature oscillations.
3. Temperature and pH oscillation frequencies are always the same.
4. Temperature and pH oscillations are in-phase for much of an individual wavetrain.
5. Temperature and pH oscillations increase in amplitude the longer the exposure to operating IIED's.
6. Temperature and pH oscillations increase in continuity the longer the exposure to operating IIED's.
7. Exposure of water to the North Pole of a DC magnet diminishes pH oscillations.
8. Exposure of water to the North Pole of a DC magnet drives the pH down.
9. Exposure of water to the South Pole of a DC magnet drives the pH up.
10. Air temperature oscillations correlate in frequency and are in-phase for periods of time across a distance of 25 feet in two rooms closed with respect to each other.

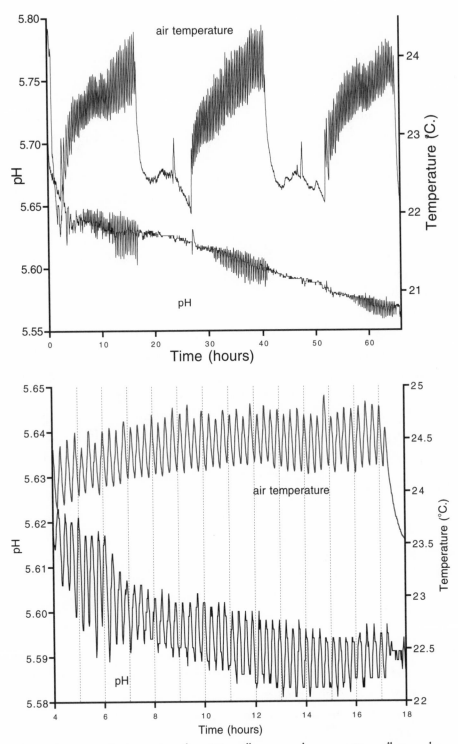

Figure 6.34   Comparison of air T-oscillation and water pH-oscillation data vs. time during Series 5 of the site-conditioning experiment, (top) S-pole up at right position and (bottom) N-pole up at left position.

As a closing observation to this section, Figure 6.34 illustrates a further relationship between the air T-oscillations and the simultaneous pH-oscillation data at the conditioned site during the 5th series. Note the strong coupling in Figure 6.34 (top) between the two kinds of oscillations as indicated by the sudden quenching of the regular pH-oscillations due to the drop in air temperature. Figure 6.34 (bottom) shows a typical sequence where, initially, the two kinds of oscillations are almost π out-of-phase with each other but, by hour 8, are in phase and remain so through hour 17. A summary of the conclusions to be drawn from this set of experiments is given in Table 6.6.

Simultaneous, Side-By-Side vs. Sequential Experiments in an Initially Unconditioned Space: Most of the experiments of Chapters 3, 4 and 5 were carried out without realizing the importance of space conditioning on the results. Further, the biology-type experiments of Chapters 4 and 5 evolved quickly into a simultaneous comparison of the four treatments: no FC, empty FC, FC + unimprinted device and FC + imprinted device. However, such an approach had not been tried for the water experiments. Finally, by September 1999, we knew unequivocally that our three years of funding was not going to be extended beyond January 31, 2000. Thus, we decided in September to write this book. WAT started writing it then, while both WED and MJK scrambled to complete unfinished experiments or perform short experiments to round out the overall study as best we could. The experiment of this section as well as that of the next both fall into this late category.

This new series of experiments using purified water in an initially unconditioned space, which was continuously monitored by computer, were initiated in November 1999. We wanted to assess and compare the results obtained from the following four treatments in both the simultaneous (side-by-side) and sequential modes:

1. Purified water in a FC with a powered, newly-imprinted, pH-lowering IIED,
2. Purified water in a FC with a powered, unimprinted device,
3. Purified water in a FC with no device present and
4. Purified water sitting alone on the table top.

To monitor a measure of R-space/D-space coupling over time, the air temperature <u>outside</u> the Faraday cages was probed with a high-resolution

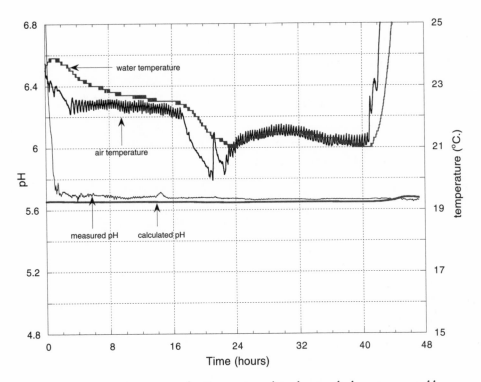

Figure 6.35   *Temperature and pH vs. time plots for purified water in equilibrium with air and simultaneously exposed to an activated pH-lowering IIED (Nov. 22-24).*

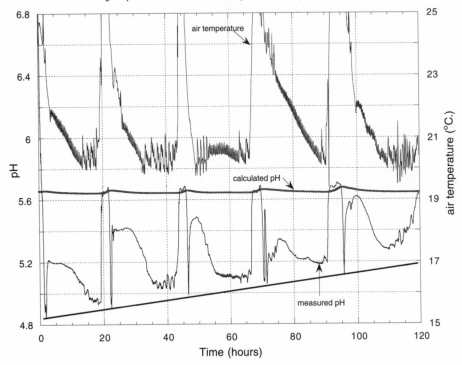

Figure 6.36   *Continuation of Figure 6.35 for the time interval Dec 12-14.*

219

digital thermometer. Three sets of experiments were performed in each mode. Unfortunately, the three simultaneous mode experiments were carried out first. Because this was an initially unconditioned space, very little change in water pH from the calculated equilibrium value was noted for any of the treatments. One would have needed to use statistical procedures to differentiate between them. The first two series of sequential measurements also showed a negligible pH-lowering effect. However, the third series in the sequential mode showed a robust pH-lowering effect.

For the first series in the sequential mode, the imprinted device had been in the "on" state for a total time of 11-14 days and yielded the data shown in Figure 6.35. Although something had started to happen with the air temperature, not much was going on with the pH. These pH-oscillations were initially observed in the water <u>not</u> in a Faraday cage although some less well developed oscillations appeared inside the FC with no device. Amplitude spectrum results showed close nesting of the T- and pH- oscillations only for the fundamental mode of 17.1 minutes. For the third sequential series, a robust change in pH was monitored (after $\sim$ 17-20 days of conditioning). This pH-lowering effect was repeated on five consecutive days (see Figure 6.36) with a maximum pH lowering of 0.8 pH units or 80% of the imprint statement. On each of these days, the pH returned to the equilibrium value for pure water in contact with air containing natural CO_2 levels. This data also shows what we think is IIED imprint-fading (rising lower baseline) at a rate of $\sim$ 0.003 pH units per hr. It is interesting to note that this imprint fading occurs while the air T-oscillations are unaffected or even grow somewhat in amplitude.

By the end of the sequential series of measurements, there was no time left to redo the simultaneous mode measurements. This, unfortunately, must be left for future experimentation.

Oscillations in Random Number Generation and the "Millennium" Effect:

Two important questions that arise as a consequence of the foregoing results are: "Does the measuring and monitoring equipment itself produce these oscillations and can a computer generating pseudo-random numbers, via an algorithm, be induced to alter its behavior in a conditioned space?". If the computer responsible for monitoring the properties of a conditioned space actually affected the generation of pseudo-random numbers in a non-random way, then maybe the computer is somehow a part of the basic oscillation phenomenon. Thus, it seemed reasonable to try generating pseudo-random numbers algorithmically in computers in both an unconditioned and a conditioned locale to see if there were any significant differences between the two locales.

Although in one two-week comparative test, no significant difference was observed between the results for the conditioned and the unconditioned sites (see Figure 6.37, Jan. 13-27), a large effect on pseudo-random number generation did appear later for the conditioned site. Unfortunately, we did not have simultaneous data for the unconditioned site during this Feb. - Mar. period in Figure 6.37 because we had been told to remove our equipment from the unconditioned site in late January so that others could use it. This time-series data representing the output of the pseudo-random number generation algorithm (see Appendix 6.A for a discussion of this method) developed oscillations during Feb. - Mar. with periods very similar to those measured for

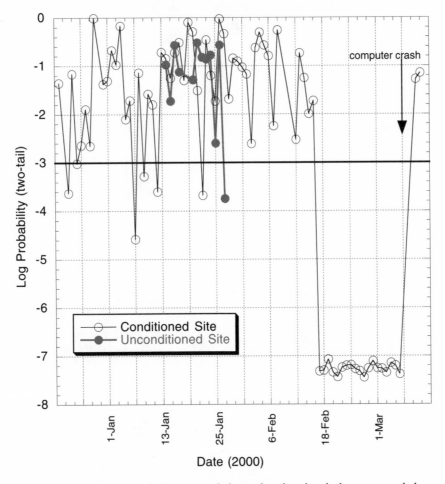

Figure 6.37   Logarithm of the two-tailed p-value for the daily means of the pseudo-random variable vs. time plot. The oscillatory period began Feb. 17, 2000 and extended for 20 days (at which time the computer "crashed").

the T, pH and σ physical parameters in various conditioned locales. Although highly complex, these oscillations were more periodic than any previous oscillation sequence. The development of these non-symmetric oscillation waveforms caused the data to deviate substantially from randomness (two-tailed p-values < 10^{-7}) as can be readily seen from Figure 6.37.

Considerable variability was initially observed in effect sizes and the p-values calculated daily from them (see Figure 6.37). Effect sizes (mean of 102600 observations per day minus 100) ranged from –0.016 to 0.093 during this period. On February 17, an entirely new regime was entered characterized by much higher effect sizes (around 0.12) that varied in an extremely narrow range compared to previous values. Observations at the unconditioned site were made for only two weeks, but p-values calculated from those means also fall in the range of high variability (prior to Feb. 17) shown in Figure 6.37.

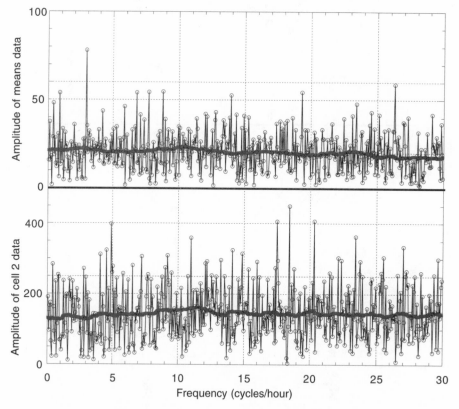

Figure 6.38   Amplitude spectra via Fourier analysis of typical real-time pseudo-random number data from pre-oscillation period (means data on top and cell 2 data on bottom). Lines through the data are 64 minute moving averages of the amplitudes.

The most significant aspect of the data collected between 2/17 and 3/6, however, was the periodicity observed in the time series for the accumulated sums from cell 2 and means that were tabulated every minute. This periodicity was evaluated by performing a Fourier analysis of the time series data. Typical amplitude spectra for the periods before and after Feb. 17 are shown in Figures 6.38 and 6.39.

The amplitude spectra shown in Figure 6.38 are derived from a Fourier analysis of the 12/29 time-series for both cell 2 and means data. Typical pre-oscillation pseudo-random data shows little if any periodicity. There are no peaks in common between the two data sets that consistently stand above the moving average. The moving averages are also fairly flat revealing no dominant frequency range. Amplitude spectra for every day prior to oscillations appear very similar to Figure 6.38.

Let us contrast Figures 6.38 and 6.39. First of all, a large number of peaks above background become apparent in Figure 6.39. Less apparent is the one-to-one correlation between most peaks in the two spectra of Figure 6.39. This is most clear for the two peaks on either side of the 5.0 cycles/day frequency. In the amplitude spectrum of means in Figure 6.38 there are few peaks above amplitude 50. However, for the corresponding plot in Figure 6.39, there are many peaks above that amplitude. Similarly, in the amplitude spectrum of cell 2 sums in Figure 6.38, there are few peaks above amplitude 350, which is not the case for the corresponding plot in Figure 6.39.

Perhaps most surprising is the fact that the first peak in both plots of Figure 6.39 is a fundamental frequency of period 113.778 minutes and most all the subsequent peaks are harmonics! Since all harmonics of this fundamental can be precisely calculated, both the fundamental and all harmonics can be easily removed from the amplitude spectra of Figure 6.39. When this is accomplished, the result is what is depicted in Figure 6.40. This figure simply displays what the spectra of Figure 6.39 looks like when the periodicity is removed. What is left is random noise that is what it all should be if the random number algorithm was behaving the way it was prior to 2/17. However, note in Figure 6.40 how the noise is significantly suppressed with decreasing frequency.

Also note how the noise amplitude toward the high frequency end approaches the general amplitude values for the higher peaks in Figure 6.38 further implying that only noise is displayed in that representation of the data collected before oscillations appeared. Figures 6.39 and 6.40 are a way of illustrating the magnitude of the periodicity in the data collected on 2/24 during the oscillatory region of the plot shown in Figure 6.37.

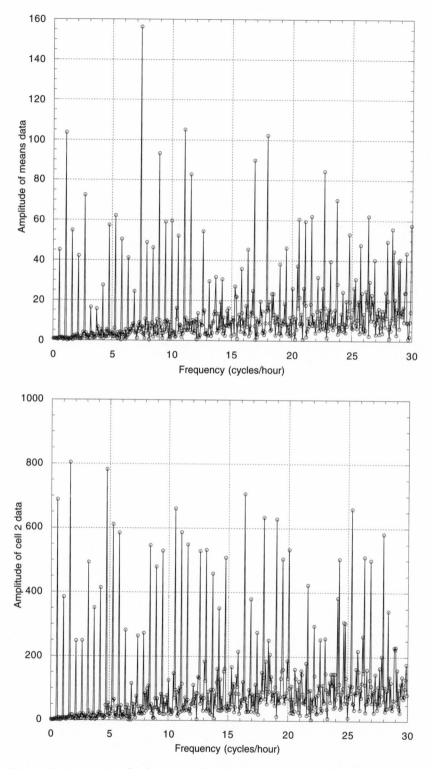

Figure 6.39   Amplitude spectra for 2/24/00 (during oscillatory period).

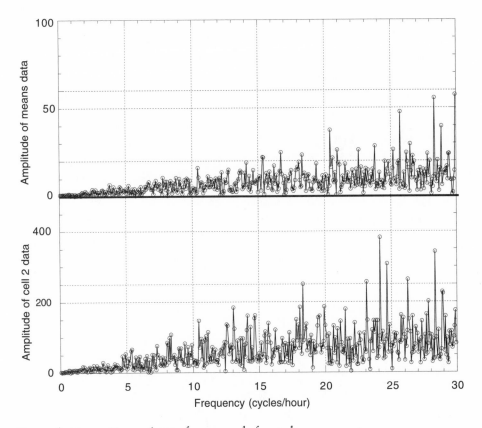

Figure 6.40   *Figure 6.39 after removal of periodic component.*

The next question is whether the periodicity can be seen in the raw data as well and, with some manipulation of the data to remove extremes, a clear picture emerges. In Figure 6.41, we plot a ten-minute moving average of the raw means data (Table 6.A.2) for the whole daily time series of Feb. 17 and Mar. 6, the first and last days oscillations appeared. The periodicity can be seen in the raw data as well, but moving averages make the waveform especially clear by smoothing out extremes.

The first thing to note is the highly regular shape of the wave and the fact that, on the two different days, the wave starts at a different point. This is true also of the means data for all the other days of the oscillatory period. <u>The time interval between major peaks is exactly 114 minutes and there are nine such intervals for a total of precisely 1026 minutes, the exact number of minutes for which the data was generated</u>. Thus, a similar standing wave in the data is produced each day during the oscillatory period. However, each wave is unique in detail and each starts at a different point in the wave train as if the system is picking up an ongoing rhythm from elsewhere.

It should be noted that the computer generating this data was left unattended starting Feb. 12 and ending Mar. 8 when it was discovered that the computer had malfunctioned (monitor was blank). No unusual temperature changes or other disturbances were noted during that time. The space was monitored every day of that period. The data for each day's run were stored in separate files on the computer's hard drive and nothing unusual about these files could be discerned. The data was downloaded on March 9 and was evaluated elsewhere as had been the practice previously.

It is obvious from examining Figure 6.41 how the effect size for the means for the whole data set could deviate from the normal pseudo-random pattern. Any asymmetry in waveforms such as those of Figure 6.41 will skew the data above or below the theoretical value of 100. Also the narrow range of the effect size is caused by the standing wave being nearly uniform from day to day.

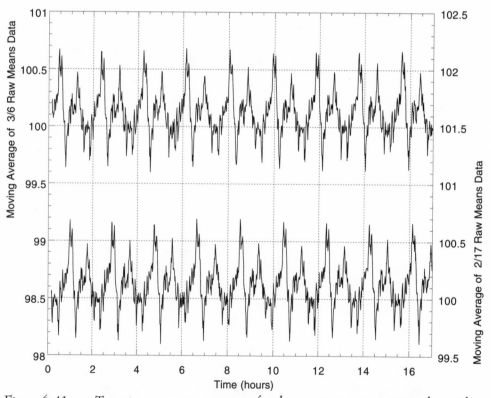

Figure 6.41   Ten-minute, moving averages for the raw means, time-series data. These means were tabulated each minute and plotted vs. time the algorithm was generating the raw data for the two particular days at the beginning and end of the oscillations.

Periodicity similar to that of Figure 6.41 was observed for accumulated sums of cell 2 and cell 100 raw data as well as the standard deviations of the means (Table 6.A.2). Examples of these are shown in Figure 6.42 for the first 8 hours of data for another day during the oscillatory period.

It can be noted in these above figures how different the waveforms can appear for the same periodicity. The simplest waveform appears in the means data followed in complexity by the standard deviations of those means. The waveforms for the sums of a cell's time series are more complex. Also note the dissimilarity of the waveforms in Figure 6.42 (bottom) for the two different cells. The waveforms for the two cells are unique. Every day during the oscillatory period the same cell has the same waveform; but, similar to the means, each starts and ends at a different point in the wavetrain. We surmise that all the cell's waveforms are similarly unique. This intricate detail regarding the daily periodicity in the data would appear to rule out some kind of gross computer malfunction as the source of the oscillations.

The analysis of periodicity in the accumulated sums of particular cells yields a higher FT amplitude than the means data. It can be noted in Figure 6.42 (bottom) that those oscillations as a percentage of the theoretical value of 50 are considerably higher amplitude than the means of Figure 6.41. FT amplitudes for the standard deviation data should be correspondingly higher. However, that is not the case, as the FT amplitudes for the standard deviations of the means are actually the lowest (not shown).

This periodicity observed in the pseudo-random number data appears to be very similar to that observed in physical-chemical measurements in a conditioned space. The two lowest frequency periods of roughly 1 and 2 hours also appear in the other data; however, the second and third harmonics are more commonly observed (30-40 minutes). These harmonics can also produce the highest amplitudes in the amplitude spectra of the pseudo-random number data.

The authors have often speculated on the influence of IIEDs and the spaces conditioned by them on the experimental equipment we use. Until now we had no direct evidence that the equipment might be affected. Other than the pseudo-random data oscillations, the computer performed normally during the time the oscillations occurred except perhaps at the end when the equipment ceased functioning. We have no reason to believe that the equipment performed unusually when other oscillations were monitored previously. We also have no reason to suspect that the computers or measuring equipment are the source of these previous oscillations. The oscillations appear in measurements of properties of differing phases including

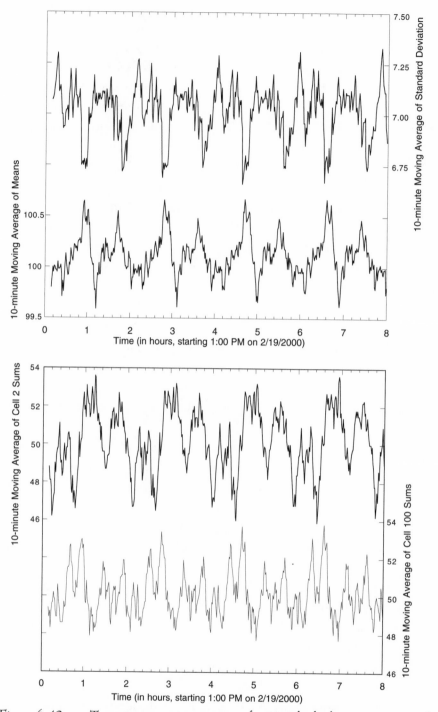

Figure 6.42 Ten-minute moving averages for (top) both the raw means and standard deviation, time-series data for one particular day of the oscillatory period (tabulated every minute and plotted vs. time the algorithm was generating the data) and (bottom) the raw sums of cell 2 and cell 100.

gases and liquids and now perhaps solids as well.

The behavior over time of the data-generating algorithm can be split into three different regimes: 1) the time before oscillations begin, 2) the oscillatory period itself and 3) the time after the oscillations. In the first and last time periods, we sometimes notice daily repetitive periodicity in the data, but the magnitude of FT amplitudes of this periodicity place it well within the noise level compared with the oscillations seen during period (2). This minor periodicity we attribute to the algorithm deviating slightly from random behavior as pseudo-random number generation is known to do, probably as a result of seed generation.

During period (2), oscillations of large FT amplitudes appear which can also be observed in the raw data. Some characteristics of these oscillations repeat on consecutive days during period (2); but, in detail, each waveform is unique. The algorithm does not simply "stick" in a particular pattern as if the same seed was used. Each data set starting at minute one consisting of means, standard deviations and sums of particular cells is absolutely unique with no repetitions. Thus period (2) represents a distinctly different computational regime, one characterized by very high periodicity. However, the sudden increase in non-randomness occurs with the mathematical routines and computer electronics performing normally otherwise. The computer did not "crash" every time the non-random behavior occurred.

The mechanism producing these oscillations in the computation of pseudo-random data is presently unknown. However, the significant difference between these oscillations and the other oscillations in material properties that we have monitored is the constancy of frequency. Because of this constancy, we observe a higher periodicity "reading" as measured by the modulus or FT amplitude. An interesting feature of the oscillations in thermodynamic properties such as temperature is the modulation of frequency that is constrained to some extent by changes in the ambient temperature. Wave trains often begin and end immediately upon a major shift in temperature (sign of dT/dt). The frequency modulation (either increasing or decreasing) also depends on dT/dt. Thus, the constraints on these oscillations are related to factors that can vary significantly over the course of a measurement period. The frequency variation observed is, in fact, directly related to these constraints varying in time.

The constraints on the frequency of the pseudo-random number oscillations are fixed, however. There are precisely nine cycles in each oscillation sequence in a time period of 1026 minutes constraining the fundamental frequency to exactly 0.5263 cycles per hour (114-minute period).

A standing wave in the time series data is produced each day during the oscillatory period and the fundamental frequency is the same each day. Presumably this frequency can change as the number of cycles per sequence changes resulting from presently unknown factors. All these frequencies can be precisely predicted, however. Also each wave on any particular day during the oscillatory period is unique in detail. Each wavetrain starts at a different point as if the system is picking up an ongoing rhythm from elsewhere. The constancy of frequency has to have something to do with the mechanism producing the oscillations. It appears that the measured rhythms are determined by factors extrinsic to the calculation and recording methods.

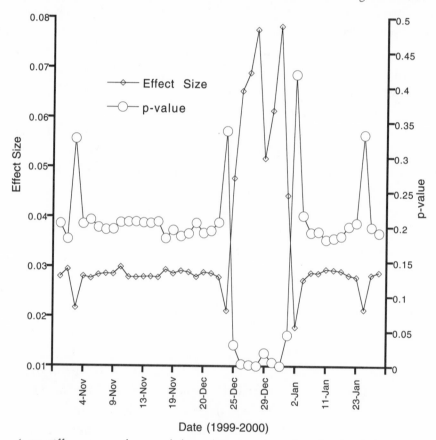

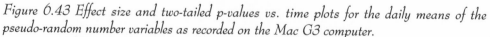

Figure 6.43 Effect size and two-tailed p-values vs. time plots for the daily means of the pseudo-random number variables as recorded on the Mac G3 computer.

As alluded to in the introduction to this chapter, this pseudo-random number oscillation data is part of a web of relationships between our physical world and the higher dimensional aspect of nature that needs to be woven into the fabric of the whole before full understanding of these effects is possible. Similar to many of the experiments we have explored, we have just barely scratched the surface with our random number generation studies. However, these results point the way toward many exciting future experiments that can be done with computers and electronic equipment in environments conditioned by IIEDs.

The Millennium Effect: The conditioned space mentioned in the previous section was used to test the effects of the conditioning on a computer generating pseudo-random numbers via algorithm. The particular PC was placed in the near field of the locus of conditioning defined previously (see Figure 6.17 next to location of Faraday cage). In the same space another computer (Mac G3) was located in the center of the room on a desk (Figure 6.17). This computer was also used to run the same EXCEL macro to produce time series data identical in format to that described above. The time span of daily operation of the pseudo-random number algorithm was also similar.

In this case, however, no highly periodic oscillations in the time series output were ever observed in either computer. Instead, significant deviation in effect sizes from "normal" behavior was observed in the Mac G3 over a particular interval of time. The effect size variation for pseudo-random number generation for this particular computer platform was significantly different from that observed for the PC. Figure 6.43 illustrates how the variation in effect size and probabilities for the Mac G3 was significantly less for the period prior to 12/25/99 and after 1/1/2000. Effect sizes tended to vary in a narrow range (0.027-0.03), with occasional excursions to lower values (and less significance), just the opposite to that for the PC behavior (see Figure 6.37 for that time period).

However, a major increase in effect size occurred starting 12/25/99 and ending 1/1/2000 for the Mac G3. The p-values for this time interval are for the most part significantly below 0.05. Also note the perturbation that occurred just before and after this time range. Similar ranges in effect sizes (0.027-0.03) were observed on another Mac G3 not in this particular conditioned space (also in a different time period) but no larger deviations were ever observed such as shown in Figure 6.43. Also note that effect sizes out of the ordinary range were not observed for the same time period segment shown in Figure 6.37.

The effects we observed in the Mac G3 data may be similar to the "field consciousness" effects described by Radin.[4] In his experiments, random-number generators were used to measure the influence that large numbers of people worldwide can have on physical reality. Possibly some mass consciousness effect relating to the year 2000 produced the effect shown in Figure 6.43 in pseudo-random number generation. Radin notes that "...the exact nature of the physical system used to detect the mass-consciousness effect does not seem to be particularly important, provided that it is a system that naturally fluctuates in some way and can be measured." It is likely that such simple computer-aided detection systems, as we used, placed in conditioned spaces may provide an ideal way to monitor changes in mass consciousness.

Experience with Conditioning Experiments at Two Remote Locations

Location 1: Experimentation began in a basement room of a family home situated about 9.5 miles distant from the laboratory complex. The house was occupied by mother, father, two girls (11 and 13) and a puppy. The experiment room was set up as a storage room serving as a catch-all of not currently used items plus a continuously running data-receiving/sending device. Our experiment was located on metal shelving fastened to the opposite wall. The occupants of the house had minimal involvement with the experiment but the father works at home in an office next to our experiment room. Our apparatus was very similar to what we were using in our regular on-site experiments[1] except that the host provided the computer and our technician spent very little time in this basement room.

Eight months of measurements were made at this site where both magnets and a conditioning device running periodically produced no noticeable effects in two months (total of 40 days conditioning). Switching to a previously utilized Faraday cage, with a pH-increasing IIED turned on, immediately produced oscillations inside the cage for the first time in this location. However, simultaneous measurements outside the cage produced no oscillations! The in-cage oscillations were not highly periodic. The next follow-up measurement (about 1-2 days later) gave improved oscillations inside the cage, especially at the low frequency end, and the baseline pH moved up slightly. The next follow-up measurement (another 1-2 days later) showed no pH-oscillations or pH-effects whatsoever. However, at the next follow-up measurement (1-2 days later), small oscillations were seen both inside and outside the cage but they were not well correlated with each other. Even with months of IIED exposure (conditioning device plus pH-increasing device), large, robust oscillations did not become established.

In trying to interpret this behavior, revisiting Equation 6.1 at the beginning of the chapter is useful. From Figure 6.30, one might conclude that the conditioning-type IIED's are not very powerful compared to the pH-decreasing or pH-increasing IIEDs and that this environment has a strong, natural leakage rate. Introducing the Faraday cage, which was probably strongly conditioned, temporarily boosted Q_C to be positive inside the cage but not outside the cage. However, this initial conditioning "charge" residing in the cage probably leaked away into the immediate environment at a faster rate than Q_D could replenish it and so Q_C became negative for some period of time before things settled down to a slowly rising Q_C condition both inside <u>and</u> outside the cage. Eventually, an asymptotic condition was reached which yielded low amplitude oscillations.

<u>Location 2</u>: A professor from a nearby university asked to collaborate with us on the reproduction of the space conditioning effect in his laboratory. We agreed and, after discussing our protocol in some detail, our technician delivered two newly constructed Faraday cages, one new pH meter with accessory temperature probe and pH electrodes plus one high-resolution digital thermometer for air temperature measurement. They supplied the computer plus software and our very capable technician was assigned the task of interfacing with this professor and his post-doc.

Almost immediately a problem arose with the water pH. Both the pH and temperature data were excessively noisy and the recorded temperatures were too high. The manufacturer replaced this meter and, except for a significantly high pH-electrode drift, it seemed OK. We had earlier wanted them to begin by measuring the air temperature with the high-resolution digital thermometer but somehow it had gone missing. Further, after telling the professor how we wanted them to perform the experiment, he wanted the protocol changed, proceeded with his own modifications and didn't seek any further assistance from us.

At this point, although we were very doubtful that the experiment would go anywhere as a reproduction vehicle of our work, we decided to allow this professor to follow his own judgement with respect to the experiment with the rationale being that perhaps we would learn something. In actual fact, we did not hear from this professor again and thus learned nothing from their experiment, except perhaps that if you work with the wrong people, who will not even follow your protocol, then you have no right to expect a successful outcome. We presume that no conditioning effect was observed in their laboratory.

What we have learned from these two experiences is that (1) we should supply all the new equipment for any future collaborative attempt to generate a conditioned space in other people's laboratory, (2) we should set up this new equipment and have it run continuously in one of our highly conditioned spaces to saturate the entire system with the conditioning "charge", (3) have a firm agreement on the following of <u>our</u> protocol, at least initially until well-developed oscillations manifest in the new space and (4) move the total system to the new space and perhaps have one of our people work with it initially in the new space until it is "up and running" satisfactorily.

Our experience has been that, in strongly coupled environments, if the experimenter is impatient and changes the experiment frequently (even by just altering the position of the equipment), a series of often conflicting and/or incomprehensible measurement results may occur. Meticulous and painstaking efforts must be made to be <u>aware</u> of all the experimental conditions when making measurements in a conditioned space. Over ten thousand hours of T-oscillation, pH-oscillation and σ-oscillation data in both water and air have been recorded in our laboratories over the past two to three years and much more must be gathered before precise understanding of these new and remarkable phenomena is at hand. Because of the foregoing, Equation 6.1 should contain an additional term, Q_{eq}, for the test equipment in order to separate its level of conditioning from that of the environmental structures and space in the locale.

Some Summary Findings for the Locale Conditioning Experiments

- Continued use of an activated IIED in a particular site or locale eventually leads to what we have labeled a "conditioned" space. The conditioning time has been observed to be ~ 3-4 months for either a pH-lowering or pH-raising IIED or for an IIED designed solely for site conditioning.

- The degree of conditioning of this locale is manifested by the appearance of anomalous measured properties in that locale relative to a distant "normal" locale. As a function of site conditioning time, the first anomaly to be detected is the onset of air T-oscillations that then grow both in amplitude and oscillation continuity with conditioning time. The second anomaly to be detected is the onset of water pH and conductivity oscillations that also grow in amplitude and oscillation continuity with conditioning time. The third anomaly to be detected is the onset of DC magnetic field polarity effects on water pH. The fourth anomaly to be detected is highly time-correlated T- and pH-oscillations between sites located at some distance from each other.

- For high oscillation continuity levels, oscillation wave trains of rising or falling frequency often appear. A model involving four coupled differential equations as utilized in some specific chemical oscillation models can closely simulate the number of cycles and the progressive change in cycle waveform in a particular oscillation wave train. This type of wave train is generally initiated or terminated by a large absolute rate of change of temperature in the locale.

- Forced air convection experiments clearly indicated that the majority of the measured air T-oscillations did <u>not</u> arise from changes in the heat content of the physical air molecules located in the experimental locale but had their origins elsewhere (perhaps the vacuum).

- The radial spatial variation of air, T-oscillation amplitude surrounding what one presumes to be the D-space source (Faraday cage with central water vessel) of the oscillations is quite anomalous relative to typical D-space phenomena. Instead of decaying monotonically toward zero, the T-oscillation amplitude profile exhibits one intermediate maximum.

- Physical removal of this expected D-space source of the oscillations did not lead to rapid collapse of this anomalous T-oscillation amplitude profile. Instead, the profile remained with only very slow decay (if any) in magnitude and thus it was labeled as a "phantom" profile. Furthermore, this "phantom" profile is a robust effect, with air T-oscillation amplitudes commonly exceeding 2-3 °C and, consequently, is easily monitored. We ascribe its continued presence in the T-measurement as largely belonging to a vacuum counterpart of the proposed D-space source.

- The additional anomalous and very robust changes in the measured "phantom" air T-oscillation amplitude spatial profile, associated with both the presence of and the orientation of a large natural quartz crystal in the central region of the profile, further indicates that we are starting to register meaningful vacuum counterpart changes.

- Pseudo-random number generation algorithms run on computers located in both unconditioned and conditioned spaces initially exhibited no anomalous behavior. However, a 20-day interval of extremely non-random and oscillatory behavior developed for one computer in a conditioned space. A second anomalous event, dubbed the "Millennium Effect", occurred in another computer from just before Christmas, 1999, until just after New Year, 2000.

- The four main factors presently identified as important for a locale to exhibit the anomalous measurement behavior we have associated with site conditioning are (1) an activated IIED at some meaningful "intention-charge" level, (2) the degree of prior conditioning of the site itself, (3) the residual "intention-charge" level potentizing the total experimental measurement equipment and (4) the degree of inner self-management of the humans occupying the locale.

References

1. C. Von Reichenback, <u>Vital Force</u>, (J.S. Redfield, Clinton Hall, New York, 1851).

2. P.P. Gariaev, A.A. Vassiliev, K.V. Grigoriev, B.P. Poponin and V.A. Shcheglov, "The DNA Phantom Effect", Short Messages in Physics, FIAN, <u>11-12</u> (1992) 63-69 (in Russian).

3. R.D. Nelson, G.J. Bradish, and Y.H. Dobyns, <u>Random Event Generator Qualification, Calibration, and Analysis</u>, (Technical Note PEAR 89001, Princeton University, Princeton, NJ, April 1989)

4. D.I. Radin, <u>The Conscious Universe</u>, (Harper Edge, San Francisco, 1997).

Appendix 6.A: Method Used for Random Number Generation Studies

On 12/20/99, an HP Vectra Series 4 PC was brought into site B, the conditioned space, while another PC was placed in a distant unconditioned site on 1/3/00. The method used to compute pseudo-random number sequences

Table 6.A.1   Minute number 1 of a typical time series output using "RANDOM".

Observation for sum 99

Cell Number Column	Bernoulli random Variable Column
Cell 1	0
Cell 2	1
Cell 3	1
Cell 4	1
Cell 5	0
Cell 6	0
Cell 7	1
Cell 8	0
Cell 9	0
Cell 10	1
.	.
.	.
.	.
Cell 199	1
Cell 200	0

Sum: 102

	Column of Sums
Sum 1	93
Sum 2	98
Sum 3	94
Sum 4	103
Sum 5	98
Sum 6	103
Sum 7	105
Sum 8	106
Sum 9	96
Sum 10	104
.	.
.	.
Sum 99	102
Sum 100	98

Mean: 99.95

employs one of Microsoft Excel's macro functions. The Excel function "RANDOM" fills a range (specified on an Excel spreadsheet) with independent random numbers drawn from one of several distributions. We used the Bernoulli distribution which is characterized by a probability (set at 0.5) of success on a given trial. Bernoulli random variables have the value 0 or 1. If the variable is less than or equal to the probability of success (set at 0.5), the Bernoulli random variable is assigned the value of 1; otherwise, it is assigned the value of 0. This process models the coin flip. It also can be used to generate an output similar to the Random Event Generator (REG) used by the PEAR[3] group among others.

The specific program used an Excel macro that filled a column of 200 cells of a spreadsheet with 0's or 1's using the "RANDOM" function. One of the arguments of this function allows a starting point boundary condition to be selected to begin random number generation. We used the function "RANDBETWEEN" to return an evenly distributed random integer between 0 and 32767 for the seed (initial condition). As part of the program, the sum of the 200 cells was computed which theoretically would be <u>100</u> for a probability of 0.5 since half of the cells should be filled with 0's and the other half 1's. Table 6.A.1 shows the compilation of data for a typical minute of the time series.

We used the function "RANDOM" in this way to fill 200 cells of a spreadsheet column with pseudo-random variables 100 times per minute. Thus, 100 sums were calculated and tabulated every minute (see Table 6.A.1). The mean of these 100 sums was also tabulated along with their standard deviation. As expected the means tended to cluster around 100 with standard deviations about 7. The output is similar to the output of REGs.[3] The tabulation ended after 1026 minutes (17.1 hours). On each day, therefore, 102600 observations of sums of random variables were made. The effect size for this number of observations is the mean minus 100, the theoretical mean. The program was run automatically every day starting at exactly the same time (1:00 PM) and could be left unattended indefinitely until the data was collected. The computers were not used for any other purpose during this experimental series.

Table 6.A.2   Typical daily time series output for cell 2.

	Means	Standard Dev.	Sums of Cell 2
Minute 1	99.95	7.46794	55
Minute 2	100.64	6.53587	47
Minute 3	100.40	6.96266	44
Minute 4	99.74	7.02161	52
Minute 5	100.49	6.3518	53
Minute 6	100.68	7.28132	49
Minute 7	101.27	7.43578	45
Minute 8	99.54	7.18367	56
Minute 9	99.90	6.99636	49
Minute 10	100.26	6.96061	50
.	.	.	.
.	.	.	.
.	.	.	.
Minute 1025	99.88	6.84828	53
Minute 1026	100.70	7.06892	47

Another tabulation performed concurrently involved recording the output of particular cells of the 200 filled by 0's or 1's. Cell numbers two (counting from the top of the column) and 100 were selected (see Table 6.A.1 for the cell 2 example). In one minute these cells were filled with 100 random variables (either 0 or 1) and their accumulated sum per minute should theoretically be 50. These accumulated sums from cell 2 and cell 100 were also tabulated (see Table 6.A.2 for the cell 2 example). A time series record (1-minute interval) of both these accumulated sums of individual cells and means of sums constituted the primary output of each daily experiment as shown in Table 6.A.2.

CHAPTER 7

Some Relevant, Quantitative Aspects of 20th Century Physics

In this chapter, we return to the central task of illuminating some of the inner workings of the QM black box, expanding on Chapter 2 to now provide a quantitative base for evaluating many of the new considerations. Therefore, this chapter will have important threads of mathematics weaving through it; however, the bulk of the mathematical details will be relegated to appendices in order not to disrupt the flow of the key ideas. The central issue to be focused on here is the detailed relationships connecting direct space (D-space or (x,y,z,t)-space) with reciprocal space (R-space or $(x^{-1},y^{-1},z^{-1},t^{-1})$-space). We start in this chapter with a common background from today's accepted physics before adding the necessary extensions of theory needed to expand the usefulness of this physics (provided in Chapter 8).

The reciprocal lattice concept: In the early part of this century, the concept of the <u>reciprocal lattice</u> was developed for x-ray crystallography. Later, in the 1930's, the theme was picked up by solid state physicists and utilized in the description of electron wave functions in solids. Since the concept of <u>reciprocal space</u> is a generalization of the reciprocal lattice concept, we first need to understand what is a reciprocal lattice.

It is well known that a crystal consists of a periodic array of atoms of the same type in three dimensions. Each of these atoms is a scattering center for an incident beam of x-rays. Along the three crystal axes, respectively, the periodic repeat distance for the atoms is defined as <u>a</u>, <u>b</u> and <u>c</u>. These atoms form planes whose collective scattering can be constructively superimposed in certain key directions, relative to the incident x-ray beam, and these scattered x-ray beams travel through a unique set of points in D-space called the reciprocal lattice of points.

To construct the reciprocal lattice for any crystal, one proceeds as follows. For each stack of planes in the D-space crystal, defined by the indices (hkl), a normal is constructed and this defines a set of interplanar spacings, d_{hkl} (see appendix 7.A to determine the connections between hkl, <u>a</u> <u>b</u> <u>c</u> and the diffraction process). All of these direction normals are arranged so as to radiate from a common origin and, on each normal, a point is placed at a distance $d^*_{hkl} = K / d_{hkl}$, where K is usually taken as unity in most theoretical work and equal to the wavelength, λ, of the incident radiation in the practical task of interpreting diffraction patterns. Thus, these points are at distances from the origin equal to the reciprocals of the interplanar spacings (for K = 1)

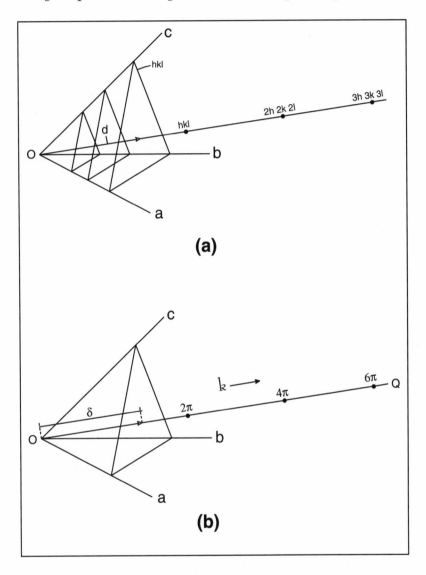

Figure 7.1 (a) Illustration that a set of rational planes of spacing d_{hkl} in direct space is represented in reciprocal space by a row of points with separation $1/d_{hkl}$ that lie on the normal to the set of planes and (b) illustration to generalize the notion of "reciprocal" for a single plane along its normal direction, OQ, and characterized by a periodic change along OQ. The phase is zero at $k=0$, 2π at $k=1/\delta$ and $n(2\pi)$ at $k=n(1/\delta)$ from this origin.

and lie on the points of a lattice that is "reciprocal" to the original lattice. These points are designated hkl, 2h2k2l, etc. in Figure 7.1a[1].

Now consider a fictitious plane with indices (nh, nk, nl) having 1/n th the spacing of the (hkl) planes. For the purposes of x-ray crystallography, the n th order Bragg reflection discussed in Appendix 7.A behaves precisely as if it were the 1st order reflection from (nh, nk, nl). Thus, all values of $d_{nh,nk,nl} = \left(\frac{1}{n}\right) d_{hkl}$ can be conceptually regarded as occurring in the direct lattice and all values of $n(1/d_{hkl})$ occur in the conceptual reciprocal lattice (see Figure 7.1a).

By following this procedure for other sets of planes in the crystal, one locates other network points of the reciprocal lattice. In this way, one obtains two lattices that may interpenetrate each other. For example, if we start with a crystal having a face-centered cubic lattice, as indicated in Figure 7.2a, so that there are atoms in the cube corner position plus atoms in every face-centered position, then it turns out that the reciprocal lattice has active points at the corners of a cube and also in the cube center (see Figure 7.2b). This is called a body-centered cubic lattice. The numbers marked at the active points of this reciprocal lattice designate the particular (hkl) set of planes in the direct lattice (Figure 7.2a) giving rise to that particular point in the reciprocal lattice.

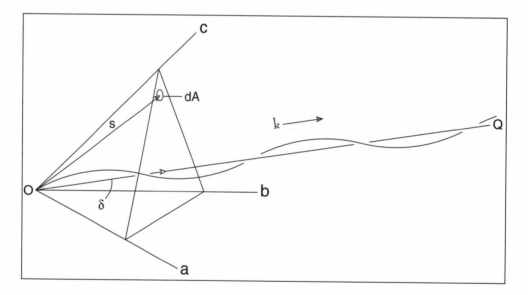

Figure 7.1c   Illustration to further generalize to a small area, dA, on the plane where δ is the projection of the vector s, which connects the origin to dA, onto the plane normal, OQ.

Because the planes of index (hkl) constitute a periodic sequence, Buerger [1] makes the point that, in the most general terms, this repetition can be described as cyclic so that the interval of repetition, d, corresponds to 2π in a harmonic wave sense. For the reciprocal representation, the interval 1/d represents 2π. Thus, if we consider the single plane in Figure 7.1b, its reciprocal representation may be defined along its normal, OQ, similar to what it was for Figure 7.1a. Let this reciprocal be characterized by a periodic change along the normal so that, in terms of phase, the phase is zero at the origin, 2π at distance of $1/\delta$ from the origin and $n(2\pi)$ at distance $n(1/\delta)$ from the origin. Here, the absolute value of the distance of the plane from the origin determines the distances from the origin where the phase of the reciprocal has values of $n(2\pi)$.

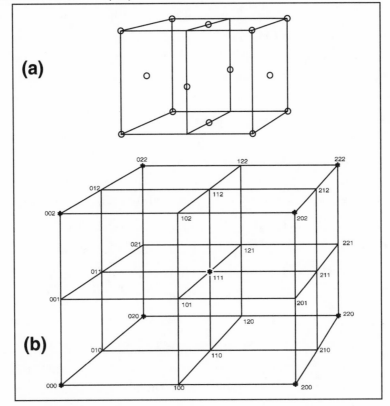

Figure 7.2 (a) Representation of a direct lattice of atoms (face-centered cubic array of circles) and (b) its reciprocal lattice (body-centered cubic array of stars). The numbers at the various coordinate points in this reciprocal lattice are the Miller indices for the various sets of parallel planes in the direct lattice.

The Reciprocal Space Concept: Generalizing further, let the phase be defined at <u>all</u> points along the normal so that the reciprocal to a plane is taken as being represented by a <u>continuous</u> phase variation along the normal to the plane. The phase variation then is linear with the change of coordinate position, k, along this normal and, since the period in reciprocal space is $1/\delta$, the phase at any distance k from the origin is $2\pi k\delta$. Using complex number notation, this phase component is given by exp $(i2\pi k\delta)$. This approach of Buerger's[1] merely states that the phase along a line in reciprocal space $((x^{-1}, y^{-1}, z^{-1}, t^{-1})$-space) normal to a plane in direct space $((x,y,z,t)$-space) is controlled by the distance, δ, of the plane from the origin.

The amplitude component of variation along the line, OQ, in reciprocal space is controlled by some quality of the plane in direct space. Let this amplitude be W for the general quality being considered. For x-ray diffraction applications, W is taken as the scattering power of the plane that is proportional to the number of electrons in the plane. Thus, the value of the reciprocal at position, k, along the normal to the plane is just given by Equation 1 in Table 7.1. Thus, the reciprocal of the plane behaves like a stationary wave of amplitude W and wavelength, $1/\delta$, along a line normal to the plane.

This generalization is quite independent of the use of planes as we will now show. From the foregoing, all points on the plane have the same phase effect, since the phase is controlled by the distance, δ, of the plane from the origin. However, the weighting, W, need not be constant over the plane and its density, ρ_w, may vary from point to point in the plane. Consider the incremental area, dA, in Figure 7.1c, to have a quality density of ρ_w. Then, its incremental effect on the phase at k is the same as that of any other part of the plane; i.e., $k\delta$. However, from Figure 7.1c, δ is just the component of the vector $\underline{s}$ along the OQ line so that $k\delta$ is just the scalar dot product of the two vectors, $\underline{s} \bullet \underline{k}$. Thus, we have the result given by Equation 2a in Table 7.1. By integrating Equation 7.1.2a over the area of the plane, we obtain Equation 2b in Table 7.1. Finally, this effect produced at position $\underline{k}$ in R-space due to an incremental region in D-space at the end of a vector, $\underline{s}$, can be integrated over a volume rather than just a plane in D-space to yield Equation 2c in Table 7.1. Equation 7.1.2c provides a completely general way by which the effects of all regions in D-space are felt at the end of a vector $\underline{k}$ in R-space (both phase and amplitude)[1]. This transformation from D-space to R-space given by Equation 7.1.2c is identical with the Fourier Transform (FT). Thus, defining ρ_s as the density of a particular quality in a D-space object, the conjugate quality in R-space is given by the FT, $F(\underline{k})$, and vice versa. In one dimension, transformation from one space to the other, T, and the reverse transformation, T^{-1}, are given by Equations 3a and 3b in Table 7.1. As is well known, and as we will see later, D-space/R-space transformation of any number of dimensions can be readily treated in this way.

Table 7.1   From a Lattice Plane Reciprocal to Reciprocal Space.

Reciprocal of a Plane,	$R_k = We^{i2\pi k\delta}$	(1)
Generalization		
The Incremental Effect, $dR_k = dW\, e^{i2\pi\,\underline{s}\,\bullet\,\underline{k}} = \rho_w\, dA\, e^{i2\pi\,\underline{s}\,\bullet\,\underline{k}}$		(2a)
The Area Effect,	$R_k = \displaystyle\int_{AREA} \rho_w\, e^{i2\pi\,\underline{s}\,\bullet\,\underline{k}}\, dA$	(2b)
The Volume Effect,	$R_k = \displaystyle\int_{D-SPACE} \rho_w\, e^{i2\pi\,\underline{s}\,\bullet\,\underline{k}}\, dV$	(2c)

The D-space to R-space Transformation Pair (1-dimensional)

$$T:\quad F(\underline{k}) = \frac{1}{(2\pi)^{\frac{1}{2}}} \int_{D-space} \rho_s e^{i2\pi\underline{s}\bullet\underline{k}}\, ds \tag{3a}$$

$$T^{-1}:\quad \rho_s = \frac{1}{(2\pi)^{\frac{1}{2}}} \int_{R-space} F(\underline{k}) e^{-i2\pi\underline{s}\bullet\underline{k}}\, d\underline{k}. \tag{3b}$$

$$T\,T^{-1} = 1;\ T^2 = \tilde{I}\ \text{ and }\ T^4 = 1 \tag{4}$$

The transformation, T, involves the phase operator $e^{i2\pi sk}$ while the inverse transformation, T^{-1}, requires $e^{-i2\pi sk}$. Ewald[2] first diagrammed the results of repeated transformation and these form a group of order 4. If $\tilde{I}$ represents the operation of inversion and 1 represents the operation of identity, then

$$T\,T^{-1} = 1;\ T^2 = \tilde{I}\ \text{ and }\ T^4 = 1\,. \qquad (7.1)$$

Figure 7.3, from Ewald[2], illustrates the process path taken by Equation 7.1.

<u>The D-space/R-space Connection in Physical Reality</u>: Historically, the foregoing have been largely applied to periodic structures like crystals and to time-domain signals of one sort or other, while the generalized applicability to any D-space object and to any quality of that object has been mislaid, or at

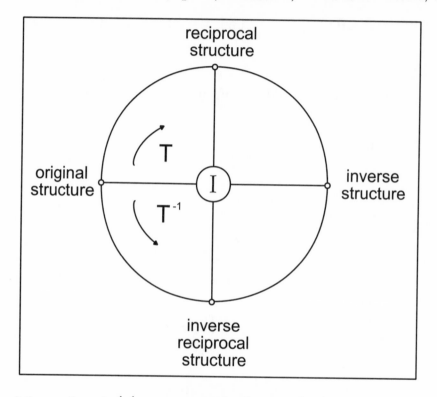

Figure 7.3   Structural changes associated with repeated Fourier transformations in a given direction (T *= clockwise and* T⁻¹ *= counterclockwise).*

least insufficiently explored. Table 7.2 presents a variety of time-domain signals in the left-hand column with their FT (or frequency domain counterparts) in the right-hand column. This connection between the two columns has been taken for granted for many decades. People have not yet associated it with the larger perspective of conjugate pattern relationships between multidimensional D-space reality and the same dimensional R-space reality. One of the most intriguing features associated with broadening our perspective on the use of these Fourier Mates expressed by Equations 3 in

Table 7.2   *Some Common Fourier Transform Pairs.*

f(x)	F(k)
(a) Math Symbol	
$\lambda\, f(x)$	$\lambda F(k)$
$f(ax)$	$(1/a)F(k/a)$
$ix\, f(x)$	$d/dk\; F(k)$
$d/dx\; f(x)$	$-ik\; F(k)$
$e^{ixk_0} f(x)$	$F(k+k_0)$
$f(x+x_0)$	$e^{-ixk_0} F(k)$
1	$\delta(x)$
$e^{-\frac{1}{2}x^2}$	$e^{-\frac{1}{2}k^2}$

(b) Line Trace

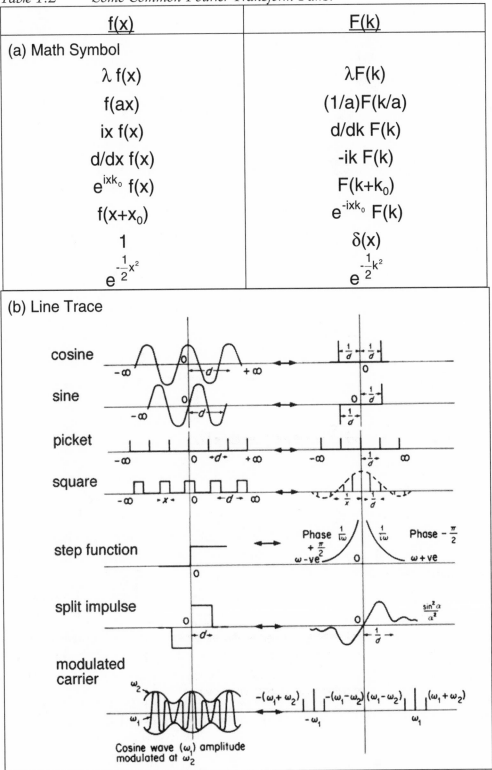

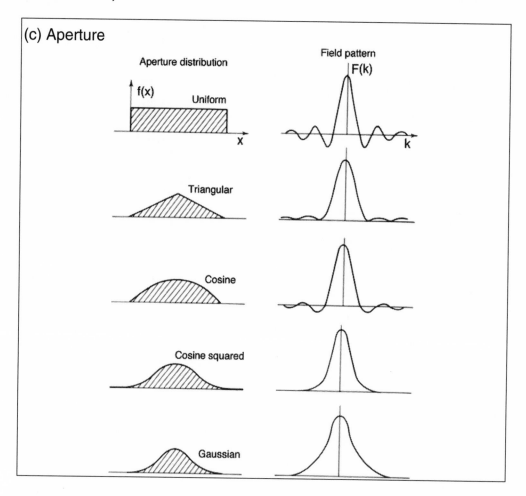

(c) Aperture

Table 7.1 is that they <u>implicitly</u> embody wave/particle aspects in the expressions of quality that one can discriminate in our D-space substance. Thus, one of the cornerstones of QM is implicitly built into our physics when one attends to both D-space <u>and</u> R-space counterparts of an object. Non-local effects are also built in because any quality density in a small region of D-space is given in terms of an integral over the entire domain of R-space so that seemingly separated D-space regions are actually connected to each other via the R-space domain. Later, we will calculate the relative variation, throughout all of the four-dimensional D-space, of the non-local force connecting two remotely located D-space objects (see Chapter 8). For the moment, and from a purely thermodynamic perspective, the Gibbs Free Energy, **G**, of a volume element of substance should include contributions from both its D-space aspect as well as its R-space aspect and may be expressed symbolically as:

$$G = G(x, y, z, t, x^{-1}, y^{-1}, z^{-1}, t^{-1})$$ (7.2a)

$$= G(x_0, y_0, z_0, t_0, x_0^{-1}, y_0^{-1}, z_0^{-1}, t_0^{-1})$$

$$+ \alpha_x \frac{\partial G}{\partial x} + \alpha_y \frac{\partial G}{\partial y} + \cdots + \beta_{x^{-1}} \frac{\partial G}{\partial (1/x)} + \beta_{y^{-1}} \frac{\partial G}{\partial (1/y)} + \cdots \quad (7.2b)$$

This Taylor series expansion about some origin illustrates the need to consider variations in R-space coordinates as well as D-space coordinates (see Appendix 7.B). It is when one is considering sub-atomic and atomic size scales that these latter terms can become large and begin to dominate Equations 7.2.

In a recent and quite elegant paper, Wheeler[3] has proposed and deeply analyzed a new eight-dimensional conformal gauging that provides a consistent geometric theory of both gravitation and electromagnetism. His procedure avoids all the problems associated with Weyl's 80-year old theory[4] and now allows full realization of its goals. By placing conformal gauging on an eight-dimensional base-space instead of the usual four-dimensional base space, Wheeler has been able to overcome the long-standing problem of object size change in models based on scale invariance. The extra four dimensions are contained in a biconformal co-space having the same mathematical structure and transformation properties as momentum space; i.e., a space having dimensions of inverse length. Thus, just as we are proposing in this book, an 8-space comprised of a direct 4-space (D-space) and a reciprocal 4-space (R-space) produces this much sought-after unification.

Three theoretical techniques have been utilized in the past for adding extra dimensions to fundamental models of physics[3]: (a) topological compactification of the extra dimensions (routinely employed in Kaluza-Klein theories), (b) construction of field equations or motion laws that dynamically reduce the scale of the extra dimensions so that they play no macroscopic role (recently employed in order to incorporate mass as a fifth dimension) and (c) identification of the extra dimensions with everyday properties of macroscopic matter (used in special relativity with time as a coordinate in a higher dimensional space rather than as an intrinsically different type of parameter on a three-dimensional space). Wheeler[3] regards the extra four dimensions of the biconformal co-space as having a type (c) local interpretation. Thus, incorporating Wheeler's elegant work into our perspective provides strong theoretical support, at a very fundamental physics level, that a D-space/R-space viewpoint is very relevant to human experience.

It is interesting that recent activity in the area of String-theory, specifically called Brane-theory, has introduced the two concepts of

Direct/Reciprocal space and electric/magnetic monopoles using quite different descriptors[5]. In the traditional view, particles such as electrons and quarks (which carry Noether charges) are seen as fundamental, whereas particles such as magnetic monopoles (which carry topological charge) are seen as derivative. In 1977, a new conjecture was made that there might exist an alternative formulation of physics in which the roles of Noether charges and topological charges are reversed. In this dual picture, the magnetic monopoles would be the elementary objects while the familiar leptons and quarks would arise as solitons. Under the rubric "Dualities of Dualities", the electric/magnetic monopole conversion goes by the name of S-Duality while a different kind of duality, called T-Duality, relates two kinds of particles that arise in string theory when a string loops around a compact dimension once (called a "vibrating" particle) or many times by stretching the string (called a "winding" particle). T-Duality states that the winding particles for a circle of radius R are the same as the vibrating particles for a circle of radius 1/R, and vice versa.

If one reduces a 6-D space-time to four dimensions by curling up two dimensions, the fundamental string and the solitonic string each acquire T-Duality with the T-Duality of the solitonic string being just the S-Duality of the fundamental string, and vice versa. This conjecture, in which the interchange of charges in one picture is just the inversion of length in the other picture, is called the "Duality of Dualities".

Experimentally Generated Fourier Transforms

As discussed in the previous section, the Fourier Transform arises in any wave diffraction process and connects the superposed diffracted wave pattern to the physical geometry of the substratum (object) causing

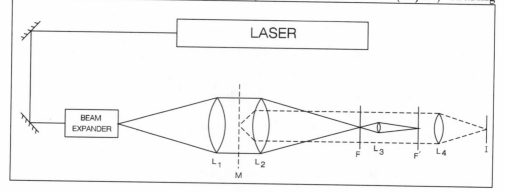

Figure 7.4   Experimental set-up used for generating the diffraction patterns at I from the mask, M (L_j = lenses and (F,F') = focal planes).

the waves to diffract. Thus, the substratum geometry is our D-space object and the diffracted wave pattern is intimately connected to its R-space counterpart. Since wave diffraction forms the basis for, or cornerstone of, holography with which most people are familiar in today's world, this is a familiar example of such D-space/R-space pattern relationships using light. A less complex, but nonetheless similar in principle, procedure for illustrating this important transformation relationship has been presented by Harburn et al[6] using the apparatus illustrated in Figure 7.4.

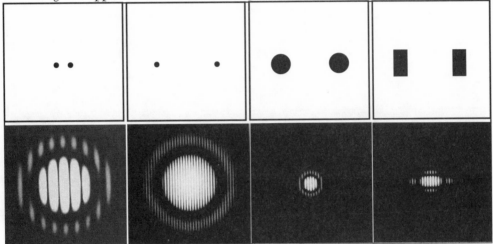

(a)

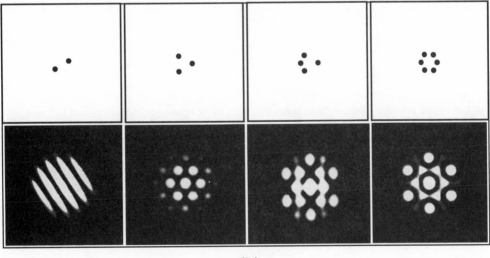

(b)

Figure 7.5a,b   Composite figure of D-space-time hole patterns and their corresponding R-space diffraction patterns as representatives of their intensity patterns; (a) illustrates size, spacing and geometry effects while (b) illustrates increasing pattern richness as the array of holes in the mask becomes more complex.

In Figure 7.4, the 50 mWatt source of coherent light passes through the beam expander which then behaves as a secondary light source of high intensity that is in the back focal plane of the collimating lens L_1 and is imaged in the focal plane F of the objective lens L_2. A mask, M, containing a number of geometrically arranged holes through which the light passes, is placed in the parallel portion of the beam so that the Fraunhofer <u>Diffraction</u> <u>Pattern</u> of this mask appears at F. Because of the high source intensity, these small diffraction patterns at F can be considerably enlarged with a projection

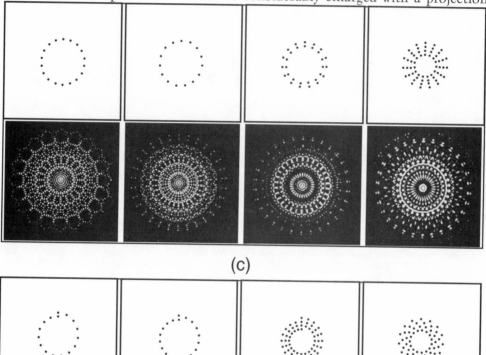

(c)

(d)

Figure 7.5c,d   Composite figure of D-space-time hole patterns and their corresponding R-space diffraction patterns as representatives of their intensity patterns; (c) and (d) further illustrate increasing pattern richness as the array of holes in the mask become even more complex than those depicted in Figure 7.5b.

lens, L_3, before being recorded photographically at F' with conveniently short exposure times.

A comparison between hole geometry in the mask, M, and diffraction pattern at F' from Harburn et al's[6] study has been given in Figure 7.5 for a few cases to illustrate the relationship between some D-space objects and their R-space counterparts. What is recorded at F' is the intensity of the diffraction pattern which, as we will see later is the modulus squared of the Fourier transform not the FT itself. The top panel in Figure 7.5a shows masks with two holes of different size, shape and spacing. The bottom panel shows the diffraction pattern corresponding to each mask above. From Figures 7.5a and 7.5b, one can see how (1) increasing the spacing between a pair of holes in D-space, increases the frequency of the perpendicularly oriented bands in the basic ring pattern that is observed from a single hole, (2) increasing the size of the hole decreases the size of the segmented ring pattern, (3) rotating the orientation of the holes in one direction, rotates the segmented ring pattern in the opposite direction by the same amount, (4) square holes lead to elliptical ring patterns rather than circular ones and (5) increasing the number and symmetry of the holes in the mask increases the complexity of the diffraction pattern. This richness of detail in the diffraction patterns is illustrated in Figures 7.5c and 7.5d for a set of holes arranged in circular and spiral patterns, respectively. These mandala-like patterns are similar to what many individuals see internally while in a deep state of meditation and one wonders about D-space/R-space perception in this regard.

Theoretically Generated Fourier Transforms

In this section, we expand on Equations 3 of Table 7.1 and will consider objects of one-dimensional, two-dimensional and three-dimensional geometry. We will calculate the Fourier Transform, $F(\underline{k})$ and it's modulus, $I(\underline{k})$, for these different objects and will display these modulus patterns to see what we can learn about D-space/R-space relationships. Most of the mathematical details are presented in Appendix 7.C. Our position vector for the object, given some chosen origin in D-space, is $\underline{s} = \underline{s}(x,y,z)$. Our position vector for the conjugate in R-space, is $\underline{k} = \underline{k}(k_x,k_y,k_z)$. In general, $F(\underline{k})$ is mathematically complex, with real (Re) and imaginary (Im) parts that depend upon the particular choice of the coordinate system that we use. Since one usually prefers to work with an invariant quantity, it is better to calculate the modulus, I, given by Equation 1a in Table 7.3. F^* is the complex conjugate of F (found by replacing $+i$ by $-i$ in $F(\underline{k})$) and I is <u>always</u> treated as a positive real quantity. For objects with circular symmetry, we use polar coordinates and obtain $I(k_r, k_z)$ where $k_r = [k_x^2 + k_y^2]^{1/2}$. From the definition of object volume, V, found by taking the integral over x, y and z, one can see that the point $\underline{k} = 0$ in R-space has an I-value that is just equal to V ($I(\underline{k} = 0) = V$). Thus, we can calculate a normalized modulus, I_n, which is size independent and is given by Equation 1b in Table 7.3. Thus, the basic R-space map can be graphed on the [0,1] interval since $I_n = 1$ as $\underline{k} \to 0$ and $I_n = 0$ as $\underline{k} \to \infty$. We shall see in Appendix 7.C, that the inner portion of I_n for simple objects has a pattern very similar to that of Figure 6.21.

For combinations of j-objects, all the individual $F_j(\underline{k})$ must be referred to the same origin by simple translations and rotations. For the simple

Table 7.3   *Theoretically Generated FT Patterns.*

Modulus,

$$I(k_x, k_y, k_z) = [F(\underline{k})F^*(\underline{k})]^{1/2} = [\text{Re}\,(F)^2 + \text{Im}\,(F)^2]^{1/2} \tag{1a}$$

Normalized Modulus (V = object volume),

$$I_n(k) = I(k)/V \tag{1b}$$

Object Translation (0,0,0) to $(\bar{x}, \bar{y}, \bar{z})$,

$$F'(k_x, k_y, k_z) = e^{i(\bar{x}k_x + \bar{y}k_y + \bar{z}k_z)} F(k_x, k_y, k_z) \tag{2}$$

Object Rotation (by angle θ),

$$k_x' = k_x \cos\theta + k_y \sin\theta$$
$$k_y' = -k_x \sin\theta + k_y \cos\theta. \tag{3}$$

<u>translation</u> of an object from its original center 0 at (0,0,0) to a new center $0'$ at ($\bar{x}, \bar{y}, \bar{z}$) in D-space, the relationship between the original FT, $\mathbf{F(\underline{k})}$, and the new one, $\mathbf{F'(\underline{k})}$, is just that given by Equation 2 of Table 7.3. Thus, this translation involves only a $\underline{k}$-dependent phase factor and I_n is not changed at all. For a simple rotation of a two-dimensional object in a plane through its center, 0, by an angle θ, one requires only the change (k_x, k_y) going to (k_x', k_y') given by Equations 3 of Table 7.3. Equation 3a of Table 7.1 and Equations 2 and 3 of Table 7.3 allow one to evaluate $I_n\mathbf{(\underline{k})}$ for an object of any shape, volume, orientation and position provided we know the quality density, ρ_s, as a function of position (x,y,z) in the object. Let us now look at $I_n\mathbf{(\underline{k})}$ for a variety of one-dimensional (1D), two-dimensional (2D) and three-dimensional (3D) D-space objects. The mathematical formulae for $\mathbf{F(\underline{k})}$ and $I_n\mathbf{(\underline{k})}$ are developed in Appendix 7.C. Here, we just focus on the $I_n\mathbf{(\underline{k})}$ patterns and what they mean. As a simple starting approximation, we will consider our objects to have a continuum and constant quality density, ρ_s, throughout the object as contrasted with a granular or atom-like quality density variation in the object.

<u>1D-Objects</u>: We start by considering the six line forms shown in Figure 7.6a and consider them to have infinitesimal but constant cross-sectional area. In Figure 7.6b, these forms are also shown in the left-hand column. The central column gives a section plot (or contour plot) of I_n as a function of k_x and k_y with y being the vertical direction and x being the horizontal direction (see Figure 7.6a) for the corresponding shape on the left. The right hand column provides a cut through this Figure along the k_y-coordinate for all shapes. These plots all correspond to the diffraction pattern of the physical aperture (object shape) under consideration.

For the single rod (or slit), the k_y-direction in R-space is colinear with the y-direction in D-space and each oscillation in I_n decays in amplitude as one moves from the center of the slit to either end. Increasing the length of the rod (slit) reduces the size of the undulation intervals, Δk_y, for the bumps in the I_n profile. This is consistent with Figure 7.5a where the larger is the D-space object, the smaller is its characteristic pattern in R-space. For the two parallel rods (slits), displaced from each other by a distance ℓ in the x-direction, from Equation 2 of Table 7.3, a phase difference of $e^{i\ell k_x}$ exists between them. This causes the second to interfere with the first to produce a dominant

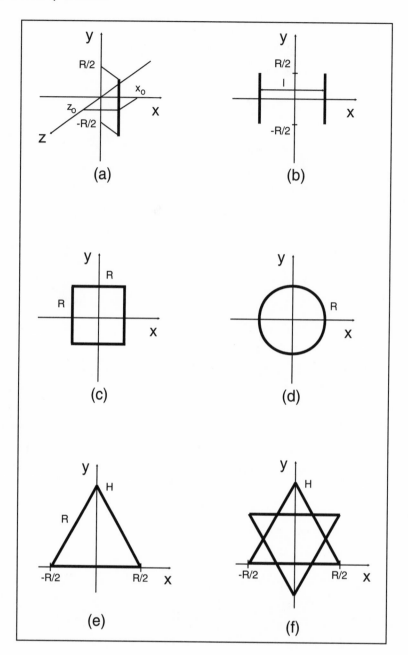

Figure 7.6a   Various 1-dimensional slit geometries (wire geometries) in D-space for which Fourier Transform representations in R-space have been calculated.

oscillation in I_n along the k_x-direction. These two results are remarkably like the classical double slit experiment of Young for either photons or electrons. Whereas a single vertical slit gives a uniform intensity in the central region of the slit on a screen behind the slit, a double slit exhibits a typical diffraction phenomenon on this screen along a line between the two slits. Perhaps what

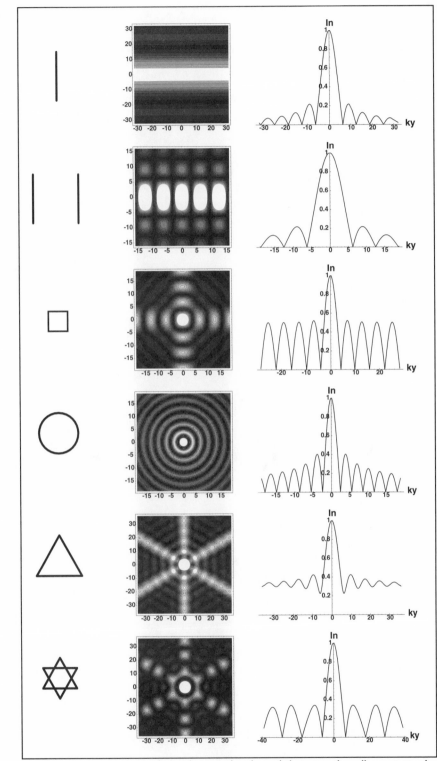

Figure 7.6b   Comparison plots of normalized modulus, I_n, for all six 1-D objects vs.
(k_x, k_y) maps in the middle column and vs. a k_y or k_n plot in the right column.

actually happens here is that the electron's pilot wave guides the electron into appropriate collision sites of this undulating R-space pattern for the two slits.

For the square line object (or slit), from the foregoing, one now expects interference effects from opposite members so that I_n exhibits both ($k_x = 0$, k_y)- and (k_x, $k_y = 0$) – type undulations. For the circular line object, the I_n (k_y) plot clearly shows the circular symmetry pattern of concentric rings. For the isosceles triangle pattern, one observes high intensity branches in R-space along directions perpendicular to each straight line (just as in the single rod case). What is remarkable here is that this intensity does not drop off as one moves to higher k-values in R-space. Finally, for the "Star of David" configuration, one sees the expected interference effects in the R-space pattern due to parallel rod segments in the D-space object. From all of this, one would expect that, for polygonal line forms having an odd number of sides in D-space, the R-space pattern would exhibit a high intensity branch perpendicular to each D-space rod segment. Further, as the number of sides in the polygon increased, the R-space pattern should approach that of the circular form.

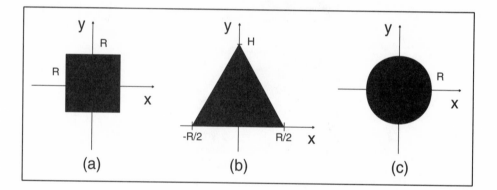

Figure 7.7a   Various 2-dimensional sheet geometries in D-space for which Fourier Transform representations in R-space have been calculated.

These calculations show that this expectation is correct but that, even a polygon of 31 sides has not yet reached the circle in terms of R-space pattern, and that, as the number of sides increases from 3 to 5 to 7 to 9, etc., the strength of the high intensity asymptote branches diminish in magnitude as one goes to large k values.

<u>2D-Objects</u>: Figure 7.7a reveals infinitesimally thin sheets of square, circular and isosceles triangle shape. The I_n results for these three shapes are just obtained from the three line shapes of Figure 7.6a by integrating over the

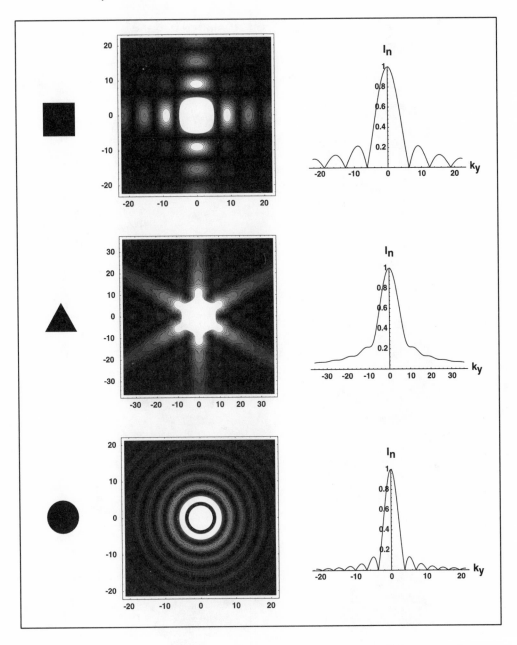

Figure 7.7b   Comparison plots of normalized modulus, I_n, for all three 2-D objects vs. k_y. Plots on the right are cross-sections of the middle 2-D I_n maps.

interior volume of these line shapes according to Eq. 3a of Table 7.1 and Eqs. 1 of Table 7.3. Figure 7.7b shows both the contour and section plots along k_y for these three shapes. The R-space patterns for these three shapes are qualitatively similar to those found for the line forms but quantitatively

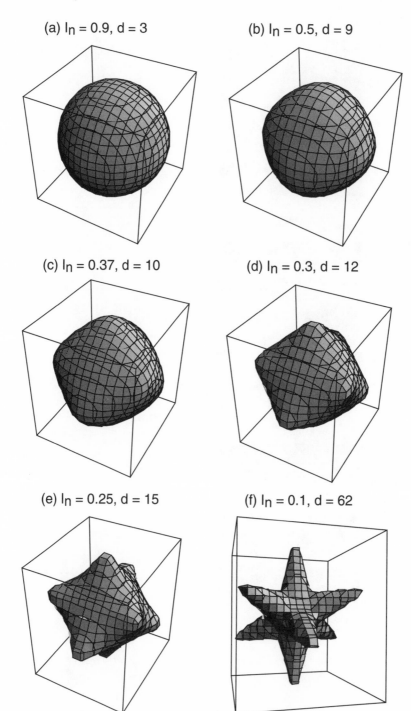

(a) $I_n = 0.9$, d = 3

(b) $I_n = 0.5$, d = 9

(c) $I_n = 0.37$, d = 10

(d) $I_n = 0.3$, d = 12

(e) $I_n = 0.25$, d = 15

(f) $I_n = 0.1$, d = 62

Figure 7.8   Various normalized isomodulus plots for a full 3-D tetrahedron at different values of I_n. *Here, d represents the maximum value of* $\{k_x, k_y, k_z\}$. *The scale of the plots extends from –d to +d in all three orthogonal directions considered in the computation.*

different in detail. In particular, we note that I_n for the triangle is a decaying function with k_y at large k_y and does not plateau to a constant value as does the line form. It should also be noted for these 2D shapes that, in the k_z-direction of R-space, I_n will appear as a long intense rod through the centroid of the sheet.

3-D-Objects: For the three 2-D-objects of Figure 7.7a, we can integrate in the z-direction to produce the cube, sphere and tetrahedron. Once again, the results are qualitatively like those found for the lower dimensional forms. At small values of k_y, I_n appears to be spherical. As k_y increases, geometrical changes develop so that the I_n-MAP distorts to form high intensity R-space channels along those coordinate directions perpendicular to the D-space faces for the object. Of course, parallel faces produce interference so that I_n along these channel-directions develop a decaying scalloped appearance. For the sphere, I_n forms a series of scalloped shells surrounding a central core. For the tetrahedron, Figure 7.8 illustrates the three dimensional I_n-MAP shapes for the particular values of I_n shown with the scale of the plots extending from $-d$ to $+d$ in all three directions of the computation (d represents the maximum value of (k_x, k_y, k_z) considered).

4D-Objects: 3-D objects moving at some velocity trace out a volume element in space-time to become a 4D-object. Thus, a uniform density spherical D-space object traces out a cylindrical shape in space-time and its R-space counterpart qualitatively appears as concentric cylindrical shells surrounding an intense cylindrical core. Of course, the orientation of this cylindrical system will change with the sphere velocity in D-space and, via Equation 2 of Table 7.3, the R-space counterpart will change in detailed quantitative ways.

Experiment/Theory Comparison

In Figure 7.5b, the experimentally-generated diffraction pattern for a mask with a hexagonal array of 6 holes was given. To prove that the Fourier Transform truly represents the diffraction pattern, we calculate I_n for the case of 6 hexagonally arranged holes and compare it with the experimental result. Figure 7.9 shows this comparison and completely supports the assertion that the Fourier Transform quantitatively reproduces the diffraction result for specific cases.

<u>**Limitations and Approximation**</u>s: The limitations of the continuum approximation used in the foregoing calculations can be explored by looking at the granularity approximation which is illustrated in Figure 7.10 for an infinitesimally thin equilateral triangle sheet. The continuum approximation is the case where <u>every</u> point in the triangle is of uniform substance density. Perhaps the simplest granularity approximation is the case where the triangle is composed of close-packed spheres of uniform substance density. A more refined granularity approximation would be one for which a small central core of each circle had a very high substance density while the outer rim of the circle had a much smaller substance density. Here, we only look at the

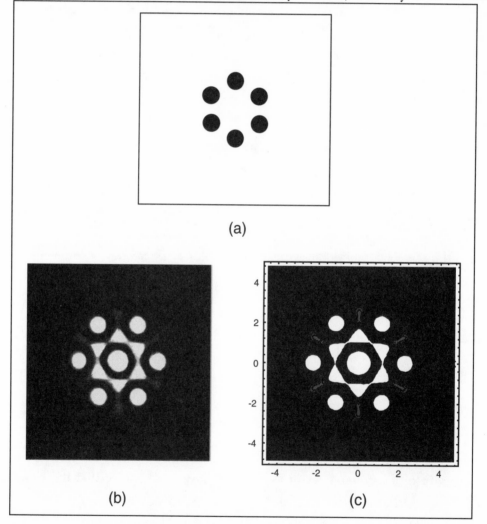

(a)

(b)

(c)

Figure 7.9 (a) The hexagonal arrangement of a 6 circular hole mask used in Figure 7.5, (b) the experimentally observed diffraction pattern from (a) and (c) the I_n pattern calculated via the Fourier Transform of (a).

262

simplest granularity approximation.

A casual glance at Figure 7.10 might lead one to presume that shrinking the radius of the circles to a very small size relative to the length, R, of the side of the triangle would allow the granularity approximation and the continuum approximation to exactly approach each other. However, this is not correct because the granularity approximation at all possible radii of the circles produces a triangle containing three types of pores: (1) P_1-type pores that are totally internal pores, (2) P_2-type pores are edge pores and (3) P_3-type pores are corner pores. In all cases, the individual pore area for each type bears a constant ratio to the circle area. Thus, as one shrinks the circle area, the number of circles increases as does the number of P_1- and P_2-type pores. Only the P_3-type pores are reduced in effectiveness as the circle size decreases. It can be readily shown that, as the number of circles in the triangle tends towards infinity, the mismatch between the area covered by all the circles to the total area of the triangle becomes a constant equal to 9.3%. This means that, in the best case, only 90.7% of the total area of the triangle will be covered by circles.

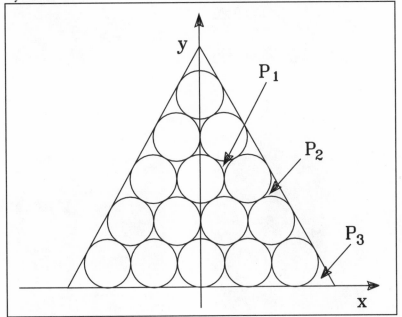

Figure 7.10   Illustration of the uniformly dense circles granularity approximation compared to the continuum approximation for a thin triangular sheet (the P_j are the three kinds of pores).

One can find the coordinates for each circle in the triangle, evaluate the FT for a single circle, then use Equation 2 of Table 7.3 to find the FT for every circle relative to a common origin and then add up all the FT's for all the circles in the triangle. For $(2N+1)$ circles in the triangle one finds that, even at N=2, the 6-fold arm pattern is present but the length of the arm in R-space is small. This arm length in R-space increases as N increases. At smaller values of I_n, many new intersecting patterns appear and disappear in kaleidoscopic fashion as N increases. Figure 7.11 illustrates some of this pattern variation for N=6.

From Equations 3 in Table 7.1, one can see that it is not really possible to pick a particular point or a limited region in R-space and see what particular locale of our D-space object relates to it on a 1:1 basis (100% confidence limit). Indeed, all points of our D-space object provide some

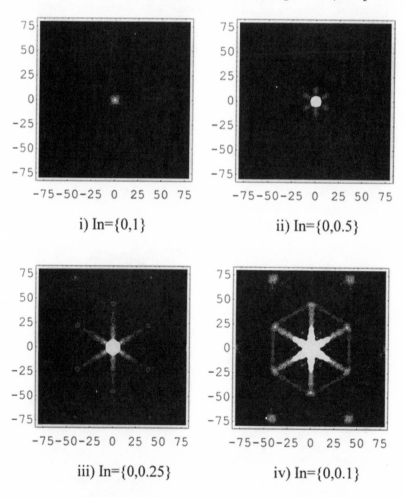

i) In={0,1}

ii) In={0,0.5}

iii) In={0,0.25}

iv) In={0,0.1}

Figure 7.11   Calculated sectional maps at various levels of the normalized modulus, I_n, as the number of rows, N, in an equilateral triangle of fixed side, R=1, increases (circle size decreases). Here, N=6 and the continuum result is given in Figure 7.7b.

contribution to the R-space map for a particular **Δk** around **k**. However, suppose one asks for a less precise result, e.g. "How closely can one approximate the D-space object by utilizing contributions from only a limited region of R-space (from $-k_m$ to $+k_m$) rather than from an infinite region (from $-\infty$ to $+\infty$)?" To answer this question, we utilize the inverse Fourier Transform (Equation 3b of Table 7.1) and consider three cases: (1) a 1D

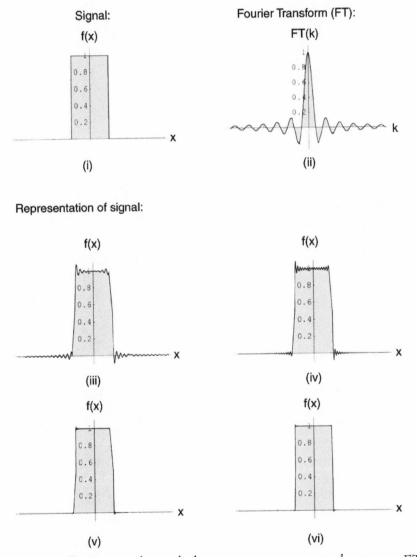

Figure 7.12a   *Illustration of signal shape approximation via the inverse FT (with percent error, ε) obtained by utilizing the finite integration limit of $\pm k_m$ in the Fourier Transform for a square signal. (i) actual square signal, (ii) exact Fourier Transform, (iii) $k_m=60$, ε=9.56%, (iv) $k_m=100$, ε= 4 . 3 % , (v) $k_m=1000$, ε=0.39% and (vi) $k_m=3000$, ε=0.2%.*

square signal, (2) a 1D triangular signal, (3a) a 1D narrow Gaussian signal
and (3b) a 1D broad Gaussian signal. These four were selected because then
one moves from a case of discontinuity in both position and slope to a
discontinuity only in slope to no discontinuity in either position or slope.
Figure 7.12 illustrates the results.

For the square signal, $f(x)$, illustrated in Figure 7.12a (i), its FT is

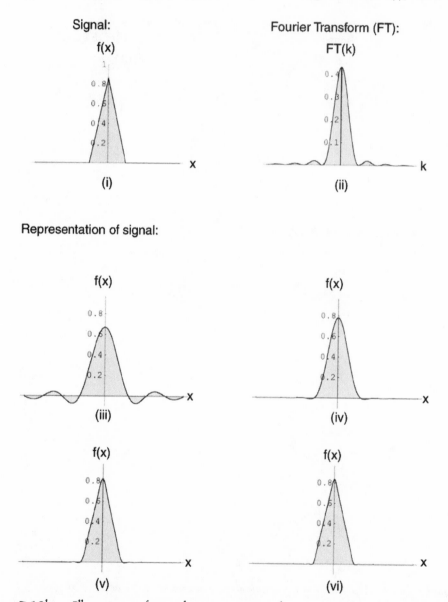

*Figure 7.12b   Illustration of signal approximation for a triangular shape, (i) actual
triangular signal, (ii) exact Fourier Transform, (iii) $k_m=2\pi$, $\varepsilon=28\%$, (iv) $k_m=4\pi$,
$\varepsilon=2.8\%$, (v) $k_m=8\pi$, $\varepsilon=1\%$ and (vi) $k_m=12\pi$, $\varepsilon=0.53\%$.*

represented in Figure 7.12a (ii) while (iii) to (vi) show how $\pm \, k_m$ approximates the true signal for [iii] $k_m = 60$, [iv] $k_m = 100$, [v] $k_m = 1000$ and (vi) $k_m = 3000$. The percent error, ε, diminishes strongly as k_m increases. In this Figure, one readily observes what is called the Gibb's phenomenon[7] in the region where $f(x)$ is discontinuous (leads to overshoot). One notes that it is necessary to go to fairly large k_m in order to reduce ε to a negligible value. For the triangular signal illustrated in Figure 7.12b (i), one finds that a reasonably

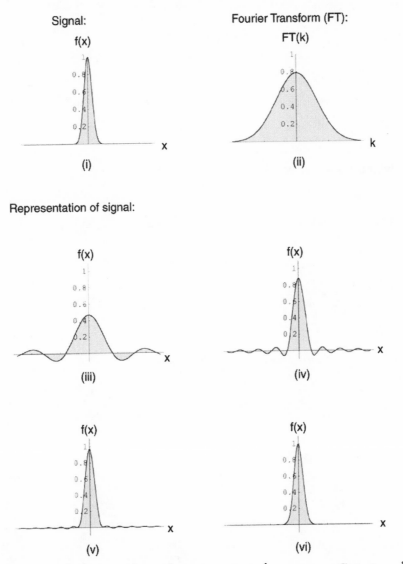

Figure 7.12c   Illustration of signal approximation for a narrow Gaussian shape, (i) actual Gaussian signal, (ii) exact Fourier Transform, (iii) k_m=2, ε=165%, (iv) k_m=5, ε=40.6%, (v) k_m=7, ε=11.6% and (vi) k_m=10, ε=0.64%.

good representation for $f(x)$ occurs when $k_m = 12\pi$ where $\varepsilon = 0.53\%$. This is much better than for the square signal. For the narrow Gaussian signal illustrated in Figure 7.12c (i), one finds a good representation for $f(x)$ when $k_m = 10$ with $\varepsilon = 0.64\%$. Thus, the removal of discontinuities in both position and slope in a D-space shape means that its R-space conjugate is reasonably

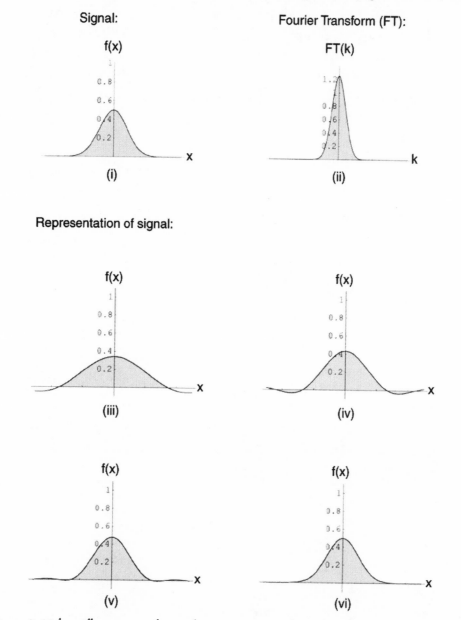

Figure 7.12d   Illustration of signal approximation for a broad Gaussian shape, (i) actual Gaussian signal, (ii) exact Fourier Transform, (iii) $k_m=1$, $\varepsilon=45\%$, (iv) $k_m=1.5$, $\varepsilon=22.4\%$, (v) $k_m=2$, $\varepsilon=7.3\%$ and (vi) $k_m=3$, $\varepsilon=0.34\%$.

well represented by a relatively small region of **k** in the low wave number domain (**0<k<k$_m$**). A similar conclusion applies even more so for a broad Gaussian signal as illustrated in Figure 7.12d where we see that **k$_m$** = 3 yields a very good approximation with ε = 0.35%.

Information Transformation in the Brain

Pribram[8] has written extensively on the brain processes involved in imaging and has a Holonomic theory to explain them. It is based solely on a slight modification of the Fourier Transform duality between D-space information patterns and spectral domain information patterns. An overly simplistic picture would be that a spacetime information pattern enters the body via the circular lens of the eye. Eventually, it activates the input and operator neurons of the brain's cortical columns. This leads to overlapping receptive fields of interneurons that are tunable by adaptation and habituation. Each interneuron thus acts like a bin in a computer that stores the averages of

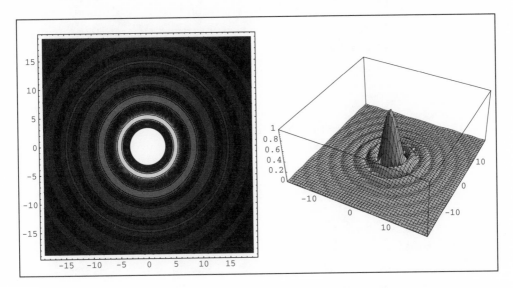

Figure 7.13   Topographic and section perspectives of normalized modulus, I$_n$, for the full circle geometry in Figure 7.7a.

the part of the patterns of input to which it is exposed[8]. The ensemble of receptive fields (bins) stores the average pattern and, when one plots these receptive fields, they bear a marked correlation to the Fourier Transform of the spacetime pattern impinging on the iris of the eye. For a uniform light intensity impinging on a circle (the iris of the eye), the Fourier Transform is given in both sectional and contour plots by Figure 7.13 and this pattern is a good representation of Pribram's experimental results[8].

The summary view, then, is that cortical neurons act like individual receiving antennas in a large array converting the spacetime information into a diffraction pattern whose mathematical representation is very close to the particular Fourier Transform. This information conversion to the frequency domain appears to be ideal for subsequent brain processing and brain perception. In the general area of antenna arrays, whether of the receiving or transmitting type, there exists the "principle of pattern multiplication" which may be stated most generally as follows: The total field pattern of an array of nonisotropic but similar sources (sinks) is the product of the individual source pattern and the pattern of an array of isotropic point sources (sinks) located at the phase center of the individual source and having the same relative amplitude and phase, while the total phase pattern is the sum of the phase patterns of the individual sources and the array of isotropic point sources. In electrical engineering, this general concept has been expanded to consider a continuous array of point sources (separated from each other by infinitesimal distances) which has been found to be equivalent to a continuous field or "aperture" distribution for an antenna[9]. One finds that it is the Fourier Transform relationship that connects the far field radiation pattern and the aperture distribution just as we found via Figure 7.9 for the simple array of six holes in a mask.

Thermodynamics and Kinetics

Our scientific experience over the last two centuries has shown us that any process of change in observable nature is driven by either a spatial or temporal gradient in the thermodynamic potential governing the system. The rate of that change is governed by the kinetics of the fundamental processes available for exchange of that thermodynamic potential. We need to look at these two aspects of natural law in order to understand in a broad sense how the system works in the material world when there is no human intention involved. Then, we will be in a position to anticipate and characterize changes associated with human intention (next chapter).

Very rarely are we concerned with completely pure materials. Rather, we are mostly interested in the properties of solutions and mixtures (multiphase solutions) where the structural state of the solutions may be solid, liquid, gas or plasma. Thus, we are more generally concerned with the thermodynamic properties of a particular component in the solution called partial molar quantities. A given component, j, (molecule, say) will have a partial molar volume, $\overline{V}_j$, energy $\overline{E}_j$, entropy, $\overline{S}_j$, enthalpy, $\overline{H}_j$, and free energy, $\overline{G}_j$, associated with it. The free energy, G, of the system is the thermodynamic potential governing the system and is given for an N-component system by Equations 1 in Table 7.4 with T = temperature and P = pressure as the two extrinsic and independent thermodynamic variables defining the state of our system so that G = G(P,T). Centuries of experiments have confirmed the specific nature of Equations 1 in Table 7.4.

Table 7.4   *Key Thermodynamic and Kinetic Relationships.*

$$G = \sum_{j=1}^{N} \overline{G}_j = H - TS \qquad (1a)$$

where

$$\overline{G}_j = \overline{H}_j - T\overline{S}_j = \overline{E}_j + P\overline{V}_j - T\overline{S}_j \qquad (1b)$$

$$\mu_j = \overline{G}_j / N_A = \mu_{oj} + kT \ln(\gamma_j C_j) \qquad (2)$$

$$(TDF)_j = \nabla\mu_j = \left(\frac{d}{dx} + \frac{d}{dy} + \frac{d}{dz} \right) \mu_j \qquad (3)$$

$$v_j = -M_j \nabla\mu_j = \frac{-D_j C_j}{kT} \nabla\mu_j \qquad (4)$$

$$J_j = -D_j \nabla C_j \qquad (5)$$

$\overline{G}$ = partial molar Gibb's free energy, H = enthalpy, S = entropy, E = energy, V = volume, T = temperature, P = pressure, μ = chemical potential, C = concentration, γ = activity coefficient, J = flux, N_A = Avogadro's number; superscript bar, $^{-}$, means a partial molar quantity, subscript j means a specific chemical species, $\frac{d}{dx}$ means differentiation with respect to the x-coordinate direction.

For electrically neutral species, it is useful to define the chemical potential, μ_j, for the j-species on a per molecule basis and it, of course, is related to the molar quantity, $\overline{G}_j$, though Avogadro's number, N_A, the number of molecules per mole ($N_A = 6.025 \times 10^{23}$). Equation 2 of Table 7.4 provides the mathematical relationship between $\overline{G}_j$ and μ_j. In Equation 2 of Table 7.4, C is the concentration of the species in the solution, γ_j is the activity coefficient for the species j, k is Boltzmann's constant (kT is the average kinetic energy for a molecule at temperature T), ln is the logarithm to the base e and μ_{oj} is the standard state or reference state value at one atmosphere pressure and 25°C. The thermodynamic driving force (TDF) for movement of any chemical species is given by the spatial gradient of μ and this is defined by Equation 3 in Table 7.4 where the *d*'s refer to partial differentials. The physical drift velocity, for a molecule of j is then given by v_j via Equation 4 of Table 7.4 where M is the mobility and D is the diffusion coefficient for the molecule species at temperature T. In the most simple circumstance ($\gamma_j = 1$), this leads to a flux J_j, (number per cm^2 per second) of the j-species given by Equation 5 of Table 7.4. Thus, the rate of supply or loss of j-species from a key reaction area in cells (e.g. mitochondria for ATP production) or other medium can be readily evaluated in a fairly simple manner.

It is a very simple step to expand the utility of the thermodynamic potential to include contributions coming from the electrostatic potential, ϕ, and thus make the description more general and fully applicable to bioelectric systems. We define this potential via Equation 1 of Table 7.5. Here, η is the electrochemical potential, μ_j is given by Equation 2 of Table 7.4, z is the electric valence and e is the electron charge. Now, both electric potential gradients as well as chemical concentration gradients are involved in the flux of j-species given by Equation 2 of Table 7.5. The next more exotic potential utilized in recent years is the photoelectrochemical potential. The photons can indeed be considered as just another species, j, where one must calculate the local concentration, C_j, from the ambient spectral intensity. However, an important ancillary role of photons in the overall system is to produce excited states of chemical species which may lead to dissociation and/or electric charge transfer with two major consequences, (1) alteration of the magnitude of ϕ and $\Delta\phi$ in Equation 2 of Table 7.5 and (2) alteration of the catalytic processes in the body (e.g. enzymes in mitochondria).

As the last step in this purely physical chain, one wants to define the complete thermodynamic potential for physical reality, ψ_p, which includes the electric field, $\bar{E}$, the magnetic field, $\bar{H}$, the gravitational potential, stored strain energy, etc. This yields Equation 3 of Table 7.5. Here, g is the gravitational constant, ρ is the density, h is the height relative to that for the standard state pressure, ε is the electric permittivity of the material while m is its molal magnetic permeability and E_M is its modulus of elasticity. Also, $\hat{\sigma}$ represents

Table 7.5   From Chemical Potential to Generalized Potential.

Electrochemical Potential

$$\eta_j = \mu_j + z_j\, e\, \phi \qquad (1)$$

$$J_j = -M_j \nabla \eta_j = -D_j \nabla C_j + (D_j C_j /kT) z_j\, e \nabla \phi \qquad (2)$$

Generalized Potential

$$\psi_{p_j} = \eta_j + \rho_j g h_j - \frac{v}{2}\frac{d}{dC_j}\left\{ \varepsilon \bar{E}^2 + m\,\bar{H}^2 + \frac{\hat{\sigma}^2}{E_M} \right\} + \cdots \qquad (3)$$

$$\psi_{p_j} = \mu_{oj} + kT \ln(\hat{\gamma}_j C_j) \qquad (4a)$$

where $\hat{\gamma}_j =$

$$\gamma_j \exp\left\{ \frac{1}{kT}\left[z_j\, e\, \phi + \rho_j\, g h_j - \frac{v}{2}\frac{d}{dC_j}\left\langle \varepsilon\, \underline{E}^2 + m\,\underline{H}^2 + \frac{\hat{\sigma}^2}{E_M} \right\rangle + \cdots \right]\right\}.$$

$$(4b)$$

---

z = valence, e = electron charge, ϕ = electrostatic potential,

η = electrochemical potential, ψ = generalized potential,

ρ = density, g = gravitational constant, h = height, v = molal volume,

ε = electrical permittivity, $\underline{E}$ = electric field strength,

m = molal magnetic permeability, $\underline{H}$ = magnetic field strength,

$\hat{\sigma}$ = stress state, E_M = modulus of elasticity,

$\hat{\gamma}$ = modified activity coefficient.

the state of stress in the material. Now, the most general expression for the flux of j is given by Equation 2 of Table 7.5 with ψ_{p_j} replacing η_j.

Before moving on, it is perhaps useful to cast Equation 3 of Table 7.5 into a form much like Equation 2 of Table 7.4. Via a simple mathematical manipulation we readily have the result given by Equations 4 of Table 7.5. Now, ψ_{p_j} is the magnetophotoelectrochemical potential in the physical domain (the U(1) Gauge domain) for the j-species and all of the various field effects have been incorporated into a modified activity coefficient, $\hat{\gamma}$. From Equation 4b of Table 7.5, one can certainly see an effect of electromagnetic fields on the thermodynamic properties of materials. Since having such materials inside a Faraday cage greatly reduces the $\varepsilon \overline{E}^2 + m\overline{H}^2$ term and thus raises the free energy of either enzymes or fruit flies, this may be one of the reasons why (1) the [ATP]/[ADP] ratio is higher and larval development time is lower for the fruit flies and (2) the activity coefficient for ALP is higher inside than outside a Faraday cage. The photons can also be "bond-breakers".

One concluding point for the thermodynamic perspective concerns the Gibbs' Phase Rule whose mathematical statement is

$$f = c - p + 2. \qquad (7.3)$$

Here, f is the number of degrees of freedom available to a system of c components when there are p coexisting phases present and only two extrinsic variables, temperature, T, and pressure, P. Thus, if we have only one component ($c = 1$, e.g. H_2O) and only one phase present ($p = 1$, e.g. water), T and P can be independently varied ($f = 2$) without changing the phase so this is called a bivariant condition. When there are two coexisting phases present ($p = 2$, e.g. two unique phases of water), it is a univariant condition ($f = 1$) that obtains and there is some constraint relationship operating between T and P (one is fixed along the univariant curve by choosing the value of the other). When there are three different material phases present ($p = 3$), it is an invariant condition ($f = 0$) that obtains and equilibrium can occur only at a single point in the entire (T, P) variable space. At all other points in this variable space, thermodynamics requires some type of material phase transformation to be occurring.

Chemical and Temperature Oscillations

<u>Natural Convection-driven Oscillations:</u> In gaseous or fluid media, convective flow of the medium can be driven by either volume or surface forces. Gravity is one example of a volume force while the electromagnetic Lorentz force due to induced electric currents is another. In general, any gradient of magnetophotoelectrochemical potential (see Equation 2 of Table 7.4 and Equations 1 and 3 of Table 7.5) can be considered as a body force. In most human experience, the gravity effect is of greatest importance in natural convection which is driven by a buoyancy density difference and impeded by the viscous inertia of the fluid. The viscosity dissipates kinetic energy while the buoyancy force releases internal energy. When the latter exceeds the former, fluid motion occurs and increases in velocity until a balance develops between them.

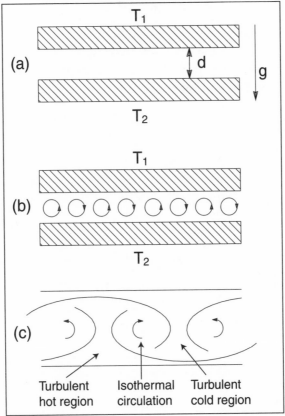

Figure 7.14   (a) Definition sketch for Bénard convection, (b) convective roll cells for Bénard convection and (c) principal features of cellular convection in the boundary layer regime.

275

The most commonly shared experience of circulatory convection is that of heating water in a saucepan placed on top of a stove. When a pure liquid is heated from below, a density inversion develops with the bottom layer temperature, T_2, becoming greater than the top layer temperature, T_1. When this density gradient exceeds a critical value (determined by the particular fluid), the fluid begins to move in periodically arranged vertical columns which close on themselves to produce continuous loops of flow (see Figure 7.14). This type of fluid flow is called Bénard convection after the first person to seriously study it. If one places a thermocouple in the fluid, temperature oscillations are continually recorded as these loops of fluid rotate. If the fluid was an alloy and one had a monitor for one particular chemical constituent placed in the fluid, one would also detect oscillations in concentration for that chemical constituent (provided that some stratification of that chemical constituent occurred when the fluid was in a quiescent state). Since different alloying elements have different densities, one can also produce density inversions due to chemical factors alone. Thus, one can generate Bénard-type convection patterns from a density inversion due to a combination of temperature gradient plus concentration gradient factors. It is the size dimension of the rolling fluid cells that indicate which factor is dominant.

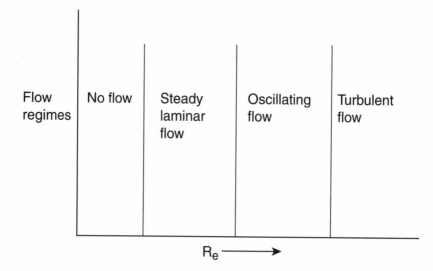

| Flow regimes | No flow | Steady laminar flow | Oscillating flow | Turbulent flow |

$R_e \longrightarrow$

Figure 7.15   The four typical fluid flow regimes as a function of Reynolds number, R_e

Temperature-driven cells are generally larger than alloying element-driven cells and convection cells in a gaseous fluid are generally larger than in a liquid fluid. In addition, the amplitude of the oscillations increases as the magnitude of the density inversion increases for a quiescent fluid. Even for a forced convection system, one finds that there is a particular range of flow conditions, defined by the key flow parameter, R_e, (called the Reynolds number) wherein oscillating flow conditions develop. This is illustrated in Figure 7.15.

Chemical Reaction-driven oscillations: Concentration oscillations have been observed by chemical engineers for decades in complex chemical solutions that are <u>far from thermodynamic equilibrium</u>. They have been observed in both "open" and "closed" isothermal chemical systems as well as electro-dissolution reactions. The chemical reaction oscillation model developed to explain this complex chemical behavior provides a compelling framework for enhancing our understanding of the oscillation behavior described in Chapter 6.

Table 7.6   The Simplest Set of Reactions for Chemical Oscillation Generation.

Reactant $\rightarrow$ A $\Longrightarrow$ B $\rightarrow$ Product   (1)

$$\text{Reactant} \overset{k_0 r}{\rightarrow} A \underset{k_u a}{\overset{k_1 ab^2}{\Longrightarrow}} B \overset{k_2 b}{\rightarrow} \text{Product} \qquad (2)$$

$$\frac{d[r]}{dt} = -k_0[r] \qquad (7.3a)$$

$$\frac{d[a]}{dt} = -k_1[a][b]^2 - k_u[a] + k_0[r], \qquad (7.3b)$$

$$\frac{d[b]}{dt} = k_1[a][b]^2 + k_u[a] - k_2[b], \qquad (7.3c)$$

$$\frac{d[p]}{dt} = k_2[b]. \qquad (7.3d)$$

k_j = rate constants (j=0, 1, u, 2)

[q] = activity of species q (q = reactant, r, component A or a, component B or b, and product, p)

Chemical oscillations, explosive ignitions, and chemical patterns have developed into an area of great interest to the world chemistry community in recent years. [10,11]. Self-sustained oscillations in a chemical system are defined as undamped oscillations arising in a system in the absence of external periodic forces. The amplitude and period of such oscillations appear to be determined only by the initial (at time $=0$) properties of the system. The simplest theoretical model applies to a closed isothermal reaction rate system whereby a reactant is converted to a product through two intermediate species A and B as illustrated in Equation 1 of Table 7.6. The key feature in this series of reactions that leads to oscillations is the step wherein A is converted to B. The double arrow is used to indicate that there are <u>two</u> possible paths for producing B from A: (1) direct conversion of A to B and (2) another simultaneous reaction converting A to B which involves chemical feedback. Some examples of feedback in chemical and biological systems are provided in Table 7.7. Of course, for any closed system, the concentration of reactant always declines with time while the concentration of product always grows with time.

Taking a detailed look at the four reactions involved in Equation 1 of Table 7.6, we have (1) Reactant $\rightarrow$ A with reaction rate $k_0[r]$ ($[r]$ is the activity (concentration) of reactant and k_0 the rate constant), (2) A $\rightarrow$ B with reaction rate $k_u[a]$ ($[a]$ is the activity of A), (3) A + 2B $\rightarrow$ 3B with reaction rate $k_1[a][b]^2$ ($[b]$ is the activity of B) and (4) B $\rightarrow$ Product with reaction rate $k_2[b]$. The third step is the critical one and is termed "autocatalytic" because the more of B that is produced, the faster does that particular step proceed (it is the essential nonlinear contribution). Including all these individual rates, we have Equation 2 of Table 7.6. This overall reaction represents the <u>minimum</u> reaction configuration needed to produce oscillations. In real oscillating chemical reactions, considerable additional complexities with more intermediate steps are generally present. However, for the minimal system of Equation 2 in Table 7.6, the concentrations of A and B begin to oscillate with time after some initial period called the induction period (see Figure 7.16). Eventually, as the concentration of reactant, **r**, runs down, the oscillations end. After that, the concentrations of **r**, **a** and **b** continue to decline until equilibrium is approached.

As already stated, Equation 2 of Table 7.6 represents one of the simplest but most general set of reactions involving feedback that allow oscillations to develop. The necessary and sufficient mathematical set of coupled time-dependent equations needed to quantitatively define the oscillations generated by this equation are given by Equations 3 of Table 7.6. These differential equations can be solved numerically and solutions such as depicted in Figure 7.16 (for $k_1 = k_2 = 1$) readily generated for the time-dependent concentration of component A subject to a particular set of initial conditions. Altering the magnitude of the rate constants and the initial conditions can change the details of the waveform.

Table 7.7 Examples of feedback and its consequences in chemical systems (after Scott[11]).

Examples of Feedback	Consequences
Gas phase (combustion processes, isomerizations)	
chain branching	ignition limits
self-inhibition	oscillations and chaos
thermal feedback	thermal runaway
chain-thermal feedback	engine knock
Solution phase (BZ family, redox reactions)	
autocatalysis	clock reactions
self-inhibition	travelling wavefronts and wave trains
	oscillations and chaos
	spatial patterns
Solid phase (pyrotechnics)	
thermal feedback	nonsteady burning velocity
	thermal runaway (haystacks, etc.)
Gas-liquid (partial oxidation processes)	
phase exchange	oscillations and chaos
Gas-solid (heterogeneous catalysis, catalytic converters)	
competitive adsorption	multistability
concentration dependent	oscillations and chaos
adsorption or phase changes	
Solid-liquid (electrodissolution, corrosion)	
pH-dependent dissolution	oscillations and chaos
potentials	
film growth	
Biological systems (enzyme processes, glycolysis, nerve conduction, life)	
allosteric effects	oscillations and chaos
chemotaxis	signal transmission
	limb development
	evolution of form

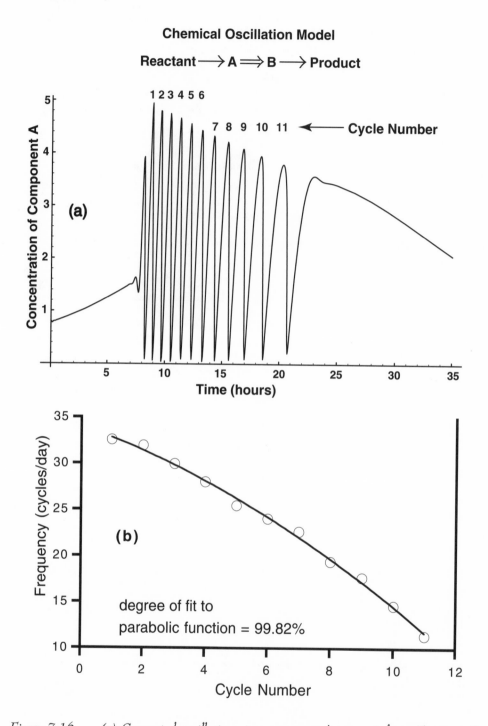

Figure 7.16   (a) Computed oscillations in component A generated via Equation 2 of Table 7.6. (b) illustration of the frequency variation of the computed oscillations in (a) with the labeled cycle number. Values for rate constants were chosen to roughly correspond to the time scales of our experiments <u>not</u> to conventional oscillating chemical reactions.

In closed systems of this sort that involve an approach to equilibrium, the oscillation frequency <u>always</u> declines, usually along with the amplitude, until the end of the oscillation train. In chemical systems where the reactant concentration, r, can be kept constant (an open system) and in the range where oscillations occur, the oscillation frequency and amplitude can remain constant as time progresses. Thus decreasing frequencies are characteristic of <u>closed</u> oscillating chemical systems that are approaching equilibrium from an initial state far removed from equilibrium. On the other hand, oscillations with frequencies that remain constant with time are found for <u>open</u> systems where the total reaction driving force is held constant through time.

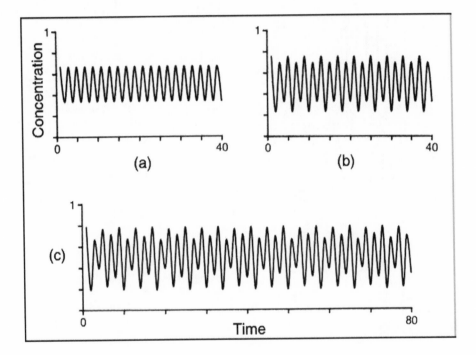

Figure 7.17   A typical period-doubling sequence leading ultimately to aperiodic waveforms and chemical chaos[10].

In conventional open system chemical oscillation experimental data, one finds that, when the oscillating chemical reactions are driven very fast, and chemical "chaos" is approached [10-12], a number of characteristic oscillation features appear. One common feature is the period-doubling illustrated in Figure 7.17. Just before period doubling occurs, the frequency is constant (Figure 7.17a). As the thermodynamic driving force is increased (usually achieved by increasing the flow rates in chemical reactors), a second period

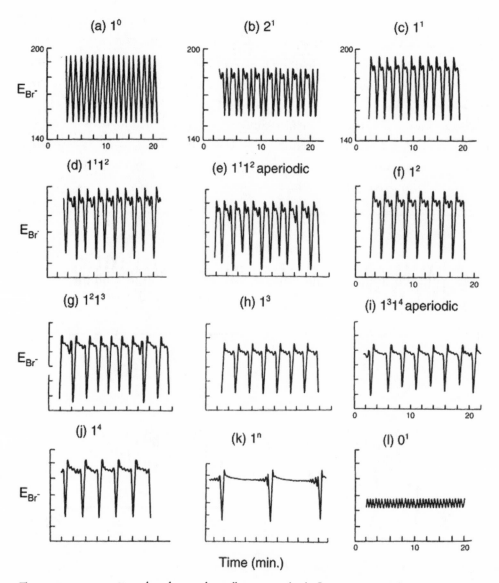

Figure 7.18a   Complex chemical oscillations at high flow rates in a flow reactor showing concatenations between states of large and small amplitude peaks (modified after Scott[11]).

becomes evident (Figure 7.17b). This period may continue doubling (Figure 7.17c) as the driving force is increased until aperiodic waveforms appear that represent the onset of chemical chaos. Such oscillation behavior (see Figure 7.19a) has also been observed in some of the data discussed in Chapter 6.

Another feature of chemical oscillations in open systems that often appears near the onset of chemical chaos is <u>peak-addition</u> as illustrated in Figure 7.18. In this Figure, the electrical output of a bromide ion electrode is

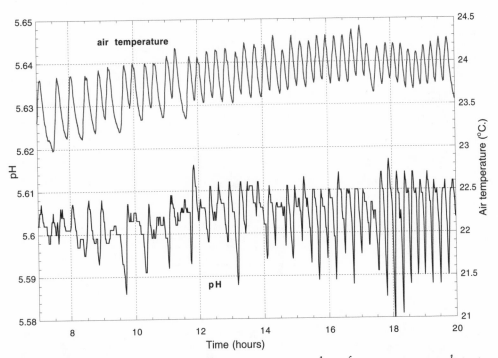

Figure 7.19a   pH and air temperature vs. time plots from magnet conditioning experiment (5ᵗʰ series, right position, no magnet) discussed in Chapter 6. Note the oscillation period-doubling region in air temperature between hours 9 and 12 (similar to Figure 7.17b) and the complex aperiodic oscillation peak-addition in the simultaneously measured pH data (similar to Figure 7.18).

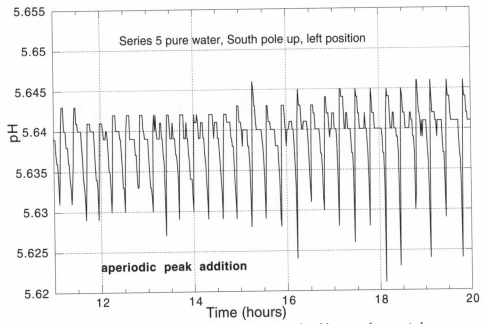

Figure 7.19b   Another example of pH-oscillation peak-addition (Chapter 6 data).

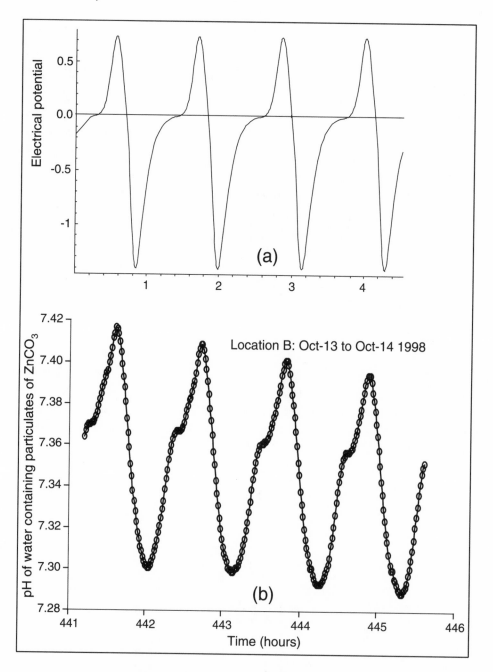

Figure 7.20 (a) Computed oscillations using the Wang et al[14] modification of the Franck-FitzHugh model of electro-dissolution and (b) observed pH oscillations for $ZnCO_3$ particulates in pure water (data from Figure 6.6).

shown plotted vs. time. At the lowest driving force, the reaction yields simple, large amplitude oscillations designated 1^0, indicating that a complete cycle has only one large and no small excursions (Figure 7.18a). As the driving force, and thus the reaction rate, is increased, the bromide ion concentration waveform becomes that shown in 7.18c designated 1^1, where each oscillation has one large and one small peak. Increasing the driving force further leads to even more complex waveforms with the one shown in Figure 7.18e designated $1^1 1^2$ aperiodic. This waveform is one with an aperiodic alternation of cycles, some with one large plus two small peaks. Once again, this category of oscillations is observed in some of the Chapter 6 data (see Figures 7.19a and 7.19b). In Figure 7.19a one can observe the pH and air temperature oscillations evolve in time from more chaotic to more ordered waveforms using the examples shown in Figures 7.17 and 7.18 as models.

Oscillations are also commonly observed during electro-dissolution reactions[12] and theoretical modeling of these reactions often assumes that there is a transition of the anodic metal between active and passive states[13]. This defines the Flade potential, E_F, at which the kinetics of the dissolution process changes discontinuously from the active to the passive form[13]. Here, the major electric current carrier through the solution of the dissolution cell is the H^+ ion and, as dissolution occurs, the interface concentration of H^+ decreases so that E_F also decreases. If E_F falls with $[H^+]$, to a value below the imposed electrode potential, E_p, the electrode becomes passivated and an adsorbed layer of sparingly soluble reaction product forms on the surface (decreases the dissolution rate). A feedback mechanism becomes possible, in this case wherein, if the diffusion rate of H^+ through the boundary layer exceeds the consumption rate of H^+ at the interface, an increase of interface H^+ may cause E_F to exceed E_p again and this, in turn, leads to a decrease in the passive film thickness so that interface H^+ is consumed at a faster rate.

Mathematically-generated oscillations using the electro-dissolution model of Wang and others[14] can also be compared to some of the pH-oscillations described in Chapter 6. The pH-oscillations observed in pure water containing $ZnCO_3$ particulates exhibit many unique waveform characteristics not observed in temperature oscillations or pH oscillations in pure water and in aqueous solutions containing dissolved salts or other particulates. Figure 7.20a shows a calculated electrode potential vs. time plot from the numerical solution of a set of differential equations similar to those used to model electro-dissolution[14]. Figure 7.20b is a real-time plot of pH oscillations measured in pure water containing $ZnCO_3$ particulates in equilibrium with atmospheric CO_2.

Coherence and Oscillating Electron Flows

The phenomenon of "ordering" is a very important one in nature and it is a quality that we have learned to somewhat manipulate from the outside. If we take the simple example of water, we know that at elevated temperature its molecules move freely in D-space without mutual correlation and exhibit a large entropy. When the temperature is lowered below 100 °C. at atmospheric pressure, liquid water is formed and the molecular motion has become highly correlated and exhibits a smaller entropy. When the temperature is further lowered below 0 °C., solid water (ice) is formed, the molecular motion is even more highly correlated and exhibits an even smaller entropy. These phase transitions towards increasingly higher states of molecular/atom correlation as the temperature is lowered is common to all materials including those that exhibit strong magnetic properties. For such materials, ferromagnets at high temperatures, their magnetic dipoles (thought to be associated with electron spins) are completely disordered (uncorrelated) and they do not exhibit ferromagnetic behavior. However, as the temperature is lowered below some critical value, called the Curie point, these magnetic dipoles become correlated and line up into an ordered array exhibiting a still lower entropy. For all materials, a similarly dramatic ordering transition for electrons occurs at a critical temperature and this is called the superconducting transition temperature. Once again, this involves enhanced correlations, this time between electrons, and thus further reduced entropy for the material.

Above absolute zero temperature, all materials absorb and emit electromagnetic photons so that, at any point in time, some of the atoms and molecules in a material exist as a disordered array of excited states (energy levels above the ground state). In some materials, large numbers of atoms/molecules can be "pumped", by an external radiant source, to multiple excited states and, for those having a suitable distribution of excited state energy levels, short bursts of intense light emission occurs. At a certain pumping power, called the laser threshold, a completely new phenomenon occurs, especially if this material is shaped as a rod and mirrors are fixed at the end faces of the rod. The emitted photons are coherent (in phase) with respect to each other and the light intensity increases dramatically with further increases of pump power. Here, these excited atomic states of the laser material have become ordered in a fashion reminiscent of the ferromagnetic phase transition but the ordering parameter is not temperature in this case. Once again, an increased state of coherence for the various moieties of the material lead to very special properties for that material.

Let us now return to that coherence domain physics associated with electron ordering, superconductivity in materials and Josephson junction behavior. The Josephson junction phenomenon relates to the coupling between two superconductors (coherent electron states) separated by a small gap. Because of electron tunneling across the gap, these two superconductors are coupled together in a similar manner to the coupling of two resonant electromagnetic cavities that can exchange energy [15]. The coupled cavities, supposed to be initially tuned to the same frequency, can only oscillate steadily if they are in phase or in an antiphase relationship (normal modes where no energy exchange occurs between the cavities.). In the superconductors there are also two normal modes wherein the electron wave-functions oscillate in phase or in antiphase. When the system is in either mode, there is no exchange of electrons between the two superconductors. However, if a phase difference, ϕ, not equal to 0 or π, exists between either of the two cavities or the two superconductors, one sees energy exchange in the former and electron exchange in the latter at a rate proportional to $\sin \phi$. In both cases, the maximum current that can flow is determined by the strength of the coupling (the smaller the spacing in the superconductor case). The steady flow of energy from one cavity to the other, or of particles from one superconductor to the other, continues only so long as the phase difference is constant. This is only possible for Josephson junctions when the voltage difference, ΔV, between the two superconductors is zero. When ΔV is not zero, ϕ changes with time so that current oscillates back and forth at the difference frequency, ν, given by

$$\nu = \frac{e\Delta V}{\hbar} = \frac{\partial \phi}{\partial t} \qquad (7.4a)$$

with

$$i_s = i_j \sin\phi \qquad (7.4b)$$

where i_j is the maximum Josephson current that the particle junction can support (determined by the nature and dimensions of the junction), e is the electron charge and h is Planck's constant ($\hbar = h/2\pi$).

In the superconductor example, $e\Delta V$ is just the electrochemical potential difference for electrons on the two sides of the junction, the electrons are very mobile in the two superconductors and the current, i_j, is sufficiently large to be easily detected. One should expect this to be a completely general

QM phenomenon in nature for the flow of species, j, in a circuit between two phases of a material having some generalized potential difference, $\Delta \psi_{p_j}$, for the j-species existing between them. Of course if the phases are not superconducting with respect to j, then conductive impedance exists in the circuit and this produces damped oscillations. Such damped oscillations may not be generally observed for many j-species because of the magnitudes involved in their case. For our experimental results with water, oscillating currents of protons would lead to both pH – and conductivity – oscillations while oscillating currents of heat or entropy would lead to temperature oscillations.

Colloids, Clusters and Electromagnetic Fields

Returning to the early part of chapter 3, when one considers all this data plus the overpowering volume of water data not referred to there, one might consider characterizing or cataloguing this data into three discriminated categories. These are (1) molecular level properties, including water clusters, so the system is considered to be single phase water and homogeneous on a size scale of $\leq 10^{-7} - 10^{-6}$ cm, (2) two-phase or polyphase water properties associated with either classical critical point phenomena or cooperative internal electromagnetic mode interactions so the system is treated as single phase and homogeneous on a size scale of $\leq 10^{-5} - 10^{-4}$ cm and (3) a heterogeneous system of the foregoing plus foreign bodies such as colloids, long-chain molecules, microscopic gas bubbles, etc. Even a flexible long-chain polymer molecule forms a type of random walk pattern in the aqueous solvent so that it becomes a sphere-like cluster with an effective radius depending upon the strength of its molecular interactions with the solvent. The better the chain is wetted by the solvent, the more open and less bunched it becomes, leading to a larger effective particle diameter for a given chain length. One can thus think of this molecular chain as a "composite colloid" of chain segments and solvent with an effective radius, R, density, ρ, electric permittivity, ε, and magnetic permeability, m, all depend on the relative strength of chain/solvent versus chain/chain interactions.

The importance of this third category is that, in an aqueous electrolyte, these microscopic moieties interact in unique ways with ambient electric, magnetic and electromagnetic fields so as to move them in certain directions

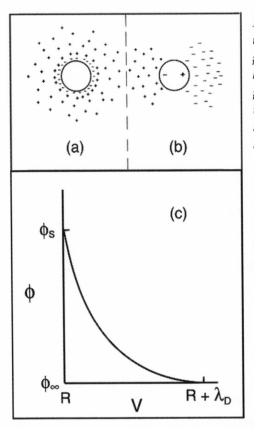

Figure 7.21   Schematic illustration of (a) the ionic double layer around a colloidal particle, (b) the neutralized electric dipole of a large molecule and (c) the electrostatic potential distribution, ϕ, varying from ϕ$_s$ at the particle surface to ϕ$_\infty$ at the edge of the space charge layer ($r = R + \lambda_D$) in the solution.

in their macroscopic environment. In turn, this produces (a) macroscopic spatial concentration changes in these moieties leading to macroscopic property variations in the overall solution, (b) activation of local thermodynamic forces to recreate, at some kinetically-limited rate, the equilibrium population of such moieties in the regions dynamically vacated and (c) activation of such forces to agglomerate or coagulate such moieties in overly enriched regions of the macroscopic solution (at rates determined by the unique kinetics of these processes). The purpose of this section is to come to an understanding of the physical chemistry behind these field effects.

To model the phenomenon, we will treat all the microscopic moieties as "effective colloids" which, because of their different electrical and magnetic nature compared to the solvent, causes some electrostatic surface potential, ϕ_s, (and magnetic surface potential, $\underline{A}_s$) to develop at the periphery of colloid/bulk solvent interface. Any electrical ions and dipoles (or magnetic dipoles) will cluster around the colloid to screen this surface potential as illustrated in Figure 7.21a. If the electric field at the particle surface is sufficiently strong, one may expect alignment of one to several layers of H_2O molecules at the colloid/electrolyte interface. Thus, the system needs to be considered as a uniform solution containing colloid-like entities surrounded by space charge sheaths of ions and dipoles that move as a unit via Brownian motion in a vast sea of solvent electrolyte. Let us now consider the interplay of forces that lead to either a stable dispersion of such colloids or an agglomeration process under two different conditions (a) the absence of external electric, magnetic, electromagnetic or gravitational fields and (b) the presence of one or more such fields.

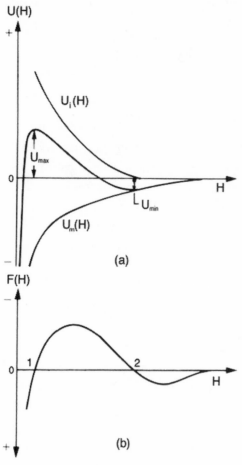

(a)

(b)

Figure 7.22   (a) Interaction energy, U(H), and (b) resultant force, F(H), between two electrically charged particles as a function of separation distance H between the surfaces of the particles.

External Field Absence Case: Two major forces determine the agglomeration tendency of colloidal suspensions; (1) electrodynamic forces of the Van der Walls dispersion type which favor agglomeration and (2) electrostatic forces (and magnetostatic forces) which favor dispersion. Figure 7.22 illustrates the total interaction energy, U(H), and the resultant force, F(H) between two colloidal particles at a separation distance H between their surfaces. $U_m(H)$ is the electrodynamic part while $U_i(H)$ is the electrostatic part. The principal features of this U(H) curve are: (i) the presence of a primary potential minimum at the particle-particle contact condition of H=0 (requires penetration of the space charge layer), (ii) a secondary potential minimum of small magnitude at relatively large distance (H ~ 10^{-6} –10^{-5} cm) and (iii) a potential barrier separating the two minima.

For a given situation, both the height of the barrier and the depth of the secondary minimum increase with colloid radius, R. Thus, one has the picture of colloids in a dilute solution moving randomly via Brownian motion, drifting diffusionally in a long range electrochemical potential gradient (including U(H)) and temporarily being captured into weakly bound clusters where the intercolloid separation distances place them in their secondary potential minima. Thermal fluctuations allow relatively easy separation to larger distances, because the colloid-colloid binding energy is only a few kT, but difficult passage to smaller separations and the primary potential well minimum unless U_{max} in Figure 7.22a is small.

For monodisperse colloid sizes and the proper solution concentration of colloids, very large (~centimeters), stable and ordered three-dimensional arrays of these particles (~10^{12} particles) bound in the secondary minima can develop. The small colloids, if they are crystalline, have the ability to freely rotate relative to each other until close crystallographic alignment, and thus a minimum free energy, has been achieved. Under small barrier conditions, a large local thermal fluctuation may occur to allow coalescence of a number of these ordered crystallites to form a larger crystal that is a slightly defective single crystal.

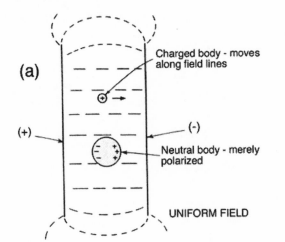

Figure 7.23

Comparison of behaviors of neutral and charged bodies in (a) a uniform electric field, (b) a nonuniform electric field.

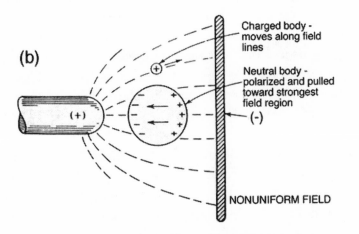

Experimentally, one can alter the height of U_{max} in Figure 7.22 via two major electrostatic effects. The electrostatic repulsive force can be increased by either (1) adding a surfactant to increase the absolute value of ϕ_s in Figure

7.21c (large positive or negative values of ϕ_s lead to a thick ion sheath around any colloid so the particles can't get close enough for the electrodynamic "attractor" to work) and (2) altering the thickness of λ_D in Figure 7.21c by changing the electrolyte concentration, c, the electrolyte valance, z, or the temperature, T, $(\lambda_D \propto (T/cz^{1/2})^{1/2})$. At present, we don't know quite as much about magnetic treatment modalities for raising or lowering U_{max}; however, we do know that increasing convective mixing of such a colloid solution enhances the kinetics of the colloid agglomeration process in quantitatively predictable ways.

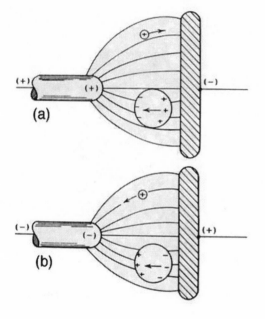

Figure 7.24 Comparison of behaviors of neutral and charged bodies in an alternating nonuniform electric field. (a) Positively charged body moves towards negative electrode. Neutral body is polarized, then is attracted towards point where field is strongest. The two charge regions on the neutral body are equal in amount of charge (but the force is proportional to the local field) and a net force towards the region of more intense field results. (b) Positively charged body moves towards the negative electrode. The neutral body is polarized, does not reverse direction when the field is reversed and moves toward the region of highest field intensity.

<u>External Field Presence Case</u>: For this case, one needs to be particularly concerned with electrophoresis, dielectrophoresis and the magnetic analogues which we shall label magnetophoresis and dimagnetophoresis, respectively. Focusing on only the electric properties for the moment, Figure 7.23 illustrates what happens to either a charged or neutral body in either (a) a uniform DC electric field or (b) a non-uniform DC electric field[17]. A charged body moves along the field lines in either case towards the opposite pole of the field (electrophoresis) at some drift velocity. A neutral body only polarizes to create an electric dipole and does not drift in a uniform field but does drift towards the high field region in a non-uniform field (the electric dipole has a decreased free energy in the high field region). This movement of electric charge dipoles is called dielectrophoresis.

Figure 7.24 shows what happens for a non-uniform AC electric field. For the charged body case, the body first drifts to the right on one half cycle and then to the left on the reverse half cycle and, for high enough frequency, there is negligible net motion over time. However, for the polarized body, it always moves towards the high field region regardless of the half-cycle polarity. Thus, in AC fields (where the electric force on a body is proportional to the spatial gradient of $\underline{E}^2$), only electric dipoles exhibit net movement and always towards the high field region. For the magnetic field case, since we only have magnetic dipoles in U(1) Gauge symmetry physics, such bodies always drift towards the high field region for either DC or AC fields.

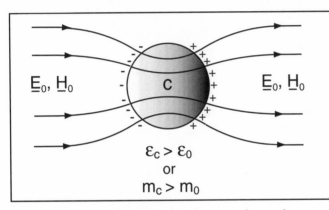

Figure 7.25

Schematic illustration of how field lines may diverge in the vicinity of a colloid, c, particle leading to increases in dipole moments and surface charge concentrations.

As we look more closely into this polarization phenomenon (electric or magnetic), Figure 7.25 illustrates how it comes about. If the "colloids" have different electric permittivity, ε, (dielectric properties) than the solvent (which is the most usual case), then the electric field lines strongly diverge in the vicinity of the particle to either concentrate in the particle (if it has a larger ε than the solvent) or avoid the particle (for smaller ε than the solvent). The induced electric dipole moment increases with both the volume of the colloid and the difference in dielectric properties. For the magnetic field case, the picture is almost exactly the same but now it is the magnetic permeability, m, difference between the "colloid" and solvent that leads to the local field line divergence in the particle's vicinity. Since, anywhere on the earth we have a DC magnetic field (~0.5 gauss) as well as an AC geomagnetic field associated largely with solar activity and we always have AC electric fields (associated with geo-fields plus our technology) and DC electric fields (associated with a non-uniform distribution of atmospheric ions), both types of local induced dipoles are generally present and a complex summation of forces is often placed on these colloids.

Perhaps a simple example from medical therapeutics will best illustrate the complexity of the issues here. Suppose we have a device placed around a human's knee which creates a macroscopically uniform AC electromagnetic field intensity ($\underline{E}^2$ and $\underline{H}^2$) outside the knee. One might quickly assume that nothing will happen inside the knee because this imposed field is macroscopically uniform. However, inside the knee, the structure is polyphase (bone, cartilage, tendons, fluid, "colloids", ions, etc.) and thus heterogeneous with respect to ε and m. This means that, <u>inside</u> the knee, the $\underline{E}$ and $\underline{H}$ fields are macroscopically very non-uniform and it is these internal environment fields that drive "colloids" and small dipoles to drift towards the local high field regions. Further, with the passage of time, these "colloids" and small dipoles concentrate in certain regions and now create <u>DC fields</u> which, in turn, initiate local ion movements to neutralize such induced DC fields.

The main point to be communicated by this final section is that the presence of <u>any</u> structural heterogeneities in water leads to local heterogeneities in electric permittivity and magnetic permeability and these, in turn, respond directly or indirectly to ambient $\underline{E}$-and $\underline{H}$-fields so as to cause drift movement of such moieties in the solution. Such long range movement upsets the homeostasis of the solution with a variety of interesting consequences.

References

1.   M.J. Buerger, <u>Crystal Structure Analysis</u> (John Wiley and Sons, Inc., New York, 1960).

2.   P.P. Ewald, "Das 'Reziproke Gitter' in der Struckturtheorie", Z. Krist. (A) <u>56</u> (1921) 129.

3.   J.T. Wheeler, "New Conformal Gauging and the Electromagnetic Theory of Weyl", J. Math. Phys. <u>39</u> (1998) 299.

4.   H. Weyl, "Sitzund D. Preuss., Akad. D. Wissensch. (1918) 465"; <u>The Principle of Relativity</u> (Dover, New York, 1923).

5.   M.J. Duff, "The Theory Formerly Known as Strings", Scientific American (February, 1998) 64.

6.   G. Harburn, C.A. Taylor and T.R. Welberry, <u>Atlas of Optical Transforms</u> (Cornell University Press, Ithaca, New York, 1975).

7.   H.S. Carslaw, Fourier Series and Integrals (Oxford University Press, New York, N.Y., 1930)

8.   K. Pribram, Brain and Perception, Holonomy and Structure in Figural Processing (Lawrence Erlbaum Associates, Hillsdale, New Jersey, 1991).

9.   J.D. Kraus and K.R. Carver, Electromagnetics (McGraw-Hill Book Company, New York, N.Y., 1973, p. 645).

10.   P. Gray and S. K. Scott, Chemical Oscillations and Instabilities (Oxford University Press, New York, N.Y, 1990).

11.   S. K. Scott, Oscillations, Waves and Chaos in Chemical Kinetics (Oxford University Press, New York, N.Y, 1994).

12.   S. K. Scott, Chemical Chaos (Oxford University Press, New York, N.Y, 1991).

13.   J.B. Talbot and R.A. Oriani, "Application of Linear Stability Analysis to Passivation Models", J. Electrochem. Soc. 132 (1985) 1545.

14.   Y. Wang, J.L. Hudson and N.I. Jaeger, "On the Franck-FitzHugh Model of the Dynamics of Iron Dissolution in Sulfuric Acid", J. Electrochem. Soc. 137 (1990) 485.

15.   A.B. Pippard, The Physics of Vibration, Volume 1 (Cambridge University Press, New York, N.Y, 1978).

16.   J. Komrska, "The Fourier Transform of Lattices", Proceedings of the International summer school on Diagnostics and Applications of Thin Films, May 27-June 5, 1991, Czechoslovakia: IOP Publishing Ltd.

Appendix 7.A: Wave Diffraction and Interference Maxima from Crystals

If one starts with two point sources of radiation as illustrated in Figure 7A.1, at a particular instant in time there are a series of locations where the two wave crests reinforce each other (black dots) and another series of locations where the wave crest from one source is cancelled by the wave trough from the other (open circles). So long as the waves remain perfect, the loci of the points where the waves cancel are time-invariant and thus one sees a set of dark bands with illumination between on a screen intercepting these waves. In a crystal, one has a periodic array of atoms and each may act as a source of radiation when excited by an incident x-ray beam. It is the superposition of all these

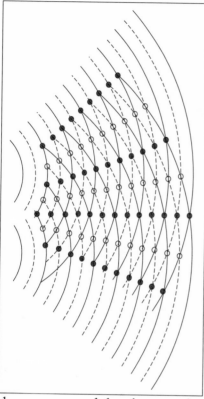

Figure 7A.1   Interference of two sets of spherical waves. Black dots show coincidences of troughs and of crests, circles show coincidences of troughs of one wave and crests of the other.

scattered wave crests that gives rise to intense illumination at specific locations in space (called the diffraction pattern) and one wants to be able to precisely predict these locations for all possible combinations of crystals and x-ray beams. Let us look into this diffraction process to see what can be learned.

Although it is the individual atoms, located at repeat distances a, b and c in the crystal that do the wave scattering, it is useful to first consider this scattering as coming from stacks of parallel planes having an orientation specified by <u>Miller indices</u> (hkl) which are determined as follows: (1) Find the intercepts of the plane on the three basic axes of the crystal in terms of the lattice constants (a, b, c) and (2) Take the reciprocals of these numbers,

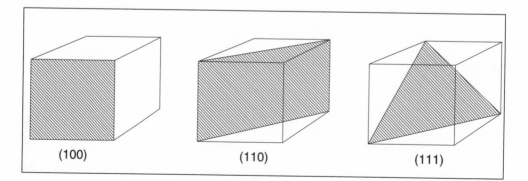

(100)   (110)   (111)

Figure 7A.2   Miller indices of some important planes in a cubic crystal.

reducing them to the smallest three integers having the same ratio. This result gives the Miller indices. For the plane whose intercepts are 4,1,2, the reciprocals are 1/4, 1, 1/2 so the Miller indices are (1 4 2). Figure 7A.2 gives the Miller indices for the three most densely packed planes of atoms in a cubic crystal.

One can account for the position of the diffracted beams via a very simple reflection model by Bragg (1913) illustrated in Figure 7A.3a. The crystal planes are spaced a distance d apart, the radiation is incident in the plane of the paper and the path length difference for rays reflected from adjacent planes is **2d(sinθ)**. Constructive interference will occur when the path length difference is an integral number, **n**, of wavelengths yielding

$$2\ d\ \sin\ \theta = n\ \lambda. \qquad (7A.1)$$

This is called Bragg's law for wavelength λ.

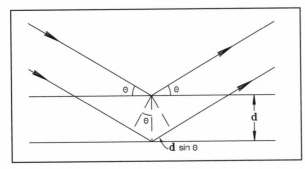

Figure 7A.3a   Derivation of Bragg's law; here d is the spacing between parallel atomic planes and $2n\pi$ is the difference in phase between reflections from successive planes.

Since a particular atom can be considered as part of many planes, one now needs to look at the scattering from individual atoms in order to derive the diffraction equations. One first looks at scattering from two lattice points, P_1 and P_2 separated by the vector, $\underline{r}$, in Figure 7A.3b. The unit incident wave

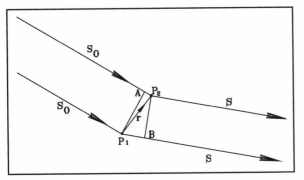

Figure 7A.3b   Calculation of the phase difference of the waves scatterred from lattice points P_1 and P_2

normal is $\underline{s}_o$ while the unit scattered wave normal is $\underline{s}$. If P_1B and P_2A are the projections of $\underline{r}$ on the scattered and incident wave directions respectively, the path length difference between the two scattered waves is

$$P_1B - P_2A = \underline{r}\bullet\underline{s} - \underline{r}\bullet\underline{s}_o = \underline{r}\bullet(\underline{s} - \underline{s}_o) = \underline{r}\bullet\hat{\underline{s}} \ , \qquad (7A.2)$$

where the vector $\hat{\underline{s}} = \underline{s} - \underline{s}_o$ has the simple interpretation as the direction of the normal to a plane that would reflect the incident wave direction into the scattered wave direction. If 2θ is the angle $\underline{s}$ makes with $\underline{s}_o$, then θ is the angle of incidence to this reflecting plane (see Figure 7A.3c) and one sees that

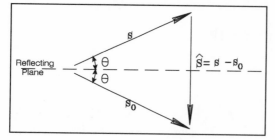

Figure 7A.3c   Construction of the normal to the reflecting plane.

$|\underline{s}| = 2 \sin \theta$ since $\underline{s}$ and $\underline{s}_o$ both have unit length. The phase difference, φ, is just $2\pi/\lambda$ times the path length difference giving

$$\varphi = \left(\frac{2\pi}{\lambda}\right)(\underline{r}\bullet\hat{\underline{s}}). \qquad (7A.3)$$

The amplitude of the scattered wave is a maximum in a direction such that the contributions from each lattice atom differ in phase only by integral multiples of 2π so, for diffraction maxima, one has

$$\varphi_a = \left(\frac{2\pi}{\lambda}\right)(\underline{a}\bullet\hat{\underline{s}}) = 2\,\pi h'$$

$$\varphi_b = \left(\frac{2\pi}{\lambda}\right)(\underline{b}\bullet\hat{\underline{s}}) = 2\,\pi k' \qquad (7A.4)$$

$$\varphi_c = \left(\frac{2\pi}{\lambda}\right)(\underline{c}\bullet\hat{\underline{s}}) = 2\,\pi l'$$

where h', k', l' are integers and not necessarily equal to the Miller indices (hkl) but are related by the factor n in Equation 7A.1 ($h'/n = h$, $k'/n = k$, $l'/n = l$).

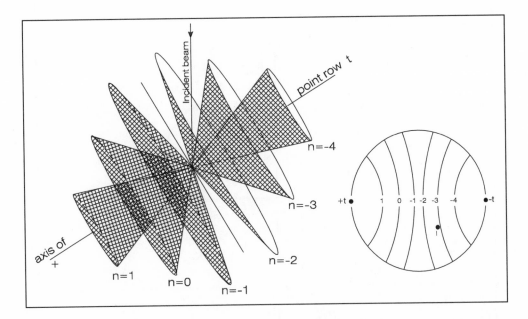

Figure 7A.4   A set of cones, each corresponding to a particular value of n in Equation 7A.1, coaxial about a selected lattice row represents solutions of the diffraction equation for the lattice row. The cones of diffracted intensity maxima are shown in perspective and in stereoscopic projection.

Thus, Equations 7A.4, which are called the Laue equations, allow one to generate Equation 7A.1, which is the Bragg equation.

Each of the Laue equations represents a set of cones of scattered radiation from a selected lattice row of atoms. This is illustrated in Figure 7A.4 for a single lattice point row **t**. For lattice point rows in the perpendicular directions, cones of scattered radiation also exist and, where these perpendicular cones of radiation constructively interfere, one finds very high intensity beams of radiation. This process is illustrated in Figure 7A.5. It is these latter beams of radiation that pass through the points for the reciprocal lattice to the original crystal lattice.

Although the foregoing has discussed reflection and diffraction, the same procedures are involved with the D-space atoms acting as individual antenna sources in a phased array with the excitation coming from R-space.

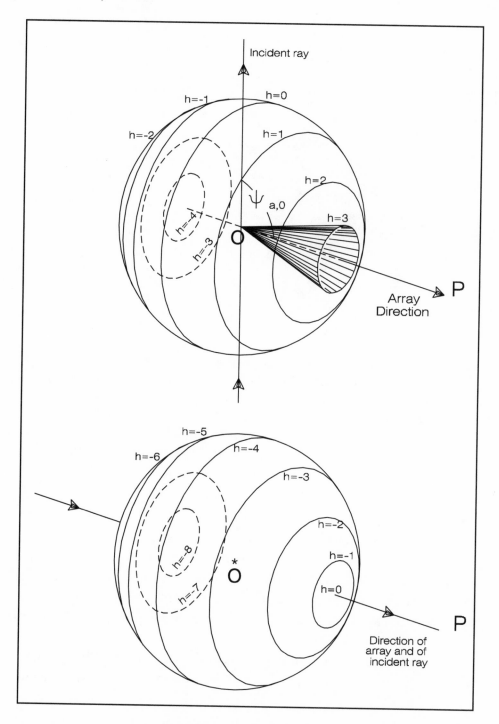

Figure 7A.5a   (top) The allowed cones of diffraction from a one-dimensional array of atoms shown by their intersection with a sphere. (bottom) The orders of diffraction that occur when the incident beam is aligned with the row of atoms.

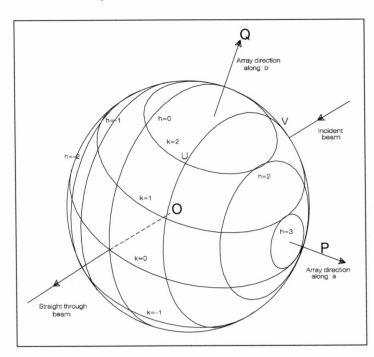

Figure 7A.5b

*The cones of diffraction corresponding to the **a** and **b** directions of the array are shown by their intersections on a sphere. Diffracted beams are formed along the lines joining O to all the intersections of circles.*

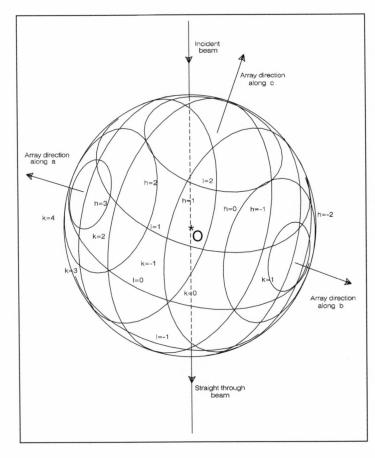

Figure 7A.5c

*The cones of diffraction corresponding to the **a**, **b** and **c** directions of the array are shown by their intersections on a sphere. A diffracted beam would be produced along a line joining O to any trisection of circles. None occurs in the case shown (except h=0, k=0, l=0).*

Appendix 7.B: Generalized Thermodynamics and Nature's Forces

On a per mole of substance basis, the Gibb's free energy function, **G**, in terms of its extensive thermodynamic variables, is expressed as

$$G(P, T, c, \phi, \underline{A}, g, \ldots\ldots) = G(w_j), \; j=1,2,\ldots n \qquad (7.B.1)$$

where P = pressure, T = temperature, c = concentration, ϕ =electrostatic potential, $\underline{A}$ = magnetic vector potential ($\underline{E}$ and $\underline{H}$ are derived from ϕ and $\underline{A}$) and g = gravitation constant. In practice, quantum mechanics currently defines these thermodynamic variables only as functions of the four space-time coordinates (x,y,z,t) while, to avoid complexification, we have proposed an eight-space, $(x,y,z,t,k_x,k_y,k_z,k_t)$, as a more appropriate base-space for calculations. Thus, each of these extensive thermodynamic variables in Equation 7.B.1 must be considered to be functions of these eight coordinates. The general procedure used in the past has been to make a Taylor's series expansion about G_o, the position $(x_o,y_o,z_o,t_o,k_{xo},k_{yo},k_{zo},k_{to})$.

As a simpler example, for a two-variable function expanded about the position (x,y), we have

$$f(x+h, y+l) = f(x,y) + \left\{ h\frac{\partial f(x,y)}{\partial x} + l\frac{\partial f(x,y)}{\partial y} \right\}$$

$$+ \frac{1}{2!}\left\{ h^2\frac{\partial^2 f}{\partial x^2} + 2hl\frac{\partial^2 f}{\partial x \partial y} + l^2\frac{\partial^2 f}{\partial y^2} \right\} + \cdots$$

$$+ \frac{1}{n!}\left\{ h^n\frac{\partial^n f}{\partial x^n} + \binom{n}{1}h^{n-1}l\frac{\partial^n f}{\partial x^{n-1}\partial y} + \cdots + l^n\frac{\partial^n f}{\partial y^n} \right\} + R_n \quad (7.B.2)$$

where R_n is the remainder. For our eight variable function, we find that

$$G = G_o + \sum_{ij} L_{ij}\frac{\partial w_j}{\partial x_i} + \sum_{ijl} M_{ijl}\frac{\partial^2 w_j}{\partial x_i \partial x_l} + \frac{1}{2}\sum_{ijl} N_{ijl}\frac{\partial w_j}{\partial x_i}\frac{\partial w_j}{\partial x_l} + \cdots \cdot (7.B.3a)$$

where

$$L_{ij} = \frac{\partial G}{\partial w_j} \partial x_i; \quad M_{ijl} = \frac{\partial^2 G}{\partial w_j^2}(\partial x_i)^2; \quad N_{ijl} = \frac{\partial G}{\partial w_j}\frac{\partial G}{\partial w_l}(\partial x_i \partial x_l). \quad (7.B.3b)$$

For the simple system of $w_j = P, T, c$, we find that

$$\left(\frac{\partial G}{\partial P}\right)_{T,c} = V; \qquad \left(\frac{\partial G}{\partial T}\right)_{P,c} = -S; \qquad \left(\frac{\partial G}{\partial c}\right)_{P,T} = \mu. \qquad (7.B.3c)$$

This expression defines the thermodynamics of <u>homogeneous</u> systems where V = volume, S = entropy and μ = chemical potential. As we move out of the linear regime into the nonlinear regime of nature's expression, the M_{ijl}, N_{ijl}, etc. terms must be considered and this defines the thermodynamics of <u>inhomogeneous</u> systems.

The foregoing is all based on utilizing a Taylor's series expansion of G about the point G_0. However, an even more general expansion is Laurent's series expansion about a point z_0. Let us consider this expansion using Figure 7.B.1. Let z' denote a point on either of two concentric circles C_1 and C_2

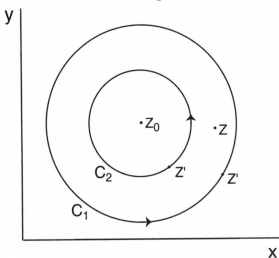

Figure 7.B.1

where $|z'-z_0| = r_1$ and $|z'-z_0| = r_2 < r_1$. Laurent's Theorem states that, if a function, $f(z)$ is analytic on C_1 and C_2 and throughout the region between these two circles then, at each point between them, $f(z)$ is represented by a convergent series of positive and negative powers of $(z-z_0)$; *ie.,*

$$f(z) = \sum_{n=0}^{\infty} a_n(z-z_0)^n + \sum_{n=1}^{\infty} \frac{b_n}{(z-z_0)^n} \qquad (7.B.4a)$$

where

$$a_n = \frac{1}{2\pi i} \int_{C_1} \frac{f(z')dz'}{(z'-z_0)^{n+1}} \qquad (n=0,1,2....) \qquad (7.B.4b)$$

and

$$b_n = \frac{1}{2\pi i} \int_{C_2} \frac{f(z')dz'}{(z'-z_0)^{-n+1}} \qquad (n=1,2....) \qquad (7.B.4c)$$

with each integral being taken counterclockwise (Figure 7.B.1).

In the case where $f(z)$ is analytic at every point on and inside C_1 except the point z_0 itself, the radius r_2 can be taken to be infinitesimally small. The expansion given by Equation 7.B.4a is then valid when $0<|z-z_0|< r_1$. If $f(z)$ is analytic at all points on and inside C_1, the integrand for b_n is an analytic function of z', inside and on C_2, because $-n+1 \leq 0$. Therefore, b_n has the value zero and the Laurent series becomes Taylor's series.

From the foregoing, it seems that the Laurent series of Equation 7.B.4a is a perfectly viable expression to substitute for a Taylor's series, especially when there are singularity points in the domain to be considered. Conversely, a Taylor's series expansion in (z,k_z), as shown in Equations 7.2 of the main text, amounts to the same thing.

Appendix 7.C: The Fourier Transform for N-space and for D-space Shapes

Komrska[16] has shown that the generalized Fourier Transform for an N-dimensional space can be given by

$$F(\underline{k}) = A^N \int_{-\infty}^{\infty}...\int f(\underline{s})e^{+ip\underline{s}\bullet\underline{k}} \, d\underline{s} \qquad (7C.1a)$$

$$f(\underline{s}) = B^N \int_{-\infty}^{\infty}...\int F(\underline{k})e^{-ip\underline{s}\bullet\underline{k}} \, d\underline{k} \qquad (7C.1b)$$

where A and B may be mathematically complex constants but p must be a mathematically real constant and the constraint connecting these three constants is

$$AB = |p|/2\pi. \tag{7C.1c}$$

If, for simplicity, we chose $N = 4$, $|p| = 1$ and $A = B = (1/2\pi)^{1/2}$, then physical substance in D-space and its counterpart substance in R-space can be related by

$$F(\underline{k}) = \frac{1}{(2\pi)^2} \int_{-\infty}^{\infty} f(\underline{r}) e^{+i\underline{r}\bullet\underline{k}} \, d\underline{r} \tag{7C.2a}$$

$$f(\underline{r}) = \frac{1}{(2\pi)^2} \int_{-\infty}^{\infty} F(\underline{k}) e^{-i\underline{r}\bullet\underline{k}} \, d\underline{k} \tag{7C.2b}$$

where $\underline{r}$ and $\underline{k}$ are four-vectors in D-space and R-space, respectively. Now, following the procedure of this chapter, we look at $F(\underline{k})$ and $I_n(\underline{k})$ for a variety of 1D, 2D and 3D objects. Using the continuum approximation following Equations 3 of Table 7.1, Equations 1 of Table 7.3, and Equation 7C.1, we will use

$$F(\underline{k}) = \frac{1}{(2\pi)^{N/2}} \int_{D-space} \rho_s e^{i(\underline{k}\bullet\underline{s})} \, d\underline{s} \tag{7C.3a}$$

with

$$I_n = [F(\underline{k})F^*(\underline{k})]^{1/2} / V \tag{7C.3b}$$

where $F^*(\underline{k})$ is the complex conjugate of $F(k)$, V is the object volume and $N = 1$, 2 or 3.

1D-Obects: For the single vertical slit (or rod) of Figure 7.6a, the Fourier Transform (FT) is given by

$$F(k_x, k_y, k_z) = \frac{1}{(2\pi)^{1/2}} \int_{-R/2}^{+R/2} e^{ik_y y} dy \int e^{ik_x x} \delta(x - x_o) dx \int e^{ik_z z} \delta(z - z_o) dz \tag{7C.4a}$$

$$= \frac{1}{(2\pi)^{1/2}} \frac{\sin(k_y R/2)}{k_y/2} e^{ik_x x_o} e^{ik_z z_o} \tag{7C.4b}$$

305

and

$$I_n(k_y) = \left| \frac{\sin(k_y R/2)}{k_y R/2} \right| \tag{7C.4c}$$

If one wished to give this slit (rod) a finite width, then integration over this thickness alters the result slightly. For the two parallel slits of Figure 7.6b, we obtain (neglecting the z-component)

$$F(k_x,k_y) = \frac{1}{(2\pi)^{\frac{1}{2}}} \int_{-R/2}^{+R/2} e^{ik_y y} \, dy \int [\delta(x - l/2) + \delta(x + l/2)] e^{ik_x x} \, dx \tag{7C.5a}$$

$$= \frac{2}{(2\pi)^{\frac{1}{2}}} \frac{\sin(k_y R/2)}{k_y/2} \cos(k_x l/2) \tag{7C.5b}$$

and

$$I_n = \left| \frac{\sin(k_y R/2)}{(k_y R/2)} \cos(k_x l/2) \right|. \tag{7C.5c}$$

For the square slit of side R with $Z_o = 0$ in Figure 7.6c,

$$I_n(k_x,k_y) = (1/4)R \left| F_{2s}(k_x k_y) + F_{2s}(k_y k_x) \right| \tag{7C.6a}$$

where

$$F_{2s}(k_x,k_y) = 2 \frac{\sin(k_y R/2)}{k_y/2} \cos(k_x R/2). \tag{7C.6b}$$

For the circular slit (Figure 7.6d) of radius R centered at $(0,0,0)$ and lying in the (x,y) plane, one uses the polar coordinate approach, $x = R \cos\theta$, $y = R \sin\theta$, to yield

$$F(k_x,0) = F(0,k_y=k_x) = 2\pi R \, J_o(k_x R) \tag{7C.7a}$$

and, with $V = 2\pi R$,

$$I_n(k_r) = |J_o(k_r R)| \quad \text{and} \quad k_r = \left[k_x^2 + k_y^2\right]^{\frac{1}{2}}. \qquad (7C.7b)$$

Here, J_o is the Bessel function of zero order.

For the isosceles triangle slit of side R and height H (Figure 7.6e) lying totally in the (x,y) plane with the point (0,0) at the slit centroid, one finds that

$$F(k_x, k_y) = \frac{\sin(k_x R/2)}{k_x/2} + \frac{\sin\left[(\frac{1}{2}k_x + \frac{\sqrt{3}}{2}k_y)R/2\right]}{(\frac{1}{2}k_x + \frac{\sqrt{3}}{2}k_y)/2} e^{ik_x \frac{R}{4} - ik_y \frac{\sqrt{3}R}{4}}$$

$$+ \frac{\sin\left[(\frac{1}{2}k_x - \frac{\sqrt{3}}{2}k_y)R/2\right]}{(\frac{1}{2}k_x - \frac{\sqrt{3}}{2}k_y)/2} e^{ik_x \frac{R}{4} + ik_y \frac{\sqrt{3}R}{4}} \qquad (7C.8a)$$

and

$$I_n = \left[F(k_x k_y)F^*(k_x k_y)\right]^{\frac{1}{2}} /3R \qquad (7C.8b)$$

For the "Star of David" slit, one just utilizes Equation 3 in Table 7.3 of the main text to modify Equation 7C.8a to the inverted triangle result and then add this new result to Equation 7C.8a to obtain $F(k_x, k_y)$ for this Star of David shaped slit.

2D-Objects: For an infinitesimally thin square sheet of side R lying in the (x,y) plane and centered at (0,0) as shown in Figure 7.7a, one finds that, neglecting the factor 2π,

$$F(k_x, k_y) = \int_{-R/2}^{+R/2} e^{ik_y y} dy \int_{-R/2}^{+R/2} e^{ik_x x} dx = \frac{\sin(k_y R/2)}{k_y/2} \frac{\sin(k_x R/2)}{k_x/2} \quad (7C.9a)$$

and

$$I_n = \left| \left(\frac{\sin(k_y R/2)}{k_y R/2} \right) \left(\frac{\sin(k_x R/2)}{k_x R/2} \right) \right| \qquad (7C.9b)$$

For the infinitesimally thin isoceles triangle sheet of side **R** and height **H** (Figure 7.7b) with its centroid at (0,0), one finds (neglecting the factor 2π)

$$F(k_x, k_y) = \int_{-R/2}^{0} e^{ixk_x} dx \int_{0}^{H+\frac{2Hx}{R}} e^{iyk_y} dy + \int_{0}^{+R/2} e^{ixk_x} dx \int_{0}^{H-\frac{2Hx}{R}} e^{ihk_y} dy$$

$$(7C.10a)$$

$$= \left[\frac{(2H/k_x)e^{ik_x R/2} - (R/k_y)e^{ik_y H}}{(2k_y H - k_x R)} \right] - \left[\frac{(2H/k_x)e^{ik_x R/2} - (R/k_y)e^{ik_y H}}{(2k_y H + k_x R)} \right]$$

$$(7C.10b)$$

and

$$I_n = \frac{2}{RH} \left[(Re(F))^2 + (Im(F))^2 \right]^{\frac{1}{2}} \qquad (7C.10c)$$

Where

$$Re(F) = \frac{4HR}{(4k_y^2 H^2 - k_x^2 R^2)} \left[\cos(k_x R/2) - \cos(k_y H) \right] \qquad (7C10.d)$$

$$Im(F) = \frac{4H}{k_x (4k_y^2 H^2 - k_x^2 R^2)} \left[2k_y H \sin(k_x R/2) - k_x R \sin(k_y H) \right].$$

$$(7C10.e)$$

For an infinitely thin circular sheet lying in the (x,y) plane and centered at (0,0) (Figure 7.7c), the FT is, neglecting the factor 2π,

$$F(k_x,k_y) = \int\limits_{-R}^{R} dx \int\limits_{-[R^2-x^2]^{1/2}}^{+[R^2-x^2]^{1/2}} e^{i(xk_x+yk_y)} dy = \frac{2\pi R}{k_r} J_1(k_r R) \qquad (7C.11a)$$

with

$$k_r = [k_x^2 + k_y^2]^{1/2} \qquad (7C.11b)$$

Since the FT must be symmetric under exchange of k_x and k_y. Here, J_1 is the Bessel Function of order one and

$$I_n(k_r) = \left| 2\frac{J_1(Rk_r)}{Rk_r} \right| \qquad (7C.11c)$$

since $V=\pi R^2$.

3D-Objects: One follows the same procedures for these objects as were utilized to extend the 1D-objects to 2D-objects. The details of this additional extension to 3D are tedious but straightforward and no significant benefit accrues to the reader by laying out these mathematical details here.

CHAPTER 8

Quantitative Theory for the New Paradigm

Physics has progressed greatly over the past 4-5 centuries, largely completing its mastery of classical physics by the end of the 19th century. This was primarily the physics of matter in its various states and forms. No effective involvement with "unseen" stuff of the vacuum was seriously considered. By the end of the 20th century, a solid foundation for quantum physics had been laid. Important involvement with the vacuum was discriminated and strange behavior at small particle size scales was appreciated. However, with the present paradigm and framework of today's physics, there is no place for human qualities to enter and become an interactive part of nature's overall expression. With the new experimental data of Chapters 3-6, it is now time to recognize these human qualities of emotion, mind, intention and consciousness as important aspects of nature's expression and to expand the framework of physics sufficiently to harmoniously incorporate them. The primary goal of this chapter is to delineate such a new framework recognizing that, since it is still a work in progress, several decades of new experiments and theory will be needed before the predictive theoretical structure is satisfyingly stable.

Because of Figure 2.1 and Equation 2.1, a massive singularity exists at the velocity of light, c, from relativity theory. From Appendix 2.C, one also notes that many mathematical singularities exist in quantum electrodynamics at the fundamental particle level. Thus, from Appendix 7.B, it should be clear that the basis for a satisfactory thermodynamics of nature, which incorporates both quantum mechanics and relativity theory, requires the use of Laurent's expansion rather than Taylor's expansion in the coordinates of the appropriate base-space for its description. This means that it is appropriate to abandon our familiar base-space (x, y, z, t) (or rather (x, y, z, jct), in order to distinguish that the quality of time is uniquely different from the quality of distance). It is much more appropriate for future human advancement and expanded understanding to recognize the importance of the reciprocal coordinate terms operating in nature and choose a biconformal base-space of the form $(x, y, z, jct; ik_x, ik_y, ik_z, ik_t)$ for viewing nature (in accord with Equation 7.B.4 of Chapter 7). Here, the new coordinates (k_x, k_y, k_z, k_t) are proportional to the mathematical residues, $\Re$, of their respective coordinate domains and the imaginary index, i, is left visible and distinguishable from j so as to identify another unique quality in nature.

One of the advantages inherent in adopting this particular base-space is that wave-particle simultaneous expression by nature is automatically built into the physics with a particular quality in one 4-space being related to its conjugate quality in the companion 4-space by a Fourier transform relationship (so the relationships of Tables 7.1 and 7.3 plus Figures 7.5 to 7.12 hold). We shall see later in this chapter (after making another pair of postulates) that this automatically gives rise to non-local forces, allows a higher gauge symmetry to be possible and starts us on our path towards discriminating substructures of the vacuum. However, the present level of modeling in this book <u>does not</u> intentionally incorporate the qualities of dematerialization/materialization of particles implicit in today's quantum theory and thus is still just a "metaphor" for the ultimate theory.

The New Framework's Foundation Stones

The Key Elements from Tiller's Multidimensional Simulator Model[1]:

(1) A network of nodal points that act as transponders/transducers for consciousness wave/energy wave conversion. The nodal point network functions on three size scales with the two larger grids being superlattice-like grids for the primary grid at the smallest size scale. (2) Spirit activates the driving consciousness wave pattern for its specific intention and the nodal points in the simulator convert these consciousness wave patterns into various kinds of energy wave patterns. These energy wave patterns communicate with the various types of particles and agglomerations of particles within the interstices of the appropriate nodal point network. (3) Because these three nodal networks, when perfectly ordered, form reciprocal hexagonal lattices to each other, any quality of substance in the space of one network is related to the complementary quality in another network via a Fourier transform relationship. To use the "Big Bang" concept for illustrative purposes, this model proposes that at the inception of our universe there preexisted the mind and emotion domain substructures of the vacuum. Thus, directed intention from the domain of spirit has a ready mechanism for creating the Big Bang process. As alluded to above, the key structural element of the mind domain is a ten-dimensional network of active nodal points in a close-packed arrangement with a lattice spacing of $\lambda_M \sim 10^{-27}$ meters (so this network forms an extremely fine grid closely related to the fundamental Planck length and

Planck time). These nodal points are undetectable by the tools of today's physics.

During the condensation phases of the Big Bang, both the substances and the nodal networks of R-space and D-space are formed. The latter via a type of self-induced coherence of superposed consciousness waves broadcast from the mind domain nodal points. We will label these three nodal networks (NN) as NN_M, NN_R and NN_D with the subscripts being used to distinguish the particular level of the model. Thus, this primary lattice of mind nodal points contains within itself two potential superlattices of nodal points that are reciprocals to each other (see Figure 7.2). The first sublattice, NN_R, is also a reciprocal of the primary mind lattice, NN_M. The use of the word "potential" here is meant to imply that these particular nodal points must first form (via some process of organization) and then they must organize themselves into an array, which originally will be a relatively random array. This then proceeds through various stages of ordering to eventually become a relatively perfect four-dimensional periodic lattice. The closest analogue to this in the world of materials science is "superlattice" formation in a host lattice of atoms. Let us now proceed with the description of the fully ordered state of these three nodal networks.

For NN_R, this first superlattice to NN_M has uniquely identifiable nodal points at $\lambda_R \sim 10^{-17}$ meters and, at a 3-space level, is also of a close-packed hexagonal type but rotated counterclockwise by $90°$ with respect to NN_M (see Figure 8.1(a)). In fact, the NN_R are located at certain sites in the NN_M separated by $\sim 10^{10}$ primary sites and have their own unique identifiable nature. The second superlattice, NN_D, is also formed from uniquely identifiable nodal points at a spacing of $\lambda_D \sim 10^{-7}$ meters. It is a superlattice to the NN_R and, at a 3-space level, is also of the hexagonal close-packed type but rotated counterclockwise a further $90°$ with respect to the NN_R. Figure 8.1(a) represents an illustrative picture of these three nodal structures in perfect lattice form (but with much reduced spacing between the superlattice nodal points); however, relative to the sites in the NN_M lattice, those in the NN_R lattice are thought to have a spacing $\sim 10^{10}$ times larger while those in the NN_D lattice have a spacing $\sim 10^{20}$ times larger.

Figure 8.1b illustrates how the situation might look when defects and disorder of the NN_R and NN_D are present. As already stated, order-disorder transformations are thought to be involved in the two coarsest networks so they can exhibit amorphous, polycrystalline or single crystal type of character. Here, one grain is thought to differ from another by the orientation of some special nodal point property, e.g. special spin vector, tensor, torsion, etc.

312

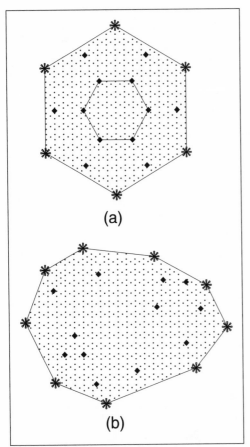

(a)

(b)

Figure 8.1   Illustrative plan view of the three nodal networks: (a) in a perfectly ordered state, (b) in the normally disordered state (except for the mind domain network). The proposed size scale change from network to network is ~ 10^{10}.

These grids of nodal points are unique in that the waves travelling through the networks exhibit qualities of consciousness as distinct from energies. The conversion from consciousness to energies occurs at the nodal points themselves. It is also thought that the major components of life energy for humans are radiated from the NN_R and NN_D. Thus, the larger is the size or number of regularly spaced radiators in the array, the greater will be the amount (and fidelity) of the information transferred from the NN_M as well as energy transferred to the human from the NN_R and NN_D making the individual more conscious and more vital.

The structural character of the nodal networks are thought to be influenced by three main forces: (1) cosmological scale forces driven from higher dimensional realms, (2) individual human internal harmony versus disharmony and (3) collective humanity's internal harmony vs. disharmony. When all the forces are beneficial, the NN form relatively perfect lattices of very large extent (e.g. Figure 8.1(a)) and humans manifest amazingly large consciousness and energy densities. When the reverse occurs, the NN form an almost amorphous arrangement and humans manifest only very small amounts of consciousness and life energy. In between, the NN structure is polycrystalline (e.g. Figure 8.1(b)) and the larger the size of the average NN grain, the greater will be the amount of consciousness and life energy flowing through the individual.

Generally, from the perspective of this model, a saint has reached a high state of inner self-management at mental and emotional levels so that the body substance radiation fields are harmonized and synchronized. This supports a superlattice ordering process to occur at the NN-level so that grain growth occurs and the average NN grain size increases. Such individuals manifest an abundant energy output even with negligible physical food intake.

Using an energy level diagram to express the "biobodysuit" metaphor of Chapter 2, one is led to Figure 8.2. Here, one can discriminate the classical physical reality (positive energy states) from the vacuum reality (negative energy states), once one defines the zero energy state as being located in the middle of what we will label the Dirac energy gap. This choice of zero energy state is historical and arbitrary. In the new paradigm it would seem more reasonable to shift it to the bottom of Figure 8.2. Then, all of the energies in the diagram are positive. The presently described quantum mechanical reality is thought to include this classical physical reality plus some aspects of the vacuum reality. The experimentally observed reality, shown by the data in Chapters 3-6 of this book, includes the classical physical reality (D-space), the mathematical modulus of the upper band (R-space) of the vacuum reality plus both the deltron activation function from the middle vacuum reality band and the intention imprint "boundary condition" imposed on the lower vacuum reality band. The details of the nodal network structures in Figures 8.1 are intimately related to the details of the energy levels in the energy bands of Figure 8.2. One goal of the present book is to expand our current quantum mechanical perspective via the "biconformal base-space interpretation" so as to develop a quantitative predictability of experimentally observable events that incorporates (1) the details of both the magnetic and the electric monopole substance levels, (2) the intention imprint as a boundary condition (BC) imposed on R-space and (3) a parameterized version of the deltron activation function. Sometime in the distant future we will have learned enough to expand the perspective sufficiently that the intention imprint, BC, can be moved to the NN_M level and the deltron activation function can be expressed in much more fundamental terms. Then we will have created a level of physics that truly incorporates the human qualities of emotion and mind into observable reality.

Empowering The Pattern: In Chapter 7, the main focus was on expressing the R-space quality pattern for an object that was the equilibrium conjugate to the D-space quality pattern for that object. Some specifics were calculated via Equations 3 of Table 7.1 for matter density, using the continuum approximation, for a variety of simple shapes. One point of clarification, here, is that the phase component in Buerger's original derivation[1] could just as easily have been taken as $\exp(-i2\pi k\delta)$ so that the exponentials in Equations 3 of Table 7.1 would have reversed signs. Many people use this reversed sign notation with equal success[2] (this amounts to integrating from $+ \infty$ to $- \infty$ instead of in the reverse direction, which is fine for mathematically Abelian, U(1) Gauge systems).

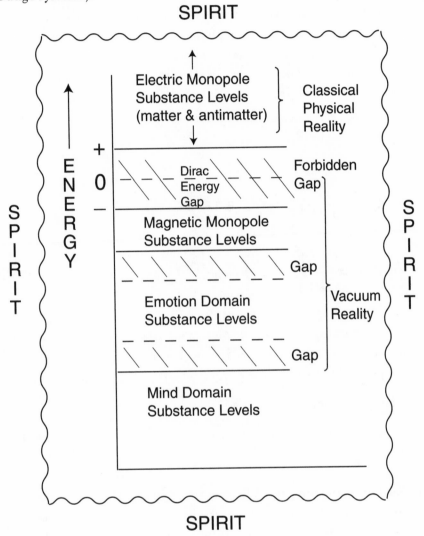

Figure 8.2   *An energy level diagram embracing both classical physical substance and "unseen" vacuum substances.*

In the U(1) Gauge experimental world, one doesn't detect any significant object shape effects, at least not for objects of macroscopic size. Presumably, this is because the magnitude of the effect in normal cases is so small that it is down amongst the "noise" for the current levels of measurement accuracy. This could be interpreted to mean that the shape's R-space modulus, **I**, is small because the cosmic background level of deltron coupling is quite small. For a system in a linear regime of deltron coupling, the deltron effect would cancel out of I_n and this becomes a baseline pattern effect for the particular shape. To empower the pattern to have a marked physical measurement contribution, through enhanced deltron activation, this additional factor must be incorporated into the theory in a mathematical fashion. At our present level of understanding, we simply define the deltron activation factor as $C_\delta(k,t,.....)$, where the ..... represent other as yet undelineated variables, and we incorporate it into Equations 3 of Table 7.1 to yield

$$T: \quad \hat{F}(k) = \frac{1}{(2\pi)^{1/2}} \int_{D-space} \hat{\rho}_s C_\delta e^{i2\pi sk} ds \tag{8.1a}$$

$$T^{-1}: \quad \hat{\rho}(s)C_\delta = \frac{1}{(2\pi)^{1/2}} \int_{R-space} \hat{F}(k) e^{-i2\pi sk} dk \tag{8.1b}$$

where the superscript $^\wedge$ notifies us that enhanced deltron activation is being taken into account. Equations 8.1 can also be used when only the cosmic background level of deltron activation, $C_\delta = C_{\delta_0}$, is present. In such a case, C_{δ_0} can be treated as a constant and brought out from under the integral sign so it disappears in the expression for the normalized modulus, I_n (see Equation 1(b) of Table 7.3).

What Does an Experimental Observation Contain?: All experimental measurements of any particular quality for a material yield a result that is comprised of two contributions, one from R-space and one from D-space. The magnitude of the former is strongly influenced by the degree of deltron activation in the measurement locale as illustrated by Equation 8.1a and by Figure 2.5 for the quantity Q_M. To quantitatively appreciate this, we define a particular R-space quality by $F(\underline{k}_4)$ via Equation 1 of Table 8.1 with it's mathematically real part, $\hat{F}'(\underline{k}_4)$, and mathematically imaginary part, $\hat{F}''(\underline{k}_4)$, in terms of the R-space four-vector $\underline{k}_4$. This yields the D-space counterparts given by Equation 2 of Table 8.1. This D-space quality and its

Table 8.1   *The Components of any Physical Measurement, Q_M.*

$$\hat{F}(\underline{k}_4) = \hat{F}'(\underline{k}_4) + i\hat{F}''(\underline{k}_4) \qquad (1)$$

$$\hat{\rho}(s) = \hat{\rho}'(s) + \hat{\rho}''(s) \qquad (2)$$

and

$$C_\delta = C_\delta' + iC_\delta'' \qquad (3)$$

with

$$Q_M'(s) = \hat{\rho}'(s) + \int_R \hat{F}'(\underline{k}_4)d\underline{k}_4 \qquad (4)$$

and

$$Q_M''(s) = \hat{\rho}''(s) + \int_R \hat{F}''(\underline{k}_4)d\underline{k}_4 . \qquad (5)$$

Here, $Q_M = Q_M' + iQ_M''$,

$$Q_M' = |Q_M| \cos\theta_3; \; Q_M'' = |Q_M| \sin\theta_3$$

and $\theta_3 = \theta_1 + \theta_2 = \tan^{-1}(Q_M''/Q_M')$ from Figure 8.3.

Equations 8.1 become

$$\hat{F}' = \int_D [(\hat{\rho}'C_\delta' - \hat{\rho}''C_\delta'')\cos(2\pi ks) - (\hat{\rho}'C_\delta'' - \hat{\rho}''C_\delta')\sin(2\pi ks)]ds \quad (6a)$$

$$\hat{F}'' = \int_D [(\hat{\rho}'C_\delta' - \hat{\rho}''C_\delta'')\sin(2\pi ks) + (\hat{\rho}'C_\delta'' - \hat{\rho}'C_\delta')\cos(2\pi ks)]ds \quad (6b)$$

$$(\hat{\rho}'C_\delta' - \hat{\rho}''C_\delta'') = \int_R [\hat{F}'\cos(2\pi sk) + \hat{F}''\sin(2\pi sk)]dk \qquad (6c)$$

$$(\hat{\rho}'C_\delta'' + \hat{\rho}''C_\delta') = -\int_R [\hat{F}'\sin(2\pi sk) - \hat{F}''\cos(2\pi sk)]dk \qquad (6d)$$

Equations 4, 5 and 6 require an iterative procedure for simultaneous solution.

R-space conjugate are connected through the deltron activation function, C_δ, of Equations 8.1 that we may define as Equation 3 of Table 8.1. Equations 8.1, when separated into real and imaginary parts provide 4 equations connecting these 6 unknown quantities.

An actual experimental measurement for **M** yields, in principle, both the real and imaginary parts of Q_M as given by Equations 8.2

$$Q_M = Q'_M + iQ''_M. \qquad (8.2a)$$

so we may assume that both Q'_M and Q''_M are known quantities with two characteristics, magnitude, $|Q_M|$, and phase angle, θ_3, illustrated by the Argand diagram of Figure 8.3. This yields

$$Q'_M = |Q_M| \cos\theta_3; \; Q''_M = |Q_M| \sin\theta_3 \qquad (8.2b)$$

as the horizontal and vertical components of this vector in Figure 8.3. By working with the constraints of vector addition in Figure 8.3, we obtain the two additional equations 4 and 5 of Table 8.1. Now we have 6 equations in the 6 unknowns so that, given Q'_M and Q''_M plus Equations 8.1, the unknowns $\hat{F}'$, $\hat{F}''$, $\hat{\rho}'$, $\hat{\rho}''$, $C_\delta{}'$ and $C_\delta{}''$ can, in principle, be completely determined. The simultaneous solution of Equations 4, 5 and 6 will be needed, probably using an iterative procedure.

As an illustrative example, this approach says that, if we take the experimentally measured voltages, $V_j(t)$, at various brain sites, j, on the skull as a function of time, t, via Equations 8.1 plus 4 and 5 of Table 8.1, we can discriminate the D-space portion, the R-space portion and the Emotion Domain contribution to the brain activity of that particular individual. At present, we just take the $V_j(t)$ and immediately Fourier transform them to yield the EEG plots without realizing what we have thrown away! The approach proposed here will provide us with a much richer understanding of the total human being. Obviously, the same approach can be applied to EKG, EMG, etc., measurements on any particular human or animal. Clearly, this approach will have many applications in the health sciences.

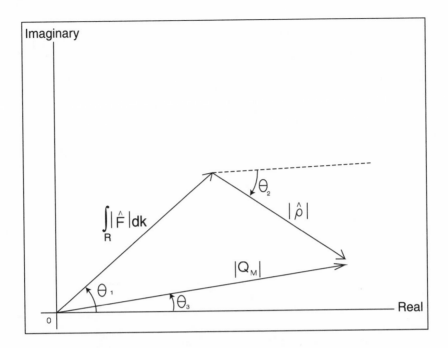

Figure 8.3   *Argand diagram for the addition of two vectors (with real and imaginary components).*

What Does This Say About the Size Scale Factor in Quantum Mechanics?:

The early experimental work after de Broglie's time showed that quantum effects became larger, the smaller the size of the moiety being considered. This is, of course, fully consistent with a D-space/R-space model because, as can be seen from Figure 7.5a, the smaller is the D-space object size the larger is the k-value needed for its R-space pilot wave counterpart. Since the energetic content of the wave components increase with $\underline{k}_4$ (frequency wave number), the more effect they will manifest on any interaction and thus on any experimental observation of that interaction. Alternatively, one might postulate that $C_\delta(k,t,.....)$ in Equations 8.1 is a nonlinear function that strongly increases with $\underline{k}_4$. Only future experiments will reveal the specific dependencies of the function C_δ on its relevant variables.

The Importance of Increasing Deltron Coupling on the Gibb's Free Energy:

Although the proper picture for the Gibb's free energy of a particular material is $\hat{G}_D$ and $\hat{G}_R$ for D-space and R-space, respectively, measurement of magnitude only yields

$$Q_G = \hat{I}_D + \int_R \hat{I}_R^n dk. \qquad (8.3)$$

319

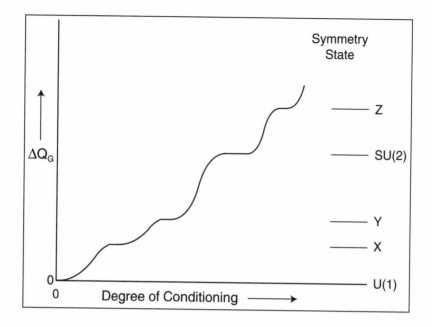

Figure 8.4   Schematic illustration of free energy change, ΔQ_G, from the ground symmetry state, U(1), as the degree of locale conditioning increases.

from Equations 4 and 5 of Table 8.1. The superscript **n** is used in Equation 8.3 because **n**=2 applies to the U(1) Gauge state but **n** changes as the degree of coupling increases (a typical diffraction pattern yields an intensity proportional to $(amplitude)^2$ – see page 352). As conditioning increases, via increased deltron coupling, all one can detect via standard measurement is ΔQ_G relative to the U(1) Gauge condition. Figure 8.4 provides a qualitative picture of the expected change of ΔQ_G, relative to the U(1) Gauge symmetry state, as the degree of locale conditioning increases. One sees that the locale symmetry state passes through the symmetries X, Y, SU(2) and Z as the degree of conditioning increases. Thus, one could say that the IIED-conditioning process stabilizes a higher symmetry state X, Y, SU(2) or Z in the locale relative to the U(1) Gauge state. Thus, if one had a device operating between any one of these higher symmetry states and the U(1) Gauge state, that device would be clearly able to deliver useful work to the U(1) Gauge domain because a free energy driving force exists between the two domains. It is via just such a process path that we have been able to produce large non-equilibrium H^+ concentrations in purified water relative to the U(1) Gauge equilibrium value. It is via this same process path that all the other remarkable phenomena of Chapters 3-6 have been produced.

Perhaps it is just this same type of process in a viable life form that characterizes its "living" state from its "dead" state. At this point in time, we are thinking of these different symmetry states X, Y, Z etc., as representing different states of order for the magnetic monopole substances that inhabit the physical vacuum.

The R-space/D-space Connection Constraints: Modern texts on Fourier Transforms[2] show that simple harmonic waves of the sine and cosine type expressed along the k_x-direction of R-space lead to a pair of δ-functions at specific locations lying on the x-axis of D-space (see Figure 8.5a). From the mathematics one finds that, as the undulation interval, Δk_x, of the R-space wave increases, the δ-functions at positions $\pm x_0$ in D-space move closer to the D-space origin. The quantitative constraint connecting x_0 to Δk_x is

$$x_0 \Delta k_x = 2\pi. \qquad (8.4a)$$

Likewise, for a harmonic wave expressed along the k_t-direction of R-space, one has a conjugate pair of δ-functions located at $\pm t_0$ along the t-axis of D-space with the quantitative constraint connecting t_0 to Δk_t as

$$t_0 \Delta k_t = 2\pi. \qquad (8.4b)$$

For a general 4-dimensional R-space simple harmonic wave of undulation interval, $\Delta \underline{k}_4$, the pair of δ-functions at $\pm r_4$ of D-space are constrained by the connection

$$\underline{r}_4 \cdot \Delta \underline{k}_4 = 2\pi. \qquad (8.4c)$$

Equations 8.4 relate to R-space waves and D-space particles. However, we also have D-space waves, although these are just spatial or temporal undulations in the density of particles or flux of particles, and we presumably have an analogue for particles in R-space that we will call "resonators". In the general model[3,4], it is the nodal points of the R-space nodal network that we will choose to act as the resonators. Thus, with this addition, we have three additional connection constraint equations:

$$k_x \lambda = 2\pi \qquad (8.5a)$$

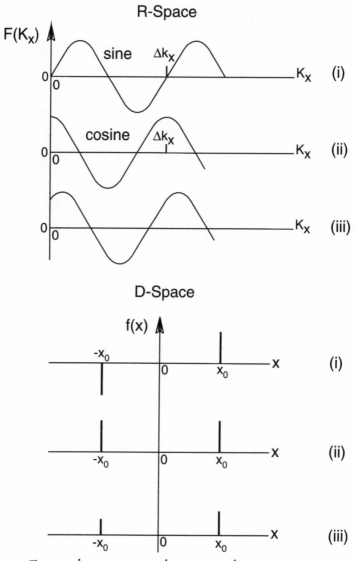

Figure 8.5a *For one dimension, complementary substance representations in D-space and R-space. Particle-like delta functions in D-space (bottom) have wave-like conjugates (top) in R-space of simple sine and cosine type.*

$$k_t \tau = 2\pi \qquad (8.5b)$$

$$\underline{k}_4 \bullet \underline{\Delta r}_4 = 2\pi. \qquad (8.5c)$$

A little later we will see how Equations 8.4 and 8.5 can be utilized to interpret the experimental reality of Chapters 3 to 6.

Although the right hand side of Equations 8.4 and 8.5 is written as

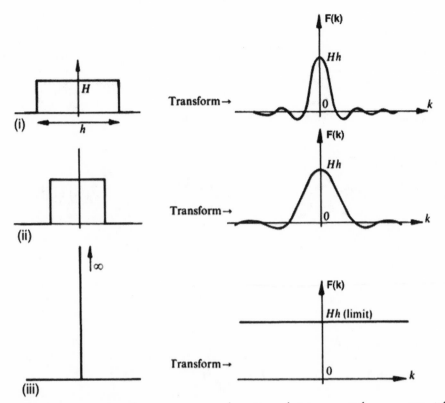

Figure 8.5b   *Progression from a square pulse, (i) and (ii), to a δ-function (iii). The area hH remains constant throughout.*

2π, in the most general case it should be written as $2n\pi$, where n is a positive or negative integer between 1 and ∞. Thus, each different integer might be considered as a unique particulate space-time world connected to the general R-space domain. If this multiworld possibility is correct, then we do not know which of these worlds contains <u>our</u> earth. Thus, a presently undetermined integer, acting as a type of scaling constant, should be present in Equations 8.4 and 8.5 and this scaling constant must be determined by future experiments.

<u>**Transforming δ-Functions Into Qualities**</u>:   To illustrate how a δ-function may be formed, consider Figure 8.5b. We start with a rectangular pulse of height H and width h at the origin of the x-axis so its Fourier transform, $F(k_x)$, is readily found to be given by Equation 1 of Table 8.2 where $F(0) = Hh$ is the $k_x = 0$ value for $F(k_x)$. For simplicity, we could even choose $H = 1/h$ for illustrative purposes so that the pulse area is unity. For

the case of constant area under the pulse in D-space as h decreases, H increases and the R-space transform spreads out in the k_x-direction. Thus, the value for the first zero of $F(k_x)$ increases as does the Δk_x between any two adjacent zeros of $F(k_x)$ (see Figure 8.5b). As h becomes smaller and smaller,

Table 8.2   *Key D-space/R-space Connections*

Rectangular Shape

$$f(x) = 0 \text{ for } |x| > h/2; \quad F(k_x) = F(0) \frac{\sin(k_x h/2)}{(k_x h/2)}; F(0) = Hh \quad (1)$$

$$= H \text{ for } |x| < h/2$$

Origin Shift

$$f(x) = \delta(x-x_o) ; \qquad F'(k_x) = e^{ik_x x_o} F(k_x)$$

$$= e^{i(2\pi k_x/\Delta k_x)} F(k_x) \quad (2)$$

Multiple δ-functions

$$f(x) = \sum_N \delta(x - x_N) ; \quad F'(k_x) = \left(\sum_N e^{ix_N k_x}\right) F(k_x) \quad (3)$$

Including Time Factor

$$f(x,t) = \delta(x-x_o,t) ; \quad F'(k_x,k_t) = e^{ix_o k_x} e^{itk_t} F(k_x) \quad (4)$$

Generalization

$$f(r_3,t) = \delta(x-x_o,y-y_o,z-z_o,t) = \delta(\underline{r}_3 - r_{3o},t)$$

$$F'(\underline{k}_3,k_t) = \exp[i(x_o k_x + y_o k_y + z_o k_z + tk_t)]F(\underline{k}_3)$$

$$= e^{i(r_{3o} \bullet \underline{k}_3 + tk_t)} F(\underline{k}_3) = e^{i[2\pi(\underline{k}_3/\Delta \underline{k}_3) + 2\pi(k_t/\Delta k_t)]} F(\underline{k}_3) \quad (5)$$

Relativity Considerations

$$d|r_4|^2 = dx^2 + dy^2 + dz^2 - c^2 dt^2 = 0 \quad (6a)$$

$$d|k_4|^2 = dk_x^2 + dk_y^2 + dk_z^2 - \beta^2 dk_t^2 = 0 \quad (6b)$$

the transform spreads out more and more seemingly losing detail contrast at each step change in h. When h approaches zero we have a δ-function and there is no detail contrast at all in the transform which becomes a constant, Hh.

Thus, a δ-function located at the origin in D-space is sustained at that location by a completely uniform amplitude spectrum over all the $\mathbf{k_x}$ of R-space from $\mathbf{k_x} = -\infty$ to $\mathbf{k_x} = +\infty$ (see Figure 8.5b).

When the origin for this δ-function is shifted to $\mathbf{x=x_o}$, its D-space representation is labeled $\delta(\mathbf{x-x_o})$ while its R-space representation is given by Equation 2 of Table 8.2. Thus, it still has an amplitude spectrum of unity but with a steadily changing phase which is directly proportional to $\mathbf{x_o}$. For multiple δ-functions at positions, $\mathbf{x_N}$, in D-space, Equation 3 of Table 8.2 provides the sustaining R-space spectrum.

Since we ultimately wish to show how such a single δ-function or an array of δ-functions can be converted to qualities in our cognitive reality, we must also account for their presence in time and their maintaining that presence in the "now" as distinct from the past or the future. If we think of our δ-function as having been created at t_0 and measure time, t, from that point, then the Fourier transform for the δ-function must always contain the phase factor $\mathbf{exp(ik_t{\bullet}t)}$ so that Equation 4 of Table 8.2 properly represents our R-space spectrum for a D-space δ-function always in the "now" at position x_0. The generalization of this picture to δ-function locations anywhere in the "now" of 3-space is given by Equation 5 of Table 8.2.

We strengthen the identifier for $\delta(\mathbf{x-x_o})$ by using the mathematical constraints of the last section, $\mathbf{x_o \Delta k_x = t \Delta k_t = 2\pi}$ so that our phase factor becomes $\mathbf{exp[i2\pi(k_x/\Delta k_x + k_t/\Delta k_t)]}$ and the $(\Delta\mathbf{k_x}, \Delta\mathbf{k_t})$ set become the undulation interval components for the wave, labeled the primordial R-space wave, identified with $\delta(\mathbf{x-x_o})$. The position $\mathbf{x_o}$ is altered merely by changes in $\Delta\mathbf{k_x}$ and the δ-function stays in the "now" by steadily decreasing $\Delta\mathbf{k_t}$.

By moving our δ-function off the $\mathbf{x}$-axis into the volume of D-space to the position $(\mathbf{x_N,y_N,z_N})$, it takes on volume characteristics with area components $(\mathbf{H_x h_x, H_y h_y, H_z h_z})$. Its R-space primordial wave has the undulation interval components $(\Delta\mathbf{k_{xN}}, \Delta\mathbf{k_{yN}}, \Delta\mathbf{k_{zN}}, \Delta\mathbf{k_t})$. This particular R-space wave is not the de Broglie pilot wave as this requires that the δ-function first be converted to a particle (see the next few pages). By considering the large range of unique δ-functions that can develop at $(\mathbf{x_N,y_N,z_N})$ just by alterations in the relative magnitudes for the components $\mathbf{H_x h_x, H_y h_y}$ and $\mathbf{H_z h_z}$, one readily sees that the precursor for a veritable "zoo" of particles exists.

For creation and annihilation of δ-functions, one can presume the spontaneous formation of both a positive-going **Hh** δ-function and a negative-going **Hh** δ-function at (x_N, y_N, z_N) in the "now" of D-space for entropic reasons. The origination of this event could be seen as the superposition of two primordial R-space waves of identical $(\Delta k_x, \Delta k_y, \Delta k_z)$ and amplitude but 180° out-of-phase with each other. The origination of this event could also be seen as occurring in 9-space and yielding both a D-space δ-function image and its R-space primordial wave image (see Figure 8.8b). In any event, as the positive-going **Hh** δ-function begins to separate from the negative-going **Hh** δ-function, the two primordial R-space waves superpose to take on the sine-wave character illustrated in (i) of Figure 8.5a.

From the foregoing one can see that, by controlling the phase of the primordial singlet k-wave in four-dimensional R-space for a D-space δ-function, it can be displaced to any position in the "now" of D-space. To have this δ-function move in a specific locus or at a specific velocity or acceleration in D-space requires additional constraints in R-space between the k_3-wave components and the k_t-wave component. Some of these are explored in Appendix 8.A.

The time factor and the unidirectional flow of time has already been introduced into Equations 4 and 5 of Table 8.2 and the equations of Appendix 8A. Einstein's great work has shown us that relativity considerations are very important in D-space, especially near the mathematical singularity at $v=c$, so that space and time become coupled into space-time. The detailed relativity aspects are beyond the scope of this book. However, time is recognized as a qualitatively different coordinate than the distance coordinates by using **ict** (i = imaginary index) for its representation in 4-space considerations and Equation 6a of Table 8.2 is a quantitative constraint needed in the description of events occurring on this space-time surface.

As stated earlier, when mathematical singularities are present in the domain relevant for consideration, it is the Laurent expansion rather than the Taylor expansion that must be used as a cornerstone for our physics. This is what really requires that we work with the R-space coordinate system described in this book, as the first order reciprocal terms of the Laurent expansion. It is also an important and surprising point that the calculated value of the contour integral around the **m** singularities, which yields what is called the sum of the mathematical residues, $2\pi i \sum_{n=1}^{m} \Re_n$, depends only on the coefficient of these first order reciprocal terms and not on any of the higher order terms. Thus, the sum of the residues can be considered as a scale factor that is incorporated into the **k**-coordinates of R-space. To distinguish these coordinates from both types of D-space coordinates, we are inclined to use the nomenclature **jk** (j = another imaginary index, perhaps different than i). Further, we anticipate a quantitative relativistic constraint equation like Equation 6b of Table 8.2 to apply for events occurring on the R-space 4-dimensional surface (here, β is an undetermined constant).

A problem that arose repeatedly in conventional physics a few decades ago involved attempts to calculate the result of even the simplest electromagnetic interactions, such as the interaction between two electrons. The most likely sequence of events in such an encounter is that one electron emits a <u>virtual</u> photon and the other electron absorbs it. Many other types of exchanges can also occur, e.g., the electrons could interact by exchanging two photons or three, etc., and the total probability for the interaction in quantum electrodynamics is given by the sum of all possible contributions. Feynman was the first one to introduce a systematic procedure for tabulating these contributions by drawing diagrams (eventually called Feynman diagrams) of the events as illustrated in Figure 8.6[5]. A particularly troublesome class of diagrams were those that include loops, such as the loop in space-time that is formed when a virtual photon is emitted and later reabsorbed by the same electron. Since the maximum energy of a virtual particle is limited only by the time needed to reach its destination, the distance covered and the time required can be reduced to zero while the maximum energy grows to infinity for such loops. For this reason, some diagrams with loops make an infinite contribution to the strength of the interaction.

These infinities spoiled even the description of an isolated electron. Because the electron can emit and absorb virtual particles, theoretically it appeared to have an infinite mass and an infinite charge. The way around this calculational roadblock was a procedure call <u>renormalization</u>. We won't explain it here but its best defense is that it works extremely well in canceling out these infinities and has yielded results that are in agreement with experiment to about one part in a billion. t'Hooft pointed out that even an isolated electron is surrounded by a cloud of virtual particles, which it constantly emits (to the vacuum) and reabsorbs (from the vacuum)[5]. These virtual particle emitters include not only neutral ones such as the photon, but also pairs of oppositely charged particles such as electrons and positrons in a dipole-like arrangement. It is the charged virtual particles in this cloud that,

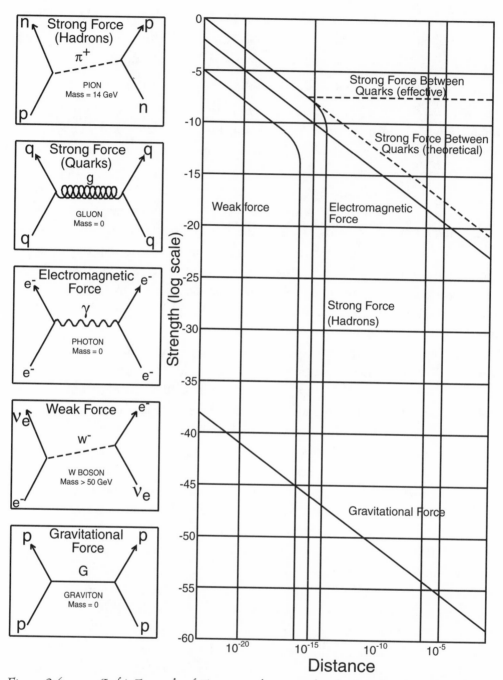

Figure 8.6   (Left) Example of Feynman diagrams for the four basic D-space forces and (Right) relative strength of these four forces as a function of particle-particle separation distance.

under ordinary circumstances, conceal the "infinite" bare charge of the electron. In the vicinity of the bare charge, the electron-positron pairs become slightly polarized with the virtual positrons situated slightly closer to the bare charge and the virtual electrons slightly repelled so that, overall, the bare charge is slightly neutralized. What is seen at long range ($>10^{-10}$ cm) from the electron is the <u>difference</u> between the bare charge and the screening charge of the virtual positrons. Just as with the bare charge, the bare mass is screened yielding a finite rather that an infinite result. Such a picture is remarkably like the "colloid" screening picture of Figure 7.21.

The foregoing conventional science description illustrates how renormalization leads to a screening atmosphere of virtual particles surrounding the seemingly infinite magnitude qualities of leptons and quarks, the fundamental building blocks of physical matter, to reduce these magnitudes to finite levels in good accord with experimental observations. We now postulate that, likewise, the D-space δ-functions illustrated in Figure 8.5 stress the local vacuum in such a way as to create a screening cloud of moieties around the bare singularity so that finite magnitudes are represented to a D-space measurement probe located outside this screening cloud. The particular quality of the δ-function plus screening cloud measured by such a probe will depend upon the specificity of the deltron activation coupling the δ-function and atmosphere to its set of primordial **k**-waves. The details of this new concept must be revealed by future experiments and theory. For now, we will just proceed as if the δ-function is a true representative of the particular D-space or R-space quality ascribed to it. Further, it is at this stage that the relevant set of primordial R-space waves combine to form the de Broglie pilot wave for the particle.

R-Space Resonators: To understand the concept of "resonators," one needs to first review the nodal network aspect of the general model described in the previous section. For the topic of resonators, we start with an original intention imprint, from the domain of spirit, activating some specific pattern of nodal points in the NN_M. For the sake of discussion, let us call this the first consciousness imprint, $C_{p_1}^*$ and it is a surrogate for the Spirit's specific intention. Of the totality of NN_M, only this surrogate pattern of nodal points is activated to broadcast this consciousness signal $C_{p_1}^*$. The phase relationships between this set of consciousness waves lead to constructive and destructive interference. This interference creates a second pattern that activates a subset of specific nodal points in NN_R and we will call this the second consciousness imprint, $C_{p_2}^*$.

These NN_R points are individual transducers/transponders[2] so they not only diffract $C_{p_1}^*$ to the NN_D but $C_{p_2}^*$ creates a new type of energy wave that is radiated in the coordinate space of the primordial **k**-waves. Constructive and destructive interference of these primordial k-waves creates what we have already called the D-space conjugate pattern (discussed at length in chapter 7). The diffraction of the $C_{p_1}^*$ pattern with the NN_R, without transduction also generates an interference pattern to activate a specific set of the NN_D points and we shall call this the third consciousness imprint, $C_{p_3}^*$. This set of activated NN_D points broadcasts a set of transduced waves in D-space that "herd" the D-space particles into wave-like patterns that are both spatial and temporal. These latter waves we shall designate as particle-modulating (see Chapter 2) or particle-herding waves (P-H waves) and their R-space conjugate or companion is the set of NN_R points that generated $C_{p_2}^*$. These latter we shall designate as "the resonators."

Following this line of reasoning, one ends up with two distinct pairs of important moieties to be concerned about: (1) the primordial **k**-waves of R-space pairing with the δ-function particles of D-space and (2) the resonators of R-space pairing with the P-H (particle-herding) waves of D-space. Both pairs of moieties are set into dynamic interaction by the first consciousness imprint, $C_{p_1}^*$. Together, these pairs form a new type of symmetry in nature. The very important quantitative feature of this dynamism is that the magnitude of $C_{p_3}^*$ is strongly dependent upon the degree of order in both the NN_R and the NN_D. Further, even if the NN_R is well ordered, if the NN_D are not on their reciprocal lattice points, $C_{p_3}^*$ will be negligible. However, if the NN_R contains significant patches of order <u>and</u> the NN_D points lie at reciprocal lattice points for the ordered patches of the NN_R, then $C_{p_3}^*$ can be very significant indeed. As an illustration example, contrasting the strength of the scattered x-ray signal from a single atom in a crystal lattice to that from a 1 micron cube of that crystal lattice or to a 1 centimeter cube of that crystal lattice, the maximum amplitude for the scattered wave goes up from 1 unit to $\sim 10^{11}$ units to $\sim 10^{23}$ units as the number of properly located scattering centers increases in this way.

Electric/Magnetic Interactions in Different Symmetry States

The Mirror Principle: When one thinks of a mirror, it is usually the familiar reflection mirror. Here, one is dealing with a kind of inversion mirror that exhibits properties like those illustrated in Table 8.3. We have had very

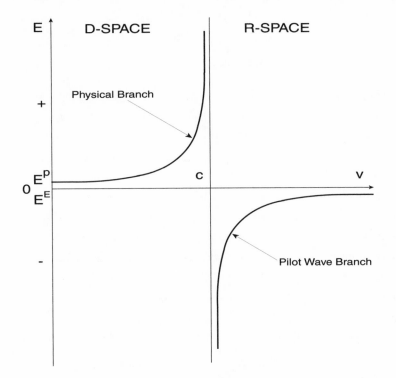

Figure 8.7   *Energy-velocity diagram for a D-space particle (v<c branch) and its R-space pilot wave conjugate (v>c branch).*

little prior experience with such inversion-like mirrors. First, the dual cognitive four-dimensional frames are reciprocals of each other, a special kind of inversion, and the substance characteristics populating the two frames are oppositely configured. In the D-space frame, one has substance with a particulate, electric nature of positive mass and positive energy that always travels <u>slower</u> than the velocity of light. By contrast, in the R-space frame, one has substance exhibiting wave-like, magnetic nature of negative mass and negative energy that always travels <u>faster</u> than physical light. The energetics of these two substances are illustrated in Figure 8.7 while a more complete spectrum of property relationships is illustrated in Table 8.3. The positive mass creates curvature effects in the D-space frame that manifests in the gravitational force while the negative mass moieties, acting via the deltrons,

Table 8.3   Aspects of the Mirror Principle

Physical	Conjugate Physical

Direct space & Direct time
    left hemisphere sensing
Nodal network grid spacing - 10^{-5} cm
Polycrystalline HCP
	Reciprocal space & Reciprocal time
	    right hemisphere sensing
	Nodal network grid spacing - 10^{-15} cm
	Disordered HCP

Electric Monopoles Forms atoms, molecules, etc. Allopathic medicine Positive mass Velocity < c Positive energy states E_p increases as velocity increases Positive entropy, S_p Positive free energy, $G_p = H_p - T_p S_p$ Positive temperature Electromagnetism Gravitation Body sensory systems delineated	Magnetic Monopoles Forms atoms, molecules, etc. Homeopathic medicine Negative mass Velocity > c Negative energy states E_E increases as velocity increases Negative entropy, S_E Negative free energy, $G_E = H_E - T_E S_E$ Negative temperature Magnetoelectrism Levitation Body sensory systems not delineated
Photons at velocity c Fastest in vacuum Slows down in dense material Faraday cage screening	Photons at velocity c' >> c ($\sim 10^{10}$c) Slowest in vacuum Speeds up in dense physical matter Screening by magnetic cage

should develop levitational force effects in the D-space frame.

To illustrate how monopoles in one space can become dipoles in another, let us consider some simple physical analogues. Suppose one has two D-space materials A and B joined at a planar interface as shown in Figure 8.8a. Let us place a singularity (electric charge, edge dislocation, etc.) in material B at some distance, z, from the interface. Mathematics, for the appropriate field associated with the singularity, shows us that some type of image of that singularity must appear somewhere in material A in order to satisfy the proper boundary conditions at the interface. Something very similar can be expected to happen at the D-space/deltron/R-space interface via part of this "mirror principle".

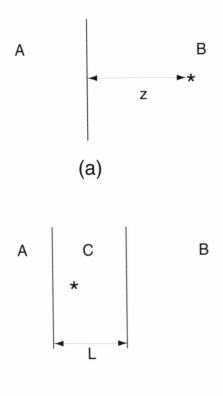

(a)

(b)

Figure 8.8 (a) Two semi-infinite D-space material domains, A and B, with a singularity, *, a distance z from the A/B interface in phase B; (b) the same as (a) but with an interface material, C, of width L that contains the * singularity.

If one places a single singularity, like an edge dislocation, in phase B at z then, in the most general case, a cluster of image singularities is needed in A to balance (1) the vector mechanical displacement continuity equations along the interface and (2) the vector mechanical traction continuity equations along the interface. Under special conditions of crystal classes for A and B, as well as crystallographic orientations for the interface planes and interface direction normals, the image singularities can reduce to quadrupole or dipole nature. If both A and B are piezoelectric materials and one is considering a simple electric charge singularity in B, one needs <u>eight</u> boundary conditions to be applied at the interface to satisfy all the mathematical constraints of the image charges (which will be multiple in general). Even if B is a simple dielectric (tensor of rank 2), five boundary conditions must be applied (three specifying tractions, one specifying continuity of electric potential and one more specifying continuity of electric displacement). As one moves to higher order tensors to describe materials A and B, the multiplicity of image singularities in material A needed to balance one singularity in B will increase. Even when B is a tensor of rank 1 and A is a tensor of rank 2, multiple image singularites will generally be needed. Thus, according to this line of reasoning, it seems quite plausible to expect that the trans-dimensional mirror proposed here may produce a special mapping transform for image transfer in the two directions across this "mirror".

To complete this discussion of the mirror effect, we must remember that the deltron domain is also involved in the interaction across the mirror. Thus, in our physical analogue, we need to consider the three-phase material system illustrated in Figure 8.8b. Let A be of semi-infinite extent and be a material of tensor rank m; let B also be of semi-infinite extent but be a material of tensor rank p > m and let C be of thickness L and a material of tensor rank s > p > m. Suppose, now, that we place a singularity at some location in phase C and consider the images that are produced in phases A and B. This example is thought to somewhat represent the situation of having a substance singularity in the nine-dimensional frame of emotion that simultaneously produces dual images in D-space and R-space. Returning to Figure 8.8b, the * singularity in phase C will have one or more primary images in phase A and phase B. These primary images, in turn, produce secondary images in B and A, etc. Thus, a single singularity in phase C will produce an array of singularities in phases A and B with some uncertainty of centroid position and array dimension. Obviously, since s > p > m, the image arrays in A and B should be quite different from each other and these differences may be partially what distinguishes the electric particle quality of phase A from the magnetic wave quality of phase B.

From our standard electrodynamics applied to the Figure 8.8b situation, even for A, B and C being isotropic materials, the force interaction between phases A and B can be readily shown to depend upon both the thickness and dielectric properties of phase C. Thus, for our D-space/deltron/R-space mirror example where non-Abelian algebra and Abelian algebra apply in different regions of the mirror, we can anticipate some uncommon interactions.

Electromagnetism (EM) and Magnetoelectrism (ME): The classical Maxwell equations of EM that one can find in thousands of textbooks on the subject are given in Table 8.4. From the top down, these are the representations, respectively, of the experimentally determined laws of Gauss, Faraday, Coulomb and Ampere. The gauge symmetry for this system of fields is the U(1) Gauge and its algebra is Abelian; i.e., the commutation law for two such fields $\underline{X}$ and $\underline{Y}$ is

$$[\underline{X},\underline{Y}] = \underline{X}\,\underline{Y} - \underline{Y}\,\underline{X} = 0. \qquad (8.6a)$$

This is to be compared with non-Abelian algebra where one has

Table 8.4   *The Classical Maxwell Equations.*

$$\nabla \bullet \underline{B} = 0 \qquad\qquad (1)$$

$$\nabla \times \underline{E} + \frac{\partial \underline{B}}{\partial t} = 0 \qquad\qquad (2)$$

$$\nabla \bullet \underline{D} = \rho \qquad\qquad (3)$$

$$\nabla \times \underline{H} - \left(\underline{J} + \frac{\partial \underline{D}}{\partial t} \right) = 0 \qquad\qquad (4)$$

with

$$\underline{D} = \varepsilon \underline{E} = \varepsilon_o (\underline{E} + \underline{P}); \qquad \underline{B} = m\underline{H} = m_0(\underline{H} + \underline{M})$$

and in S. I. units, $\varepsilon_o = 8.854 \times 10^{-12}$ $(J^{-1}C^{-2}m^{-1})$,

$$m_0 = 4\pi \times 10^{-7} \ (J\,s^2C^{-2}m^{-1}).$$

$\underline{B}$ is the magnetic flux density, $\underline{H}$ is the magnetic field strength,

$\underline{E}$ is the electric field strength, $\underline{D}$ is the electric displacement,

ρ is the electric charge density, $\underline{J}$ is the electric current density,

$\underline{P}$ is the electric polarization, $\underline{M}$ is the magnetization,

ε is the electric permittivity, (ε_o is the vacuum value), and

m is the magnetic permeability (m_0 is the vacuum value).

$$[\underline{X},\underline{Y}] = \underline{X}\,\underline{Y} - \underline{Y}\,\underline{X} \neq 0. \qquad\qquad (8.6b)$$

Maxwellian electrodynamics is generally thought to be one of the most elegant and perfect theories in physics. However, towards the end of the last century, many began to realize that there were several flaws inherent in its linear structure.

It is well known that nature generally displays properties of symmetry (when looked at from the proper reference frame). Surprisingly, although magnetism is a physical observable, it does not observationally manifest as a monopole but only as a dipolar quality. This is inherent in the "source free" implication of Equation (1) in Table 8.4. Although 20th century science looked long and hard for these magnetic monopoles, no satisfactory experimental evidence has been found to reveal their physical existence. As might be expected, this has not totally deterred some individuals from incorporating these moieties into their theoretical considerations. Harmuth[6], while attempting to calculate transient EM behavior from antennae, showed that the Maxwell's Equations of Table 8.4 fail for waves with non-negligible losses because of singularities encountered in the course of the calculation. However the equations succeed when a magnetic current density (moving magnetic monopoles) is introduced into the equation set and then shrunk to zero when one has reached the last singularity (but not before). As one other example among many, Seiberg and Witten[7] found that, in the four-dimensional quantum field theory, supersymmetry, certain key mathematical singularities could be eliminated by introducing magnetic monopoles. They were able to show that the magnetic monopoles became massless right when the equations, in the absence of these monopoles, explode to infinity.

Barrett[8] may have cleared up the dilemma by pointing out that the Maxwell equation Gauge symmetry is of the U(1) form when only electric charge and electric currents are present but is of the more complex SU(2) form when magnetic charges and currents are also present. U(1) fields are known to have fewer local degrees of freedom than SU(2) fields and SU(2) fields can be transformed into U(1) fields by the process of symmetry breaking. However, after symmetry breaking, only some topological charges are conserved; electric charge is conserved while magnetic charge is not. Harmuth's[6] amended Maxwell's equations and Barrett's[8] identity relationships between the SU(2) symmetry and the U(1) symmetry are shown in Table 8.5.

When we turn, now, to a D-space/deltron/R-space frame of reference and a partially conditioned locale, we must expect something very close to that shown in Table 8.6 to hold, following the notation of Table 8.5. Because this new approach is still a work in progress, it is more illustrative than exact

Table 8.5   *Amended Maxwell's Equations with Symmetry Parameters.*

$$\nabla \bullet \underline{B} = \rho_m \qquad (1)$$

$$\nabla \times \underline{E} + \frac{\partial \underline{B}}{\partial t} + g_m = 0 \qquad (2)$$

$$\nabla \bullet \underline{E} = \rho_e \qquad (3)$$

$$\nabla \times \underline{H} - \left(g_e + \frac{\partial \underline{D}}{\partial t}\right) = 0 \qquad (4)$$

$$g_e = \sigma \underline{E} \quad ; \quad g_m = s \underline{H} \qquad (5)$$

U(1) Symmetry   SU(2) Symmetry

$\rho_e = \dot{J}_0$ $\qquad\qquad \rho_e = \dot{J}_0 - iq(\underline{A} \bullet \underline{E} - \underline{E} \bullet \underline{A})$

$\rho_m = 0$ $\qquad\qquad \rho_m = -iq(\underline{A} \bullet \underline{B} - \underline{B} \bullet \underline{A})$

$g_e = \underline{J}$ $\qquad\qquad g_e = iq[\underline{A}_0, \underline{E}] - iq(\underline{A} \times \underline{B} - \underline{B} \times \underline{A}) + \underline{J}$

$g_m = 0$ $\qquad\qquad g_m = iq[\underline{A}_0, \underline{B}] + iq(\underline{A} \times \underline{E} - \underline{E} \times \underline{A})$

$\sigma = \underline{J}/\underline{E}$ $\qquad\qquad \sigma = (iq[\underline{A}_0, \underline{E}] - iq(\underline{A} \times \underline{B} - \underline{B} \times \underline{A}) + \underline{J})/\underline{E}$

$s = 0$ $\qquad\qquad s = (iq[\underline{A}_0, \underline{B}] + iq(\underline{A} \times \underline{E} - \underline{E} \times \underline{A}))/\underline{H}$

Here, g_e, g_m, ρ_e, ρ_m, σ, s and $\underline{A}$ stand, respectively, for electric current density, magnetic current density, electric charge density, magnetic charge density, electric conductivity, magnetic conductivity, and magnetic vector potential, respectively.

(particularly the R-space component). It is the degree of conditioning that determines the magnitude of the coupling parameters δ_D, δ'_D, δ_R and δ'_R. As a pathway to solving this set of equations and to gaining some understanding of Table 8.6, we first recognize that $(\underline{E}_D, \underline{H}_D)$ come from solving the equations

Table 8.6   EM and ME Equations in a Partially Conditioned Locale

D-space	R-space	
$\nabla_D \bullet \tilde{\underline{B}} = \delta_D \rho_m$	$\nabla_R \bullet \tilde{\underline{D}} = \delta_R \rho_e$	(1)
$\nabla_D \times \tilde{\underline{E}} + \dfrac{\partial \underline{B}}{\partial t} + \delta'_D \underline{g}_m = 0$	$\nabla_R \times \tilde{\underline{H}} + \delta'_R \underline{g}_e + \dfrac{\partial \tilde{\underline{D}}}{\partial k_t} = 0$	(2)
$\nabla_D \bullet \tilde{\underline{D}} = \rho_e$	$\nabla_R \bullet \tilde{\underline{B}} = \rho_m$	(3)
$\nabla_D \times \tilde{\underline{H}} - (\underline{g}_e + \dfrac{\partial \tilde{\underline{D}}}{\partial t}) = 0$	$\nabla_R \times \tilde{\underline{E}} - (\underline{g}_m + \dfrac{\partial \tilde{\underline{B}}}{\partial k_t}) = 0$	(4)
$\underline{g}_e = \sigma_D \tilde{\underline{E}}$	$\underline{g}_m = s_R \tilde{\underline{H}}$	(5)
$\tilde{\underline{E}} = \underline{E}_D + \int_R \hat{I}(\underline{E}_R) d\underline{k}$	$\tilde{\underline{E}} = \underline{E}_R - \int_D \hat{I}(\underline{E}_D) d\underline{s}$	(6)
$\tilde{\underline{H}} = \underline{H}_D + \int_R \hat{I}(\underline{H}_R) d\underline{k}$	$\tilde{\underline{H}} = \underline{H}_R - \int_D \hat{I}(\underline{H}_D) d\underline{s}$	(7)
$\nabla_D = i\dfrac{\partial}{\partial x} + j\dfrac{\partial}{\partial y} + l\dfrac{\partial}{\partial z}$	$\nabla_R = i'\dfrac{\partial}{\partial k_x} + j'\dfrac{\partial}{\partial k_y} + l'\dfrac{\partial}{\partial k_z}$	(8)
$\delta_{D_0} \leq \delta_D \leq 1$	$\delta_{R_0} \leq \delta_R \leq 1$	(9)
$\delta'_{D_0} \leq \delta'_D \leq 1$	$\delta'_{R_0} \leq \delta'_R \leq 1$	(10)

of Table 8.4 for the fully uncoupled condition (set $\delta_D = \delta'_D = 0$). Likewise, $(\underline{E}_R, \underline{H}_R)$ comes from the analogous set of fully uncoupled R-space equations (set $\delta_R = \delta_R' = 0$). Thus, for any values of $\delta_D, \delta_D', \delta_R$ and δ_R' not equal to zero we can, in principle, calculate $\hat{I}(\underline{E}_R), \hat{I}(\underline{H}_R), \hat{I}(\underline{E}_D),$ and $\hat{I}(\underline{H}_D)$ so that an internally self-consistent set of $\tilde{\underline{E}}, \tilde{\underline{H}}, \tilde{\tilde{\underline{E}}}$ and $\tilde{\tilde{\underline{H}}}$ can be determined by an iterative procedure. This set $(\tilde{\underline{E}}, \tilde{\underline{H}})$ yields what we have heretofore called <u>augmented electromagnetism</u>[2,3,9-11] involving the use of IIED's. One of us[9] has already speculated on the possibility that the $(\tilde{\tilde{\underline{E}}}, \tilde{\tilde{\underline{H}}})$ set yields **Qi**. If this supposition is correct then, just as the broad EM spectrum provides us with a connection between many seemingly diverse phenomena, the overall ME spectrum may do likewise for the many forms of **Qi**.

As a closing perspective on this section, it is important to recognize that a variety of other investigators have also used higher dimensional frameworks as base spaces for the expression of nature's laws[12-16]. The closest one of these to the model utilized in this book is that utilized by Wheeler[12] mentioned in Chapter 7 (see page 249). The general advantage of such an approach is that one has an additional set of uncommitted field components and material parameters with which to rationalize heretofore unexplained phenomena. In addition, one usually has a detailed quantitative vehicle with which to match such experimental data and one may make specific predictions as a basis for future experiments. Only detailed experimental assessment, using clearly defined protocols, allows one to meaningfully discriminate between these various possibilities.

In the Inomata[13] framework, complex components were introduced into the electric and magnetic field vectors with imaginary magnetic charge and current. This led to "mirror" type Maxwell equations with one set being mathematically real and the other set being imaginary. In the Rauscher[14] framework, an 8-space was utilized with 4 real (x,y,z,t) and four imaginary (x',y',z',t'). She generates longitudinal components of $\underline{E}$ and $\underline{B}$ as a projection from the complex 8-space onto the mathematically real 4-space. Evans[15,16], on the other hand, somewhat follows Barrett[8] by introducing a non-Abelian gauge and also a complexification of $\underline{E}$ and $\underline{B}$. However, he focuses on terms of the form $\underline{E} \pm i\underline{B}$ and generates a longitudinal field which he calls $\underline{B}^{(3)}$. He maps the U(1) Gauge onto the O_2 symmetry group, which describes rotation in a plane (a 2-D group). He also maps the SU(2) Gauge onto the isomorphic O_3 symmetry group, which describes rotation in three dimensions. In reference 16, an entire journal issue has been devoted to these symmetry questions, particularly as they relate to electromagnetism.

Some Applications of the Theoretical Constructs

Non-Local Forces: One of the difficult to understand outcomes of Quantum Mechanics (QM) is the prediction of non-local forces or action at great distances. If the theory proposed by this book is on an approximately correct track, one should be able to use it to predict some measure of these non-local forces in space-time. Let us see if this is so!

Since in D-space, we know that the force between two objects is given by the space derivative of their interaction energy, we shall start by considering the total free energy, $\hat{G}_T$, for the objects given by Equation 1 of Table 8.7.

Table 8.7   *Mapping the Non-local Force, $\hat{F}_{nl}$, Throughout D-space.*

$$\hat{G}_T = \hat{G}_D + \hat{G}_R \tag{1}$$

$$\Delta\hat{F}_{nl} = \lim_{\Delta\underline{r}\to 0}\left(\frac{\partial\hat{G}_R}{\partial\Delta\underline{r}}\right)_{r_0} \tag{2}$$

where

$$\hat{G}_R(\underline{k},\underline{r}) = e^{i(\underline{r}-\underline{r}_0)\bullet\underline{k}}\hat{G}_R(\underline{k},\underline{r}_0) \tag{3}$$

Thus,

$$\Delta\hat{F}_{nl} = \lim_{\Delta\underline{r}\to 0}\left[\frac{e^{i\Delta\underline{r}\bullet\underline{k}}-1}{\Delta\underline{r}}\right]\hat{G}_R(\underline{k},\underline{r}_0) \tag{4a}$$

$$\cong i\underline{k}\cos(\theta_{r_0})\hat{G}_R(\underline{k},\underline{r}_0) \tag{4b}$$

$$\cong -\underline{k}\cos(\theta_{r_0})\mathcal{J}_m[\hat{G}_R(\underline{k},\underline{r}_0)] \tag{4c}$$

and

$$\hat{F}_{nl} = \int_{R-space}\Delta\hat{F}_{nl}dk \tag{5}$$

$$\hat{I}_{nl} = [\hat{F}_{nl}\hat{F}_{nl}^*]^{1/2} \tag{6}$$

Thus, the force, $\hat{F}_{nl}$, between the objects at separation distance $\underline{r}$ is obtained by displacing one of them by distance $\Delta\underline{r}$ (the other is considered to be at the origin) and taking the limit as Δr shrinks to zero. The equation for $\Delta\hat{F}_{nl}$ is given by Equation 2 of Table 8.7. We can evaluate $\Delta\hat{F}_{nl}$ for the special case wherein the two objects are identical to each other. To do this, we utilize Equation 2 of Table 7.3 that we list in Table 8.7 as Equation 3. Inserting Equation 3 of Table 8.7 into Equation 2 leads to Equations 4. In Equation 4c, $\mathscr{Y}_m$ represents the imaginary part of $\hat{G}_R(\underline{k},\underline{r}_0)$ while the angle θ_{r_0} is between the two vectors $\underline{k}$ and $\Delta\underline{r}$ at $\underline{r}_0$. To obtain $\hat{F}_{nl}$ one needs to integrate over all $\underline{k}$ and this leads to Equation 5 in Table 8.7. Finally, the physically observable value of this non-local force is given by some power, n, of its modulus (see Equation 8.3) via Equation 6 of Table 8.7. It is Equation 6 that has important ramifications for non-local healing.

Time-dependent D-space Oscillations: From what has already been written in this chapter about resonators, it should be obvious that the activation of multiple specific R-space resonators, k_{tj}^* (with j=1,2,3...), will generate many D-space, time-dependent P-H (particle-herding) waves with periods inversely proportional to the specific k_{tj}^*. Thus, via such a procedure, <u>any</u> desired wave shape in D-space could be generated. Likewise, it can be shown that such oscillations naturally arise when phase entrainment of waves occur via enhanced coupling (see pages 352-353). What is not so clear, and is much more challenging, is to understand how a particular D-space "trigger" like $|dT/dt|$, the absolute magnitude for the rate of temperature change in the space, can appear to create a train of such P-H waves. Perhaps the activation of a single k_t^* in R-space plus a particular rate of temperature change in D-space are sufficient to manifest a D-space wave train with wave shapes that yield multiple harmonics. The detailed mathematics for this example is given in Appendix 8.B while only the summary features are laid out here.

We start with the appropriate version of Equation 8.1a as Equation 1 of Table 8.8. Here, $\hat{f}(t)$ represents our temperature change rate which is considered to be zero for times, t, less than zero and to grow or decay linearly with time for times greater than zero (see Equation 2a of Table 8.8). The form to be chosen for C_δ is a great unknown at this time so we just start by considering a simple Taylor's series expansion in what we think are relevant variables as in Equation 2b of Table 8.8. Later, by matching theoretical predictions with available experimental data, we will be able to learn something

Table 8.8   *D-space Temperature Oscillations in Time for a Single Activated R-space Resonator.*

$$\hat{F}_R(k_t) \quad = \frac{1}{(2\pi)^{1/2}} \int_{-\infty}^{+\infty} \hat{f}(t') C_\delta(k_t, t', I^*, \dots) e^{ik_t \bullet t'} dt' \qquad (1)$$

where

$$\hat{f}(t') = 0 \text{ for } -\infty < t' \leq 0$$

$$= a' + b' t' \text{ for } 0 \leq t' \leq t \qquad (2a)$$

and

$$C_\delta = a'' + b'' t' + c'' k_t + \dots \qquad (2b)$$

so that

$$\hat{f}(t') C_\delta = a + b t' + (ct')^2 + \dots \qquad (2c)$$

Integrating, $\hat{F}_R(k_t) =$

$$\frac{1}{(2\pi)^{1/2}} \left\{ \left[\frac{\alpha - 2\gamma}{i} + \beta \right] \left[e^{ix} - 1 \right] + \left[\left(\frac{\beta}{i} + 2\gamma \right) x + \frac{\gamma x^2}{i} \right] e^{ix} \right\} \qquad (3)$$

and

$$\hat{I}_R(k_t) = (\beta / 2^{1/2} \pi) \{ A(x) + B(x) \cos x + c(x) \sin x \}^{1/2} \qquad (4a)$$

with

$$A(x) = \{ [1 + (\alpha' - 2\gamma')] + \alpha' x + [1 + \gamma'(\alpha' + 2\gamma')] x^2 + 2\gamma' x^3 + \gamma'^2 x^4 \} (4b)$$

$$B(x) = -\{ [1 + (\alpha' - 2\gamma')] + \alpha' x + \gamma'(\alpha' - 2\gamma') x^2 \} \qquad (4c)$$

$$C(x) = -\{ [1 - 2\gamma'(\alpha' - 2\gamma')] x + \gamma' x^2 \} \qquad (4d)$$

$$\alpha = a/k_t, \ \beta = b/k_t^2, \ \gamma = c/k_t^3, \ x = k_t t$$

$$\alpha' = \alpha/\beta = a k_t/b \text{ and } \gamma' = \gamma/\beta = c/bk_t$$

about these initial choices. Combining Equations 2a and 2b in Table 8.8 leads to Equation 2c with three undetermined coefficients.

In Equation 2a, $a' \sim 300°$ Kelvin and $b' \sim \pm(10^{-3}$ to $1)$ °K per second. In Equation 2b, $a'' = C_{\delta_0}$ while Equation 2c requires that $a = a'(a''+c''k_t)$, $b = b'a''+b''a'$ and $c = a'c''$ so these three coefficients need to be determined by later matches with experiment in order to provide internal self-consistency for the theory.

Via simple integration of Equation 1 in Table 8.8, we determine $\hat{F}_R(k_t)$ and its modulus $\hat{I}_R$ as Equations 3 and 4, respectively, in Table 8.8, where $\alpha = a/k_t$, $\beta = b/k_t^2$, $\gamma = c/k_t^3$, $x = k_t t$, $\alpha' = \alpha/\beta = a k_t/b$ and $\gamma' = \gamma/\beta = c/bk_t$. A couple of important points to note about $\hat{I}_R(k_t)$ from Equations 4 in Table 8.8 is that (1) we ultimately need to plot $\hat{I}_R(k_t)/\beta$ or $\hat{I}_R^2/\beta^2$ vs. $x = k_t t$ for a range of the two parameters so as to determine which values give close fit with the T-oscillations of Chapter 6 and (2) we can express $\hat{I}_R/\beta$ or $\hat{I}_R^2/\beta^2$ in the form of a general series of cosines of argument nx; i.e.,

$$[(\pi 2^{1/2})/\beta]\hat{I}_R(k_t) = \sum_{n=0}^{\infty} a_n \cos nx. \qquad (8.7)$$

Equation 8.7 has the inherent capacity to exactly match the specific forms of the pH-oscillations and the T-oscillations of Chapter 6. The detailed procedure for evaluating the magnitudes of the coefficients, a_n, in Equation 8.7 is given in Appendix 8.B. In this book, we do not take the time to actually calculate these numbers as much work is entailed in doing that properly. Here, we are content to merely show that it is straightforwardly possible to do so, thereby provisionally justifying our initial presumption that activation of a single resonator in R-space can provide rather complex but lawful temporal oscillations to be measured in D-space.

Aspects of Homeopathy: Let us consider the basophil cell staining experiments of Benveniste and his group as reported on by Michel Schiff[17]. The initial publication in the journal "Nature" (June 1998) of data very similar to that presented in Figure 8.9 caused what came to be called "The Benveniste Affair". This oscillatory data covering a dilution range from 21 to

43 decades (well below Avogadro's number) so disturbed the fixed mind-sets of Nature's editor (and a great many other scientists) that a deplorable period of very inhuman behavior, directed at Benveniste, ensued. Here, we will analyze the dilution/succussion process utilized in the preparation of a homeopathic remedy via our D-space/δ/R-space procedures to see if this perspective can account for the essential features of Figure 8.9.

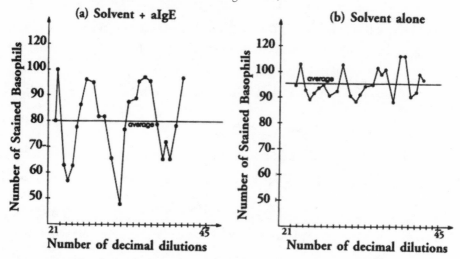

Figure 8.9   *Experimental plot of basophil cell staining at extremely high dilutions of aIgE as a function of the number of decimal dilutions, n.*

Like many biological cells, basophils have a jelly-like appearance so they need to be stained with some sort of dye to make them visible. In the research on high dilutions (homeopathic levels), the factor being analyzed was the manner in which the molecule anti-immunoglobulin E, aIgE, behaved. This molecule acts as a kind of "eraser" to the point where they sometimes all become invisible, as if they had never been stained[17]. The percentage of basophils that become invisible depends on the quantity of aIgE used. Thus, the more it is diluted, the less efficient it should become as an eraser. However, from Figure 8.9, one sees that aIgE's ability to act as an eraser is present even at dilutions where there is not even a single aIgE D-space molecule left in the solution.

A considerable variability exists in the eraser's efficiency and differs greatly from one person's blood to another's. In some cases, a given amount of aIgE will succeed in preventing the staining of practically all basophils. In others, practically no effect is seen. Thus, the maximum proportion of basophils losing their visibility is usually somewhere between the two extremes[17]. In Figure 8.9 a series of 25 decimal dilutions of aIgE in solvent is compared with a corresponding series of decimal dilutions in the control (solvent alone). Here, the range of dilutions is very large, from 10^{-21} to 10^{-45}.

From Figure 8.9, one sees that, on average, the number of basophils that remain stained is lower for the solvent plus aIgE solutions (~80% remain stained) than for the solvent alone (~96% remain stained). In addition, the solvent plus aIgE erasing ability is much more variable with change of dilution than for the solvent alone. Finally, and perhaps most important, the solvent plus aIgE erasing efficiency seems to oscillate with a fundamental periodicity of about 8 decades as a function of dilution. The basic task we set for this section is to show you, the reader, both how we set up an evaluation of $\hat{I}_R(k_t)$ for this case and what constraints must be placed on C_δ to have the calculated integral of $\hat{I}_R(k_t)$ match this fundamental periodicity in this aIgE dilution range. Expansion of such an approach would then allow one to completely match (point-to-point) such data in a straightforward way.

One begins by defining the time-dependent D-space aIgE concentration in solution, $C_D(t)$, during the dilution/succussion process, where Δt is taken as the average time interval per decade of dilution. This yields Equation 1 of Table 8.9 where $\alpha = 1/\Delta t$. We then use Equation 8.1a to obtain $\hat{F}_R(k_t)$ and the definition for the modulus, $\hat{I}_R(k_t)$ (see Equation 6 of Table 8.8). If we assume the simplest possible case where $C_\delta = C_{\delta_0}$ is independent of time, t, then it can be taken outside the integral sign and Appendix 8.C shows that Equation 2 of Table 8.9 results. Equation 2 is indeed an oscillating function (the cosine term) of the aIgE dilution index, n, where $n = t/\Delta t$ and, if we were to set $tk_t^* = \Delta n \Delta t\, k_t^* = 2\pi$ with $\Delta n \sim 8$, then the D-space fundamental periodicity of Figure 8.9 could be matched by the activation of a single R-space resonator at $k_t^* = \pi/(4\,\Delta t)$. However, when one looks at the oscillation amplitude of Equation 2 in Table 8.9 for the dilution range $\alpha t = n \geq 21$, one finds that it is insignificant in magnitude and $\hat{I}_R(k_t)$ goes to the constant given by Equation 3 in Table 8.9.

For the next mathematically simplest case, suppose we assume that, on average during the succussion/dilution step, a factor β of the available inherent deltron concentration in the water, C_δ^*, is activated. This would yield Equation 4 of Table 8.9. Thus, for β smaller than ~9, one obtains the same result as for C_δ = constant (Equation 3 of Table 8.9). However, for β close to 10 (just

Table 8.9   *Modulus, $\hat{I}_R$, for the Succussion/dilution Process in Preparing a Homeopathic Remedy*

$$C_D(t) = C_D(0)10^{-\alpha t} \; ; \; \alpha = 1/\Delta t. \tag{1}$$

For $C_\delta = C_{\delta_0}$,

$$\hat{I}_R(k_t) = \frac{C_D(0)C_{\delta_0}}{\sqrt{2\pi}} \left\{ \frac{1 - 2 \bullet 10^{-\alpha t}\cos(tk_t) + 10^{-2\alpha t}}{(\alpha\ln10)^2 + k_t^2} \right\}^{1/2}. \tag{2}$$

For $\alpha t \geq 21$,

$$\hat{I}_R(k_t) = \frac{C_D(0)C_{\delta_0}}{\sqrt{2\pi}} \left\{ \frac{1}{(\alpha\ln10)^2 + k_t^2} \right\}^{1/2} \tag{3}$$

For $C_\delta = C_\delta^*(\beta)^n$,

$$\hat{I}_R(k_t)$$

$$= \frac{C_D(0)C_\delta^*}{\sqrt{2\pi}} \left\{ \frac{1 - 2 \bullet (10/\beta)^{-\alpha t}\cos(tk_t) + (10/\beta)^{-2\alpha t}}{(\alpha\ln10)^2 + k_t^2} \right\}^{1/2}. \tag{4}$$

For $C_\delta = C_{\delta_0} + \beta t$,

$$\hat{I}_R(k_t) =$$

$$\frac{C_D(0)C_{\delta_0}}{\sqrt{2\pi}} \left\{ \frac{1 - 2(1 + bt/C_{\delta_0})10^{-\alpha t}\cos(tk_t) + (1 + bt/C_{\delta_0})^2 10^{-2\alpha t}}{(\alpha\ln10)^2 + k_t^2} \right\}^{1/2}$$

$$\tag{5}$$

when b = mathematically real and $C_{\delta_0} = a" + c"k_t$.

above or just below), this equation would produce a finite amplitude for the oscillatory components and could potentially provide some match to the data of Figure 8.9. Although this case is pedagogically useful, before exploring it a bit, let us return to the more general form for C_δ as expressed by Equation 2b in Table 8.8. Appendix 8.C shows us that Equation 5 of Table 8.9 is the result. If we had included higher powers of t in the expansion for C_δ, a series with slightly modified coefficients for these higher powers of t would replace the $(1+bt/C_{\delta_0})$ term in Equation 5 of Table 8.9 and it would then potentially exhibit the desired oscillatory behavior. This means that the $C_\delta(t)$-term can generate a growing function of time sufficient to offset the decaying function of time coming from the $C_D(t)$-term. Much more theoretical and experimental work will be needed to concretize the full functional form for $C_\delta(t, k_t, I^*,...)$ but at least we have made a start.

Before closing this mathematical assault on the quantitative exploration of homeopathy, we evaluate the integral of $\hat{I}_R(k_t)$, where $\hat{I}_R(k_t)$ is given by equation 4 of Table 8.9, under the condition that β is a constant independent of n. This is a somewhat tedious calculational process so all of the details are relegated to Appendix 8.D. Defining $A = C_D(0)C_\delta^*/(2\pi)^{1/2}$ and $\phi = \int_R \hat{I}_R dk_t/A$, Figures 8.10 show calculated plots of ϕ vs. n for $10/\beta$ varying from 1.01 to 1.06 and for $10/\beta$ varying from 0.99 to 0.94.

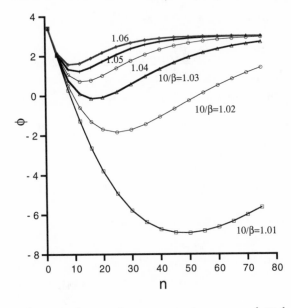

Figure 8.10a   Calculated plots of ϕ vs. n for $10/\beta$ varying from 1.01 to 1.06 ($\phi=A^{-1}\int_R \hat{I}_R dk_t$ with $A=C_D(0)C_\delta^*/(2\pi)^{1/2}$).

Three important conclusions can be drawn from these plots: (1) Choosing $\beta=a$ constant independent of n <u>cannot</u> yield an oscillatory result for ϕ no matter what value is chosen for A, (2) A range of β definitely exists that yields positive values for ϕ with $21< n <45$ as required for any match to the data of Figure 8.9 and (3) Selecting an appropriate value for the constant A allows ϕ to pass through the middle of the experimental data even though it does not oscillate in phase with the data. From these conclusions one expects that, by allowing β to be a general oscillatory function of n and with all of these values of β yielding positive values for ϕ in Figures 8.10, <u>the experimental data of Figure</u>

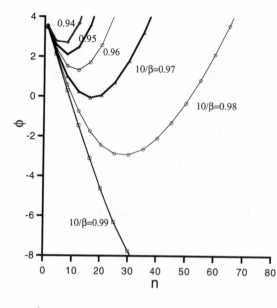

Figure 8.10b Calculated plots of ϕ vs. n for $10/\beta$ varying from 0.99 to 0.94 ($\phi = A^{-1} \int_R \hat{I}_R dk_t$ with $A = C_D(0)C_\delta{}^*/(2\pi)^{1/2}$).

8.9 should be able to be closely matched. This final step requires a very large number of calculations to be run and the visual benefit to be gained from making such an effort is not warranted at this time. However, a much simpler computational path exists if we define $\phi = \int_R \hat{I}_R^2 dk/A^2$ which is quite proper for the U(1) and near U(1) Gauge states (see pages 352-353).

A Possible D-space Structural Mechanism for Homeopathic Action: As discussed in Table 7.4, it is the chemical potential, μ_j, of the j-species that drives its chemical reactions. From thermodynamics, μ_j is given by the slope of the total free energy, G_T, as a function of j-species concentration, c_j, and is plotted in Figure 8.11 as a function of c_j.

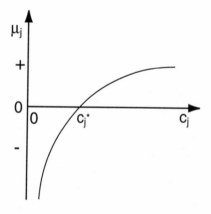

Figure 8.11 Plot of the chemical potential, μ_j, for a j-species as a function of concentration, c_j, of this species in the solution.

This shows us that (1) μ_j goes to $-\infty$ as c_j in D-space approaches zero, (2) μ_j has a fairly substantial region of negative values (between 0 and c_j^*) followed by (3) a very large region of positive values ($c_j^* < c_j < 1$) and an equilibrium concentration, c_j^*, where the configurational entropy (multiplied by the absolute temperature) associated with either dissolving this species in the solution, or creating it in the solution, exactly balances the heat of formation associated with adding j to the solution.

Nature abhors large negative μ_j and will do anything kinetically possible to change μ_j to a zero value. At any negative thermodynamic driving force (TDF) for molecular change, $\Delta\mu_j$ is given theoretically by

$$\Delta\mu_j = -kT \ln(c_j^*/ c_j). \qquad (8.8)$$

At room temperature, $kT \sim 2.6 \times 10^{-2}$ electron volts (eV) so that, when c_j^*/ c_j $\sim 10^{-16.7}$, $\Delta\mu_j = 1$ eV. In contrast, a single hydrogen bond in water has a strength of ~ 0.22 eV (~ 5 kilocalories per mole). This can be readily provided when c_j^*/ c_j is smaller than $10^{-3.7}$.

When one puts a specific physical biomolecule into water, two very important things happen. First, an H-bond cage forms around the molecule in all its conformations[3] so that, so far as configurational entropy of mixing in aqueous solutions is concerned, the presence of that specifically structured water cage indicates the specific biomolecule is present. Second, the R-space information pattern for that biomolecule, although not 100% fulfilled, is a good approximation based solely on the detailed water cage structure.

The procedure of dilution/succussion with archetypal intention (via Hahnemann and subsequent practitioners) is particularly interesting when μ_j falls into the negative region of Figure 8.11. Then, three important considerations come into play, (1) assuming that D-space/R-space equilibrium for the solution existed prior to the D-space dilution process, the R-space conjugate pattern for j is still at full strength and exerts a real force, proportional to the activated deltron content, on the D-space domain (this force is such as to stimulate some thermodynamically beneficial changes in the hydrogen bond network), (2) the D-space thermodynamic forces also try to resist the loss of entropy of mixing for j as the D-space dilution process continues and (3) the succussion process itself is a very chaotic process acting very non-linearly on this H-bond network so that more thermodynamically desirable H-bond network changes can be nucleated (provides the critical magnitude energy fluctuations needed for rearranging this H-bond network).

This specific development of patches of unique order in the H-bond network is thought to involve the enhancement of deltron activation at each step of the succussion/dilution process so that D-space/R-space coupling increases. The consequence of this increased force transfer from the R-space counterpart of j to the very dilute water is thought to be the creation of empty

H-bond cages of close to the exact conformation of the D-space biomolecule cage. The presence of this structure stabilizes the R-space counterpart of j and provides the needed D-space entropy of mixing, as a surrogate for j, to lower the free energy of the system and stabilize the entire process. But, if it takes ~0.2 eV to create an H-bond and this j-surrogate, image H-bond cage needs hundreds to thousands of H-bonds to configure its outer surface, where do they come from? Further, what D-space forces keep this "image cage" from collapsing? Let us now consider Nature's building blocks for such j-surrogate cages.

Nanobubbles in Water: As discussed in Chapter 3 (see pages 69-70), a very good case can be made that nanometer-sized bubbles of gas, probably from dissolved air and CO_2, appear to form naturally in water. It is known that O_2, O_2^+, O_2^-, H_2, H_2^-, N_2^-, N_2^+, CO_2^+, CO_2^-, etc., all have magnetic properties so that, if bubbles are formed from these gasses, the magnetic permeability of the bubbles will be positive compared to the surrounding water (diamagnetic with negative permeability). Thus, the diverging flux lines at such bubble surfaces, from the earth's magnetic field passing through the water, create magnetic dipoles at each bubble (see Figure 7.25). A similar circumstance develops if an electric field is present and one considers the difference in electric permittivity of the bubble interior compared to the aqueous solution (electric dipole formation). These both stabilize the bubbles thermodynamically and allow them to interact with each other to form fragile chain-like arrays of bubbles of some very small size. The thermodynamic calculation of gas bubble nucleation and stabilization at some unique size is a fairly complex one that needs to be carried out before complete faith in the magnetic field or electric field driving force can be established. However, if this supposition is even approximately correct, and the data qualitatively support that supposition, then the array of nanobubbles provides two things for the j-surrogate image concept, (1) a supply of H-bonds surrounding each bubble and (2) internal gas pressure to convert the surrogate image into a balloon-type entity that keeps the walls from collapsing together. Of course, the detailed thermodynamic balance of internal energy gains and losses plus configurational entropy gains and losses between consumed nanobubbles and created j-surrogate images is a complex one that needs to be worked out. However, it seems to be a completely doable calculation, but now we must again ask the question – "So what?".

Artificial Enzymes: It is particularly interesting to note an important recent development in biochemistry[18]. Scientists are developing and using a new technique called molecular imprinting. They etch a material to create molecule-size, carefully-shaped, pores in the surface of a polymer, or plastic, that mimic the geometry for the active sites of specific enzymes (called plastizymes). These precisely shaped imprints are cavities with antifunctionality – just like the active site of an enzyme.

Such imprinted polymers have been utilized to effectively separate chiral forms of benzodiazopenes, a class of drugs that serve as sedatives and muscle relaxants. Although the plastic versions are somewhat primitive compared to the best protein recognition sites, they are much more robust than proteins which are very sensitive to pH, heat, etc. Some individuals have also crafted molecularly imprinted polymers into films that act as semipermeable membranes. One constructed film allows adenine to pass through the membrane but blocks the other three bases that carry the code in DNA molecules. On another front, a body implant made of an imprinted polymer could attract proteins that would encourage the body to integrate the implant with natural tissue. This has been demonstrated for large proteins like bovine serum albumin, immunoglobuline G and fibrinogin. As a final example, industry uses catalysts to speed many chemical processes, but often at higher temperatures than the imprinted polymers can manage. Thus, they have extended the imprinting technique to silica, the main component of glass.

Research into imprinted materials is still in its early stages and some critical issues still need resolving before it can become practical in a widespread sense. However, the work shows that approximate geometry at the D-space level carries critical information for biological processes. Figure 7.7 illustrates an aspect of this unseen information from the R-space level that is intrinsically imbedded in a particular D-space geometry. If such geometric imprints in polymers, such as discussed in this section, can be effective and specific in mimicking important biochemical molecules, then so can the "negative image" H-bond cages in water proposed above. But is there some type of conventional mechanism that can be used as an analogy to help us understand the information transfer involved in this j-surrogate H-bond image model?

Magnetic Quantum Cellular Automata: At a slightly deeper level of information transfer logic than utilized above, much interest has recently been focussed on single electron transistors (SETs) as viable candidates for replacing conventional silicon processors and memory devices. A particular interesting configuration of SETs called quantum cellular automata (QCA) has been recently shown to perform logic operations[19]. Even more recently, QCA architectures using linear arrays of relatively large magnetic metal dots (~100 nanometers in diameter) with spacings of 500 nanometers have been demonstrated to work at room temperature[20].

IIED's and SU(2)/U(1) Mixed Gauge Symmetry: One important distinction between U(1) Gauge symmetry and SU(2) Gauge symmetry via the theory of this book is thought to be the state of organization of the nodal network points at the R-space level. These NN_R are in an amorphous arrangement for the U(1) gauge condition but in a lattice-like arrangement for a relevant region of **k**-space for the SU(2) Gauge condition. Since the radiation from these NN_R activate the magnetic substance of R-space plus the NN_D, and thereby the electric substance of D-space, this determines the energy exchange details in D-space.

Working in real numbers, a single vibrational source in D-space of the form $a \cos(\omega t+\phi)$ has an instantaneous intensity, $I(t)$, given by $a^2 \cos^2 (\omega t+\phi)$ and, since the mean value of $\cos^2 p$ is 0.5, $\bar{I} = 0.5\, a^2$ (here, the bar designates the mean). Considering a large number of superposed D-space sources, one can similarly write for the simultaneous intensity

$$I(t)= \left[\sum_i a_i \cos(\omega_i t + \phi_i) \right]^2 = \qquad (8.9a)$$

$$\sum_i a_i^2 \cos^2(\omega_i t + \phi_i) + \sum_i \sum_{ji} a_i a_j \cos(\omega_i t + \phi_i)\cos(\omega_j t + \phi_j) \quad (8.9b)$$

For a very large number of <u>randomly phased components</u>, the phase angle distribution is fairly uniform through the range 0 to 2π. Thus, the mean value of $\cos^2(\omega_i t+\phi_i)$ is 0.5 while the double summation vanishes. This yields

$$\bar{I} = 0.5 \sum_i^N a_i^2 = (N/2)\,\bar{a}^2 \qquad (8.9c)$$

for N sources. Equation 8.9c is the well-known result that randomly phased vibrations are to be combined by the summation of intensities. Ultimately, this randomization of signal phases is thought to come from the amorphous nature of the nodal networks in our model.

When one looks more deeply into this superposition of signals phenomenon, one sees that the total effect is given as the product of (1) a source effect and (2) an array geometry effect for a set of identical sources. It is the array factor that interests us here. If the array of sources is geometrically amorphous, both spatially and temporally, then we can't have anything but the U(1) Gauge result. However, if the array is ordered spatially in either 1-D, 2-D or 3-D and phased sequentially in time, then a very different result ensues. In this latter case, even if the source effect is isotropic, the array factor can produce strong superposed <u>beam</u> effects (as in crystal diffraction) which can be fixed or scanned. From antenna theory, it is relatively easy to show that the directivity of a linear array can be as large as N, the number of identical source elements in the array[21]. This directivity turns out to be a measure of the coherence of radiation from the linear array. Furthermore, this directivity is independent of scan angle. Thus, when patches of order develop in R-space, one can expect the overall character of $\hat{I}_R$ to change dramatically.

Returning to the second term of Equation 8.9b, let us suppose that two waves, p and q, phase entrain ($\phi_p = \phi_q$), then this sum becomes

$$\sum_i \sum_{ji} a_i a_j \cos(\omega_i t + \phi_i)\cos(\omega_j t + \phi_j) = \{a_p a_q/2\}\{\cos(\omega_p - \omega_q)t +$$

$$\cos[(\omega_p + \omega_q)t + 2\phi_p]\} \approx (a_p a_q/2)\cos(\omega_p - \omega_q)t \qquad (8.9d)$$

since the second term is either greatly diminished, completely cancels due to random phase effects or is at too high a frequency to be experimentally registered. Let us now suppose that three waves, p, q and r phase entrain plus that $\omega_j = j\omega_0$ for all j. Then, we have

$$\sum_i \sum_{ji} a_i a_j \cos(\omega_i t + \phi_i)\cos(\omega_j t + \phi_j) \approx 1/2[(a_p a_q + a_q a_r)\cos(\omega_0 t) + a_p a_r$$

$$\cos(2\omega_0 t)]. \qquad (8.9e)$$

When four waves, p, q, r and s all phase entrain, the RHS of Equation 8.9e becomes

$$1/2[(a_p a_q + a_q a_r + a_r a_s)\cos(\omega_0 t) + (a_p a_r + a_q a_s)\cos(2\omega_0 t) +$$

$$a_p a_s \cos(3\omega_0 t)] \qquad (8.9f)$$

and so on as more and more waves phase entrain. This is exactly what we see happening to our T- and pH-data as conditioning develops in our experimental space. First, the Equation 8.9c term dominates as a kind of noise. Then, some order begins to develop with the FT of the data showing only a single weak peak $(a_p a_q)$ at ω_0 in the frequency spectrum. Then, with further conditioning, this ω_0 peak grows in amplitude $(a_p a_q + a_q a_r)$ and its first harmonic, $2\omega_0$, develops some amplitude $(a_p a_r)$, etc. Thus, for a partially conditioned space, Equation 8.9c should be replaced by

$$I(t) = \sum_i a_i^2 \cos^2(\omega_i t + \phi_i) + \sum_{n=1}^{j} b_n \cos(n\omega_0 t) \qquad (8.9g)$$

and this is probably how our oscillations come into being.

It is probable that, for a largely U(1) Gauge condition, one should use $\hat{I}_R^2$ in place of $\hat{I}_R^n$ in Equation 8.3; however, for a largely SU(2) Gauge condition, probably the first power of $\hat{I}_R$ is appropriate. For the mixed Gauge condition, perhaps both these terms should be present or one should parametrically use $\hat{I}_R^n$, where n is between 1 and 2. Because so little is known about this new physics at the moment, for illustrative purposes we will simply treat $\hat{I}_R$ as a vector of positive magnitude and use it in the first power format.

When a particular site is fully "conditioned" by an IIED, it is thought to be almost 95%-100% in the SU(2) Gauge symmetry state for some region of R-space. The U(1) Gauge symmetry state is due to amorphous nodal networks at both D-space <u>and</u> R-space levels. The mixed SU(2)/U(1) Gauge symmetry state is thought to be largely due to a disordered NN_D with patches of NN_R order at the 1-D, 2-D, 3-D or 4-D level.

From this perspective, our working hypothesis with respect to IIEDs is that, after a successful imprinting session, these particular IIEDs are largely in the SU(2) Gauge symmetry state. Because they are, therefore, at a higher free energy state than the surrounding U(1) Gauge symmetry state, <u>any</u> process path capable of being driven by a thermodynamic driving force will be kinetically driven at some rate. To block one or more of these active pathways, we wrap the devices in aluminum foil and store them in electrically-grounded Faraday cages. Another working hypothesis that we hold is that some higher intelligence in the universe assists us in (1) providing the critical free energy fluctuation needed to nucleate a critical size patch of NN_R-order and (2) sealing off other free energy leakage paths in R-space and D-space of which we are presently totally unaware.

When we ship the IIED's to Minnesota for use in the experiments, some time adjustment is generally required at the new location before effective use commences. This varies from a long time when the space is totally unconditioned to a very short time when it is fully conditioned. We have discovered experimentally that a conditioned space can remain in this higher symmetry state for several months to over a year without input from an IIED. There seems to be no absolute reason why the IIED's need decay even in a year provided the larger environment is supportive. Even as we humans go on breathing automatically in a normal, healthy air environment, these devices, in a supportive environment, should be able to keep sending out their augmented-EM signal for a very long time.

Extending this line of reasoning, if one created a "conditioned" space in a trailer-type laboratory, it could be pulled around the country to demonstrate the higher symmetry physics at a multitude of locations. Of course, it would be necessary to be able to overcome any negative (leakage) aspects associated with both particular sites, materials and people during such an adventure (see Equation 6.1). Such a process as this, involving spatial displacement of a localized conditioned domain, opens up many interesting application opportunities.

Long-distance Communication Between Vessels of Water: In Chapter 6, data was provided that demonstrated seeming long distance communication between vessels of water. Figure 6.15a shows us that, with an IIED only at site A and pH-measurement at sites A (unconditioned), B (conditioned), C (unconditioned) and D (unconditioned). pH-oscillations generated by the IIED at A led to the presence of highly correlated pH-oscillations at B but not at C or D. Figure 6.18 shows us that, with or without fan-driven convection, the temperature oscillations at site B do not originate from oscillating heat content changes in the particulate aspects of the air due to natural convection. Instead, the T-oscillations probably arise from oscillatory changes in the vacuum within all the air molecules of site B. Both of these observations are fully consistent with a strong $\hat{I}_R(k_t)$ contribution at site B. Such a contribution arises from R-space, which we have identified with the coarsest level of the vacuum. This contribution would be largely independent of D-space position and has a large magnitude only when a large deltron coupling occurs between the wave-like substance operating within this level of the vacuum and the particle substance operating within physical atoms and molecules.

From a spatial symmetry perspective, suppose we consider a rectangular piece of homogeneous solid material and want to describe a particular quality, X, of that material as a function of position from the center of the rectangle. The partial free energy of the system might be expressed as a Taylor's series expansion in ascending powers of X, with each term being a function of position. If the vacuum substance is isotropic and one rotates the rectangle through 180 degrees, the quality X sees no difference in its environment. This means that all coefficients of the odd powers of X must be set to zero because this type of rotational symmetry exists. This is typical of the U(1) Gauge symmetry state for magnetism. On the other hand, if some measure of ordering develops in the substance of this coarsest level of the vacuum, and if this could take the form of ordering in some of the phase factors associated with the k_x, k_y, k_z, k_t, primordial waves, the vacuum environment would no longer appear to be isotropic. In this case, if we rotated our rectangle by 180°, the quality X would now see a difference in its environment. This means that some or all of the coefficients of the odd powers of X will be non-zero. This is typical of the SU(2) Gauge symmetry state for magnetism.

Decay of the Temperature Oscillation Amplitude with Distance: In Chapter 6, data was provided to demonstrate a seemingly non-monotonic decay of the temperature oscillation amplitude with distance. Figure 6.21 shows us that the T-oscillation amplitude relative to the central vessel of water is relatively isotropic around the vessel (or previous location of the vessel), decaying to a relative minimum at ~12" from the vessel before ascending to a relative maximum at 60" from the vessel and then decaying monotonically to small values at > 120" from the vessel. Because of the coarseness of our position measurements, Figure 6.21 might be a type of approximate envelope for $\hat{I}_R(k_t, r)$ as illustrated in Figure 8.12.

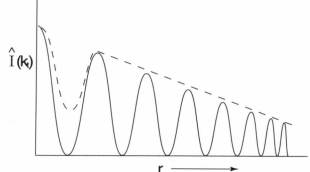

Figure 8.12 Schematic drawing of possible relationship between $\hat{I}_R(k_t)$ and r, the distance from the water vessel.

We can calculate $I_R(k_r)$ for a cylindrical object of radius r_c and it exhibits such a scalloped appearance with the first zero occurring at $k_r r_c \approx 2\pi$. Thus, the "effective" k_r of this water vessel/Faraday cage system would be ~ 0.5 cm^{-1}.

Fine Structure Observed in Many Physical Processes: To close this applications section, some preliminary assessment concerning the relationship of the present modeling to understanding the presence of fine structure in the experimental data observed for many physical processes has been initiated. The reason for including such an incomplete assessment here is that it has pedagogical value towards helping the reader see something of the larger perspective provided by this model. Much more work needs to be done to complete this assessment so the reader is cautioned not to jump to any firm conclusions at this time – it is very much a work in progress.

For the past several decades, Shnoll and his colleagues in Russia, via careful measurements of many natural processes in nature over a long period of time, have revealed a remarkable fine structure to the statistical distributions of certain key characteristics for these natural processes[22,23]. Furthermore, this fine structure exhibits repetitive periods of 24 hours, ~ 27 days and 365 days (the earth's rotational period about its axis, $\sim$ the sun's rotational period about its axis and the earth's rotational period about the sun)[22,23]. This behavior has been observed in biochemical reactions with protein macromolecules, in homogeneous chemical reactions with low molecular weight compounds, as well as in a variety of diverse physico-chemical measurements such as (a) velocities of latex particles in an electric field, (b) the discharge time delay in a neon lamp RC-oscillator, (c) transverse relaxation time, τ_2, of water protons using spin-echo techniques, (d) amplitude of the concentration fluctuations in the Belousov-Zhabotinsky reaction and (e) radioactive decay of various isotopes.

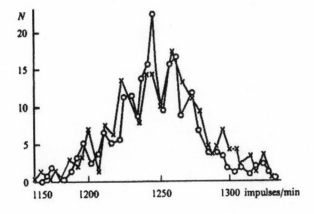

Figure 8.13a Synchronous measurements of the radioactivity of two ^{14}C preparations using two independent automatic measuring stations.

Simultaneous β-activity of ^{14}C, measured with automatic recording equipment at two widely separated locations (from 100 miles to 1000 miles apart) produced essentially identical histogram profiles during simultaneous recording (see Figure 8.13a). Likewise, for measurements of two very different processes simultaneously taking place in nearby buildings, closely nested histogram profiles were observed (see Figure 8.13b). The stochastic nature of radioactive decay and its compliance with Poisson statistics <u>are not questioned</u>. Shnoll and colleagues[22,23] feel that the conventional Gaussian or Poisson distributions are, as a rule, the result of smoothing of histograms so that the fine structure is averaged out.

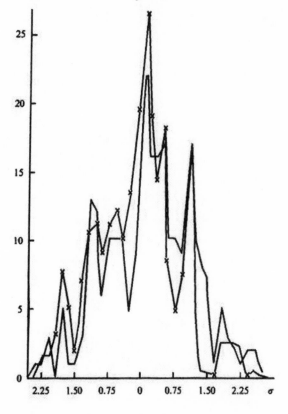

Figure 8.13b Similarity of histograms obtained from simultaneous measurements of processes of entirely different nature. Juxtaposition of two histograms: one is plotted from 250 measurements of the reaction AA and DCPIP, the other from the same number of simultaneous measurements of the beta decay of ^{14}C.

Because the Shnoll and others[22,23] data seems to be relatively independent of position and are in-phase temporarily, it suggests that this fine structure might have its origins in the R-space component, $\hat{I}_R(k_t)$, of their measurement. Of course, it is additionally possible that these experimental spaces had become partially "conditioned" over the years. Let us broadly explore, just a little bit, to see how cosmological periodicity might enter such data by focussing only on radioactive decay.

Radioactive decay is a process, somewhat like the homeopathic dilution/succussion process, involving a specific nuclear reaction that reduces the concentration, C_j, of a parent species, j, with time. At a specific point in time, τ, a natural distribution of j exists in the earth, $C_j^E(r,\phi,\theta,\tau)$, and probably in the sun, $C_j^S(r,\phi,\theta,\tau)$. For a particular laboratory on the surface of the earth, which we will approximate as a sphere, the D-space concentration is given by $C_j^E(r^*,\phi^*,\theta^*,\tau)$ relative to some coordinate system fixed to the center of the earth. The equilibrium R-space conjugate for this particular radioactive sample in the laboratory we will designate by $FT_j^E(\underline{k}_4)$. Although we know that $FT_j^E(\underline{k}_4)$ changes as the earth rotates around its axis and as it translates around the sun which is, in turn, rotating and translating through the Milky Way, $\hat{I}_{R_j}^E$ does not (the phase factor cancels out via the definition of $\hat{I}_R$ given in Equation 6 of Table 8.7). Thus we must look deeper.

In D-space, $C_j^E(r,\phi,\theta,\tau)$ may be altered not just by radioactive decay but also by a variety of transport processes carrying j into or out of a specific D-space locale at different rates. By analogy, there must also be an R-space counterpart to this conservation equation for j so that $FT_j^E(\underline{k}_4')$ at the coordinate $\underline{k}_4'$ will also be influenced by $FT_j^E(\underline{k}_4'')$ at adjacent coordinate locales, $\underline{k}_4''$, to produce incremental changes in the magnitude of $FT_j^E(\underline{k}_4')$. In turn, these transport-type changes, $\Delta FT_j^E(\underline{k}_4')$, produce a thermodynamic force in the D-space conservation equation for j.

If the sun also has this j-species radioactive decay process with $C_j^S(r',\phi',\theta',\tau')$ representing its D-space distribution and $FT_j^S(\underline{k}_4)$ representing its equilibrium R-space distribution, then $FT_j^S(\underline{k}_4)$ can interact with/interfere with $FT_j^E(\underline{k}_4)$. Now we need to recall that objects far removed from each other in D-space have their R-space conjugates closely spaced and, for both the earth and the sun, these conjugates will be largely located in the low frequency region of R-space. This means that, for the j-species, its total R-space conjugate, FT_{jT}, must be given by

$$FT_{jT}(\underline{k}) = FT_j^E(\underline{k}) + FT_j^S(\underline{k}) \qquad (8.10a)$$

and its total modulus by

$$\hat{I}_{RT_j}(\underline{k}) = \{ [FT_j^E(\underline{k}) + FT_j^S(\underline{k})][FT_j^{*E}(\underline{k}) + FT_j^{*S}(\underline{k})] \}^{1/2} \qquad (8.10b)$$

359

$$= \{ (\hat{I}_{R_j}^{S})^2 + (\hat{I}_{R_j}^{E})^2 + [FT_j^{E}(\underline{k})FT_j^{*S}(\underline{k}) + FT_j^{*E}(\underline{k})FT_j^{S}(\underline{k})] \}^{1/2} \quad (8.10c)$$

Now, we see that, although translation and rotational periodicities are not present in $\hat{I}_{R_j}^{S}$ or $\hat{I}_{R_j}^{E}$, they are present in $\hat{I}_{RT_j}(\underline{k})$ via the FT_j product terms in Equation 8.10c. Thus, if only the earth and sun are important in the R-space map for the j-species conjugate, the earth's rotation period about its axis, the sun's rotation period about its axis and the earth's rotation period about the sun will be present in the numerical magnitude of $\hat{I}_{RT_j}$ and, therefore, in the careful measurement of radioactive decay for the j-species. Of course, other planetary bodies may also play a role in the R-space, j-conjugate interaction so they would need to be included in Equations 8.10. Hopefully, this brief exercise has added to the reader's awareness of R-space implications for <u>all</u> physical measurements.

<u>Biconformal Base Space as an Alternative Interpretation for Quantum Mechanics</u>: In a recent article[24], one gains a simplified version of the key perspectives and questions being seriously pursued by physicists working in the area of QM. The QM mathematical solutions are based on Schroedinger's wave equation with the wave function being interpreted in terms of probabilities. The <u>Copenhagen Interpretation</u> of QM grew out of discussions by Bohr and Heisenberg in the 1920's wherein observers see a random outcome, with the probability of that outcome being given in terms of the amplitude of the wave function. The advantage of this interpretation is that only a single outcome (amongst other possibilities) occurs, matching what we observe experimentally. The residual problem with this interpretation is that it requires the wave function to "collapse". However, no equation was available to specify "when" this collapse was to occur. In spite of this problem, the Copenhagen Interpretation survived because it gave a strikingly successful recipe for doing calculations that accurately described the outcome of experiments.

A second possible interpretation was given more recently by Everett[24]. He proposed the <u>Many Worlds Interpretation</u> wherein the list of possible result superpositions will seem like alternative worlds to their inhabitants. The advantage of this particular view is that the Schroedinger equation always works and the wave function never needs to collapse. A third possible interpretation by Zeh[24] has been labeled <u>Decoherence</u>, wherein tiny interactions with the surrounding environment rapidly dissipate the peculiar nature of quantum superposition and explains why the everyday world looks "classical" instead of quantum mechanical.

Now we are adding the <u>Biconformal Base-space Interpretation</u> to the mix and, beyond what has already been said about it in this book, we select the Young Double Slit Experiment to illustrate its utility. From either a photon source or an electron source, the D-space particles are ejected towards the slits, uniformly over some solid angle. The R-space aspect of the photon or electron interacts with the slit interference pattern to produce a total R-space modulus for the dual system, slits plus particles, much like Equations 8.10 for the Shnoll experiments.

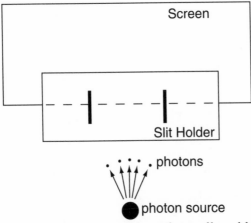

Figure 8.14   Schematic illustration of the Double Slit experimental system geometry.

The system geometry for (1) the slit holder, (2) photon and (3) screen is illustrated in Figure 8.14 (the slit spacing is greatly accentuated). For simplicity and as an approximation, we will neglect the screen and just consider the two-body interaction event. This will yield useful information but not complete information without inclusion of the screen. In Table 8.10, Equations 1 give both the system Fourier transform, $FT_T(\underline{k})$, and its modulus, $I_{R_T}(\underline{k})$. Expanding Equation 1b leads to Equations (2a) and (2b), where the superscripts ' and " refer to the real and imaginary parts, respectively. The measured light intensity on the screen we call Q_M and it is given by Equations 3 using I_{RT} instead of I_{RT}^2 for illustrative purposes in Table 8.10. It is the third term on the right in Equation 3b that interests us because, since both the slit holder and the photon have mathematically real FT's, this product is just the FT of their convolution (given by Equation 4 of Table 8.10). Because of the intimacy of the convolution process, this would yield a calculated value for the system modulus that illustrates interference effects in the photon pattern on the screen. Thus, it seems that this FT product result in the mathematics means that the primordial wave components making up the de Broglie pilot wave for the photon have been irrevocably altered so that, from

Table 8.10   *Superpositions for a Two-body System Event*

System FT

$$FT_T(\underline{k}) = FT_1(\underline{k}) + FT_2(\underline{k}) \tag{1a}$$

and

$$I_{RT}(\underline{k}) = \{A + (FT_1 FT_2^* + FT_1^* FT_2)\}^{1/2} \tag{1b}$$

with

$$A = I_1^2 + I_2^2 \tag{1c}$$

Expanding Equation 1b

$$I_{RT}(\underline{k}) \approx A^{1/2}[1 + 1/(2A)(FT_1 FT_2^* + FT_1^* FT_2) + \ldots] \tag{2a}$$

$$\approx A^{1/2} + (FT_1' FT_2' + FT_1'' FT_2'')/2A^{1/2} + \ldots \tag{2b}$$

Measured Light Intensity

$$Q_M = Q_D + \int_R I_{RT}(\underline{k})d\underline{k} \tag{3a}$$

$$\approx Q_D + \int_R A^{1/2}d\underline{k} + \int_R \left[\frac{FT_1' FT_2' + FT_1'' FT_2''}{2A^{1/2}}\right]d\underline{k} + \ldots \tag{3b}$$

Convolution Theorem

$$\int\int_{-\infty}^{\infty} f(x')\phi(x-x')\, e^{ikx}dx'dx = \int_{-\infty}^{\infty} f(x')e^{ikx'}dx' \int_{-\infty}^{\infty} \phi(y)e^{iky}dy$$

$$= FT_1 FT_2 \tag{4}$$

Table 8.2, the photon trajectory must quickly move in a lateral direction to accommodate these changes associated by convolving with the slit holder's interference pattern. At this point, one begins to see a weakness with the present level of modeling in that we are unable to give enough specific details on the lateral photon movement. That will need to wait until we more fully explore an enriched model.

To experimentally prove the efficacy of the biconformal base-space interpretation, I propose an experiment to be carried out by a capable physicist amongst this book's readership. Construct a slit holder with three slits, the usual pair at spacing l_1 and the third at spacing l_2 where $l_2 \neq ml_1$ with m a sizable integer. Further, add a shield between the photon source and the slit holder in Figure 8.14 so as to leave the pair of slits at spacing l_1 fully unobstructed but completely blocking the passage of photons into slit 3. In this case, since the FT for the three slit, slit-holder is different than the FT for the two slit, slit-holder, the photon pattern on the screen should be different for the two cases. Of course, now, from a computational point of view, we are dealing with a four-body interaction event, (1) slit holder, (2) photons, (3) screen and (4) shield.

It has been asked that, if a tree falls in the forest and no one is there to observe it, does the event really occur; i.e., does the QM wave function for the event really collapse? From the content of this section, the answer is a definite "yes". However, if a human observer is also present and aware of the event, their R-space nature plus their D-space neural response to observing the event unfold, requires expansion of the experimental system to include the observer's FT in the overall system modulus, $\hat{I}_{R_T}$, for the event. Thus, the mathematics describing the event is quantitatively different when an observer is present than when the observer is absent. The details surrounding such differences are part of our collective future while, here, our intent is only to show a pathway leading towards our fuller understanding of those details.

Some General "Wrapping up" Comments

The biconformal base-space refinement of the simple direct-space concept is realistically required by thermodynamics and produces a "separation of variables" type solution for the quantum mechanical perspective. This simplifies the quantum entanglement issue facing our present day physics community. Higher dimensional structures, such as required by present day Brane Theory, may or may not need to utilize a "rolled-up" version of this biconformal base-space. That issue is beyond the scope of the present book.

Certainly a supersymmetry philosophy is supported by our work since the magnetic monopole holds such a central place in it.

For astronomy and cosmology, the "Big Bang" concept is not inconsistent with the model proposed in this book; however, it is largely limited to changes occurring at the magnetic monopole band of the vacuum reality plus the electric monopole band of the classical physics reality. The lower two bands of the vacuum reality plus the spirit domain reality are thought to have pre-existed the "Big Bang". Because the mirror principle in this biconformal base-space acts on mass singularities as well as on charge singularities, mass image effects can be expected to influence measurable gravitational forces, just as charge image effects influence electromagnetism.

Although we have provided a qualitative model of how human intention, from the level of spirit, ultimately manifests as effects in physical reality, the quantitative expression of the model only extends to the R-space/Emotion Domain boundary. For the quantitative model, today we must treat the intention imprint and the deltron activation as boundary conditions applied to R-space. This will be sufficient to clarify a variety of misconceptions in today's physics and set the stage for the next major step in quantitative development – that of pushing the boundary conditions to the Mind Domain/Spirit interface.

References

1.   M.J. Buerger, <u>Crystal Structure Analysis</u> (John Wiley and Sons, Inc., New York, 1960).

2.   R. Bracewell, <u>The Fourier Transform and its Applications</u> (McGraw-Hill Book Company, New York, 1965).

3.   W.A. Tiller, <u>Science and Human Transformation: Subtle Energies, Intentionality and Consciousness</u> (Pavior Publishing, Walnut Creek, CA, 1997).

4.   W.A. Tiller, "Towards a Predictive Model of Subtle Domain Connections to the Physical Domain Aspect of Reality: The Origins of Wave-Particle Duality, Electric-Magnetic Monopoles and the Mirror Principle", J. Scientific Exploration, <u>13</u> (1999) 41.

5.   G. 't Hooft, "Gauge Theories of the Forces Between Elementary Particles", Scientific American, <u>242</u>, 6 (1980) 104.

6.   H.F. Harmuth, "Correction of Maxwell's Equations for Signals I ", IEEE Transactions on Electromagnetic Compatibility, <u>28</u> (1986) 250.

7.   N. Seiberg and E. Witten, "Electric-Magnetic Duality, Monopole Condensation and Confinement in N=2 Supersymmetric Yang-Mills Theory", Nuclear Physics B, <u>426</u> (1994) 19.

8.   T.W. Barrett, "Comments on the Harmuth Ansatz: Use of a Magnetic Current Density in the Calculation of the Propagation Velocity of Signals by Amended Maxwell Theory", IEEE Transactions on Electromagnetic Compatibility, <u>30</u> (1988) 419.

9.   W.A. Tiller, "Augmented Electromagnetic Waves and Qi Energy", Coherence – International Journal of Integrated Medicine, <u>1</u> (2000) 13.

10.   M.J. Kohane and W.A. Tiller, "Energy, Fitness and Information-augmented Electromagnetic Fields in *Drosophila Melanogaster*", J. Scientific Exploration, <u>14</u> (2000) 217.

11.   W.E. Dibble Jr. and W.A. Tiller, "Development of pH and Temperature Oscillations in Water Containing $ZnCO_3$ Crystallites Using Intention Imprinted Electronic Devices", Subtle Energies and Energy Medicine, <u>8</u> (2000) 75.

12.   J.T. Wheeler, "New Conformal Gauging and the Electromagnetic Theory of Weyl", J. Math. Phys. <u>39</u> (1998) 299.

13.   S. Inomata, "Consciousness and Complex Electromagnetic Fields", (Electrotechnical Laboratory, MITI, 5-4-1 Mukodai-cho, Tanaski-city, Tokyo, 1976).

14.   E.A. Rauscher, "Some Physical Models Potentially Applicable to Remote Reception", in <u>The Iceland Papers</u>, Ed. A. Puharich (Essentia Research Associates, Amherst, Wisconsin, 1979).

15.   M.W. Evans, "Electrodynamics as a Non-Abelian Gauge Field Theory", *Frontier Perspectives* 7, (2) Fall (1998) 7.

16.   Alpha Foundation's Institute for Advanced Study (AISI), "The New Maxwell Electrodynamics Equations", Journal of New Energy, 4 (3) Winter (1999) pp. 3-335.

17.   M. Schiff, The Memory of Water (Thorsons/Harper-Collins, San Francisco, CA 1994).

18.   C. Wu, "Molecules Leave Their Mark: Imprinting Technique Creates Plastic Receptors that Grab Specific Chemicals", Science News, 157 (2000) 186.

19.   I. Amlani, A.O. Orlov, G. Toth, G.H. Bernstein, C.S. Lent and G.L. Snider, "Digital Logic Gate Using Quantum-dot Cellular Automata", Science, 284 (1999) 289.

20.   R.P. Cowburn and M.E. Welland, "Room Temperature Magnetic Cellular Automata", Science, 287 (2000) 1466.

21.   R.C. Hansen, Editor, Microwave Scanning Antennas, Vol. II: Array Theory and Practice (Academic Press, New York, NY, 1966).

22.   S.E. Shnoll, V.A. Kolombet, E.V. Pozharskii, T.A. Zenchenko, I.M. Zvereva and A.A, Konradov, "Realization of Discrete States During Fluctuations in Macroscopic Processes", Physics Uspekhi, 41 (1998) 1025.

23.   S.E. Shnoll, T.A. Zenchenko, K.I. Zenchenko, E.V. Pozharskii, V.A. Kolombet, and A.A, Konradov, " Regular Variation of the Fine Structure of Statistical Distributions as a Consequence of Cosmo Physical Agents", Physics Uspekhi, 43 (2000) 205.

24.   M. Tegmark and J.A. Wheeler, "100 Years of Quantum Mysteries", Scientific American, 284 (2001) 68.

Appendix 8.A: Some R-space Undulation Interval Recipes for Specific D-space δ-function Loci

One might begin by asking "What abrupt changes in R-space shift the δ-function from x_0 to $x_0 + \Delta x_0$?". This only requires an abrupt change in the undulation interval of the appropriate k_x-axis de Broglie wave component from Δk_x to $\Delta k_x{}'$ where

$$\Delta k_x = 2\pi/x_0 \text{ and } \Delta k_x{}' = 2\pi/(x_0 + \Delta x_0). \qquad (8A.1)$$

For constant velocity movement of this δ-function along the x-axis over the time interval $t_0{}'$ to $t_0{}' + \Delta t_0{}'$, one requires that

$$\Delta k_x = 2\pi/x_0 \text{ for } t \le t_0{}' \qquad (8A.2a)$$

$$\Delta k_x{}' = 2\pi/(x_0 + v_x \Delta t_0{}') \text{ for } 0 \le \Delta t_0{}' \le \Delta x_0/v_x \qquad (8A.2b)$$

$$= 2\pi/[\,x_0 + v_x((2\pi/\Delta k_t) - t_0{}')] \qquad (8A.2c)$$

where v_x is the velocity along the x-axis and Δk_t is the k_t-axis undulation interval. Of course, in this fixed space-time frame, Δk_t shrinks as Δt increases. However, the shrinkage rate may be very small if t_0 is very large (e.g., if the origin of t_0 is the "Big Bang"). In a similar fashion, one could state the specific R-space conditions needed for δ-function movement at constant acceleration, a_x, along the x-axis of D-space over the interval x_0 to $x_0 + \Delta x_0$ and $t_0{}'$ to $t_0{}' + \Delta t_0{}'$. One ends up with a somewhat more complex expression than Equation 8A.2c connecting $\Delta k_x{}'$ to Δk_x, x_0, $t_0{}'$, v_x and a_x.

To have our δ-function perform simple harmonic motion along the x-axis, the connections required for

$$x_0(\Delta t') = x_0(0) + A\sin\omega t' \; ; \; t' = t_0{}' + \Delta t_0{}' \qquad (8A.3a)$$

with

$$\Delta k_x' = 2\pi / x_0 (\Delta t_0') \; ; \; \Delta k_t = 2\pi / (t_0' + (\Delta t_0')) \qquad (8A.3b)$$

are

$$\frac{dx_0}{dt_0} = \frac{dx_0}{d\Delta t_0'} \;\; = A \; \omega \cos \left[2\pi\omega \left(\frac{1}{\Delta k_t} - \frac{t_0'}{2\pi} \right) \right]$$

$$= \left(\frac{\Delta k_t}{\Delta k_x'} \right)^2 \frac{d\Delta k_x'}{d\Delta k_t} \qquad (8A.3c)$$

using the differential chain rule. To have our δ-function perform circular motion in the xy-plane of D-space requires coordinated changes of $\Delta k_x'$ and $\Delta k_y'$ in terms of Δk_t in R-space. The procedure is straightforward following the example of Equations 8A.3 with the two relationships

$$x_0 (\Delta t') = x_0(0) + A \cos(\omega_1 \Delta t')$$

and

$$y_0 (\Delta t') = y_0(0) + A \sin(\omega_1 \Delta t') \qquad (8A.4a)$$

Motion of our δ-function over an ellipsoidal path in D-space requires coordinating changes in $\Delta k_x'$, $\Delta k_y'$ and $\Delta k_z'$ in terms of Δk_t utilizing the three relationships

$$x_0 (\Delta t') = x_0(0) + A \cos(\omega_1 \Delta t')$$
$$y_0 (\Delta t') = y_0(0) + A \sin(\omega_1 \Delta t') \sin(\omega_2 \Delta t') \qquad (8A.4b)$$
$$z_0 (\Delta t') = z_0(0) + A \sin(\omega_1 \Delta t') \cos(\omega_2 \Delta t').$$

In all of the foregoing changes, the "River of Time" flows in an undisputed fashion while the undulation intervals for the other $\underline{k}$-wave coordinate directions change in well-defined and specific ways to cause our δ-function to execute specific motions in D-space. It should be clear from these few examples that a recipe can be given for R-space undulation interval changes that will guarantee <u>any</u> type of δ-function motion wished in D-space.

Appendix 8.B: Theoretically Matching Temporal D-space Oscillations

Our starting point is Equation 8.7 and Equations 4 of Table 8.8 of the main text, both expressions for $\hat{I}_R(k_t)$. Our goal is to gain a pathway for determining the a_n in Equation 8.7 in terms of the parameters of Equation 4. Because the square root in Equation 4a is difficult to work with, we begin by squaring both sides of Equation 8.7 so that

$$Q^2 = (2\pi^2/\beta^2)\,\hat{I}_R^{\ 2} = \left[\sum_{n=0}^{\infty} a_n \cos nx\right]^2 \tag{8.B.1a}$$

$$= a_0 \sum_{n=0}^{\infty} a_n \cos nx + a_1 \sum_{n=0}^{\infty} \frac{a_n}{2}\left[\cos(n+1)x + \cos(n-1)x\right] + \cdots$$

$$+ a_m \sum_{n=0}^{\infty} \frac{a_n}{2}\left[\cos(n+m)x + \cos(n-m)x\right] + \cdots \tag{8.B.1b}$$

We can now use standard orthogonality procedures to obtain

$$a_p = \frac{2}{\pi}\int_0^{\pi} Q^2 \cos px\,dx \tag{8.B.2}$$

From simple integration tables, we utilize

$$\int \cos x\,dx = \sin x;\ \int \sin x\,dx = -\cos x;\ \int \cos^2 x\,dx = \frac{x}{2} + \sin 2x;$$

$$\int \sin^2 x\,dx = x - \int \cos^2 x\,dx;\ \int x\cos x\,dx = \cos x + x\sin x;$$

$$\int x\sin x\,dx = \sin x - x\cos x;$$

$$\int x\cos^2 dx = \frac{x^4}{4} + \frac{x}{2}\sin 2x + \frac{1}{8}\cos 2x;$$

$$\int x^2 \cos x\, dx = 2x\cos x + (x^2 - 2)\sin x;$$

$$\int x^2 \cos^2 x\, dx = \frac{x^3}{6} + (\frac{x^2}{4} - \frac{1}{8})\sin x + \frac{x}{4}\cos 2x$$

$$\int x^2 \sin x\, dx = 2x\sin x - (x^2 - 2)\cos x . \qquad (8.B.3)$$

This leads to, for the first five terms,
p=0;

$$a_0^2 + \sum_{n=1}^{\infty} \frac{a_n^2}{2} = \frac{2}{\pi}\int_0^{\pi} Q^2 dx \qquad (8.B.4a)$$

p=1;

$$[2a_0a_1 + a_1a_2 + a_2a_3 + ...]\int_0^{\pi}\cos^2 x\, dx = \frac{2}{\pi}\int_0^{\pi} Q^2\cos x\, dx \qquad (8.B.4b)$$

p=2;

$$[2a_0a_2 + \frac{a_1^2}{2} + a_1a_2 + a_2a_4 + ...]\int_0^{\pi}\cos^2 2x\, dx = \frac{2}{\pi}\int_0^{\pi} Q^2\cos 2x\, dx \quad (8.B.4c)$$

p=3;

$$[2a_0a_3 + a_1a_2 + a_1a_4 + ...]\int_0^{\pi}\cos^2 3x\, dx = \frac{2}{\pi}\int_0^{\pi} Q^2\cos 3x\, dx \qquad (8.B.4d)$$

p=4;

$$[2a_0a_4 + a_1a_3 + \frac{a_2^2}{2} + a_1a_5 + ...]\int_0^{\pi}\cos^2 4x\, dx = \frac{2}{\pi}\int_0^{\pi} Q^2\cos 4x\, dx \quad (8.B.4e)$$

Equations 8.B.4 provide us with $n+1$ equations in $n+1$ unknowns (the a_n) and thus can be solved. If we wish to know the amplitude of only the first four harmonics, then we truncate the series at p=4, set $a_5 \sim 0$ and we then use straightforward algebra to solve five equations in the five unknowns a_0, a_1, a_2,

a_3 and a_4. The single most important point of all this for the reader is that, for a single value of $k_t = k_t^*$, many harmonics beyond the fundamental appear in $\hat{I}$ and thus in the physical measurement. The amplitudes of these harmonics can be straightforwardly but tediously obtained via the set of equations given by Equations 8.B.4.

Appendix 8.C: Modulus Evaluation for Remedy Preparation in Homeopathy

Defining the time-dependent D-space concentration, $C_D(t)$, via the succussion/dilution process as

$$C_D(t) = C_D(0)10^{-n} \text{ where } n=\alpha t =t/\Delta t \tag{8.C.1}$$

and where Δt is the average time for each succussion/dilution step. This yields an R-space counterpart given by

$$\hat{C}_R(k_t) = \frac{C_D(0)}{\sqrt{2\pi}} \int_0^t C_\delta 10^{-\alpha t'} e^{-itk_t'} dt' \tag{8.C.2}$$

since $C_D(t) = 0$ for $t<0$. Because we have the mathematical relationship

$$a^x = e^{x \ln a} \rightarrow 10^{-\alpha t} = e^{-\alpha t \ln 10}, \tag{8.C.3}$$

if $C_\delta = C_{\delta 0} = $ constant, Equation 8.C.2 becomes

$$\hat{C}_R(k_t) = \frac{C_D(0)C_{\delta_0}}{\sqrt{2\pi}} \left\{ \frac{1-e^{-t(\alpha \ln 10 + ik_t)}}{\alpha \ln 10 + ik_t} \right\} . \tag{8.C.4}$$

This yields the modulus, $\hat{I}_R(k_t) = [\hat{C}_R \hat{C}_R^*]^{1/2}$ as

$$\hat{I}_R(k_t) = \frac{C_D(0)C_{\delta_0}}{\sqrt{2\pi}} \left\{ \left[\frac{1-10^{-\alpha t} e^{-ik_t}}{\alpha \ln 10 + ik_t} \right] \left[\frac{1-10^{-\alpha t} e^{+ik_t}}{\alpha \ln 10 - ik_t} \right] \right\}^{1/2} \tag{8.C.5a}$$

$$= \left\{ \frac{1 - 2 \bullet 10^{-\alpha t} \cos(tk_t) + 10^{-2\alpha t}}{(\alpha \ln 10)^2 + k_t^2} \right\}^{1/2} \tag{8.C.5b}$$

$$\text{since } \cosh(itk_t) = \frac{e^{-ik_t} + e^{+ik_t}}{2} = \cos(tk_t). \tag{8.C.5c}$$

If $C_\delta = a" + c" k_t + bt = C_{\delta_0} + bt$, Equation 8.C.2 yields

$$\hat{C}_R(k_t) = \frac{C_D(0)C_{\delta_0}}{\sqrt{2\pi}} \left\{ \frac{1 - (1 + bt/C_{\delta_0})10^{-\alpha t} e^{-ik_t t}}{\alpha \ln 10 + ik_t} \right\} \tag{8.C.6a}$$

so

$$\hat{I}_R(k_t) =$$

$$\frac{C_D(0)C_{\delta_0}}{\sqrt{\pi}} \left\{ \frac{1 - 2(1 + bt/C_{\delta_0})10^{-\alpha t} \cos(tk_t) + (1 + bt/C_{\delta_0})^2 10^{-2\alpha t}}{(\alpha \ln 10)^2 + k_t^2} \right\}^{1/2}$$

$$\tag{8.C.6b}$$

Finally, since

$$\int x^m e^{ax} dx = \frac{1}{a} x^m e^{ax} - \frac{m}{a} \int x^{m-1} e^{ax} dx, \tag{8.C.7}$$

if

$$C_\delta = a" + \sum_{m=1}^{M} c_m^" k_t^m + \sum_{m=1}^{P} b_m t^m = C_{\delta_0} + \sum_{m=1}^{P} b_m t^m, \tag{8.C.8}$$

then

$$\hat{I}_R(k_t) =$$

$$\frac{C_D(0)C_{\delta_0}}{\sqrt{\pi}} \left\{ \frac{1 - 2P_1(t)10^{-\alpha t} \cos(tk_t) + P_2(t)10^{-2\alpha t}}{(\alpha \ln 10)^2 + k_t^2} \right\}^{1/2} \tag{8.C.9}$$

where P_1 and P_2 are straightforwardly determined polynomials in ascending powers of t (as in Equation 8.C.8).

Appendix 8.D: Calculation of $\int_R \hat{I}_R dk_t$ for $10/\beta = 1 \pm$ a small constant

From Equation 4 of Table 8.9, $\hat{I}_R$ is given by

$$\hat{I}_R = AB\{1 - C \cos(n\Delta tk_t)\}^{1/2} \qquad (8.D.1a)$$

with

$$A = C_D(0)C_\delta^*/(2\pi)^{1/2}; \quad B = \left\{\frac{[1 + (10/\beta)^{-2n}]}{[(\Delta tk_t)^2 + (\ln(10/\beta))^2]}\right\}^{1/2} \Delta t \quad ;$$

$$C = 2\left[\frac{(10/\beta)^{-n}}{1 + (10/\beta)^{-2n}}\right] \qquad (8.D.1b)$$

and $n = \alpha t = t/\Delta t$. For simplicity, we will also define $x = \Delta tk_t$. Now, binomial expansion of Equation 1a becomes

$$\hat{I}_R = AB\{1 - (C/2)\cos(nx) - (C^2/8)\cos^2(nx) - (C^3/16)\cos^3(nx) -$$
$$(5C^4/128)\cos^4(nx) - ...\} \qquad (8.D.2a)$$

$$\approx AB\{[1 - C^2/16 - C^4/68 - C^6/156 - ....] - C/2[1 + C^2/10 + C^4/50$$
$$+ C^6/538 + ...]\cos(nx) - C^2/16[1 + C^2/3 + C^4/6 + ...]\cos(2nx) -$$
$$C^3/64[1 + C^2/2 + C^4/5 + ...]\cos(3nx) - C^4/205[1 + 4C^2/5$$
$$+ ...]\cos(4nx) - C^5/640[1 + C^2 + ...]\cos(5nx) - ...\} \qquad (8.D.2b)$$

$$\approx AB \sum_{m=0}^{\infty} a_m \cos(mnx). \qquad (8.D.2c)$$

Here, the standard formulae connecting the higher powers of $\cos(nx)$ to its higher harmonics, $\cos(mnx)$, have been utilized to go from Equation 2a to Equation 2b. By inspection of Equations 2b and 2c, the various a_m are readily determined.

Integrating $\hat{I}_R$ from Equation 2c yields

$$\int_R \hat{I}_R dk_t = \frac{2A}{\Delta t} \int_0^{x^*} a_0 B dx + \frac{2A}{\Delta t} \sum_{m=1}^{\infty} \int_0^{x^*} a_m B \cos(mnx) dx \qquad (8.D.3)$$

where $x^* = \Delta t k_t^* \geq 10\ln(10/\beta)$ was chosen to yield an error of less than 1%. Because B and $B\cos(mnx)$ are both even functions of x, the integral from $-\infty$ to $+\infty$ becomes twice the integral from zero to $+\infty$. The a_0 term is just the area under a monotonically decaying function as x increases. The a_m terms are more complex because of the superposed oscillations multiplying this monotonically decaying function. Proceeding, we find that

$$\frac{2A}{\Delta t} \int_0^{x^*} a_0 B dx = 2A a_0 \gamma \ln\left\{ \frac{x^*}{\ln(10/\beta)} + \left[1 + \left\langle \frac{x^*}{\ln(10/\beta)} \right\rangle^2 \right]^{1/2} \right\}$$

$$\approx 2A a_0 \gamma \ln(20) \qquad (8.D.4a)$$

where

$$\gamma = [1 + (10/\beta)^{-2n}]^{1/2} \qquad (8.D.4b)$$

From published tables, one finds that

$$\int_0^{\infty} \frac{\cos(zx)\, dx}{[x^2 + a^2]^{1/2}} = K_0(az) \text{ for } a > 0, z > 0 \qquad (8.D.5a)$$

where K_0 is a Bessel function of the second kind and zeroth order. Since the asymptotic form for $K_0(az)$ is

$$K_0(az) = \left[\frac{\pi}{2az}\right]^{1/2} e^{-az} + O\left[\frac{1}{(az)^{3/2}}\right], \qquad (8.D.5b)$$

where $O(1/y^{3/2})$ means a quantity less than $C/y^{3/2}$ where C is a positive constant, the region where $az<1$ could lead to appreciable error in the integral. Thus, we decided to use a numerical solution, wherein the denominator of Equation 5a is a constant over any single quarter cycle of the cosine function but increases abruptly to a new value for the next quarter cycle, etc. Our cosine term in Equation 3 now becomes

$$\frac{2A}{\Delta t} \sum_{m=1}^{\infty} \int_0^{x^*} a_m B\cos(mnx)dx \approx 2A\gamma \sum_{m=1}^{\infty}\sum_{j=1}^{\infty} a_m\alpha_j \int_{x_j}^{x_{j+1}} \cos(mnx)dx$$

$$(8.D.6a)$$

$$\approx 2A\gamma \sum_{m=1}^{\infty}\sum_{j=1}^{\infty} a_m\alpha_j \left\{\frac{1}{mn}\left[\sin(mnx_{j+1}) - \sin(mnx_j)\right]\right\} \qquad (8.D.6b)$$

$$\approx (2)^{1/2} A\gamma \sum_{m=1}^{\infty}\sum_{j=1}^{\infty} a_m\alpha_j \cos\left[\left(j-\frac{1}{2}\right)\frac{\pi}{2}\right] \qquad (8.D.6c)$$

where

$$\alpha_j = \frac{1}{\left[\left\langle\left(j-\frac{1}{2}\right)\frac{\pi}{2mn}\right\rangle^2 + \left\langle\ln\left(\frac{10}{\beta}\right)\right\rangle^2\right]^{1/2}} \qquad (8.D.6d)$$

and

$$mn(x_{j+1} - x_j) = mn\Delta x_j = \pi/2 \text{ with } x_1 = 0 \text{ so } \Delta x_1 = x_2 = \pi/2(mn).$$

Our final step in evaluating the integral of $\hat{I}_R$, for a variety of $10/\beta = 1\pm\Delta$ over the range of n of interest, is to numerically calculate C, a_0, a_1, a_2, a_3, a_4,..., γ and α_j for $1 \leq j \leq 50$ before generating the needed products and sums. Two of the output results are provided in Figures 8.10 of the main text.

CHAPTER 9

Some Implications for Religion, Philosophy, Psychology and Integrated Medicine

The boundaries between these areas of professional activity are quite diffuse so that, unless one has substantial formal training, one unintentionally slips back and forth between them. That weakness will be readily apparent in this chapter and the authors beg the indulgence of sophisticated readers in this regard.

Religion

In the field of religion, some concept of spirit residing in both the without and the within of humans has always been paramount. The specific images and the specific dogmas utilized by the various religions have been, on the one hand, seemingly designed as a set of guidelines whereby their group, sect or cult may live what is deemed to be a proper, valued life. These particular guidelines have often been ascribed to honest inspiration and often to unique revelation from the "divine". From the viewpoint of various religious positions, each seems equally valid in their general expression with their core picture of reality being related just as much to our connectedness as to our seeming separateness and differences. All wonderful contrasts in God's "garden" of life! On the other hand, various religions have, more-often-than-not, become power vehicles for control of these masses of humans via mindset molding and constraint mechanisms in the evolving human cultures. Most of them propose the existence of some unseen deity, remote and separate from themselves, that requires worship and proper behavior on the supplicant's part.

Over the years, many major points of contention have arisen between these various religions and the consensus science of the time. This is to be expected because science has been able to develop a wide spectrum of probes for experimentally perturbing nature and recording nature's responses while religion has not. These two areas of human activity have much in common in that they both seek to understand the "truth" about nature although religion focuses it's attention largely upon "divine" nature while present science excludes this aspect. Religion must build its pictures largely on theories, inspired or revelatory, without viable experimental probes with which to refine the theories. Science, on the other hand, is committed to accepting only testable and repeatable experimental data for building its world picture. Perhaps the

377

biobodysuit metaphor briefly enunciated in Chapter 2 is a suitable vehicle whereby science and religion may eventually find an area for mutual investigation. In the interest of such a future cooperative effort, let us revisit this metaphor in much greater detail.

The Biobodysuit Metaphor: The working hypothesis is that we are all spirits having a physical experience as we ride "the river of life" together. Our spiritual parents dressed us in our biobodysuits and put us in this playpen, which we call a universe, in order to grow in coherence, in order to develop our gifts of intentionality and in order to ultimately become what we were meant to become -- effective cocreators with our spiritual parents.

These biobodysuits come in a wide variety of colors and two unique morphologies, that we choose to call genders. Each biobodysuit has four main layers: (1) the outer layer is the electric monopole substance layer, (2) the first inner layer is the magnetic monopole substance layer, (3) the second inner layer is the emotion domain substance layer and (4) the third inner layer is the mind domain substance layer -- and inside that is a portion of our spirit self that drives the vehicle. So think of this multilayered suit as a kind of "diving bell" or apparatus that our spirit self uses to sense and experience this peculiar earth environment.

All of these inner layer substances function in what we presently call "the vacuum" and, the more structurally refined are these layers, the larger is the amount of our high spirit self that can inhabit the biobodysuit. What are known as the four fundamental forces of present-day science all function in the outermost layer and somewhat in the first inner layer of the biobodysuit. What are presently called "subtle energies" all function in the three inner layers which are substructures of the vacuum.

In terms of some of the characteristics of these suits, it is well known that, at least at the moment, our eyes detect only a very small fraction of the total electromagnetic spectrum and our ears detect only a very small fraction of the total available sound spectrum. Thus, it is perhaps not so surprising when I suggest that we generally detect only one band in the total spectrum of reality!

For most of us, we are presently only cognitively aware of the outer layer of our biobodysuits and the outer layer of the world that surrounds us. However, some individuals are, today, cognitively aware of these unseen bands in the spectrum of reality[1,2]. This means that such a capability is a natural part of the multidimensional human genome and that all of us have the latent capability for achieving these expanded levels of cognition. This generally occurs via intentional and diligent practice of self-management techniques.

We are all familiar with such processes at the outer layer level of the biobodysuit for gaining various athletic, artistic or strength coordinations. Now, we want to extend such efforts to the emotional and mental levels as well. This allows us to build new infrastructures at the inner levels of our biobodysuits.

At least three or more inner self-management techniques at emotional and mental levels are readily available to us:

(1) <u>Yoga</u> -- The oldest and best known. It focuses on the brain in order to still the mind and then make significant contact with our larger self.

(2) <u>QiGong</u> -- The next oldest, and the basis for all the martial arts. It focusses on the Dan Tien point just below the belly-button in order to still the mind and then make contact with our larger self.

(3) <u>HeartMath</u> -- The newest, which focuses on the heart in order to still the mind and then make significant contact with the larger self.

There are a variety of other procedures, Sufism being one. In almost all cases, sufficient diligent practice leads to various levels of adeptship and this naturally manifests as what we presently call "superphysical" abilities. I prefer to call it <u>actualizing</u> our latent abilities[1,2] which involves becoming more coherent and therefore more conscious.

In this metaphor, consciousness is a concomitant or byproduct of spirit entering dense matter. If only a little can enter because insufficient structural organization exists in the dense matter, then the individual consciousness will be low. This means that the individual's awareness will also be low and very little flexibility will exist in the course of action to be taken in response to a stimulus or event that occurs in the environment. However, by the diligent application of personal effort, one can increase the structural refinement in their biobodysuit so that it exhibits a greater capability. Thus, more of our high spirit self can enter the body and the individual exhibits a higher level of consciousness. This manifests, in part, as greater personal awareness, the recognition of new possibilities, more flexibility, more adaptability, a greater ability to just love and not judge another human, the recognition that only win-win situations are enduringly stable, the recognition of others as part of our larger self, etc. This continual "bootstrap" process is the way we grow. And we have grown quite a bit since we first invested a part of our spirit-selves in the biobodysuits of the mammalian ape. However, we still have a very long way to grow before we reach <u>home</u>!

What we see here is that "we are the product of the process and we are built by the process!" By directed intention, we engage in activities outside of ourselves and, by the quality of our actions there, have the possiblity of building a better biobodysuit (a major experience in spirit creation) and developing a higher consciousness -- both of which greatly enrich the human family!

At the outer layer of our biobodysuits, our neural systems function only on the basis of contrast or differences. Thus, our sensory systems in this layer detect only the differences between things and this is why we appear to be separate from each other. At the level of the first inner layer of the biobodysuit, a special kind of "mirror-type" relationship exists and the coordinates for experience are not distance and time but are the reciprocals of these (1/distance = number per unit distance or a spatial frequency and 1/time = number per unit time or a temporal frequency). Thus, this coarsest level of the vacuum is a four-dimensional frequency domain and, there, there is no separation between us. There, we form a unity, and the events that occur in that presently unseen domain are the <u>precursors</u> to all the events that materialize at the space-time level. If you like, it is the prephysical reality where we collectively create our future at the space-time level.

At present, we don't cognitively access the vacuum domains in the reality spectrum for a variety of reasons. Three of these are:

(1) We are seldom quiet enough at the outermost layer level in order to reliably sense the information signals present at the more subtle levels -- they are buried down in the noise.

(2) We have not yet developed a sufficiently coherent structural organization at these inner levels to allow large amplitude signals to exist and be sustained in the vacuum domains and

(3) Perhaps most important of all is that our mindsets are such that we believe the four dimensions of space-time are all that exists and, therefore, we have built a cognitive jail for ourselves with walls so high that it is almost impossible to tunnel through them and break free of this confining mindset!

Now, let us address some of the key points in this biobodysuit metaphor:

<u>(a) The Vacuum</u>: Most of the general public hold the idea that the vacuum is not only the absence of physical matter but is also devoid of anything! However, for quantum mechanics and relativity theory to be internally self-consistent, the vacuum is required to contain an amazingly large inherent energy density. This vacuum energy density is so large that, for a "flat" universe, the intrinsic total energy contained within the volume of a <u>single</u> hydrogen atom is about one trillion times larger than that contained in <u>all</u> the physical mass of all the planets plus all the stars in the entire known cosmos out to a radius of 20 billion light-years. This makes the energy stored in physical matter an insignificant whisper compared to that stored in the

vacuum. Uncovering the secrets of the vacuum is obviously a very important part of humankind's future!

(b) <u>Coherence</u>: To illustrate this principle, let us consider the case of a typical home-use 60 watt light bulb. It provides some illumination but not a lot of illumination. This is primarily because the emitted photons destructively interfere with each other so that most of the bulb's potential effectiveness is destroyed. However, if we could somehow take the <u>same number</u> of photons emitted by the light bulb per second and orchestrate their emission to be in phase with each other, then we would have constructive interference between these photons and now the energy density of the surface of the light bulb would be thousands to millions of times larger than that emitted by the surface of the sun. This illustrates the unutilized potential in the present light bulb. Perhaps the best example of the development of coherent energy emissions from humans comes from studies of QiGong masters[1]. They appear to emit beams of infra red radiation (1 to 4.5 microns) from their palms that have healing benefits.

(c) <u>Mindsets</u>: One of the most striking experiments concerning the power of one's mindset was carried out in the mid-1930's by a psychologist named Slater who designed what might be called "upside down" glasses[1]. Subjects were asked to continually wear these glasses that distorted one's perception so that the wearer saw everything in an upside down configuration. It was very destabilizing for the wearer but after about two to three weeks (depending on the wearer), there was a sudden "flip" and they saw everything right side up. Then, if the subject permanently removed the glasses, the world was abruptly upside down again for about two to three weeks before the images returned to a normal perspective. Here, we see that the original mindset was so strong concerning the upright orientation of familiar objects that, when the special glasses inverted this orientation, a force developed in the brain to seemingly cause neural dendrites to grow into a configuration that essentially created an inversion mirror in the optical information path. Once this neural structure was "hardwired", it took the old mindset several weeks to deconstruct the special signal inversion network. We now call this "neural learning" and we humans do it all the time. It is how we build additional infrastructure into the various layers of our biobodysuits!

(d) <u>The Cause/Effect Process</u>: Via specific intentions, the in-the-biobodysuit aspect of our spirit self produces actions in the infrastructures of the various layers and these ultimately manifest as events in space-time. Specifically, the intention from the domain of spirit imprints an initial pattern on the mind domain (the innermost layer). The detailed intralayer connections[1] transfer the imprint in a correlated pattern to both the magnetic monopole layer (second layer) and to the emotion domain layer (third layer) where it activates an important coupling substance, called deltrons, in this layer

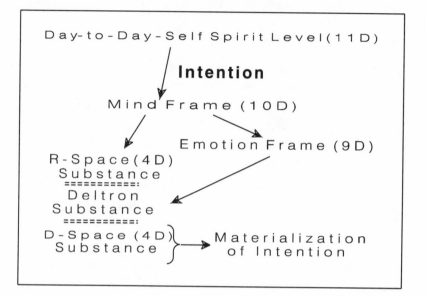

Figure 9.1   Illustration of one possible process path whereby spirit produces action in the physical domain.

(see Figure 9.1). The deltrons allow coupling between the magnetic monopole substance of the second layer and the electric monopole substance of the first layer (outermost layer). This coupling agent acts much like the "toner" needed in a standard copy machine to produce a clear and legible copy[1]. When the original intention imprint reaches the outermost layer of the biobodysuit, it activates the built-in mechanisms for action in the surrounding domain -- physical reality.

It is via this process that we collectively and continuously create our future in space-time. Our individual responses to the events we perceive in space-time are in the form of thoughts, attitudes and physical actions (and probably reciprocal space actions). This is feedback to the mind and emotion domains which make incremental changes to the patterns that generated the initial events in space-time. The superposition of all the responses to the initial events from all of humankind leads to the new pattern at the mind level that generates a new set of events in space-time[1]. Iteration of this incremental step, which can be considered as a single frame in the "movie" called the "River of Life", is how we collectively create our cognitive reality and how our spirits learn the pros and cons of applied intentionality.

The experimental studies described in Chapters 3 to 6 of this book provide peripheral evidence in support of this metaphor. These are all very remarkable experimental results which are certain to confound many of our physics, biology and medical colleagues. However, the experimental data speaks for itself in spite of the entrenched belief systems held by others. Adding the "space conditioning" aspect of the IIED studies to the "neural learning" aspects of Slater's upside-down glasses experiment plus the inner self-management aspect of accomplished Yoga, QiGong and HeartMath practitioners, one sees that "serious" transformation is occurring in the various layers of our and nature's biobodysuit. This looks like important infrastructure development, particularly at the various levels of the vacuum.

In closing this section, It seems that the more we explore these new concepts and experiments, the more we come to feel that there is only a single reality being expressed by nature but that we have limited access to it. Our access appears to be limited by our level of cognitive development and this, in turn, is limited by the quality of our focussed intentions to develop more infrastructure in the various layers of our biobodysuits.

Philosophy

Humankind is concerned with scientific enquiry because he/she wants to understand the milieu in which they find themselves. She/he wants to engineer and reliably control or cooperatively modulate as much of their environment as possible to sustain, enrich and propagate their life. Following this path, the goal of science is to gain a reliable description of all natural phenomena so as to allow accurate prediction (within appropriate limits) of nature's behavior as a function of an ever-changing environment. As such, science is incapable of providing us with absolute truth. Rather, it provides relative knowledge, internally self-consistent knowledge, about the relationships between different phenomena and between different things.

The goal of engineering, on the other hand, is to build on this fundamental understanding in order to generate new materials, devices, structures, attitudes, moralities, philosophies, etc., for producing tangible order, harnessing the latent potential in nature's phenomena and expanding human capabilities in an ever-changing environment. In this context, medicine is to human biology as engineering is to physical science.

As each of us rides the "river of life", the great consciousness adventure, we perceive events occurring around us but, more often than not, we do not perceive the total information content inherent in those events nor the complete reality of those events. As for the latter point, this is so because what we take as the reality of an observation is actually a convolution of (1) what our presently developed sensory system actually senses and (2) our mindset or belief structure that filters and/or selectively amplifies segments of the neurally-gathered data stream. As for the former point, only what we call the five physical senses are at present reliably developed and functionally integrated within our overall sensory system so that only a fraction of the total available data reliably registers itself as our neurally-gathered, internal data stream. We are thus always making personal observations through the distorting and spectrally-limited lens of our mindsets and we have no way at present to perform a deconvolution and perceive the pure information inherent in our neurally-gathered, internal data stream. By using designed instruments to access information patterns in nature, we gain a more objective perspective of these events. However, we must always remember that these instruments were designed to be consistent with the logic of our present, average, cognitive development. Therefore, they also have a limited access to the total information spectrum associated with these events occurring in nature.

Pathways To Scientific Understanding: Over the course of the past 4-5 centuries, we have learned how to conduct true scientific investigations, first under the label of classical mechanics, and more recently, quantum mechanics. Let us review how this is generally done.

The time-honored method of scientific inquiry for a new phenomenon is to treat it as a "black box" whose internal characteristics are unknown but are amenable to probing and analysis. One applies some appropriately selected input stimulus (IS) to the box and determines its output response (OR) to the specific stimulus. By varying IS and correlating the OR with the IS, one deduces information about the most probable behavior of the box for this magnitude of stimulus. One then speculates on models of nature that would first qualitatively and then quantitatively reproduce such a spectrum of responses. Then one proceeds to design critical tests for discriminating between the initially acceptable models.

Since the true and lawful nature of the box would have a much more complex and "rich" expression than we can obtain by this limited probing, the exact and complete response function for the box may be characterized by the following general functional form[1]

$$\frac{OR}{IS} = f\left(\varepsilon_1, \varepsilon_2, \varepsilon_3, \ldots \varepsilon_n; x_1, x_2, x_3, \ldots x_n\right) \quad . \tag{9.1a}$$

Here, f represents the exact and complete functional relationship between all the possible material parameters, ε_j, and all the possible experimental variables, x_j, of the system where unlimited range of magnitude is allowed for these parameters and variables.

Because, at any point in time, one has limited cognitive awareness of all these parameters and variables, a limited array of probe stimuli, probe measurement accuracy, financial resources for the probing and limited patience for endless data gathering, one settles for the following functional expression as the "operational" response function for the box

$$\frac{OR}{IS} = f'\left(\varepsilon_1, ..., \varepsilon_j \; ; \; x_1, ..., x_j\right) \text{ for } \varepsilon_j' < \varepsilon_j < \varepsilon_j'' \; ; \; x_j' < x_j < x_j''. \quad (9.1b)$$

This operational response function, f', involves a limited but sufficient number of parameters and variables with bounded ranges ($\varepsilon_j' - \varepsilon_j''$ and $x_j' - x_j''$) for a satisfactory degree of reliability. It is this type of response function that one tries to match with a model so that our successful models simulate "idealized" nature rather than "actual" nature.

This is a practical procedure that has been very fruitful for an evolving humanity and it provides meaningful but relative truth concerning this aspect of nature. Over time, people tend to become attached to the theoretical model that has been fashioned to fit idealized nature (Equation 9.1b) and tend to forget that they are not dealing with actual nature (Equation 9.1a). This attachment can become so strong that a rather rigid mindset can develop in the scientific community concerning it and it becomes the scientific world view or paradigm for an extended period of time. However, periodically in time, the prevailing paradigm is unable to accommodate some new sets of experimental observations so pressure begins to develop to change the accepted form of Equation 9.1b and this would constitute a paradigm shift.

Paradigm shifts in physics do not occur easily because the old mindset of the establishment has great inertia to change for a variety of reasons. Such a shift began a century ago with the, then, new concepts of discrete quantum packets of change plus the relativistic coupling of the separate coordinates, distance and time, into an indivisible space-time. These new concepts violated certain basic assumptions inherent in the prevailing perspectives of classical mechanics and they were strongly resisted. Today, such concepts are well accepted but it took a century of productive and fruitful work to make it so.

Now, a century later, the prevailing physics model is unable to incorporate the robust experimental observations concerning, psychoenergetics,

ESP, remote viewing, distant healing, homeopathy, mind and emotions into it's internally self-consistent picture. Thus, physicists must either deny the existence of such observations as being valid observations or they must expand their model of nature sufficiently to incorporate them into a larger view of nature. Unfortunately and perhaps predictably, at the moment, most of the scientific establishment has preferred to "sweep all these observations under the rug" rather than accept the limited nature of their present perspective and thus proceed forward to define and explore the larger truth.

Because humankind continues to grow steadily in consciousness while continuing to refine and expand its experimental tools for probing nature, a wise society would periodically assess whether or not their current formulation of Equation 9.1b is still a valid approximation to the truth of <u>all</u> the experimental observations gathered by their community. One must really expect that, with the passage of time, our old relative truth must be periodically replaced with a new relative truth as a course correction for our trajectory towards enlightenment (Equation 9.1a).

The work laid out in this book, both experimental and theoretical, suggests a single reality with a postulated absolute aspect and a relative aspect. The absolute aspect is considered to be eleven-dimensional and above while the relative aspect is considered to be ten-dimensional and lower. These various dimensions can all be considered to be states of symmetry or organizations of spirit in this single reality framework, from the fundamental bits of matter that we call quarks to that state of spirit that we call "the divine". Depending upon the state of sensory development in the various layers of our biobodysuits, humans access only various fragments of this single reality, which are played out within the cognitive framework of those humans. Most of them, today, cognitively access only the U(1) gauge level of symmetry expression in the larger reality. The physics development based upon this cognitive limitation has been formally expressed in the four-dimensional framework of space-time, our designated D-space. Some humans appear to cognitively access higher dimensional aspects than just D-space; i.e., R-space and higher but not with the same degree of reliability and acuity that they do with D-space events and phenomena. This appears to be a statistical variation in the evolutionary unfoldment of that latent capacity inherent in the multidimensional human genome. It is presumed that this undoubtedly relates to additional infrastructure development in the various vacuum layers of their biobodysuits.

In terms of Equation 9.1b, the present-day quantum mechanical description for the electron would be approximately expressed as

$$\left(\frac{OR}{IS}\right)_e \approx f'(h,c,q_e,m_e,g,k,\varepsilon_E,\varepsilon_H\,;\ \mu_e,x,y,z,t) \qquad (9.2a)$$

with $\qquad \mu_e = f''\left(\mu_{e_0},c_e,P,T,\phi,E,H\right).$ $\qquad\qquad$ (9.2b)

Here, the parameters are h = Planck's constant, c = velocity of light, q_e = electron charge, m_e = electron mass, g = gravitational constant, k = Boltzman's constant, ε_E = electric permittivity of the medium and ε_H = magnetic permeability of the medium. The variables, x, y, z, t are our familiar D-space coordinates while μ_e is the generalized potential for the electron in the medium, given by Equation 9.2b in terms of the various thermodynamic contributions: C_e = concentration of electrons, P = pressure, T = temperature, ϕ = electrostatic potential, E = electric field, H = magnetic field and μ_{e0} is the ground state potential due to its interaction with the vacuum. The subscript, e, stands for electron and one or two second order parameters have been neglected.

Based on the work laid out in this book, an expanded and more useful perspective would be

$$\left(\frac{OR}{IS}\right)_e \approx$$

$$f'\left(h,c,e,m_e,g,k,\varepsilon_E,\varepsilon_H,\alpha_{\delta_e},\beta_{I^*e},...;\ \mu'_e,x,y,z,t,k_x,k_y,k_z,k_t\right) \text{ (9.3a)}$$

with $\qquad \mu'_e = f''\left(\mu'_{e_0},c_e,P,T,\phi,E,H,C_\delta,I^*\right).$ $\qquad$ (9.3b)

Here, the new parameters $\alpha_{\delta e}$ and β_{I^*e} have been added to help define the effective contributions of the activated deltron concentration, C_δ, and the intention, I', on the altered generalized potential, μ'_e, as seen by our measurement instruments. One of the wonderful challenges that lie ahead for us is the discovery of the correct formulation for Equation 9.3b, both experimentally and theoretically. As we come to do this, we will probably begin to distinguish D-space and R-space as two aspects of physical reality (lower and higher, respectively) and will probably find that Figures 6.1 and 6.2 have multiple levels as the magnitude of C_δ and I^* increase significantly in our environment.

Psychology

The fields of psychology and psychiatry are very important parts of integrated medicine since they deal with the mind, the emotions and the behavior patterns of humans. The practitioners observe these behaviors and seek to restore internal balance at mind and emotion levels so as to reduce and eliminate what are considered to be aberrant behavior patterns. As such, all of the cornerstones for these practitioner's actions fall outside the foundations of present day physics and biology. This is because there is no place in current quantum mechanics descriptions of nature where one can meaningfully incorporate specifics concerning emotion and mind.

Any model is better than <u>no</u> model as it provides a target at which experiments may be aimed. The perspective and theoretical model underpinning the present work provide the outlines of a framework wherein mind and emotion play a central role in the cognitively observable events found in physical reality. As such, it should be useful as (1) a beginning template for organization of the existing experimental data in psychology and (2) as a vehicle for designing specific experiments to illuminate the key details needed for eventual quantitative understanding in this field. Before proceeding to "nibble" around the edges of this conceptual approach, we should first be clear on the fact that, to many individuals, all aberrant human behavior arises because of their <u>perception</u> that there is a separation between them and God and this is not true. Second, although spirit is in everything and thus is present at all levels of the biobodysuit, we will focus largely on the mind, emotion, R-space and D-space aspects of the model.

Psychologists study the behavior (O.R.) of humans to various seen or hidden input stimuli (I.S.) and use the Equations 9.1 approach to try to understand and help humans alter aberrant behavior. Since the scope and difficulty of such an endeavor needs to be appreciated, it is useful to place an operational number on the size of $\varepsilon_j + x_j$ in Equation 9.1b for a typical problem in various fields of human activity. This, then, provides us with a relative measure of the cost in either dollars or human years of research effort needed to bring the various fields to the same level of reliability. These $\varepsilon_j + x_j$ numbers for a typical problem in various fields are: Physics ($\sim$4), Engineering ($\sim$7-9), Materials Science or Geology ($\sim$20-30), Medicine ($\sim$50-100), Psychology ($\sim$200-500) and Sociology ($\sim$1000-3000). The more complex is the system, the larger is the network of experimental grid points needed to survey the $\varepsilon_j + x_j$ space. The cost and human-years of research effort increase as a power law depending on the grid spacing, d, selected and the degree of reliability chosen with $\varepsilon_j + x_j$ as the exponent; i.e.,

$$\text{Cost} \propto (n/d)^{\varepsilon_j + x_j} \qquad (9.4)$$

where n is the average extent of investigation along any particular coordinate $\varepsilon_j + x_j$. When $n/d \sim 10$, a reasonably good level of quantitative modeling can be achieved and thus reliability of prediction attained. Using the above $\varepsilon_j + x_j$ values for typical problem solving in various fields for the same level of reliability, one can readily see why physics today generates an acceptably reliable science-based technology while several of the other fields are still in an art-based technology stage of development[3]. In particular, for psychology, at this point in human evolution we cannot expect much more from past research than some useful recipes and, even with the present model, one is still only "nibbling around the edges".

Although Equations 9.3 have been designed for electrons, a similar but much more complex form of the equation could be designed by experts for application to the field of psychology. To non-experts like the authors, one would expect, at the D-space level, an array of ε_j relating cerebral cortex functionality, limbic system functionality, old brain-stem functionality and heart system functionality to human behavior. Then, there would be a corresponding set of ε_j needed to express the functionality of their R-space counterparts. Next, the single α_{δ_e} of Equation 9.3a would probably require replacement by a whole new set of ε_j to express the deltron activation spectrum for a range of mind domain imprints. Finally, another set of parameters would need to be defined to properly express the intentionality spectrum for the individual and replace β_{I^*e} in Equation 9.3a.

As we all know, there is a wide spectrum of personality traits from which one may select to create their behavior patterns. Many may be present simultaneously but with quite different proportions of each. This is not unlike the situation that one finds for many complex chemical reactions, although the final desired product molecule is produced by the reaction at a percentage yield which depends on the thermodynamic variables set for the overall reaction, the final chemical soup contains a variety of unwanted chemical intermediates and other isomer products at different yields. Thus, even here, the O.R. for the initial I.S. is a spectrum of the primary possibilities.

Genetic predispositions, in the absence of other factors, create particular time-unfolding infrastructure "wiring" in the various layers of our biobodysuits. And, of course, some of these may be defective relative to the norm. Habituation reinforces the prevailing infrastructure while traumatic or sensitizing life experiences lead to alterations in this infrastructure. An example that is useful to recall at this point is "Wolf's Law of Bone Structure". If one of our bones receives a non-uniform stress for an extended period of time, the bone will grow new trabeculae (a type of bone girder) in the exact location needed to maximally support this stress distribution. The physical strain field probably interacts with the electrostatic field of the system (via the piezoelectric effect) producing certain field changes, and these changes cause ions and molecules to be transported to specific locations where they can agglomerate into the specific tissue and structural components of the trabeculae. Carrying this idea further, one can conceive of emotional and mental field patterns as acting like a stress to influence the key potentials in the other layers of the biobodysuit and leading thereby to new infrastructure development in these layers.

In terms of this "trabeculae" picture, it is important to realize that, when we remove the body stress that initially created a certain pattern of trabeculae in the bone, these trabeculae do not dissolve at once, rather, they may dissolve only very slowly (under a proper regime of physical exercise) because of the detailed molecular dynamics involved. Thus, they may maintain the body in a distorted shape for quite a long time. The same may be said for those infrastructure changes generated as a response to emotional or mental stress. Finally, since mind is the builder, long term, sustained and focussed intention can be utilized by any of us to alter the infrastructure of the various layers in our biobodysuits.

Before closing this section, it is perhaps important to point out that the fine structure temporal periodicities noted in the Shnoll et al type of data (see pages 357-358) can be expected to appear in some form within psychological data. Much more can be learned by trying to quantitatively understand this type of experimental data. Perhaps even more important for psychologists will be to come to a full understanding of why some ITC (instrumental transcommunication) sites on earth yield clear audio and video communication between our cognitive domain and the "unseen" domains of nature while others, with the same type of technical equipment, do not! Clearly, the technical equipment is a <u>necessary</u> but not a <u>sufficient</u> condition for replication of the ITC phenomenon. It obviously does not belong to the U(1) Gauge symmetry paradigm of our current physics' worldview. Instead, it belongs to a higher symmetry paradigm that manifests significant non-random <u>coupling correlations</u> with higher dimensions of the universe. In this higher symmetry state, proper human motivations, intentions, sincerity, etc., are very important parts of the set of "sufficient" conditions for replication of the ITC phenomenon.

To create a successful consciousness bridge for such interdimensional communication and cooperation, all scientists must come to recognize that their entire personal set of physical and vacuum-level broadcast fields are important variables influencing the phenomenon under investigation. Thus, they must become highly inner self-managed in order to stabilize the intensity of these personal fields during the course of any experiment of this type.

Integrated Medicine

The old view of medicine's relationship to human treatment is much like that of an auto mechanic to a car. First, the car is a finite thing with specific parts that need adjusting or replacing. Second, the mechanic utilizes his learned knowledge, motor skills and basic intelligence to perform these manipulations. Finally, only the outer layer of the biobodysuit has relevance to this auto mechanic model of health care.

The new view of medicine is an integrated multidimensional view wherein the subtle domain levels of the practitioner, the patient and the universe, to some degree, all cooperate in the repair, balancing and transformation process. This means that the attitudes, intentions and personal energy fields along with intellectual, knowledge and motor skills plus tools of the practitioner are combinatorially important in the treatment process. It also means that the attitudes, intentions, personal energy fields, etc., of the patient are also critically involved in the treatment process. It also means that the unseen forces of nature may be encouraged to cooperatively participate in the treatment process. Finally, it also means that the health care practitioner, the treatment locale, the patient and the unseen forces of nature can all, via sustained and specifically directed intention, increase the level of coherence in their local selves and environment so that the in-phase power density of the energies involved in the overall cooperative treatment process can be greatly enhanced.

This new view of medicine also sheds strong light on the so-called placebo effect. The prevailing medical view is that nothing real has occurred and that any improvement is only delusional. In Benson's work among patients receiving a variety of treatments they believed in, but for which medicine finds no physiological basis, the treatments were effective 70% to 90% of the time. However, when the physicians began to doubt whether these treatments really worked, their effectiveness dropped to 30% to 40%[4]. Similar belief-related success was observed in Wolf's work with women who experienced persistent nausea and vomiting during pregnancy[5]. Sensors were positioned in their stomachs so that contractions could be recorded. Next, they were given a drug that they were told would cure their nausea. In fact, they were given ipecac. However, because of their belief, the women reversed the laboratory-proven action of the drug, and their measured stomach contractions damped down to negligible values. From these studies and more like them, it can be seen that belief fuels expectations and expectations, in turn, marshal intention at both unconscious and conscious levels to fulfill expectations. The experiments described in this book tend to both scientifically validate that perspective and also illuminate some of the key factors involved.

References

1.   W.A. Tiller, <u>Science and Human Transformation: Subtle Energies, Intentionality and Consciousness</u> (Pavior Publishing, Walnut Creek, CA, 1997).

2.   D.I. Radin, <u>The Conscious Universe</u>, (Harper Edge, San Francisco, 1997).

3.   W.A. Tiller, Science, <u>146</u> (1964) 871.

4.   H. Benson and M. Stark, "Timeless Healing: The Power and Biology of Belief," (Scribner, New York, NY, 1996).

5.   S. Wolf, "Educating Doctors," (Transaction Publishers, New Brunswick, N.J., 1997) pp. 109-114, 135-145.

CHAPTER 10

Some Implications For Science and Technology

As a foundation for this chapter, it is useful to begin by listing, first the general experimental facts discovered during this work and, second, the theoretical premises upon which our deductions have been made. These will form the basis for our statements concerning this book's implications for science and technology.

The General Experimental Facts

1. A decidedly non-physical processing procedure involving human consciousness has been applied to one of two identical physical devices (electronic) so as to significantly expand the capabilities of the processed device (labeled IIED) compared to the unprocessed device (labeled the "control").

2. Unless the processed and unprocessed devices are effectively isolated from one another, even while in the "off" state, the unprocessed device acquires a significant measure of the processing and begins to manifest the capabilities of the processed device (IIED) so that the initial "control" for the experiments is lost.

3. At the moment, an effective isolation procedure is to wrap each device in aluminum foil and store it in it's own electrically-grounded, Faraday cage.

4. At present, a single "imprinting" process session keeps a device "charged up" with respect to it's specific intention for an effective use time of 3-4 months if properly shielded between use periods.

5. Reimprinting of a specific device with it's specific intention on a 3-4 month cycle leads to no apparent reduction in the device's capability to broadcast the assigned intention when in the "on" state.

6. Recharging the device's electrical batteries does not appear to interfere with the strength of the intention imprint residing in the device.

7.   The present processing procedure involves the meditation of four accomplished human processors who mentally hold a specific intention for the specific device placed on a table before them (in the "on" state) while they are in this special meditative state. The device performance subsequently expresses that intention into the physical space of the target experiment when it is placed nearby and is turned on.

8. The experimental data robustly supports the IIEDs use to either increase or decrease the pH of purified water by one full pH unit, a result that is 50-100 times larger than the measurement accuracy for the device. This data also indicates that water in the presence of an "on" IIED leads to significantly more coherent pH-behavior than in the presence of an "on" control device.

9.   The experimental data robustly supports ($p<0.001$) the IIEDs use to significantly increase the [ATP]/[ADP] ratio in developing fruit fly larvae (*Drosophila melanogaster*) so as to reduce larval development time, $T_{1/2}$, by a significant factor. This data also indicated that the ambient, unshielded, electromagnetic fields inside the incubator were a significant stressor for the growth of [ATP]/[ADP] ratio and decrease of $T_{1/2}$. Likewise, the specific MHz electromagnetic fields due to the control device (power less than 1 microwatt) was a statistically significant ($p<0.001$) stressor. Importantly, although the electromagnetic radiation was expected to be identical for the IIED as for the control device, the growth of [ATP]/[ADP] ratio and decrease of $T_{1/2}$ were significantly different ($p<0.001$) for the IIED compared to the control device.

10.   The experimental data robustly supports ($p<0.001$) the IIEDs use to significantly increase the *in vitro* thermodynamic activity of the liver enzyme, alkaline phosphatase (ALP) by a statistically significant factor. The data also indicated that both the ambient, unshielded EM fields and the ambient shielded, specific MHz, EM fields of the control device inside the incubator significantly reduced ($p<0.001$) the ALP activity while the IIED in the same environment significantly increased ($p<0.001$) the ALP activity.

11.   The experimental data robustly supports ($p<0.001$) the IIEDs use to significantly increase the [ATP]/[ADP] ratio via electron transport chain activity for *in vitro* larval homogenates. The data indicated that the presence of NAD (nicotinamide adenine dinucleotide) significantly ($p<0.001$) amplified the effects of four simultaneous and specific purified water treatments applied to these homogenates inside the incubator: (1) control, (2) inside a Faraday

cage with no device, (3) inside a Faraday cage with an IIED in the "on" state and (4) inside a Faraday cage with a control device in the "on" state. Most importantly, statistically significant ($p<0.001$) differences were found to be present after just the four water treatments with no additional NAD present.

12. The experimental data robustly supports ($p<0.001$) the use of the liver enzyme, ALP, as a detector of what certainly appear to be non-direct space, physical effects. Statistically significant ($p<0.001$) variations in ALP activity were found for the ALP-detector placed inside the incubator when: (1) an empty Faraday cage (electrically grounded) was placed on the incubator shelf remote from the ALP-detector and the number of copper layers, n, in the walls of the cage changed, (2) $n=0$ compared with $n=1$ while adding either an unimprinted or imprinted device (on or off) at different locations in the cage and (3) replacing the device of (2) with one to three ALP-vessels.

13. The experimental data robustly supports the occurrence of some type of "conditioning" taking place in the local physical space surrounding an activated IIED so that, after some critical conditioning time, the IIED can be removed and significantly different property measurements are observed in that locale compared to an unconditioned locale located ~20-50 feet away.

14. Our best present estimate of the treatment time needed to condition a new experimental locale is ~3 months whether one uses a "water" IIED or a specific IIED designed only to produce locale conditioning. This conditioning time appears to vary somewhat depending upon the consciousness of the humans entering/staying/leaving that locale.

15. The experimental data shows that, in a partially conditioned locale compared to an unconditioned locale, small temperature oscillations first begin to appear in the air. This is followed, at slightly longer conditioning times, by the appearance of pH-oscillations, σ-oscillations and T-oscillations in the water. At still longer conditioning times, the amplitudes of all these oscillations grow in magnitude and one begins to detect significant values of ΔpH_s^N, the pH change associated with a north-pole DC magnetic field polarity applied to the water versus with a south-pole DC magnetic field polarity applied to the water (magnitudes sometimes larger than 1 pH unit). The magnitude of these oscillations can often attain 2-3° C and 0.25 pH units.

16. The experimental data shows that the well-developed oscillations are of both a long period nature (~diurnal) and a short period nature (~20-80 minutes) with 4-6 harmonics making up the periodic short period wave. In almost all cases, the T-oscillation waveform and the pH-oscillation waveform are highly correlated with closely nested power spectra. It appears that, when the absolute magnitude of the rate of ambient temperature change, $|dT/dt|$, exceeds a certain value, a short period oscillation train is either initiated or terminated.

17. The present experimental data shows that a conditioned locale, in the absence of an IIED, can continue to exhibit such anomalous behavior for a very long time -- over a year in one locale (to date).

18. In experiments with two monitored water vessels displaced a considerable distance apart (100-900 feet), with each vessel in it's own electrically-grounded Faraday cage and with both locales being conditioned locales, the initiation of short period oscillations in one vessel leads to highly correlated short period oscillations in the other. If only one of the locales is conditioned but a water-type IIED in the "on" state is present at the unconditioned locale and short period oscillations initiated, then highly correlated short period oscillations appear in the vessel located in the conditioned locale.

19. With the measurement apparatus in a conditioned locale, if one removes one of the system components (such as a computer) and replaces it with a new one, the oscillations disappear for several to many hours and then gradually reappear.

20. For some materials, when one adds even a small amount of a specific material into a conditioned locale, the oscillations may disappear for a very long time (many weeks) before weakly reappearing.

New Meaning For Humanity From These Facts

(a) Under some conditions, it is indeed possible to attach an aspect of human consciousness, a specific intention, to a simple electrical device and have that device, when activated, robustly influence an experiment conducted in its vicinity in complete accord with the attached intention. Thus, if they do it right, humans can influence their environment via specific, sustained intentions.

(b) Under the specific conditions surrounding the four accomplished meditators, their procedural techniques and their seeming connections to levels of the universe different than normal physical reality, they appear to precipitate something with intelligence into these electrical devices and the devices then become potent surrogates for communicating the prime directive intention to the target experiment. Moreover, the level of nature at which this communication occurs appears to be dominant over events in the physical domain.

(c) When activated, an IIED appears to manifest a thermodynamic potential of sufficient magnitude and specificity so as to cause energy flows and chemical reactions in the physical domain to drive in those necessary directions needed to fulfill the specific prime directive imbedded in the device. Furthermore, this seems to apply to inorganic and organic as well as inanimate and animate materials.

(d) Continued use of these activated IIEDs in a particular locale, seems to change the substratum of that locale so that nature expresses itself differently than in normal locales even after the IIED has been removed and deactivated. This different expression of nature manifests itself as anomalous but reproducible property measurement.

(e) Some new field appears to be involved in the information passage that occurs between conditioned locales that are widely separated from each other in physical space. Even with transmitters and receivers located inside electrically-grounded Faraday cages, highly correlated patterns of information appeared in the remotely located locales.

(f) Some type of field is present that is able to transfer the specific intention, in the unshielded device case from an "off" IIED to an "off" unimprinted control device, even when the two devices are separated in physical space by very large distances. Thus, in this type of experiment, great care is needed to ensure effective isolation between the "control" and the IIED.

(g) Although we don't fully understand them, we now have some new tools with which to probe the deeper structures of the universe and a new adventure is underway for humanity!

Implications for Some Fields Of Science

The most general implication of this experimental work for all scientific fields is that human intention can have a significant time-averaged contribution to the spectrum of thermodynamic potentials that affect the basic processes involved in physical phenomena. Under certain circumstances, these effects can be quite large; thus, future scientific investigations must all evaluate the magnitude of the human-field contribution to the measurement. The second general implication is that the substratum (vacuum baseline) of an experimental locale appears to be stable in at least two states of quite different symmetry so that physical materials have different property measurement behavior according to which state of symmetry is being manifested by the locale. Thus, in the future, one must consider measurement locale as a possible variable in the measurement process. In a recent editorial by Philip Anderson[1], he cites the importance of the chiral anomaly (and similar phenomena) raised by Jackiw in his Dirac Prize lecture[2] and this may be relevant here as a key subtle effect in quantum field theory. To quote Anderson[1],

"When one expects the currents of right-handed and left-handed massless Dirac fermions to be separately conserved, in fact it is only their sum, the so-called vector current, that is perfectly conserved when there are interactions, as a result of things that happen at high energies within the supposedly inert sea of negative energy states. The fact that the two chiralities of Dirac fermions are not independent leads to large effects like the mass of the P meson. This poses, again, a serious problem for condensed matter theorists: when can we ignore the dynamics of our Fermi seas of filled states? When do separate left-spinning and right-spinning (that is, chiral) quasi particles suffice, and when do they decay into something else? The notorious "linear T" resistivity observed in the cuprates (the observed scattering rate whose frequency and temperature dependence is incompatible with quasiparticle theory) is very likely to be a manifestation of just this kind of decay."

Perhaps Anderson[1] is unknowingly revealing to us that the states of the vacuum are characterized by more than just their relative, negative energy but perhaps also by some other quality (maybe an aspect of consciousness).

Let us now become more specific and consider the implications for a few specific fields.

Physics: This is a paradigm-changing body of work because it demonstrates (a) a significant new thermodynamic potential functioning in nature, presumably at the level of the vacuum, (b) this new potential is associated with an aspect of consciousness, specifically, sustained human intention, (c) this new potential can be mentally imbedded into a simple electrical device (IIED) so that the device then manifests a type of intelligence closely related to the specific imbedded intention and can broadcast that intelligence to a nearby target experiment. This target experiment then manifests measured property changes consistent with this imbedded intention. It is presumed that this physical property control occurs via this imbedded intelligence influencing the coherence condition of the negative energy states in the vacuum and (d) continued use of these devices in a particular locale leads to what appears to be a structural phase transition in the vacuum so that, what was once a single-phase, highly-disordered vacuum appears to have become at least a binary-phase vacuum. This second phase manifests a higher level of symmetry (higher Gauge, reflective of the presence of magnetic monopoles) than the primary phase vacuum (lower Gauge, amorphous-like). Significant property measurement changes of the oscillating type (very reminiscent of standard coherence phenomena seen in a two-phase system) is associated with the development of this higher symmetry vacuum phase.

The theoretical modeling used to rationalize and perhaps understand these new phenomena is a ten plus-dimensional one with the original intention being injected from a higher dimensional space (like a boundary condition) onto an ordered array of nodal points existing at the 10-dimensional vacuum level.[3] This consciousness imprint pattern is diffracted (broadcast) from this 10-D mind nodal network, NN_M, onto a 4-dimensional superlattice-type network of uniquely distinguishable nodal points (relative to this NN_M primary set) called the reciprical-space nodal network, NN_R, which may or may not be disordered. This pattern, in turn, is diffracted (broadcast) onto an even larger superlattice-type network of uniquely distinguishable nodal points (relative to both NN_M and NN_R) called the direct-space nodal network, NN_D, which may or may not be disordered. It is these nodal networks that communicate information, via consciousness/energy conversion, to the various substances operating in these spaces.

Through the agency of a nine-dimensional coupling substance in the vacuum, called deltrons, the faster than light magnetic monopoles functioning in reciprocal space (the coarsest level of the vacuum) can interact with the electric monopole substance functioning in the direct space of physical matter. The vacuum phase transition mentioned above involves an ordered phase formation of magnetic monopole substance phase of R-space. These magnetic monopoles of R-space travel so fast that they "write" the waves, thought to be the de Broglie pilot waves, controlling the movement of particles in D-space.[4]

A symmetry principle, called the mirror principle is thought to operate between D-space substances and R-space substances so that the monopole charge singularities in one space produce dipole images through this mirror into the other space.[4] Likewise, the monopole mass singularities in one space produce images through this mirror into the other space. Thus, the negative monopole mass singularities of R-space are thought to be the origin of the "dark matter" we currently detect with our instruments in D-space. Whether or not this image is also of the dipole type or is a higher multipole image depends upon the tensorial qualities of this mirror for mass singularities.[4] In this model, what we presently call particle spin in current descriptions of physics is directly related to the character of the de Broglie pilot wave that surrounds and guides the particle.

Maxwell's equations, that we utilize in standard D-space electromagnetic (EM) calculations, arise as a consequence of the electric monopoles plus magnetic dipole images in D-space. A corresponding set of equations in R-space involving magnetic monopoles and electric dipole images generate a new field in the vacuum (in R-space) labeled magnetoelectrism (ME).[3,4] As deltron coupling increases between these two monopole substances functioning in their respective spaces, non-linear coupling occurs between Maxwell's equations and this corresponding set of equations in R-space to produce what has been labeled augmented-electromagnetic fields.[4,5] These various augmented-electromagnetic fields are thought to be the various forms of Qi mentioned in Asian literature.[6]

Since the primary model is a wave diffraction model[3], the equilibrium relationship between a particular quality in R-space substance and that same quality in D-space substance is given by a Fourier transform over the dimensionality of the coordinate space involved. Thus, any physical measurement we make involves the sum of the mathematically real modulus (with deltron coupling) from each space. This means that, as human intention or IIEDs significantly increase the local deltron coupling, the magnitude of the result for the property being measured can change, often by very large factors. This will clearly be a challenge to tomorrow's physics.

One might ask why we have decided to communicate our work to the scientific community in this form rather than publish it in a series of papers in respected physics and biology journals. We have, of course, tried to follow that accepted path; however, the results so boggle the mindsets of most reviewers that the work is unconsciously (and maybe consciously) looked upon as a form of heresy so the papers are always rejected. Some of our work has been published in lesser known journals more accepting of anomalous material. Because of space limitations, however, the overall perspective has not been easily available to the public in this format. With the present book format, the scope and implications of the overall study can be more clearly seen by the reader.

Here, we have laid out our results with experiments carried out at both Stanford and Minnesota sites by the same experimenters (with added technician help in Minnesota). An important step, yet to be achieved in the "birth" of this new science, is to have other investigators, independent of us and in their own laboratories, reproduce and extend this type of work. An equally important intermediate step, yet to be initiated (when and if new funding becomes available), is to have us "seed" this type of work in three or four laboratories around the country to "prime the pump" so to speak. Only then will the full requirement of science for new ground-breaking work be satisfied, "reproducibility by others". One slight difficulty with this was laid out via Equations 1 of Chapter 6; i.e., some minimum level of inner self-management of the experimenters involved is needed to keep the "leakage" rate from exceeding the "pumping" rate due to the IIEDs so that the vacuum coherence level of the experimental locale grows with time.

Biology: One important side issue of the present work is that ambient broadband EM radiation as well as low power MHz EM radiation act as a significant biological stressor which (1) reduces the [ATP]/[ADP] ratio in at least one simple life form (*Drosophila melanogaster*), (2) reduces the thermodynamic activity of at least one enzyme, alkaline phosphatase and (3) structures water in a long-term memory-inducing way. This is probably an indication of a more general effect that is important for all of biology. This doesn't mean that all EM effects are negative for biological systems but some certainly are.

The fact that IIEDs can profoundly affect the pH of purified water, and can probably do likewise with many other water properties, indicates a central role for this type of device for *in vitro* cell biology research and *in vivo* research on living organisms, including humans. The IIEDs produce a manifested increase in the level of coherence of the water (presumably and primarily at the vacuum level which influences the physical level) compared to an unimprinted device with its above-mentioned EMF effects. This is expected to have profound implications for all levels of biological systems. Certainly, the IIED-effect on increasing [ATP]/[ADP] ratios in both *in vivo* fruit fly studies and in *in vitro* larval homogenate studies support such a view. Clearly, the electron transport chain is being significantly influenced in both cases.

The present biological community seriously appreciates the importance of enzyme conformations in aqueous solutions towards their catalytic efficiency; however, they do not yet appreciate that their free energy, via their R-space modulus, is also strongly conformation dependent and that this contribution can be significantly altered by focussed human intention, whether stored in an IIED or not. This is a very important area for future research investigations.

The importance of R-space potentization, as in homeopathic practices, is neither appreciated nor understood by today's biological community. Their old mindsets are seriously distorting their perceptions of the topic which has great power for application in future biology. It is very important for biology to move to a new world view wherein changes at both the level of physical substance and the level of the vacuum can seriously affect biological functioning.

As a final note to this section, it is important to highlight the achievement that biological detectors of subtle energies are now available and that they can be meaningfully utilized to help us understand qualitatively, and predict quantitatively, interactions between the R-space aspect (coarsest level of the vacuum) and the D-space aspect (physical substance) of biological systems. We have a rare opportunity to open our eyes here to a larger perspective of nature to the greater benefit of both biology and humankind!

Electrical Engineering: In this area of activity, the present work has many strong implications for new understanding and new technology. In particular, when one delineates EM-waves from ME-waves from augmented-EM waves, one sees that there appear to be new possibilities for communication that do not have some of the limitations of the present, purely D-space, EM-communication modalities. This is somewhat expressed by Figures 7.5 to 7.8 and the surrounding discussion. There, we see the R-space modulus in k_j-coordinate format for a variety of D-space shapes. Now, if we wish to construct a simple dipole antenna from the superposition of such line objects, its R-space modulus for this D-space form can be readily calculated following the procedures described in Chapter 7. Now, when we activate this dipole antenna form with a driving voltage, $V(w^*, t)$, of resonant frequency, w^*, for the specific dimension of this dipole antenna, the following questions come to mind: (1) what are the D-space and R-space field moduli maps associated with the time-dependent charge distribution in this antenna?, (2) what is the mechanism of photon generation within this antenna material?, (3) what is the photon spectrum and time-dependent spatial distribution emitted from this antenna?, (4) how does (3) change as the conductivity, electron mobility and electron mean free path change for the antenna material? and (5) how do the magnitudes of these factors change as one increases the deltron coupling between the R-space and D-space substances?

Another common example to further illustrate the point of the previous paragraph comes from considering present-day EEG (electroencephalogram) measurement procedures. The present procedure is to take the time-varying voltages measured at various locations, r_j, on the head, $V(r_j, t)$, and look at the power spectrum distributed over the frequency domain of delta, theta, alpha and beta brain waves. However, following the basic procedures of Equations 8.1 and 8.2 plus Table 8.1 allows us to learn more discrete information concerning the various biobodysuit layers of the individual's brain.

The increased coherence in a measurement that one observes with the use of an IIED in comparison to an unimprinted but otherwise identical device is considered to be a general phenomenon that could be characterized by its signal/noise ratio. The IIEDs appear to generate a higher signal to noise ratio by reducing the noise level in the environment. Thus, their use is appropriate for information systems of all sorts. Existing technological devices, like computers, should benefit from their use as would any information system needing increased channel capacity. This should apply particularly well to quantum computers now under development because, with the IIEDs one appears to be reducing noise fluctuations that arise from the vacuum level (the wave aspect in quantum mechanics). Since any physical measurement involves both a D-space contribution as well as an R-space contribution and, since the D-space particle behavior is controlled by the R-space wave behavior[4], it seems reasonable to propose both higher fidelity and larger channel capacity for electrical engineering systems wherein more coherence exists in the "primary driver".

The questions "what is the intelligence that is somehow "housed" in the larger aspects of the IIEDs?" and "where in this "structure" does this intelligence reside?" are certainly intriguing ones. Because the prime directive of the particular IIED is able to be effectively communicated to seemingly all aspects of the chemical reaction systems involved in the associated target experiments, this intelligence is thought to largely reside in the various substructures of the vacuum. Obviously, much work needs to be done to gain some real understanding of this new phenomenon in nature.

As a final input to this section, it seems worthwhile to address the question of superconductivity with all its technological implications for future humanity. As is well known, the phenomenon of superconductivity is related to a condition or conditions of coherence in the material which are sustained in that state in spite of the increasing magnitude of D-space energy fluctuations as the temperature is increased. In low temperature superconductivity, it is thought to be highly correlated movements of lattice phonons with conduction electrons in the paired state. In high temperature superconductivity, it is a more complex picture, seemingly related to electron populations in s and d-states. In both of these cases, the D-space conditions rest upon a seemingly amorphous (with respect to magnetic monopole positions) R-space vacuum substratum. However, now we seem to have a vehicle for influencing the basic coherence level in the vacuum which, in turn, influences all particle behavior at the D-space level[4]. This may be the pathway humanity needs to develop a science of room temperature superconductivity!

Implications For Some Technologies

Perhaps the most general point to be emphasized, when one wants to put IIEDs to work to either upgrade an existing technology or to create a new one, is illustrated by revisiting Equations 1 of Chapter 6. These are:

$$Q_C \approx Q_D + Q_{LS} + Q_{Eq} + Q_E \qquad (10.1a)$$

$$\approx (Q_D' - \int_{t_1}^{t_2} q_D dt) + (Q_{LS}' - \int_{t_1}^{t_2} q_{LS} dt) + (Q_{Eq}' - \int_{t_1}^{t_2} q_{Eq} dt)$$

$$+ (\int_{t_1}^{t_3} Q_E' dt - \int_{t_1}^{t_2} q_E dt) \qquad (10.1b)$$

Here, Q_C is the total coupling effect between D-space materials plus the processing space and the levels of the vacuum, the subscripts, D, LS, Eq and E stand for Device (IIED), Local Space, Equipment and Experimenter (people working in the space). Equation 10.1b expresses the fact that each of the contributions in Equation 10.1a contain some intrinsic leakage rate, q_j, whose integral over the time interval t_1 to t_2 may be large enough to convert Q_C from initially positive to negative values. Thus, not only is device design important so the Q'_D can be a large positive value and q_D a small positive value, but one wishes to minimize the values of q_E and q_{LS} while maximizing the value of Q'_E. For this ambient human contribution to the conditioning process, one places a premium on employees who are highly inner self-managed and encourages the practice of Siddha Yoga, Qigong and heart focus techniques by all workers. Further, although it is important to recognize that inner self-management gives an employee access to intuition-type skills, these do not completely compensate for the lack of precise, formal knowledge so as to be able to efficiently put the intuitive insights to work in this physical reality. Thus, one would like both qualities to be present in employees for these new technologies.

Let us now consider various technological applications.

1. Water Treatment For Health Care: The most obvious application from the work done to date is to produce bottled purified water for human consumption with special properties. One would be purified water with a pH of ~8, when in equilibrium with atmospheric CO_2. The purpose for this water would be to allow humans to balance the pH of their body fluids in spite of a normally acidic diet that most people consume these days. A variant of this water for the same commercial market would be to utilize an IIED that increases the oxygen solubility of purified water 5-fold to 10-fold. This water would be an energizing metabolic boost for the human body either at work or during athletic endeavors. Of course, it would have great medical benefits for people with a variety of ailments. On a more industrial scale, combinations of such waters would find great utility in community sewage processing plants, water treatment plants, garden and farm watering systems as well as reclamation projects for lakes and waterways. It would be interesting to see if nitrogen solubility in water could be significantly increased with special IIED technology so that we might reduce our dependence on commercial fertilizers that have the unwanted byproduct of polluting our ground water systems. Many obvious extensions exist in this area.

2. Enhancing Brain Coherence In Humans: Although utilizing a different device processing technique than the IIEDs discussed in this book, there is already a commercial device on the market that purports to do this so that extracts from their advertising literature will illustrate the point.[7] The device is a pendant worn around the neck and contains, supposedly, sympathetic resonant technology that helps the wearer stay more focused and balanced. They advertise the QLink for people to lower their golf scores with the following specific statement "the QLink is the best tool for reducing stress and enhancing your overall sports performance. The QLink helps you get into that "sweet spot" called the Zone -- and helps you stay there! So you play better, score lower, and enjoy your game more." Many laudatory, unpaid testimonials have been provided by golf professionals in support of such a statement. They also make the following advertising statement, "Both alternative and traditional doctors have tested the QLink pendant and report that it neutralizes the EMF mind/body stress effects from computers, cell phones and other electronic devices."

Most of the supporting data for the QLink is in the form of testimonials. However, because the EMF consequences for humans are potentially so significant, and because of the strong EMF effects we have reported in Chapters 3-6 of this book, Dr. C. Norman Shealy and one of us have recently conducted a double blind clinical test of human EEG-response to both an electromagnetic (EM) stressor and a Clarus QLink device.[8] The detailed analysis of this data is currently in process; however, preliminary assessment of this data indicates that wearing the Clarus QLink beneficially moderates the influence of our particular EM stressor on the subjects' EEG's.

Future home, business or hospital use of IIEDs, specifically designed and imprinted for strengthening the human immune system against EMFs, chemical toxicity, mental and emotional stress, etc., is expected to play an important role in our evolving human society. An obvious extension of these considerations to sophisticated military and space-flight vehicles should be noted.

3. Chemical and Pharmaceutical Industries:

In these industries, large processing plants exist that are dedicated to producing particular chemical isomers or biological enantiomers. These are very profitable ventures, with sales often in the billions of dollars per year, even when the yield of the desired product in the basic process is fairly small and it must be carefully separated from the unwanted byproducts. Specially designed and carefully imprinted IIEDs prepared for this application area could be utilized to "tilt" the chemical reaction process path so as to generate an enriched yield of the desired isomer or enantiomer.

To seriously investigate such a possibility one would start with a simple laboratory bench top apparatus and well known separation procedures which statistically produce a given yield of the desired product. Then, one would add the appropriate IIEDs into the environment, just as was done in Chapters 3-5, to see what increase in yield can be attained. Then, one would "condition" a separate space and, when ready, one would transport this original apparatus into that space and, with the old or upgraded IIEDs, redo the yield experiment. With a satisfactory result, the next step would be to condition a larger space for the smallest, realistic pilot plant that scales up the process towards profitable commercialization. Finally, one would tackle the challenge of "conditioning" a true commercial plant scale operation so as to produce the enhanced yield of the desired product. There is expected to be a significant "learning curve" involved with growing Q_C (see Equations 10.1) into the positive range and materialize large yield enhancements from such a large-scale enterprise.

4. Semiconductor Fabrication Lab Facility: The semiconductor processing involved in modern integrated circuit (IC) manufacturing is extremely complex and "high tech". The key to profitability is to be found in the device yields of the various sequential stages in this manufacturing process. As we go to smaller and smaller IC sizes plus larger and larger number of ICs per wafer, the requirements become increasingly stringent and the local intelligence imbedded in nearby IIEDs is expected to make such requirements more manageable. The initial proof of principle and scaling-up steps to a practical system is expected to follow those outlined in the previous example.

5. Crystal Growth With An Ordered Internal Vacuum Phase: This example is a test case for any materials processing application (such as superconductors, magnetic disks, lasers, solar cells, etc.) so let us consider it to be the growth of commercial size silicon crystals. The goal would be to manufacture such crystals so that, when they are finally pulled from the furnace, the substratum of vacuum, internal to the D-space single crystal of silicon atoms, will be in the form of an R-space single crystal of the magnetic monopole counterpart substance to these silicon atoms. The experimental approach would be similar to that laid out for the two previous examples; i.e., one would begin with a small laboratory size, silicon crystal puller and fully "condition" both the apparatus and the surrounding space before attempting to grow such vacuum-ordered single crystals. Of course, the development of experimental testing procedures to determine the presence and defect nature of such a vacuum-ordered phase will be no mean feat in itself. Once such techniques are available and reliable, the scale-up to commercial size would follow the stages mentioned for the two previous examples.

6. Enhanced Computer Coherence: Because IIEDs reduce the noise level in the vacuum and thus enhance the signal to noise ratio in information systems, one expects that some interesting consequences might be forthcoming by imprinting an IIED for use with a specific type of computer. Different computers behave differently with respect to environmental conditioning as was demonstrated to us during the 1999 holiday season when we discovered what we have called the "millenium effect". In a conditioned space (a 9' x 9' room) we placed two maximally separated computers with a proximal pseudo-random number generator associated with each. One computer was a Macintosh while the other was a PC. We set the PC running on Dec 20 (October 29 for the Mac) and let the systems continuously record until late in January and no one entered the room during the holiday period. Figure 6.43 shows the results for the Macintosh that clearly reveals the change in randomness recorded by its pseudo-random number generator. This change is what we have dubbed the millenium effect. Figure 6.37 shows the results for the PC and it also shows the millenium effect but with a reverse pattern of randomness with time during this interval. Without attempting any detailed explanation, it seems clear that different brands of computers respond differently to subtle energies. Such differences are expected to have great practical value.

7. Integrated Medicine Applications: This is a vast area with many, many components. To illustrate, let us begin with some specifics and then move to the general. IIEDs could be developed to beneficially adjust the body functioning of individuals with specific categories of serious ailments such as diabetes, kidney dialysis needs, arthritis, high blood pressure, etc. IIEDs could be created to beneficially modify the needs of individual critically ill patients. Perhaps they could be utilized to ameliorate the conditions of AIDS or cancer patients or premature babies since they can adjust internal chemical reactions. For more general use, IIEDs could be utilized to condition the office space for general practitioners, psychologists or psychiatrists so that greater clarity of perception is available or where intention effects need to be enhanced to "prime the pump" of key change for the patient. IIEDs could be generated for application in hospital rooms to produce a sense of well-being, to enhance healing rate and to reduce suffering, especially for terminally ill patients, and to encourage individual fitness for newborn babies in the nursery. Finally, even for the surgery, IIEDs could be designed to enhance alertness and focus of the operating room team while simultaneously relieving their tensions. Beyond all of the foregoing, the use of IIEDs in the development of new diagnostic and treatment instrumentation plus therapeutic modalities promises to be an interesting adventure. As we begin to tap some of the potential associated with ordered phases being present in the vacuum, the face of medicine will drastically change -- and for the better!

References

1.   P.W. Anderson, "Reference Frame, Brainwashed by Feynman?", Physics Today, February 2000, p. 11-12.

2.   R. Jackiw, Helv. Phys. Acta 59 (1986) 835.

3.   W.A. Tiller, Science and Human Transformation: Subtle Energies, Intentionality and Consciousness (Pavior Publishing, Walnut Creek, CA, 1997).

4.   W.A. Tiller, "Towards a Predictive Model of Subtle Domain Connections to the Physical Domain Aspect of Reality: The Origins of Wave-Particle Duality, Electric-Magnetic Monopoles and the Mirror Principle", J. Scientific Exploration, 13 (1999) 41.

5.   W.A. Tiller, "Augmented Electromagnetic Waves and Qi Energy", Coherence, 1 (2000) 13.

6.   K.S. Cohen, The Way of Qigong: The Art and Science of Chinese Energy Healing (Ballantine Press, New York, 1997).

7.   QLink, Clarus Products International, L.L.C.; 1330 Lincoln Avenue, Suite 210; San Rafael, California 94901.

8.   C.N. Shealy, T.L. Smith, P. Thomlinson and W.A. Tiller, "A Double-Blind EEG-Response Test For A Supposed Electromagnetic Field-Neutralizing Device, Part I: Via The Clinician Expertise Procedure", Subtle Energy and Energy Med., 9 (2000) 231.

Index

A

allopathic medicine, 2, 32

4-Nitrophenol (4NP), 109

4-Nitrophenyl Phosphate (4-NPP), 109

Abelian algebra U(1) Gauge, 1, 53, 314, 334, 339

activation barrier, 102, 103, 104, 107

active sites, 105, 351

adenosine triphosphate (ATP), 20, 107, 123, 124, 144, 146, 147, 148, 149, 150, 157, 158, 159, 272

adsorption, 96, 101, 279

agglomeration, 75, 289, 290, 292, 311

albumin, 68, 351

algebra (Abelian, non-Abelian), 1, 53, 334, 370

algorithm, 220, 221, 223, 226, 228, 229, 231, 236

alkaline phosphatase (ALP), 13, 20, 102, 108-119, 125-127, 130-136, 139, 274, 394, 396, 401, 402

ALP activity (ALP), 108, 110, 112, 113, 114, 115, 116, 118, 119, 125, 130, 131, 135, 136, 394, 396

amended Maxwell equations, 336, 337

amorphous, 312, 313, 352, 353, 399, 404

amplification, 194

ANOVA, 112, 113, 116, 118, 121, 123, 132, 133, 134, 136, 137, 138, 139, 140, 141, 153, 154, 166, 167

antimatter, 35

antiparticle, 35

archetypal intention, 349

Argand diagram, 318, 319

art-based technology, 42, 389

artificial enzymes, 350

assays, 112, 123, 148, 152, 163

[ATP]/[ADP] ratio, 120, 122, 123, 126, 134, 135, 141, 147, 148, 149, 150, 152, 153, 154, 158, 161, 163, 164, 166, 167, 274, 394, 401, 402

augmented-electromagnetism, 36, 339

Avogadro's number, 271, 272, 343

B

bare charge, 328, 329

basophil cell, 343, 344

Bénard convection, 275, 276

Bessel function, 307, 309, 375

biconformal base-space, 23, 310, 314, 360, 361, 364

big bang, 32, 311, 312, 364

biliary obstruction, 108

biobodysuit, 27, 28, 314, 378, 379, 380, 382-383, 386, 388, 390, 391, 403

biochemical pathways, 106

biochemical reactions, 357

bioelectric, 96, 272

bioenergetics, 144

black box, 21, 22, 24, 40, 41, 42, 240, 384

blinded research (single, double), 5, 406

body force, 275

box plot, 112, 116, 118, 123, 129, 130, 131, 132, 133, 134, 135, 153, 159, 161, 163

Bragg reflection, 242

brain cortical columns, 269, 270

Brane theory, 363

Brownian motion, 289, 290

bubble arrays, 56, 288, 350

buoyancy force, 275

C

calcite precipitation, 73

carbonic acid, 98, 105

carbonic anhydrase, 103, 105

catalyst, 75, 103, 351

cell sums, 223, 227, 228, 229, 237, 238, 239

chaos, 279, 281, 282

chemical chaos, 281, 282

chemical feedback, 278

chemical oscillation model, 186, 235

chemical oscillations, 185, 186, 277, 282

chemical potential, 271, 272, 273, 303, 348

closed system, 278, 281

CO_2 solubility, 70, 93, 405

coagulation, 289

coenzyme, 102, 105, 106, 120, 125, 126, 146

cofactors, 105

cognitive domain, 21, 24, 39, 391

coherence, 155, 170, 214, 286, 287, 312, 353, 360, 378, 381, 391, 399, 401, 403, 404, 405, 408

coherence (length, time, domain), 61, 92, 94, 170, 214, 287, 353, 401

coherence (self-induced), 312

coherent electron states, 287

colloid (surface science), 69, 70

colloids, 188, 288, 289, 290, 291, 292, 293, 294, 329

communication (long distance), 190, 355, 390-391, 397, 402

concept (reciprocal lattice, reciprocal space), 240, 242, 243, 249, 329, 363

conditioned space (locale), 30, 31, 39, 170, 174, 175, 177, 179, 182, 194, 202, 203, 220, 227, 231, 232, 234, 236, 355, 407

conditioning (space), 11, 13, 20, 169, 170, 172-175, 177, 190-182, 186, 189, 192, 194, 201, 206-208, 210, 212, 214-218, 220, 231-236, 283, 320, 338, 383, 395, 405, 407, 408

confidence limit (CL), 129, 264

configurational entropy, 348, 349

conformal gauging, 249

conjugate physical, 244, 246, 253, 254, 268, 305, 311, 314, 318, 321, 322, 330, 331, 332, 349, 360

consciousness, 1-5, 7, 10, 20, 170, 171, 231, 232, 310-313, 329, 330, 379, 380, 384, 386, 391, 393, 395, 396, 398, 399

consciousness imprint, 329, 330

consciousness waves, 312, 329

continuum approximation, 262, 263, 305, 314

convolution, 361, 362, 384

convolution theorem, 362

cooperative phenomena, 171

correlations, 94, 110, 142, 154, 175, 177, 179, 190, 191, 193, 201, 207, 213, 223, 269, 286, 391

coupling, 20, 146, 147, 169, 171, 173, 186, 187, 206, 214, 218, 287, 316, 319, 320, 329, 338, 349, 355, 382, 385, 391, 399, 400, 403-404

coupling (weak, strong), 24, 27, 30, 36, 37, 38, 44, 169, 187, 218, 234

coupling substance, 24, 382, 399

critical point, 56, 60, 288

critical temperature, 286

critically conditioned locale, 189

crystal growth - $ZnCO_3$, 73, 93

crystallite dissolution, 88-93

crystallites ($ZnCO_3$, $CaCO_3$), 54, 88, 89, 291

cultures, 142, 148, 150-152, 164, 377

cycle number, 185, 280

D

de Broglie pilot wave, 23, 36, 325, 329, 361, 400

deionization, 101

δ-function (delta-function), 321-326, 329, 330, 367, 368

deltron activation, 27, 30, 31, 36, 314, 316, 318, 329, 349, 364, 389

deltron activation function, 314, 318

deltrons, 24, 25, 27, 314, 316, 318, 319, 320, 329, 331, 333, 334, 336, 345, 349, 355, 364, 382, 387, 399, 400, 403

dematerialization, 22, 311

development time, 120, 143, 144, 147, 153, 154, 161, 162, 164-166, 274, 394

devices (isolation, storage, IIED), 1, 2, 4, 5, 10, 11, 13, 14, 17-20, 54, 70-88, 93, 94, 101, 110-120,

125, 126, 128, 132, 133, 136, 138, 148, 150, 152, 154, 162, 164, 166, 167, 168, 171, 206, 218, 220, 232, 294, 320, 351, 355, 383-384, 393-397, 399-401, 403-407
dielectric loss tangent, 62
dielectrophoresis, 292
diffraction patterns, 241, 250-253, 255, 261, 262, 270, 295
diffraction process, 240, 250, 296
diffusion coefficient, 272
dilution/succussion, 344, 345, 346, 349, 358, 371
dimensions (extra, higher), 8
Dirac energy gap, 314
direct space (D-space), 23-29, 33-38, 125, 126, 169, 171, 180, 186, 194, 199, 202, 206, 214, 218, 235, 240, 241, 244, 246, 248-253, 255, 256, 258, 261, 264, 265, 268, 269, 286, 299, 304, 305, 312, 314, 316, 318, 319, 321, 322, 324, 325, 326-334, 336, 338, 340-346, 348-355, 359, 361, 363, 367-369, 371, 386-389, 395, 400, 402, 403, 404, 407
dispersion, 289, 290
distant healing, 33, 386
distillation, 100
Drosophila Melanogaster, 122, 142, 143, 144, 147, 149, 154, 394, 401
duality of dualities, 250

E

effect size, 113, 115, 116, 118, 154, 222, 226, 230, 231, 238
electrostatic, 55, 107, 115, 272, 273, 289-291, 302, 387, 390
electric conductivity, 64, 337
electric permittivity, 273, 288, 293, 294, 335, 350, 387
electrochemical potential, 272, 273, 287, 290
electro-dissolution, 277, 284, 285

electrodynamic, 61, 290, 292, 310, 327, 334, 336
electrodynamic excitations, 33
electromagnetic, 1, 13, 19, 65, 69, 110, 146, 147, 152, 274, 275, 286-288, 290, 294, 327, 394, 400, 402
electromagnetism, 25, 26, 36, 48, 50, 53, 249, 332, 334, 339, 364
electromagnetism (normal, augmented), 339, 400
electron transport chain, 106, 123, 144, 146-150, 154, 157-159, 394, 402
electrophoresis, 292
EM shielding, 73, 110, 113, 123, 125, 128, 394
emotion domain, 27, 28, 311, 318, 364, 378, 382
emotional (states, domain, frame), 4, 14, 68, 310, 311, 313, 314, 318, 334, 364, 378, 379, 382, 386, 388, 390, 406
endergonic reaction, 103
energy levels, 152, 286, 314, 315
energy metabolism, 144, 146, 147, 150, 152, 157
energy waves, 311, 330
enthalpy, 271
entropy (configurational), 55, 56, 57, 59, 60, 271, 348-350
entropy of mixing, 349, 350
enzymatic activity, 11, 20, 109, 110
enzyme, 1, 12, 20, 69, 102-110, 113, 114, 120, 125-128, 157, 158, 272, 274, 279, 350, 351, 394, 395, 401, 402
enzyme (inhibitor, activator), 105
etheric, 24
experimenter effect, 171, 234, 401, 404
exposure (simultaneous, sequential), 73, 81-83, 86, 115, 116, 125, 132, 137, 150, 152, 161-164, 188, 207, 208, 212, 213, 216, 232, 252
exposure periods, 115, 116, 125, 132, 137, 150, 152, 162, 164

F

Faraday cage, 13, 19, 30, 36, 72, 73, 83, 89, 90, 110-120, 123, 125, 128, 129, 131-134, 150-152, 155, 161, 162, 170, 172, 176, 177, 179, 183, 184, 186, 189, 191, 193, 195, 196, 200-202, 218, 220, 231-233, 235, 274, 332, 354, 357, 393, 395-397

Faraday cage (layer number effect), 114, 131, 132, 136

ferromagnets, 286

Feynman diagram, 327, 328

field effects, 27, 70, 289

filtration, 100, 101

fine structure effects, 357, 358, 390

fitness, 142-144, 146-148, 150, 152, 154, 161, 162, 164, 409

Flade potential, 285

flux lines, 350

forced convection, 195, 199, 201, 277

forces (non-local), 22, 25, 38, 311, 313, 340

Fourier amplitude spectrum, 177, 179, 207, 208, 220, 223, 325

Fourier transform, 176, 178, 179, 194, 210, 212, 244, 246, 247, 250, 253, 256, 258, 261, 262, 265-270, 304, 305, 311, 318, 321, 323, 325, 361, 400

Fourier transform pairs, 247

Fraunhofer diffraction, 252

free energy (Gibb's), 55, 62, 267, 271, 302, 319

frequency, 63, 65, 66, 67

frequency spectrum, 177

frequency wave number, 319

fructose, 105

fruit flies, 11, 20, 36, 120, 122, 126, 134, 135, 141-143, 274, 394, 402

fruit fly homogenates, 122, 134, 135, 141

G

gas bubbles, 56, 288, 350

Gauge symmetry, 30-32, 39, 51, 293, 311, 320, 334, 336, 352, 354, 356, 391

gene expression, 143, 144, 146, 147

genes, 142, 143, 146

genetics, 142-144, 147, 150, 390

geocosmic factors, 4

Gibb's free energy, 55, 62, 267, 271, 302, 319

Gibb's phase rule, 34, 274

global symmetry, 50-53

glucoses, 105, 147

granularity approximation, 262, 263

gravitational constant, 28, 273, 387

H

harmonics, 177-179, 208, 209, 212, 223, 243, 321, 341, 367, 370, 371, 374, 396,

H-bond network, 56, 349

healing (remote), 2, 33, 38, 341, 381, 386

heart (ordered mode), 5, 19, 38, 379, 405

hexagonal lattice, 311

Higg's mechanism, 53

high pressure liquid chromatography (HPLC), 123, 148, 149, 152

holography, 251

holonomic theory, 269

homeopathic, 5, 19

homeopathy (law of similars, potentization), 68, 69, 332, 343, 344, 346, 347, 348, 358, 371, 386, 402

human internal harmony, 313

hydrogen bond, 55, 56, 57, 60, 70, 349

I

IIED (see devices)

images, 24, 181, 252, 326, 332-334, 350, 351, 364, 377, 381, 400

imprint charge, 79, 171

imprinting (process), 13, 19, 20, 38, 65, 75, 79, 87, 113, 354, 393, 408

imprinting effect, 75, 79

in vivo, 102, 142, 147, 148, 150, 154, 159

information transfer, 33, 36, 67, 313, 351

information wave, 23

inner self-management, 14, 19, 29, 37, 38, 171, 236, 313, 379, 383, 391, 401, 405

instar, 122, 142, 152, 164

intention (mind-body), 1, 2, 4, 5, 10-13, 18-20, 24, 26-29, 32, 34-39, 70, 73, 75, 82-84, 87, 93, 94, 110, 120, 125, 142, 146, 148, 150, 154, 155, 161-163, 180, 183, 189, 190-193, 236, 270, 310, 311, 314, 329, 349, 364, 378, 380, 382-383, 387-404

intention broadcasting, 93

intention-augmented EMFs, 36, 110, 146, 150, 154, 163

intention-transmission, 180, 191-193

interference interactions, 125

intermediary metabolism, 119, 145, 147

irradiation, 100, 101

isofemale strain, 143, 147, 148, 164

isomodulus plots, 260,

isotopic-spin, 49, 50, 52, 53

J

Josephson junction, 287

K

Kaluza-Klein, 249

kinetic, 34, 43, 44, 56, 93, 99, 270, 271, 272, 275, 285, 289, 292, 349, 354

L

larval (development), 142, 149, 150, 152, 154, 155, 161, 162, 164-166

larval development time, 11, 13, 20, 120, 143, 144, 147, 148, 153, 154, 161, 162, 164-166, 274, 394

larval homogenates, 122, 123, 126, 148-150, 152, 394, 402

laser, 57, 214, 286, 407

Laurent series, 303, 304

Laurent's expansion, 303, 310, 326

light, 8, 23, 101, 171, 251, 252, 269, 286, 310, 331, 361, 363, 387, 399

local symmetry, 50-53

lyophilate, 127

M

magnet polarity effect, 30, 172-174, 206, 207, 235, 395

magnetic field effect, 4, 13, 30, 31, 36, 62, 64-66, 69, 147, 172, 173, 206, 273, 293, 335, 339, 350, 387

magnetic monopole, 22, 24, 27, 28, 31, 249, 250, 321, 332, 336, 364, 378, 382, 399, 400, 404, 407

magnetic permeability, 273, 288, 293, 294, 335, 350, 387

magnetic vector potential, 36, 65, 146, 302, 337

magnetoelectrism, 25, 332, 334, 400

magnetophoresis, 292

magnetophotoelectrochemical potential, 274, 275

mathematical residues, 310, 326

matter, 1, 4, 6, 8, 9, 28, 31, 39, 45, 49, 51, 52, 61, 100, 171, 249, 310, 314, 329, 332, 379, 380, 386, 398, 400

matter-mind interaction (MMI), 4

Maxwell equations, 25, 36, 61, 334-336, 339

means amplitude spectrum, 176-179, 202, 203, 208, 220, 223, 325

median, 129, 130, 159, 161, 165

medicine (era I, II, III), 2
meditation, 19, 20, 34, 35, 37, 253, 394
mental (states, domain, frame), 4, 68, 313, 379, 390, 406
meta-analysis, 8
metabolic pathways, 146
metabolism, 119, 144-148, 150, 152, 157
metamorphosis, 142
metaphysics, 3, 4, 7, 8, 12
metastable phase formation, 88
microorganisms, 100, 101
millennium effect, 231, 236
Miller indices, 243, 296, 297, 298
mind domain, 27, 28, 311-313, 364, 378, 382
mirror (principle, relationship), 8, 10, 24, 51, 154, 163, 181, 286, 331-334, 339, 364, 380, 381, 400
mitochondria, 157, 158, 272
mobility, 28, 272, 403
models (conceptual, analytic), 9
molecular imprinting, 351
molecular information, 67
multidimensional reality, 40, 45
mu-metal shield, 65

N

NAD – nicotinamide adenine dinucleotide, 102, 106, 107, 119-124, 126, 127, 134, 135, 141, 144-154, 157-159, 163, 166, 167, 394
NAD (breakdown products), 123, 124
nanobubbles, 350
nodal points, 311-313, 321, 329, 399
non-local forces, 22, 25, 248, 311, 340, 341
normalized modulus, 254, 257, 259, 264, 269, 316
nutritional stress, 147

O

open system, 281, 282

organism (development, fitness), 68, 69, 100, 102, 106, 143, 146, 148, 154, 401
oscillation continuity, 214, 215, 234, 235
oscillation period doubling, 281
oscillations (pH, temperature, conductivity, property, short period, diurnal, wave train), 37, 46, 81, 88-90, 92, 93, 172, 175, 177, 179-210, 212-218, 220-223, 225-227, 229, 335, 255, 256, 275-282, 284, 285, 286, 288, 341-345, 355, 356, 369, 395, 396
oxidative phosphorylation, 144, 158, 159

P

paradigm, 21, 32, 33, 119, 310, 385, 391, 399
paradigm (scientific), 1, 2, 9, 12, 119
parapsychology, 3, 6
partial molar quantities, 271
particle modulation waves (particle-herding wave), 23
particulates, 28, 54, 94, 174, 175, 177, 179, 187-190, 207, 284, 285, 323, 331
Pearson correlation coefficient, 154
perception (extra sensory), 3
pH (definition), 11, 13, 20, 54
pH (device-mediated changes), 34, 54, 70, 72, 74-94, 98, 99, 394, 395, 401, 405
pH (equation, device calibration, electrode), 30, 66, 71, 72, 77, 78, 82, 86, 87, 89, 90, 98, 172-175, 177, 179-182, 188-194, 206-213, 216-220, 222, 232-235, 279, 283-286, 343, 351, 355, 394, 395
pH-lowering, raising, 83-86, 91, 182, 206, 207, 212, 216, 218-220, 234
pH-oscillations, 89, 90, 92, 172, 175, 179, 180, 189, 192, 193, 206, 207, 209, 212, 213, 217, 218,

220, 232, 234, 283, 285, 343, 355, 395, 396

phantom effect, 201, 202

phase, 33, 34, 38, 44, 49-51, 58, 60-62, 73, 88, 93, 98, 100, 171, 188, 189, 216, 218, 227, 241, 243-245, 255, 270, 274, 279, 286-288, 297-299, 312, 314, 318, 325, 326, 329, 333, 334, 348, 352, 352, 356, 358, 359, 381, 391, 399, 400, 407-409

phase difference, 255, 287, 292, 293

phase rule (Gibb's), 34, 274

phenotype, 143, 144, 150

photoelectrochemical potential, 272, 274, 275

photons, 19, 35, 36, 46, 51, 52, 69, 102, 128, 256, 272, 286, 327, 332, 361, 363, 381, 403

physics (new, classical, quantum), 21, 25, 30, 31, 35, 39, 45, 49, 50, 53, 125, 146, 173, 240, 248, 249, 250, 287, 293, 310-312, 314, 326, 327, 336, 354, 355, 363, 364, 383, 384-391, 399, 400, 401

physics Gauge (U(1), SU(2)), 30-35, 39, 48-53

physiology, 142

piezoelectric, 33, 333, 390

placebo, 7, 8, 391

plastizymes, 351

polycrystalline, 312, 313, 332

porcine kidney, 110, 127

potential, 1, 19, 34-37, 43, 50, 58, 60, 61, 65, 69, 70, 84, 115, 146, 150, 155, 158, 270, 275, 279, 285, 287-291, 302, 303, 312, 333, 337, 346-348, 381, 383, 387, 387, 397-399

primary lattice, 312

primordial δ-wave, 326, 329, 330, 356

primordial R-space wave, 325, 326, 329, 330

protocol (experimental), 10, 12-14, 38, 71, 77, 78, 83, 86, 87, 111, 150, 233, 234, 339

pseudo-random variable, 221, 230, 238

psychoenergetic, 8, 20, 386

pumping (optical, consciousness), 171, 286, 401, 408

Q

Qigong, 33, 37, 379, 381, 383, 405

quantum cellular automata, 351

quantum electrodynamics, 61, 310, 327

quantum mechanics, 21, 26, 35, 302, 380, 384

quantum mechanics (Copenhagen interpretation, biconformal base interpretation, decoherence interpretation, many worlds, space interpretation), 310, 314, 319, 340, 360-363, 387, 388, 403

quartz, 56, 202-205, 235

quartz crystal effect, 202-205, 235

R

radiators, 313

random event generator, 237

random number generation (RNG), 4, 220, 221, 229, 231, 232, 236, 238, 408

reality, 1, 2, 9, 10, 24, 27, 29, 34, 35, 38, 39, 45, 115, 231, 246, 273, 314, 325, 364, 377, 378, 380, 383, 386-388, 397, 405

reciprocal space (R-space), 23-25, 27-29, 33, 35-38, 125, 126, 169-171, 186, 206, 214, 218, 240, 241, 243-246, 248-256, 258, 259, 261, 264, 265, 268, 299, 305, 312, 314, 316, 318, 319, 321-327, 329-331-333, 334, 336, 338, 341-345, 349-355, 359-361, 363-364, 367, 368, 371, 382, 386-389, 399, 400, 402-404, 407

reflecting plane, 298

re-imprinting, 79, 112

relativistic constraint, 327

relativity theory, 23, 24, 28, 51, 310, 380

remote viewing, 3, 33, 386

renormalization, 327, 329

replicate, 38, 67, 87, 112, 120, 123, 151-153, 164, 391
replicate assays, 112, 123
resonance, 61, 63, 65-67
resonance absorption, 63
resonators, 321, 329, 330, 341-345
Reynold's number, 276, 277

S

scattering, 240, 244, 296, 297, 330, 398
science-based technology, 43, 389
screening atmosphere (mass, charge), 329
s-duality, 250
serum ALP, 108, 109
shielding, 19, 65, 69, 110, 113, 123, 125, 128
side-groups, 56, 105
simple harmonic wave, 321, 367
simulator model, 311
singularities, 60, 304, 310, 326, 329, 332-334, 336, 364, 400
solenoidal coil, 64, 65
solution shaking effect, 54, 85, 89, 91-94, 189
space (physical, base, higher dimensional, direct, reciprocal, biconformal, general), 1-5, 8-12, 19-21, 23-30, 33-35, 41, 46, 48, 49, 56, 170, 171, 249, 274, 289, 290, 296, 302, 304, 310-314, 316, 326, 330, 332, 334, 339, 340, 352, 359, 360-363, 389, 394, 395, 397, 399, 400, 404, 406
(see direct space; reciprocal space)
space conditioning, 169, 170, 172, 180, 182, 189, 206, 214, 218, 233, 383, 404
space-time, 4, 9, 21-23, 25, 50, 51, 84, 250-252, 261, 269, 270, 302, 323, 326, 327, 340, 367, 380-382, 385, 386
spectrophotometric method, 109
spirit, 26-28, 329, 364, 377-383, 386, 388
statistical analysis, 164

statistical probability,
stressor, 154, 394, 401, 406
string theory, 250
substrate, 93, 105, 106, 109, 127, 147, 158
subtle (domain, energy), 5, 11, 12, 36, 38, 39, 70, 113, 132, 378, 380, 391, 398, 402, 408
subtle energy detector, 113, 125, 126, 132
succussion, 344-346, 349, 358, 371
sucrase, 105
sucrose, 105
superconductivity, 286, 287, 280, 404
superconductors, 287, 288, 407
superlattice, 311-313, 399
superlattice ordering, 313
surfactant, 128, 291
surrogate image, 350
symmetry, 1, 2, 11, 173, 180, 226, 253, 254, 258, 320, 321, 330, 331, 336, 337, 339, 355, 356, 386, 391, 398-402
symmetry (gauge, broken), 22, 29-32, 39, 49-53, 56, 173, 180, 293, 311, 320, 334, 336, 339, 352, 354, 356, 386, 391
symmetry group, 339

T

Taylor's expansion, 249, 302-304, 310, 326, 341, 356
t-duality, 250
temperature-oscillations, 88, 89, 93, 175, 181, 182, 184, 197, 199, 203, 206, 216, 275, 276, 285, 288, 342, 356, 356, 395
tensor, 312, 333, 334, 400
tetrahedra, 55, 56
thermistor, 180
thermodynamic (activity, activity coefficient), 11, 13, 20, 108-110, 154, 155, 229, 387, 394, 400
thermodynamic driving force, 93, 144, 158, 272, 281, 289, 302, 310, 349, 350, 354, 359

thermodynamic equilibrium, 34, 183, 277, 348
thermodynamic potential, 34, 37, 270-274, 397-399
thermodynamics of inhomogeneous systems, 303
trans-dimensional, 333
transformation (human), 1, 4, 383, 391
transmitter/receiver experiment, 89, 93
TUKEY post hoc tests, 112, 113, 116, 118, 121, 123, 130, 132, 134, 136-139, 141, 167, 168

U

uncertainty principle, 22
undulation interval, 256, 321, 325, 367, 368
unimprinted device, 37, 54, 72, 77, 94, 110, 111, 113, 125, 218, 402
universe (relative, absolute), 26, 311, 378, 391, 391, 397, 398
universe, (non-local), 3, 8

V

vacuum, 4, 10, 12, 22, 33, 34, 53, 125, 155, 170, 171, 235, 310, 327, 329, 332, 335, 356, 378, 380-383, 387, 398-403, 407
vacuum (substructure, physical), 11, 12, 28, 34-36, 45, 311, 314, 315, 321, 378, 380, 391, 398, 403, 407
vacuum ordering, 30, 170, 171, 206, 407, 409
virtual photon, 327
vitros DT system, 109, 110, 127

W

water, 7, 11-14, 19, 20, 30, 32, 34, 36, 102, 113, 120, 122, 123, 125, 126, 130, 134, 135, 141, 172, 173, 175-182, 186, 189-191, 194-196, 200-202, 206, 216-218, 220, 233-235, 274,

276, 286, 288, 345, 350, 355-356, 394, 397, 405
water (Evian, Castle Rock, ASTM type 1), 54, 72-77, 79-89, 98, 99, 188
water (memory), 62, 69, 74, 75
water (physico-chemical properties), 62, 187, 349, 351
water (purified, molecule), 34, 54-58, 63, 68, 72, 77, 79-84, 87-89, 92, 94, 99-101, 110-112, 120, 149, 152, 154, 163, 166, 168, 173, 174, 183, 187-190, 192, 193, 207, 212, 218-220, 284, 285, 320, 394, 401, 405
water (structure), 5, 12, 294, 349, 400
water clusters, 288
wave cycle number, 185
wave superposition, 296, 326, 352, 360-362
wave train, 182-185, 226, 229, 235, 279, 341
waveform symmetry, 180

Y

Young double-slit experiment, 361

Z

zero point fluctuations, 61